D1356506

The Christian Warfare

The Christian Warfare

An Exposition of Ephesians 6:10 to 13

D. M. LLOYD-JONES

THE BANNER OF TRUTH TRUST

THE BANNER OF TRUTH TRUST
3 Murrayfield Road, Edinburgh EH12 6EL
PO Box 621, Carlisle, Pennsylvania 17013, USA

© 1976 D. M. Lloyd-Jones
First published 1976
ISBN 0 85151 243 7

Printed and bound in Great Britain by
Morrison & Gibb Ltd., London and Edinburgh

Preface

This volume consists of a series of sermons preached in Westminster Chapel as part of a systematic exposition of the Epistle to the Ephesians. As explained in the Introduction it consists of a final word of warning and exhortation by the Apostle Paul to these early Christians.

My contention is that the same warning and exhortation are urgently needed today, and perhaps more so than at any time since they were originally written.

These are my reasons for saying this.

Our age is one that has largely ceased to believe in the supernatural at all. This is partly due to the advance of science in its various branches. Man is regarded as the master of his own fate and the determiner of everything.

But even in the Church, and among those who claim to believe in a supernatural realm, there is evident and increasing forgetfulness of what the Apostle Paul teaches here – indeed an open denial of it.

In a recent television programme Bishop Butler of Westminster R.C. Cathedral stated openly that he did not believe in a personal devil, but was ready to bow to the teaching of his Church which, he said, on the whole still seemed to believe in his existence.

Earlier this year some 68 men describing themselves as Academics, and belonging to the Anglican Church, in a letter to The Times stated openly that they likewise did not believe in a personal devil or in demons.

Even among evangelical teachers the same tendency is seen, for we have been told recently by a popular writer on Counselling that we need not consider the possibility of demon possession in our pastoral work, as that ended with the apostolic era.

Moreover the new emphasis on political and social matters as being the key to the restoration of the influence of the Church points in the same direction. But nowhere is it seen more plainly than in the pathetic belief that the Church can expect a response to her appeal to godless citizens to discipline themselves for the sake of the country.

It is my belief, as I have tried to show in my exposition of the Apostle's warnings, that the modern world, and especially the history of the present century, can only be understood in terms of the unusual activity of the devil and the 'principalities and powers' of darkness.

Indeed, I suggest that a belief in a personal devil and demon activities is the touchstone by which one can most easily test any profession of Christian faith today.

I make no apology, therefore, for having considered the matter in such detail. It is essential for the successful living of the Christian life and for the peace and happiness and joy of the individual Christian, and also for the prosperity of the Church in general.

In a world of collapsing institutions, moral chaos, and increasing violence, never was it more important to trace the hand of 'the prince of the power of the air, the spirit that now worketh in the children of disobedience', and then, not only learn how to wrestle with him and his forces, but also how to overcome them 'by the blood of the Lamb and the word of our testimony'. If we cannot discern the chief cause of our ills, how can we hope to cure them?

May God bless this volume to that end!

As ever I am profoundly grateful for the invaluable help of Mrs E. Burney, Mr S. M. Houghton and my wife.

London August 1976   D. M. Lloyd-Jones

Contents

[7]

Ephesians 6:10—13

Finally, my brethren, be strong in the Lord and in the power of his might. Put on the whole armour of God, that ye may be able to stand against the wiles of the devil. For we wrestle not against flesh and blood, but against principalities, against powers, against the rulers of the darkness of this world, against spiritual wickedness in high places. Wherefore take unto you the whole armour of God, that ye may be able to withstand in the evil day, and having done all, to stand.

I

Introduction

'Finally, my brethren, be strong in the Lord, and in the power of his might.' These words introduce a statement which, beginning at this point, runs on more or less to the end of this Letter to the Ephesians. It is one of the Apostle's ringing and most eloquent statements of how the Christian life should be lived.

The word 'Finally' must first engage our attention, because we must be clear as to its meaning. 'Finally, my brethren,' says Paul. What does he mean by 'Finally'? Is he just saying, 'I have really said all that I intended to say'? Is it just an indication that the letter is about to end? Of course in a sense it is that. But if we regard it merely in that light, we shall miss the real point of what is being said here. This is not just a kind of postscript; it is not an afterthought. It is not that the Apostle, having said all that he wished to say, finished his letter and then remembered that there was just one other thing to be mentioned.

In other words there is a very direct connection between what Paul begins to say here and what he has just been saying. Indeed I go further. There is a direct and immediate connection between this and the whole of the Epistle up to this point. He carries the case he has been making right through to the end, and when he comes to this statement it is but a further outworking of the great theme. It is most important, therefore, that we should get this great statement into its true setting and perspective.

In the first place let me remind you of the major themes of this Epistle. Speaking generally we can say of the first three chapters that the Apostle is reminding these Ephesians, and reminding us through them, of the great doctrines, the fundamental postulates of the Christian faith. He is letting them know who they are, what they are, and how they have become what they are. That is his theme. All the major doctrines of the Christian faith are to be found in these first three chapters. Of course Paul has his own way of putting them before us. Undoubtedly his chief aim is to give a picture of the glory and of the exalted character of the Christian life. He works up to that in the second half of the third chapter, where he says some almost incredible things. He says that he is praying for the Ephesian believers, that 'they might be filled with all the fulness of God', and reminds them that 'God is able to do exceeding abundantly above all that we ask or think, according to the power that worketh in us'. Here we have a great picture of what the Christian should be. Paul has told us how we become Christians – it is by the blood of Christ (Ephesians 1:7). It is all a part of God's great plan in eternity, as he tells us in the first chapter. Christ came and His saving work is being worked out. Jews came in, Gentiles came in, and we are together in this body, this new man, the Church (2:16).

But the Apostle desires the Ephesians to understand above all else the privileges that belong to such a life. So he has prayed thus in the first chapter: 'the eyes of your understanding being enlightened, that ye may know what is the hope of his calling, and what the riches of the glory of his inheritance in the saints, and what is the exceeding greatness of his power to us-ward who believe.' In other words, if we but realized the exalted character of what he calls our 'high calling', the whole situation would be transformed. He writes three chapters to bring them face to face with this teaching.

Then, having done that, the Apostle begins to appeal to them, and plead with them to live in a manner that is worthy of their calling. Such is the apostolic method. Paul never starts with morality and behaviour. Invariably we have this grand context. No man can ever live the Christian life until he is a Christian, until he knows what it is to be a Christian, until he has some conception of the glory of the Christian position. So the Apostle begins chapter 4 by saying, 'I, therefore, the prisoner of the Lord, beseech you that ye walk worthy of the vocation wherewith ye

are called', and from that point to the end of the Epistle he
continues making this great and grand appeal.

But we observe that even after having started on that practical
theme Paul still cannot leave the doctrine, for in verses 1 to 16 of
chapter 4 we have one of the most wonderful expositions of the
nature of the Christian Church that can be found anywhere in the
Scripture. Not until verse 17 does he again come back to this
matter of the practical application: 'This I say therefore, and
testify in the Lord, that ye henceforth walk not as other Gentiles
walk, in the vanity of their mind . . . (but) put on the new man,
which after God is created in righteousness and true holiness'. In
other words he says to them, Now that I have reminded you of
what you are, and how you have become what you are, I want
you to see that it is essentially a matter of logic, and of application
of the truth, that you have to live the kind of life that pleases God.
He says, You have been born again, you are no longer like those
other Gentiles who continue to live in sin and in enmity to God.
Well, do not go on living as if that were still the case with you.
It would be inconsistent, it would be irrational to do so. So he
reminds them that, as they are born again, they must evidence the
fact in their lives. He reminds them also that the Holy Spirit
dwells in them; He does not dwell in those who are not
Christians. And they must manifest His indwelling. They must
not 'grieve the Spirit'. Then he reminds them that they are God's
'dear children'. The others are not children of God. One only
becomes 'a child of God' in Christ Jesus. God has made all men
and sometimes the term 'children' or 'offspring' is used in that
sense (e.g. Acts 17:28). But in the normal New Testament sense,
to be 'children of God' is a relationship that is given to us; as
John puts it, 'authority is given to us to become the sons of God'
through faith in Jesus Christ (John 1:12). Paul therefore argues,
Because you are God's dear children, you do not behave as other
people, there is something special about you, and you show this
constantly in your demeanour. Then, finally, he reminds them
that they are children of light. He says, 'You were sometimes
darkness, but now you are light in the Lord: walk therefore as
children of light' (Ephesians 5:8). You have come from those
underground caverns in which the children of iniquity spend their
time, and have their conversation. You have come into God's

daylight, into the broad sunshine, therefore do not go groping about in the dark, but live as children of the light, glorifying your Father.

Then we come to another section beginning at verse 18 in chapter 5, where the Apostle says, 'Be not drunk with wine, wherein is excess; but be filled with the Spirit'. This new section runs on to verse 9 of chapter 6. Paul's argument is that as we are filled with the Holy Spirit we must live in a way that is unique, a thing we can never do unless we are filled with the Spirit. He works that out along various lines. If you are filled with the Spirit, he says, when you meet together in church fellowship, there will be great praise and thanksgiving. 'Speaking to yourselves in psalms and hymns and spiritual songs, singing and making melody in your heart to the Lord, giving thanks always for all things unto God and the Father in the name of our Lord Jesus Christ.' What a picture of the Christian Church, and what a contrast to what is so often seen today!

Then the Apostle proceeds to say that we are all to be subject one to another, and he works that out in three main respects. Wives are to be subject to their husbands, children are to be subject to their parents, servants are to be subject to their masters. But he always puts it in a doctrinal manner. The husband is to love his wife 'even as Christ loved the church and gave himself for it'. You cannot find such subjection in anybody except Christians. But every Christian husband and wife should be manifesting the fact that they are 'filled with the Spirit'; and they should be an astonishment to the world. The same is true of the relationship of children and parents. It is to be the exact opposite of what we are witnessing today – not lawlessness, but 'honouring father and mother'. And the father must not 'provoke his children to wrath'. On the contrary, because he is 'filled with the Spirit', there is understanding, tolerance, patience and everything that is necessary. And it is to be the same with Christian masters and servants, and with Christian servants and masters. Paul always deals with the two sides. He tells the servants, who were slaves in those days, how they are to behave; he tells the masters also to remember 'that your Master also is in heaven, neither is there respect of persons with him'. In these ways Paul shows how, in life's various relationships, this 'life in the Spirit' manifests itself.

Having done all that, the Apostle now says 'Finally, my brethren', as if to say, Now in the light of all I have been telling you about yourselves, and of the kind of life you have to live, is that all? 'No', he says, 'there is still one other matter.' That is the matter he now introduces for our consideration. He cannot stop at the end of the ninth verse in chapter 6, and for this reason, that we do not live this Christian life in a vacuum. It is not just a matter of, 'Well, there it is all set out for you; now go and do it.' There is another matter that must be considered, there is another factor that in a sense Paul has not mentioned yet, namely, the mighty opposition to Christian living which we all inevitably encounter in this world of time.

That is the subject Paul introduces here. He has reminded us of what we are, he has shown us the possibilities that belong to our new position, and there is no limit, no end, to them. 'That ye might be filled with all the fulness of God.' 'That ye might apprehend with all saints what is the breadth, and length, and depth, and height; and to know the love of Christ, which passeth knowledge.' Limitless! endless! 'Oh,' you say, 'how wonderful!' Wait a minute! says Paul. Let me remind you that you have to live that kind of life in a world in which there is a tremendous power working against you, that you will be engaged in a terrible conflict with the devil and all his forces. If you do not realize that, he says, and take the appropriate action with respect to it, you will undoubtedly and inevitably be defeated. So he is compelled to introduce this subject. Hence 'Finally' does not just mean, 'Well, now, I have said this, that, and the other thing. Ah! there is just one matter more!' Not at all! What we have here is a vital part of the whole picture. We might very well translate the word, which in our Authorised Version appears as 'Finally', as 'Wherefore' or 'Henceforth', or 'For the rest'. It does not matter which of those terms we employ. There, then, we have the setting for this word 'Finally'. It is not enough to know all that he has already told us about the Christian life; we must also realize and accept what he is now about to say to us. It is still part of the whole picture, and of his essential teaching.

As we introduce this great subject our first business is to give a broad analysis of the section, to show the divisions of the subject matter, in order that we may have the picture clearly in our minds. This done, I shall make some few general comments on it before we proceed to the detailed analysis. But in dividing this section starting at verse 10 and going on roughly to verse 19 or 20 I find myself faced with a difficulty, although it is not vital to the truth. There is a very famous work on this subject by William Gurnall, a great Puritan who lived 300 years ago, called 'The Christian in Complete Armour', a massive volume that is fortunately again available in this country. It is a great classic which has given food for the soul to countless thousands of Christian pilgrims during the last 300 years. Now, to my disappointment and almost dismay, I cannot accept William Gurnall's division of the subject. This is in a sense a mechanical point, and yet it seems to me to be of importance. Gurnall divides it up thus. He says there are two main sections here, the first being verse 10 itself, verse 10 alone. Then section two, he says, includes verses 11 to 20. He states the matter thus: Section 1, verse 10 – 'A short but sweet and powerful encouragement' to this Christian warfare. Section 2, verses 11 to 20 – Here we have 'several directions for their managing this war the more successfully, with some motives here and there sprinkled among them'.

I really cannot accept that division; and I make bold to suggest a better one. I agree that there are two main sections, but I suggest that the first section runs from verse 10 to verse 13 where we have a general exhortation. The second section, verses 14 to 20, gives detailed instructions with regard to the general exhortation. That seems to me to be the natural division. First, the general, then the particular. In verse 14 the Apostle is clearly taking up what he had just said in general; he is now going to work it out in particular. 'Stand therefore, having your loins girt about with truth, and having on the breastplate of righteousness', etc. Verse 14 onwards is clearly the detailed application of what he has said in general in the first section, verses 10 to 13.

But we must sub-divide the first section. In verses 10 to 13 we have what I call a general exhortation, or what could be still better described as 'a call to battle'. I cannot quite understand how Gurnall can introduce the word 'sweet' here. He does add 'powerful' I admit – 'A short but sweet and powerful encouragement.' And it is the power that strikes me; it is a stirring call to battle, a resonant exhortation. But the Apostle divides that up. First, he tells us how to prepare ourselves for this battle, and there are two sub-sections: (1) Verse 10: 'Be strong in the Lord, and in the power of his might.' (2) Verse 11, and repeated in verse 13 for emphasis: 'Put on (take unto you) the whole armour of God.' Secondly, at the end of verse 11, and in verse 12, he supplies the reason why he gives this call to battle.

The first question is, How do I prepare for the battle? And there is the double answer, 'Be strong in the Lord, and in the power of his might', and 'Put on the whole armour of God'. But then he does something which is found without variation in all his letters. He tells us why we need such a preparation. Now that is typical of the Scripture, which never tells you to do a thing without explaining why you must do so. Why should I be 'strong in the Lord and in the power of his might?' Why is it absolutely essential that I should put on, not merely one or two pieces of armour, but 'the *whole* armour of God?' Here is the answer, again sub-divided. In verse 11 he says, You had better put on the whole armour of God 'that you may be able to stand against the wiles of the devil'. Then he proceeds to elaborate the point in verse 12, which is but an analysis of 'the wiles of the devil'. 'Why should I put on the whole armour?' asks someone. 'Why should I be careful that I am strong in the Lord and in the power of his might?' Here is your answer. 'We wrestle not against flesh and blood, but against principalities, against powers, against the rulers of the darkness of this world, against spiritual wickedness in high (or heavenly) places.' That is why you need it all, and you are a fool if you fail to realize it, and to act accordingly. You are confronted, he says, by that kind of enemy and opposition.

But Paul also adds, 'that you may be able to stand in the evil day'. Life is always a battle, but there are certain times which are worse than others. There are 'evil days'. You sometimes feel when you wake up in the morning (do you not?) as if everything is about to go wrong? It is an evil day, and the devil seems to be busy following you everywhere, threatening you, taunting you, jeering at you, mocking you, throwing fiery darts at you! Well, there are evil days and a man who does not realize their occurrence is certain to be defeated. If you want to be able to 'stand in the evil day', 'be strong in the Lord and in the power of his might', 'take unto you the whole armour of God'. You will need it all. And then, as if to drive the point right home to us, he says, 'and having done all, to stand'. It is a great thing to be able to 'stand' in a world like this. People are falling right and left, everywhere. You see it in the world, you see it, alas, in the church. The great thing is to be able to 'stand'. That is the reason for the exhortation, and the Apostle's explanation of the only way whereby anyone can stand.

Such, then, is our analysis of the first main section which I am calling, A general exhortation, or A call to battle. And then in the second main section Paul proceeds to give us the detailed instructions. He does not take any risks. Like a good teacher he never takes anything for granted. He asks, Have you put on your armour, are you starting with your loins girt, is your breastplate in position, are your feet, head, and all parts covered? Every part has to be catered for; so he takes them through it all in detail. He does not stop at a general instruction, he proceeds to detailed instructions as to how every part is to be guarded and safe-guarded.

Is the picture clear in our minds? I have got to realize who I am and what I am, and it is inevitable that I should be anxious to live in a manner that is worthy of my calling. When you visit a foreign country you should remember that you are a Britisher, and you should not let your country down. You should be careful of your conduct for that very reason. This is a principle we apply everywhere in life. Children are told to behave themselves at parties. Why? Because they are representatives of the family. And it is the same with us no matter what our age. But that is not enough, we have to realize something further, and we have to be prepared to meet it, namely, this opposition of the devil.

I wish to make some general comments about the Apostle's teaching at this point before we come to the detailed treatment. Take, for instance, this question of the relationship of this section to all that has gone before. Somebody may say, 'Well now, in what respect is this different from what Paul has already been telling us?' The difference is that up to this point Paul has been dealing with the Christian life mainly in terms of the conflict we have with the world that is around and about us, and with the 'flesh'. He knows that the Ephesian believers, though they are true Christians, have still something of the old nature in them. There is sin still left in the body, in the flesh, and so far he has really been dealing with that evil. There is an enemy *within*, there is a lurking power that is always ready to take control of our flesh, and, as Paul says in writing to the Romans, to 'reign in our mortal body'. Now that is what he has been dealing with, in a sense, so far. But now he deals with the enemy that is *outside* us – the devil and his forces. He has not touched on that so far. Verse 12 emphasizes the difference immediately. 'For we wrestle not (not only) against flesh and blood.' Not only have we to wrestle against flesh and blood, but also 'against principalities, against powers, against the rulers of the darkness of this world, against spiritual wickedness in high places'. So there is an essential difference between what Paul is going to deal with now and what he has been dealing with hitherto.

We must not press this into an absolute distinction. It is a vital distinction in thought, but it is not an absolute distinction in practice. I mean this, that the devil does work in us and can work in us through our bodies, through our instincts. The devil can make use of anything. I shall be pointing out later how he can even produce illnesses and sicknesses and depression and misery. The devil can do all this within us, so we must not make it an absolute division. And yet it is a very real division. In other words, we must never forget the devil, we must never forget the 'principalities and powers'. I must never think that my whole problem is confined to that which is within me and in other people. Above and beyond that is this other mighty power arrayed against me, the mightiest of all powers apart from God Himself. Not to remember this basic fact is to court certain defeat and disaster. The great trouble with the world today, and with the Church unfortunately, is that they know so little about the devil and the 'principalities and powers'. Much teaching concerning holiness and sanctification never even mentions the devil and these powers at all. The problem is regarded solely as something confined to ourselves. Hence the total inadequacy of many proposed solutions.

But, further, as I have been hinting already, this section of the Epistle is of vital importance in connection with the whole problem of the biblical doctrine of sanctification and holiness. It is one of the crucial passages with regard to that doctrine, but one, as I have said, which is curiously and strangely forgotten and neglected. What does it tell us?

The Christian life, in the first place, is a warfare, it is a struggle. 'We wrestle.' The whole section is designed to impress this fact upon us. There is no grosser or greater misrepresentation of the Christian message than that which depicts it as offering us a life of ease with no battle and no struggle at all. There are types of holiness teaching that teach just that. Their slogan is, 'It is quite easy'. They say the trouble is that so many Christian people remain ignorant of this fact, and therefore go on fighting and struggling. That is the essential characteristic of the teaching of the Cults. That is why they are always popular. 'Quite easy! a life of ease!' You cannot fit that into this Epistle with its 'We wrestle!' 'Be strong in the Lord, and in the power of his might. Put on the whole armour of God, that ye may be able to stand.' The first thing we have to realize is that the Christian life is a warfare, that we are strangers in an alien land, that we are in the enemy's territory. We do not live in a vacuum, in a glasshouse. The teaching which gives the impression that the pathway to glory is all easy and simple and smooth is not Christianity, it is not Paul's Christianity, it is not New Testament Christianity. It is the hallmark of the quack remedy always, that it cures everything so easily! One dose, and there is no more trouble!

Secondly, this is a warfare that you and I have to wage. 'Be strong in the Lord, and in the power of his might.' YOU have to be strong. 'Put on the whole armour of God, that YOU may be able to stand', 'and having done all, to stand'. 'Stand therefore'—YOU! It is not only a warfare, it is a warfare that you and I have to wage. Let us be clear about this. There is a teaching which says, 'Christian people, you have been making a great mistake; you have been trying to fight this battle; you must stop doing so'. It says that there is only one thing to do, 'Hand it over to the Lord' and all will be well. 'Hand it over to the Lord, He will fight for you.' But you cannot fit that into the teaching we have here. I do not find the Apostle telling me to hand it over to the Lord and

[20]

that He will fight my battles for me while I just sit back and enjoy the fruit of His victory. It is not here! *I* have to fight! Another way in which that teaching is put sometimes is: 'Let go and and let God.' 'Let go,' they say, 'you have been holding on to it, you have been trying . . . Let go, let God. It is all right, you will have victory. It is quite simple, no effort is required.' But surely what we read here is the exact opposite of such teaching. It is you and I who have to do the fighting. Thank God, we are given strength and power and the arms, but *we* have to do it. I am given everything I need and I am given the power to use it. I do not relax and merely look on and reap the fruits of the victory of Another. No, *He* makes *me* more than conqueror; but it is my battle and I have to wage it. These are fundamental principles in connection with the doctrine of sanctification. And I believe that much of the decline in the Christian Church today is due to the fact that that other teaching has had such a vogue.

But, thirdly, observe the way in which we are called to this battle. Notice the way in which Paul puts the call, this general instruction, or general exhortation. I have referred to it as a 'call to battle'. The other teaching to which I have been referring has sometimes represented itself as providing a kind of clinic for sick souls. They say, 'You are spiritually ill and spiritually wounded and spiritually defeated. There is a clinic for you and there is a message that will soothe you and help to heal your wounds, and lead you to a way of victory without struggle.' A clinic! But there is no clinic here; it is rather a barracks!

Or let me put it in another way. There is nothing sentimental here. I would lay it down as a fundamental proposition that if any teaching concerning holiness and sanctification is sentimental it is not scriptural! There is a series of books which betray themselves, it seems to me, by their very title. An example is, 'Quiet Talks on Power'. Can you fit that notion into the words which the Apostle uses here? There is a contradiction in the terms used. You cannot have a quiet talk on power; you cannot have a quiet talk on Niagara, you cannot have a quiet talk on the explosion of an atomic bomb. A quiet talk on power! It is sentimental, it is flabby, it is weak. That is not what we have here!

Dare I go further and say that surely nothing has done so much harm to the true doctrine of sanctification as what are generally described as 'devotional talks'. It is a part of this same 'nice teaching' – quiet devotional talks, with simple affecting illustrations! But that is not what the Apostle is talking about. What we have here is the exact opposite. We have a martial atmosphere, we have a rousing, stimulating call. It is a trumpet call – 'BE STRONG IN THE LORD, AND IN THE POWER OF HIS MIGHT. PUT ON THE WHOLE ARMOUR OF GOD.' Do you not hear the bugle, and the trumpet? It is a call to battle; we are being roused, we are being stimulated, we are being set upon our feet; we are told to be men. The whole tone is martial, it is manly, it is strong.

Then go on to realize that there is nothing quick and easy about all this. You have to go on doing it. 'Put on the Gospel armour. Each piece put on with prayer.' You do not simply do one thing and then all is right and well. No, Paul gives us all these details, and it takes time to work them out. There is nothing quick and ready-made about this; you have to work it out in detail.

Finally, you have to keep on doing it. There is 'no discharge in this war'. While you and I are alive in this world the devil will be there with all his evil and malignity; and he will fight us to the end, he will fight us to our deathbed. Is this hopeless? It is the reverse! It is glorious. We are given the privilege of following in our Lord and Master's footsteps; 'As he is, so are we in this world' (1 John 4:17). It is a mighty conflict; but I can be 'strong in the Lord and in the power of his might', I can clothe myself with 'the whole armour of God'. Are you ready for the battle? Are you on the alert, are you on your feet? Are you just indulging your weaknesses and whims and fancies, and pitying yourself, and grumbling and complaining about this and that problem or situation? Rise up, shake them off, stand on your feet, be a man! Realize that you are a member of this mighty regiment of God, fighting the battle of the Lord and destined to enjoy the glorious fruits of victory throughout the countless ages of eternity. Have you heard the trumpet call? 'Be strong in the Lord and in the power of his might. Put on the whole armour of God.'

2

The Only Way

We come now to the detailed consideration and analysis of this most important statement: 'Finally, my brethren, be strong in the Lord, and in the power of his might. Put on the whole armour of God, that ye may be able to stand against the wiles of the devil.' The Apostle is exhorting these Ephesians to realize something of the nature of the battle in which we are all inevitably engaged as the result of being Christians. Indeed this battle exists whether we are Christians or not. The teaching of the Bible throughout is that this world in which we live is a battle-ground, is a place in which we literally have to fight for our souls, to fight for our eternal welfare.

The Apostle gives these Ephesians some very specific instruction with regard to the nature of that battle, and as to the only way in which it can be waged successfully. Clearly the exhortation is primarily for Christian people; his whole argument is based upon that consideration. At the same time, however, it has a message for everyone; for it is true to say that this is a conflict which affects all persons whether they realize it or not. Those who are not Christian do not understand their own world at this present time; they cannot understand why it is as it is, and why various things are happening. So while we are looking at the Apostle's instruction with regard to the way to fight this great battle, we shall, incidentally, be seeing the exposure of the complete failure of all who are not Christian even to understand their problem, and still more their failure to deal with it in an adequate and successful manner. In other words, we are confronted here with the

Apostle's teaching as to the way in which we can fight successfully the forces that are arrayed against our souls and their highest and best interests.

Perhaps the best way to approach this subject, and to put it into its modern setting in order that we may realize the relevance of all this to life as it is today, would be for me to quote some words which I read in a newspaper recently. A certain senior lecturer in education in a college in Great Britain said this: 'The Church should take a firmer lead in moral matters; woolly generalizations must go. The Church must give answers to real modern problems, including sex. While the religious basis offers the best prospect of success it should never be regarded as the only way to teach morality, otherwise we would become narrow-minded.' This is a very typical statement of the attitude of so many in the world at the present time to the problem which is dealt with here by the Apostle Paul. I refrain from making certain obvious comments upon it, for I am interested in it simply because I think it will help us to understand the Apostle's teaching. Setting detailed considerations aside for the moment, we shall consider the Apostle's teaching in general as it gives an answer to this kind of statement. The lecturer uses the word 'woolly' – he does not want 'woolly generalizations'. Yet, poor man, his own statement is nothing but a woolly generalization! However, let us ignore that. It is one of the typical modern clichés – 'The Church must do this and not do that; it is about time the Church . . .' We are all familiar with such remarks.

Statements of this type are invariably based on an ignorance of what the Church is, and what is the nature of her teaching. In the Ephesian passage before us, the Apostle is really saying that what he is teaching is the only way to deal with the problem of conflict. The lecturer says that 'while religion offers the best prospect of success, it should never be regarded as the only way to teach morality, otherwise we would become narrow-minded'. The Apostle, on the other hand, specifically and openly says that the way he propounds is the only way to victory. That is why there is such a note of urgency in his teaching, and why, as I have said, it is a kind of trumpet-call: 'Be strong in the Lord, and in the power of his might. Put on the whole armour of God.' If you fail to do this you are defeated, you are already finished before you start. The Apostle's is the only way. We make no apology for saying so. We are not at all afraid of this charge of 'narrow-mindedness'. When you know that to take a certain course is the only cure for a disease, that it is specific, that it cures it to a certainty, and that nothing else can do so, you do not regard it as being narrow-minded to use that remedy and to refuse to waste time with other remedies. That is not being narrow-minded, it is just being sensible and sane and rational.

Every kind of specialization is in this sense narrow. We are living in an age of specialization; but I have never heard anyone suggesting that an atomic scientist is narrow-minded because he gives the whole of his time to the science of the atom. Of course not! That is just common sense, that is wisdom; it is to concentrate on what matters, what is powerful, what really does yield results.

But let me state my thesis positively. The claim of the Christian faith quite openly and specifically is that it – and it alone – can deal with this problem. The Gospel of Jesus Christ is not one of a number of theories and teachings and philosophies confronting the world. It is unique, it stands absolutely alone. The Bible is not one book among many books. It is God's Book, it is a unique Book, it is *the* Book, standing apart from all the others. We must emphasize this because it is the whole basis of the Christian faith. The Church is not one of a number of institutions; she claims to be quite unique as an institution; she says she is the body of Christ. We speak because we have a revelation. The Bible does not provide us with a theory, a speculation, an attempt to arrive at truth. The position of all the men who wrote the books of the Bible is akin to what the Apostle says about himself in the third chapter of this Epistle to the Ephesians: 'For this cause, I, Paul, the prisoner of Jesus Christ for you Gentiles, if you have heard of the dispensation of the grace of God which is given me to you-ward: how that by revelation he made known unto me the mystery'.

The Apostle does not address the Ephesians saying: 'Listen, many people have been offering you advice and teaching; well, I have studied a great deal also, and I have come to this conclusion; so this is what I suggest.' That is not the case at all! He says, 'a revelation was given to me'. It is not a message devised by Paul;

[25]

it was given to him by the Lord Himself, the Lord of Glory, on the road to Damascus. He apprehended him and arrested him and said, 'I am going to send you as a minister and a witness to the people and to the Gentiles' (Acts 26:16–18). Divine communication is the whole basis of the Christian faith. It is therefore foolish to regard that faith as one amongst many. No, as the Apostle Peter stated it once and for ever at the very beginning of the Church when he and John had been arrested and were arraigned before the authorities in Jerusalem, 'There is none other name under heaven given among men whereby we must be saved' (Acts 4:12). None other! There is not even a second! He is the only One, and He is enough; you do not need any addition. This and this alone! And that note is found in everything the Apostle says. That is why he is so urgent, so insistent as he presses his message upon them. This is the only hope. Were it not for this there would be nothing at all. It is a dogmatic pronouncement; and anyone who apologizes for his Christianity, or tries to accommodate it, or to say that it is the best amongst a number, is virtually denying the most essential point in the Christian position.

We must not stop, however, at a mere dogmatic assertion, but must proceed to demonstrate it. I suggest that if you take the evidence of history you will be driven to the conclusion that it is the only way. Go back, review the history of the centuries as far as it is known, look at secular history-books, take history as it is recorded in the pages of the Old Testament, and you will find beyond any doubt or question that the asseveration of the Apostle is fully and completely substantiated.

You find it in miniature, as it were, in the story of the children of Israel themselves. Their story is that whenever they were true to God, and worshipped Him, and obeyed His commandments, all went well with them; they were a pattern and an example to the nations, and highly successful; but every time they turned away from God and looked at the idols of other nations, or took up their religion or their philosophies, everything went wrong with them. It is the principle that emerges as you read through the pages of the Old Testament.

But the most impressive statement of all, the perfect summary of this entire argument, is provided by the Apostle Paul in the Epistle to the Romans, beginning at verse eighteen and going on to the end of the first chapter. He says that as nations and peoples in supposed 'wisdom' have turned their backs upon God the Creator, they have always become fools – 'Imagining themselves to be wise, they became fools'. Then he proceeds to give an account of their terrible moral degradation, the perversions and obscenities into which they fell. 'Ah,' says our modern lecturer, 'the Church must speak specifically about sex . . .' Very well, the Church does so! If you want to know what she has to say, read the second half of the first chapter of the Epistle to the Romans, and you will find an account of all the modern perversions, all the foulnesses that are disgracing life at the present time. They have occurred many times before. But when has that happened? It is always when man in his supposed wisdom has turned from the Creator and has given his worship to the creature. The whole history of the human race substantiates what the Apostle claims. Before Christ ever came into the world everything else had had its opportunity. The Greek philosophers had flourished, the greatest of them had already taught their beliefs. But they could not deal with the problem of sin; their teaching was not adequate and had already failed. There was also the great Roman Empire with its system of law; but there was a canker at the very heart of the Empire; and it finally collapsed, not because of the superior prowess of the Goths and the Vandals and the Barbarians, but because of the moral rot at its very heart. That was the cause of the 'Decline and Fall' of the great Roman Empire, as is admitted by all. In other words, history substantiates the Apostle's teaching.

But, unfortunately, modern history, contemporary history, proves my thesis also. This is where we see the relevance of this teaching. And how up-to-date it is! how it speaks to us at this present time! We have read in our newspapers during the last week statements such as that of the Medical Officer of Health for the City of Edinburgh, and of various other Medical Officers of Health who have been giving their annual reports. 'The Church,' says the lecturer I have quoted, 'must supply an answer to the problem of sex.' What the Medical Officers of Health are reporting is that there is an appalling increase in venereal diseases and especially amongst adolescents and juveniles. Such is the problem confronting us. This moral problem has become the most acute and the most urgent – there is a serious breakdown of morality.

[27]

They tell us that we are confronted by an amoral generation, by people who do not seem to have a moral sense at all! But let us not forget that this situation must be considered in the light of the exceptional educational facilities and opportunities and advantages which have been available since 1870. This man who tells us that religion is not the only solution is a lecturer on education, and there has been an abundance of such lecturers and lectures since 1870. And yet here is our great problem – immorality and vice and evil! The world has multiplied its institutions for dealing with the moral and social problems in this present century more than ever before. Clubs, institutions, cultural agencies, have been multiplying one on top of another. Never has the government of any country spent so much in an attempt to deal with moral and social problems as has been done in this country in the present century. And yet here are these men saying one after another that moral standards are deteriorating almost hourly, week by week, and that the problem is becoming appallingly difficult of solution. They are asking what can be done? The lecturer in question says that things have come to such a pass that the Church must do something, the Church must begin to speak. But then he spoils it all by telling the Church what she is to say; and what he says, as I shall show, is completely wrong!

What then is the position? It is as religion has declined in this century that the moral problem has become more acute. Let us remember that we have two lots of statistics. There are the statistics of the Medical Officers of Health, proving that all these terrible problems and diseases are on the increase. But there are other statistics, church statistics. The number of church members is going down year by year; the number of adherents is declining; the number of Sunday School scholars grows less and less. The two things go together. As religion has gone down all these other things have gone up. I am simply saying all this to justify the assertion of the New Testament that its teaching is the only way, and that there is none other. The modern situation is proving it before our eyes, and yet our education lecturer says that Bible teaching must not be the only teaching. He says that 'perhaps it will give the best hope of success', but would be 'narrow-minded' if we said that this is the only answer and solution. Well, let him mention the others! What has he got to mention? Education?

We have tried it. Let him mention various clubs. We have tried them also, and cultural agencies. We are still trying them all. How foolish, how ridiculous, to utter these general clichés and not face the facts!

But there is a further reason why this is inevitably the truth; it is because of the nature of the fight in which we are engaged. The whole of past history proves it, the modern position proves it. But apart from that the nature of the fight itself makes this proposition inevitably true. How? Man's own nature makes a warfare absolutely certain. The fatal mistake made constantly about man is to regard him only as a mind and an intellect, and therefore, the whole basis of secular teaching is that all you need do is to tell men about the evil nature of certain things, and the evil consequences of doing them, and then they will stop doing them. Conversely, if you tell them to do certain things because they are right and good and true and noble, they will jump at them and do them. What ignorance of human nature!

I am not alone in speaking thus. I was interested recently to read a review of part of the autobiography of a well-known sceptical, irreligious, modern writer, Leonard Woolf. The review was written by another literary sceptic, Kingsley Martin. But the reviewer, at any rate, had reached the conclusion that the trouble with this whole school to which Leonard Woolf belongs is just this, that they will not see that man in the main is irrational. He used what seemed to me to be a very good illustration. 'What Leonard Woolf and all his companions, such as Bertrand Russell and others, have always failed to grasp is this,' he said, 'that man is a kind of iceberg.' Standing up above the water is a certain amount, about a third perhaps, which may look very white, but underneath are two-thirds out of sight in the depth, in the darkness. Writers like Leonard Woolf, says Kingsley Martin, do not realize that man is mainly irrational. What he means, of course, is that man is not governed by his mind, his intellect, his understanding, but by desires, impulses, and instincts, by what the psychologists call 'drives'. These are the things that control and master a man; and the problem which is confronting the world in the present era is that of these instinctive 'drives'.

All this can be seen on the national and international plane as

[29]

well as in the case of the individual; and that is what makes all optimistic statements about some world organization that is going to banish war so childishly ridiculous. Nations, like individuals, are not governed by common sense. If the world were governed by common sense there would never be a war. War is sheer madness, from every standpoint. It is a waste of money, it is a waste of life, it is a childish way of settling a dispute and a problem. How can you settle a problem of government or any other problem by just killing one another? I repeat, war is sheer madness; there is nothing to be said for it. Why then do the nations fight and prepare for war? The answer is that they are not governed by their minds and intellects but by the two-thirds that is underneath the surface, the part of the iceberg that you do not see – greed, avarice, national pride, the desire to possess and to become greater than others. These are the things that ever cause wars. 'Whence come wars among you?' asks James. 'Come they not hence, even of your lusts, that war within your members?' (James 4:1). That is true of the individual as well as of nations; and because it is true it follows that nothing but that which can deal with this hidden powerful two-thirds can really provide a remedy for the situation. It is the claim of the Gospel that it, and it alone, can do so. Nothing else can.

In the next place consider the enemy that stands against us. 'We wrestle not against flesh and blood, but against principalities, against powers, against the rulers of the darkness of this world, against spiritual wickedness in high places.' 'Take unto you the whole armour of God,' says Paul, 'that ye may be able to stand against the wiles of the devil.' Put up all your moral schemes and teachings against the wiles of the devil and he smiles at you in contempt. Of course! How utterly inadequate it all is! We shall elaborate that later.

Furthermore, consider the standard to which we are asked to attain. Christianity not merely tells us to be nice and good and clean and moral. A Christian is not simply a nice respectable person. It is because so many have thought that mere respectability is Christianity that they have left the Church. They say that such a result can be achieved outside the Church, and point to the nice, good, moral people who are not Christians. And that is a perfectly fair argument. But the answer to it is that that is not

Christianity. A Christian is not merely a person who does not do this, that, or the other. A Christian is positive. He is called to 'hunger and thirst after righteousness'; to be 'pure in heart'; to be 'perfect even as your Father which is in heaven is perfect'. That is Christianity! To be like Christ, to live as He lived! And the moment you consider the standard you see how utterly impossible and inadequate are all these other suggestions that are being put forward. We can, therefore, sum it all up by asserting openly, frankly, avowedly, and unashamedly, as the Apostle does here by implication, that this, and this alone, is the only way of victory and of triumph. It was because this is so that the Son of God came into the world. If anything else could have sufficed He would never have come. There would never have been an Incarnation, still less a death upon the Cross, were it not that this is true. 'The Son of man is come to seek and to save that which was lost.' This is the beginning and foundation and basis of the Christian position. Christ came because, in a sense, He had to come if there was to be any salvation at all. He came because man had completely failed.

> *O loving wisdom of our God,*
> *When all was sin and shame,*
> *A second Adam to the fight*
> *And to the rescue came.*

It was and is the only way, there is no other. Let the world in its supposed wisdom call it 'narrow-minded'. As long as it does so it will continue to degenerate morally and ethically, and fester in its own iniquity. The Christian way is the only way.

But let us consider a second general point. It is obvious from the statement of the lecturer which we have been considering that Christianity is capable of being misunderstood and this, unfortunately, is something that has kept recurring throughout the centuries. There has been nothing so tragic as the misunderstanding of Christianity and the Christian message. There are people like this lecturer in education who are very ready to say, 'The Church must make her contribution. Christianity, perhaps, is the best hope we have got. It is not our only hope, but perhaps it is one that is most likely to lead to results, so the Church must play her part.' Governments are very ready to say this in times of crises. When the problem gets out of hand they ask, 'Well now, what has the Church to say?' And they expect the Church to make some general statements which will improve the moral tone of society. The Church must play its part! Yes, but this attitude betrays, as I say, a complete ignorance as to what the message of the Church really is.

There have been two main misunderstandings in this particular context. The first is that Christianity and its message is nothing but a teaching that we ourselves have to apply. This lies at the root of the misunderstanding of the lecturer whose statement we are examining. It is a very old fallacy. It was the real trouble at the beginning of the eighteenth century before the great Evangelical Awakening took place. It was the over-all fallacy of the men who were called Deists, and others. They said that God had created the world like a watchmaker winding-up a watch and then had no further concern with it, except that He had given it a certain moral teaching. So they merely equated Christianity with a teaching and morality which tell people to live a good life. Thomas Arnold, headmaster of Rugby in the nineteenth century, was guilty of exactly the same fallacy: that was his teaching also. It is sometimes known as 'Public School religion' and teaches that Christianity is that which makes you 'a good little gentleman'. You refrain from certain things and you do certain other things. It is just moral, ethical teaching.

Now this is a tragic misunderstanding of the whole position, for it regarded Christianity merely as one teaching among a number of other teachings, for example, those of Plato, Socrates, Aristotle, Seneca, and others who supplied high, idealistic, moral teaching. Christianity is but another, and perhaps the best of them all; so let us give great attention to it. And do not forget that the late Mr Gandhi of recent date held a very exalted and noble teaching; and there are various others. They add to their list of great teachers the name of 'Jesus', as they call Him, and He generally comes somewhere about the centre. Some rise superior to Him, others are esteemed His inferiors. But such thinking and talking simply reduces Christianity to nothing but a moral, ethical teaching – just a variant of the theme of 'Goodness, Beauty and Truth' to which we are to aspire. It is because such multitudes of people, especially in the present century, regard that as Christianity that the Church is as she is.

Such was the teaching of the theological school called Modernism or Liberalism which came in about the middle of the last century in this country. Its theme was 'the Jesus of history'. They took out miracles, indeed the entire supernatural element, and the substitutionary atonement. What is Jesus? 'Ah,' they said, 'Jesus is the greatest religious teacher the world has ever known. Listen to His teaching, emulate His example, follow Him; and if you do so you will be a good Christian. Do not bother about doctrines, they are not important; it is Jesus' teaching that matters.'

So Christianity has been reduced to a moral and an ethical code and teaching. That leads inevitably to failure and to disaster, for it leaves the whole business to us as individuals. I have got to admire the teaching, next I am required to accept it, and then I have to proceed to put it into practice. It is left entirely to me. 'Ah but,' they say, 'look to the example of Jesus.' Example of Jesus? I know of nothing that is so discouraging as the example of Jesus! As I look at His moral stature, at His absolute perfection, as I see Him walking through this world without sin, I feel that I am already condemned and hopeless. Imitation of Christ? It is the greatest nonsense that has ever been uttered! Imitation of Christ? I who cannot satisfy myself and my own demands, and other people still less – am I to imitate Christ? The saints make me feel ashamed of myself. I read of men like George Whitefield and others, and I feel that I have not yet started. And yet I am told to take this ethical teaching of the Sermon on the Mount, this idealistic social teaching, and to put this into practice! 'It is so marvellous,' they say, 'it will stimulate you; look at Him and follow Him!'

It is not surprising that failure has resulted, and that people have left the Christian Church; it is not surprising that we are faced with a moral collapse in this country, and in all the countries, at the present time; for the non-Christian ethical teaching leaves it all to me, strengthless and powerless though I am. I am like the Apostle Paul by nature and I say, 'Alas, with my mind I see what is right, but I find another law in my members dragging me down. With my mind I receive and accept and admire the law of God,

[33]

but there is this other law, this other thing, working within me, and making me captive to the law of sin and death which is within me' (cf. Romans 7:14-25). There is this third of the iceberg, as it were, above water and it is looking at the sun; but I am aware of the other two-thirds that is dragging me down to the depths and the darkness. 'O wretched man that I am! who shall deliver me?' That is the inevitable position. If Christianity is but a moral ethical teaching it is as useless as all the others. The 'Christian' way has always been proved to be useless when it is reduced to such a level.

But Christianity is no mere code of ethics. Our educationalists cannot just turn to us and say, 'Well now, come along, you representatives of the Christian Church. Do not be narrow-minded, but give us your help, give us your teaching, we want to know what you think about sex, and many other factors in life.' I answer that what is needed is not what I think about sex, but a power that will deliver a man from being mastered and controlled by it. There is ample knowledge about sex. Alas, people today know far too much about sex; they know much more than their forefathers knew. They are reading books about it – novels, text-books, and so on – and the more they read the worse they get. Their reading only serves to aggravate the problem. It is not knowledge we need; it is power. And that is where your moral ethical systems break down and fail completely. They have no power to offer, none at all. We must beware, therefore, of reducing Christianity to a mere moral, ethical teaching. God forbid that anybody should still be held in that ignorance and blindness! All that teaching has been tried very thoroughly for a hundred years and more, and it has failed completely, both in the case of the individual, and also in the national and international realms.

But I must say a word about the other misunderstanding. Here, again, is an interesting and fascinating story. There have been those who have said, 'No, it is not just enough to hold this teaching before men and to tell them to get on with it, because the forces against us are too great. We are up against the world and the flesh and the devil. There is all that I am conscious of within myself, and then as I walk about the streets and see the hoardings and the placards and read newspapers, sin is insinuating itself and tempting me. I see it everywhere around me, in advertisements, in dress, and in all that characterizes the life of a great city like London. How can I fight against all this?' 'No,' they say, 'there is only one thing to do. If a man is to save his soul and to live a good and pure life he has got to get away from all this, he has got to segregate himself.'

In other words, the second great misunderstanding of the Christian teaching is that which we can sum up under the whole notion of monasticism. Here is a wonderful story. There is something about the people who started the monastic idea which calls forth one's admiration. At any rate they were men who were serious and concerned about their souls and their lives and their daily living. This was the biggest thing in life to them; so much so that they would give up a profession, they would give up home, they would give up all that had been dear to them and retire into a monastery, there to live what they called the 'religious' life. The idea was that the only way in which you could fight this battle was to get away from the enemy as much as possible. Now in that principle, as I shall explain, there is something which is right and true. The Apostle Paul, addressing the Romans in chapter 13 of his Epistle, says, 'Make no provision for the flesh'. It would be good for all of us if we spent less time reading our newspapers, kept our eyes straight ahead as we walked the streets of London, did not look at certain things, and did not go to certain places. So far, so good! But certain people carried that further; they said that you must get right out of the world. You must concentrate on this alone, you must give up ordinary life and living, and isolate yourself; you must go into a monastery, or become a hermit on top of a mountain, or get away into some cell somewhere; that being the only way of escape. And they did not stop even at that. They said that you have to keep down the body; so you have to fast twice, perhaps three times a week. You have to do other things also, perhaps put on a camel-hair shirt, and in various ways knock down this body of yours and insult it as much as you can. They indulged in what were called 'flagellations'; they would beat their bodies, scarify their flesh, all in an attempt to overcome these powers that are against us in this great fight of which Paul is speaking. The best description of all this that I have ever read is to be found in a book called *The Vision of God*, the Bampton Lectures delivered about 1928 by Kenneth E.

Kirk. There you will find an account of how this idea came in, and at a very early period in the history of the church. And that same school of thought has persisted ever since.

But that is not Christianity, and for the following reasons. Though you leave the world and all its prospects, and go and live as a monk or a hermit in a cell; though you have left the world, you have not left yourself – the two-thirds submerged part of the iceberg is still with you! You do not leave your sinful nature outside the monastery. Evil imaginations and thoughts are with you still; you cannot get rid of them. Wherever you go they go; yourself, your nature, this part that drags you down will be with you in the cell exactly as it was on the streets of London. Not only so, the evil powers are also there as much as they were when you were living your life amongst other people. 'We wrestle not against flesh and blood, but against principalities and powers, against the rulers of the darkness of this world, against spiritual wickedness in high places.' Stone walls do not keep them out, iron bars do not keep them out, locked doors do not keep them out; wherever you are they will be there. They are spiritual, they are unseen, they can penetrate everywhere, and they are with you in your cell. You cannot get rid of them. And for these reasons the great system of monasticism finally broke down completely.

The whole matter can be summed up in the story of one person, Martin Luther. What exactly did Luther discover? He was a monk there in his cell, fasting, sweating, praying, trying to get rid of the body, trying to get rid of this problem, trying to conquer these spiritual enemies. But the more he tried the nearer he seemed to be to complete failure and utter hopelessness. And at last he saw it! His monastic ideas were a travesty of Christianity; they were not Christianity at all. Christianity was something essentially different. He saw that you could be a Christian in the midst of the world, you could be a Christian 'sweeping a floor', as he puts it. You need not be a coenobite, you need not take vows of chastity and remain unmarried, in order to be a preacher. No, as a married man you are as eligible as a man who renounces sex. He suddenly saw that the monastic way was not God's way, and that was the beginning of the great Protestant Reformation. Thank God that that which Luther had to unlearn is not the Christian teaching, for the logical

[36]

end of the monastic argument is that you cannot be a true Christian and still live in the world. Of course the Roman Church did not teach that, but divided Christians into 'religious' and 'laity', and taught that the latter could be helped by borrowing from the over-plus of righteousness of the former – the utterly unscriptural doctrine of supererogation. You see how essentially different that is from the New Testament teaching. Here were ordinary people, servants, slaves, husbands, wives, parents, children. The Apostle does not say to them, 'Off, all of you, into a monastery; get away somewhere from the world.' Not at all! Thank God it is not that! That would be a gospel for wealthy people alone. And not only so; there would be no Christian witness and testimony in the world.

What a denial it is, ultimately, of the glory of the Christian faith! What is the Christian method? I end with a text. It is not, 'Set about imitating Christ, adopt His moral ethical teaching, and try to put it into practice'. It is not, 'Get away and become a monk or a hermit'. But just where you are in the midst of the world, with evil and sin rampant round and about you, and everybody and everything doing all they can to discourage you and to drag you down, just as and where you are, 'Be strong in the Lord, and in the power of his might. Take unto you the whole armour of God, that you may be able to withstand the wiles of the devil.' It is not retreat, it is not escape, it is not attempting something that is impossible. No, it is this supernatural, miraculous Gospel that enables us to be 'more than conquerors' over everything that is set against us.

I have dealt with all this because of the terrible misunderstanding of Christianity found in the newspapers, and their failure to understand the very basis of the Christian faith. Thank God, this faith of ours is entirely different from what men imagine. It is supernatural, it is 'the life of God in the soul of man', and being that, it holds out before me not only a hope, it offers me a certain victory.

3
The Enemy

'Henceforth,' says the Apostle, 'this is the thing you have to bear in mind' – and he proceeds from this tenth verse until the twentieth verse to deal with the most urgent matter confronting all Christian people. It is the fight, the conflict which everybody coming into this world has inevitably to wage. We have so far been looking at it in a general manner, introducing it, and dividing up the statement into its two main component parts. We have also seen that the Apostle presses his instruction upon these Ephesians, and upon us, because it is clearly the only way whereby this warfare can be waged successfully. Christianity is an exclusive religion; it claims that it, and it alone, is the truth of God. And not only is it the one and only way, it also does not need any help or assistance. There is no need to add a little Buddhism or Mohammedanism or Confucianism, or any other 'ism' to it. It is itself the way, and it is complete, it is entire. Hence the Apostle urges Christians not only to consider it, but to understand it, and above all to apply it.

We come now to the Apostle's explication as to why he presses this upon them in a most urgent manner. This is most characteristic of him. He does not just make statements, he gives reasons for his statements. We are to put on the whole armour of God – *for*, or *because*, 'we wrestle not' etc. This is one of the most glorious aspects of the Christian faith. You cannot reason yourself into it, but the moment you are in it you find that it is the most reasonable thing in the world, full of understanding, full of explanations.

Christianity, unlike so many of the cults, is not merely something which teaches you to persuade yourself in a thoughtless manner. It does not just tell you to say something, and to go on saying it mechanically, whether it be true or not, and whether you feel it or not. That is not Christianity. It always gives reasons. So here the Apostle goes on to give us the explanation as to why he exhorts us to 'be strong in the Lord and in the power of his might', and 'to put on the whole armour of God'. We need it all; and he tells us why particularly in verses 11 and 12.

These verses constitute a most striking and remarkable statement. I wonder whether anyone is surprised that we propose to consider it, and is tempted to say, 'Well, in the midst of life in the world as it is today, with conditions and situations as they are, are we really going to spend our time in looking at and considering what the Bible has to say about the devil and these principalities and powers?' If you have such a feeling, all I can say is that, far from being a realist, as you probably imagine yourself to be, you are of all people the one who is not really facing the world situation as it is at this moment. There is nothing more realistic at this hour than what we are going to consider. There is nothing in the whole world that is so urgently needed at this moment as an understanding of this very thing the Apostle tells us here.

I shall not mention the name of any statesman, or of any political party, of any country or any political or social organization – and yet I venture to assert that what we are about to consider is more relevant to the condition of the world than all talk about politics and international relationships and everything in which statesmen and their followers indulge. That is a strong and a bold statement, as I am well aware; but if you believe the Bible at all, it must inevitably be true. We are dealing, remember, with the ultimate cause of the world situation, and for this reason I can say that this is more urgently relevant than anything else. Let me use a comparison which I have often employed. It seems to me that what modern thinkers so constantly fail to do is to differentiate between a disease itself and the possible symptoms of a disease. A disease may give rise to many symptoms. Take any example at random. With influenza prevalent you may get pneumonia. The primary disease is, in a sense, in your lungs. Let that do for the moment as a rough definition of pneumonia. But you will find that you have many other symptoms. You will have a headache, you will feel flushed, you may have odd aches and pains all over your body, and there may be sweating and so on. There are very many symptoms of the disease, and the danger is that we should spend our time in medicating the symptoms only. You can take various things to relieve your headache, such as aspirin, and your head will feel better for a while. But it will not make any difference to the pneumonia. And so you can go on dealing with one symptom after another. You will find that you are kept very busy, and that you will have to go on dealing with fresh symptoms constantly. But the disease itself, and not the symptoms, is the thing that really matters.

What is the chief trouble with the world at this moment? Here are all the statesmen and others meeting busily in conference, quarrelling, breaking up, and then meeting again. What is the matter? The trouble is that they do not realize the nature of the disease, they have never understood the cause. And the greatest tragedy of all is that the Christian Church which alone has the message that can expose the cause and recommend the only remedy that can cure – I say that the Christian Church herself, instead of teaching the remedy, is half her time and more but saying things which the statesmen and the politicians can say. She does so, of course, because she wants to give the impression that the Christian message is 'relevant'. People think that a message is revelant only if one is talking in worldly and temporal terms. If you talk about these statesmen by name, and take up particular manifestations of the problem, such as bombs and so on, you are being tremendously relevant! How pathetic it is! How tragic! Medicating the symptoms and not recognizing the disease!

The business of the Christian Church is to get down to the root cause of the trouble. It alone can do so. And it is because what we are looking at here gives the only true understanding of the world situation, and what can be done about it, that I am claiming for it that it is the most urgently relevant message in this troubled world of ours today. But, naturally, as I shall proceed to show, it is something that is utterly ridiculed by the world. Nevertheless, and indeed because of that, let us look at it.

First of all the Apostle directs us to the fact of the conflict. You notice his terms, 'We wrestle.' Now this term 'wrestle' causes the commentators a great deal of trouble. The trouble arises because the Apostle starts by saying 'We wrestle', and then when he comes to describe the 'armour' uses terms that have nothing at all to do with 'wrestling'. When he comes to the details of the armour he seems to be thinking rather of two armies meeting in conflict, and of fiery darts, and swords. There seems to be a certain amount of confusion. It is very difficult to determine exactly why the Apostle used this term 'We wrestle' – his only use of the word. The obvious explanation must be this, that he is anxious to show the intimate nature of the conflict. While it is right, as we shall see, to think of great massed battalions, and two great opposing forces, we must realize at the same time that it is an individual matter. The notion of wrestling brings us immediately to that – two men grappling with one another. So we have to bear the two aspects in mind. We are participators in this mighty spiritual conflict that is going on round and about us and in us. But we are also individually engaged, every one of us. We have not only to watch as parts of an army, we have also to watch individually. I believe that Paul used the expression 'We wrestle' in order to show that aspect of the truth.

But then he uses these other terms, 'Put on the whole *armour* of God, that ye may be able to *withstand* in the evil day' – and then – 'having done all, *to stand*'. He uses these terms for one reason only, namely, to bring out the fierceness and the terrible nature and character of the conflict. As Christian people we are set in this tremendous conflict, wrestling, standing against, withstanding an enemy that is attacking. The first thing you have to do is to repulse the attacks, and you have to keep on doing so because he continues to be the enemy. And even though you get a temporary victory you do not say, 'Well, it is all over, I can take my ease now, and go away on holiday.' Not at all! 'Having done all things, to stand.' The idea is that this is a relentless war, that 'there is no discharge in this war', as the Book of Ecclesiastes puts it, but that as long as we are in this life and world we have to be aware of the fact that we are engaged in a fight, a struggle, a conflict.

This clearly needs to be emphasized, because there are so many who do not realize it. And not to realize that you are in a conflict means one thing only, and that is that you are so hopelessly defeated, and so 'knocked out' as it were, that you do not even know it – you are unconscious! It means that you are completely defeated by the devil. Anyone who is not aware of a fight and a conflict in a spiritual sense is in a drugged and hazardous condition. And then, of course, on the other hand the Cults are always with us; and the whole teaching of the Cults – I do not care which of them you specify – is always that you can be delivered right out of the conflict somehow or another. 'Oh yes,' they say, 'it is quite true that there is a problem; but all is well, you do this and that and all will be well.' That is the essence of Christian Science teaching. There is no conflict, there is no such thing as disease, there is no such thing as pain. These things are non-existent, they say, and you must keep on saying this to yourself, and persuade yourself, and for the time being you feel very happy. But it is done by evading facts, by turning your back upon truth, by fooling yourself. All the Cults do that in some shape or form. They want to give you the impression that you can relax and be at ease; that there is no conflict, no fight; whereas the Apostle says 'We wrestle'. You are 'withstanding', there is an enemy who is always attacking you, and even though you get your victory, 'stand', and make sure that you continue so to do. Always keep on your feet. In other words, the difficult thing in this world is to keep on your feet, for there is an enemy who is ever threatening you and trying to knock you down. The great task of life, the great business of life is to keep standing! Now this is the Apostle's representation of the matter. It is not mine; it is his. He multiplies his terms, and repeats them in order to bring home to us this notion that we are in the midst of a mighty conflict.

We now go on to see what he has to say about the nature of the conflict. Here, as is again not unusual with him, he starts with a negative. At this point we come to the very essence of the matter, to what I would call one essential and peculiar character and nature of the biblical message from beginning to end. This is something peculiar to the Bible. The Bible must not be classed with any other book, because not only does it differ in details, its whole point of view is different. It is *essentially* different. It is a 'peculiar', a 'special' book. And this is the point at which it departs from every other teaching offering itself to mankind. Look at the depth of its insight, look at its understanding. That is what makes this book so marvellous, and proves it to be the book of God Himself. It gets down to the depths, it goes down to the roots. There is nothing superficial, nothing glib and light in it. It is indeed a divine revelation.

I am making these preliminary remarks because to me the most important thing we can grasp at this hour is that in the world as it is at this moment we have a text-book, a manual of life, that really gives us an understanding. Nobody but the Christian understands the world. But he does so, for he accepts this teaching as an essential part of the divine message. But I go further; our knowledge of this, and our acceptance of this, is a thoroughgoing test of our profession of the Christian faith. Let me ask a question therefore before we go any further. Do these phrases form a part of your essential thinking – 'that ye may be able to stand against the wiles of the devil'? 'We wrestle not against flesh and blood, but against principalities and against powers'? Are they always in your thinking as a part of your Christian philosophy, and always present in your mind? As you look at the world today, do you say at once, 'Here is the explanation'? Do you normally think like that? All I say is, that if you do not, you have a very defective sort of Christianity. Ephesians chapter 6, verses 10–13 is a vital and essential part of the Christian faith.

What then does the Apostle say? Let us take the negative first – 'We wrestle not against flesh and blood.' Those who are familiar with their Bibles will know that the term 'flesh' in the New Testament, and especially in the epistles of Paul, is very generally used for the old sinful nature. Not the old man, but the old nature, the sinful nature still residing within us. But this is not the only sense in which the term 'flesh' is used, and, obviously, it is not the sense in which it is used here. The addition of the word 'blood' establishes it beyond any doubt. Actually, in the Greek, 'blood' comes before 'flesh': 'We wrestle not against blood and flesh.' It just means human nature, it means man. So Paul says that we are fighting not men only. Our problem is not that of 'man' or of 'mankind' only, it is something else also.

Here we have one of these fundamental propositions of the Scripture. Here, also, we see how much it differs from the worldly point of view even at its best and highest. The first thing you have to realize, says the Apostle, is that the problem confronting you as an individual, and the problem confronting the whole of mankind, is not merely a human, earthly problem. It is much greater than that and therefore much more difficult.

Let us look at the difference between this and what is believed by those who are not Christian. The world, of course, does not believe this, it has not got hold of this negative. What, then, according to the world, is the cause of our troubles? Throughout the centuries the world has tended to believe in various explanations. In the times when the Church was first established, the world generally believed in a variety of gods. There was a god of war, there was a god of love, there was a god of peace, and so on. To this extent, you see, men had a certain amount of insight, for they thought that the world was being influenced and governed by certain unseen powers and forces. They felt that there must be a god who shows himself in all his power in war. Then there was clearly a god of love also. And so they felt that the one thing to do was to please and to placate these gods. When the Apostle Paul visited the famous city of Athens he found it cluttered up with altars to the various gods. Their idea was this, that as these gods had such influence upon man and his life in this world, obviously the thing to do was to put yourself on the right side of the gods. So they had a multiplicity of altars and took their offerings to the various gods and offered them their worship. They believed that their troubles were due to their failure to please the gods. Some of them believed in spirits in trees and in stones, in the sun, the moon, the stars; it is all a part of the same idea. Polytheism, animism, all these things, were merely a recognition on the part of mankind that there are other forces and powers which we do not see but which seem to exert a very great influence upon us.

Then, moving a little from that, others began to see that these were no gods, but obviously the creations of men's minds and imaginations. Accordingly they began to speak in terms of fate. 'Nobody knows what fate is,' they said, 'all we do know is this, that there seems to be something that is influencing us and governing us, and it is very powerful, indeed much more powerful than we are. If you are fated to do such and such a thing you will do it; if it is fated that such a thing should happen to you it will

[44]

happen to you.' Fatalism was a belief in an unseen power that men could not define but which governed their circumstances and controlled what happens to them. But, speaking generally, by today men have moved away from such a belief, although of course there are many who still believe in fate. There are many who, in spite of modern education, believe in astrology and things of that type in this sophisticated twentieth century of which we are so proud. Astrology! – the influence exercised by the stars, the month in which a person is born, and so on!

I am calling attention to all this because it is indicative of an awareness in man that there is something outside himself which makes a tremendous difference to his life. On the other hand, the modern scientific man, on the whole, does not believe in matters to which I have just been referring. His position is, that there is nothing outside himself, that the problem is really man himself and alone. Such is the typical, modern, educated moral man. He is not a Christian. Of course not! He does not believe in the spiritual realm at all. That is why he does not believe in God, in the deity of Jesus Christ, in the Holy Spirit; that is why he does not believe in the existence of the devil and of 'principalities and powers', 'the rulers of the darkness of this world'. There is no such thing to him as a spiritual realm. Belief in it is, to him, nothing but a kind of hangover from those primitive times and conditions in which people believed in spirits in trees and brooks and stones and everywhere else. But, he says, we have outgrown such fantasies. Man has been fooling himself throughout the centuries with fate and all these things, and the nonsense of astrology! Here is your supposed realist, the man who claims to govern everything with his mind and who believes that the sole problem is man himself. In other words, all our troubles are due to man's ignorance, his lack of knowledge and understanding, and his lack of development.

To speak generally, this is surely the most urgent problem facing the world today, because, if you take modern man's standpoint, the spiritual realm is entirely banished. But such is the position of large numbers of our fellow-men.

If, then, the problem is only that of man, and man's ignorance, what is the solution? Such people say that that is a perfectly fair question, and that during the last hundred years or so at least two answers have emerged. First is the idea of progress, development, evolution. We must not lose hope, they say, for, after all, man is only on the threshold of the realization of his own greatness and glory and endless possibilities. They urge us to look back and to see that there has already been development and advance. We have already left animism, we have turned our back upon polytheism, we have got rid of mere fatalism. We now think, and we reason. Man is really beginning to come into his own. And this is inevitable because there is a force in life, some *élan vital*, some vital force. That is how they put it; they are not fatalists, they do not believe in unseen powers! But there is in matter some life-force and power that is pushing everything upwards and forwards! This is the view of the modern rationalist who only believes in things that can be reasoned about and felt and touched and measured and handled! You see, he has to fall back upon a 'vital force', 'Force' with a capital F. That is part of his explanation, it is a part of the comfort he is trying to give us. He tells us not to be impatient, but to hold on, and to wait. There is this evidence of advance and improvement, and it will go on and on until eventually all problems are banished and the world becomes perfect. There are many variations and modifications of that view. We need not trouble to deal with them. Communism is one of them, of course, with its teaching about dialectical materialism and the struggle between capital and labour, supply and demand. It is all part of the process we have to go through until we arrive at that classless perfect society. The real philosophic basis of communism is the evolutionary view of life. There are many people who confess themselves Christians who seem to me to be adopting the notion of evolution more and more.

Then the other answer given by modern man is, that we must not rely passively on this inevitable progress and forward march. We must, in addition, educate one another, spread knowledge, apply our reason to the situation and get everybody else to do so. And they claim, quite confidently, that if we but do so our problems are really going to be solved.

Is it not clear that this is a most vital and urgent matter? The world has been living on this teaching during this present century. It is being given much publicity at the present time, and we are told that if only we can teach the masses and educate them, and

[46]

teach them how to reason, there would never be another war. They would soon see that war is ridiculous and that we must get together and hold conferences and settle all disputes amicably, by which means we shall all live happily ever afterwards! Many really believe in such a programme; and the result is, of course, that when it does not happen they are disappointed; they cannot understand it and are bewildered. But that is the prevailing notion and the prevailing theory.

So we are given the comfort of the evolutionary process and the spread of knowledge and culture and education. It is to me almost beyond understanding that anybody who looks at the modern world and reads a newspaper can still go on believing such theories. Indeed, if they never even read a newspaper, how can anybody who has ever known an educated, cultured, reasonable man, who nevertheless fails drastically in his own personal life, possibly believe such things? How can they believe that wisdom and knowledge and learning, and the ability to reason and to use logic, is the solution to the problem, when what is to be seen daily in the lives of men and women proves the exact opposite? It is amazing! But what I am concerned to emphasize particularly is that these theories are the opposite of what the Apostle teaches here in Ephesians chapter six.

'We wrestle not against flesh and blood.' The problem is not merely on the human level. Man supplies problems certainly, but they are the symptoms of the disease, the real cause is further back – 'not against flesh and blood'. It is at this point that I justify my original statement that it is the Gospel, and the Gospel alone, that holds out any hope for this troubled unhappy world. The whole basis of man's conduct of affairs rests on the supposition that we are wrestling only with flesh and blood, that the problem is man, and that the problem can therefore be solved by human, earthly media, and by ways and means of man's own devising. Always it is man, flesh and blood, that is being considered, and only man. The natural man's thoughts never rise higher. The spiritual is never mentioned. This is surely something that is absolutely basic.

So far I have stated the matter negatively: but now let us look at it positively. 'We wrestle not against flesh and blood, *but* against principalities, against powers.' Notice how Paul repeats this word 'against' for the sake of emphasis. 'Bad style,' you say. 'We wrestle not against flesh and blood, but against principalities, against powers.' Your pedantic little editors would knock out these repetitions of 'against', would they not? '*Against* principalities, *against* powers, *against* the rulers of the darkness of this world, *against* spiritual wickedness in heavenly places.' Here, once more, we are looking directly at what is most essential in biblical and Christian teaching. What is the problem of this world? What is the ultimate cause of our troubles? It is not man! It is the devil and his unseen forces and powers. That is the proposition. This is what we have to analyse, or rather, we have to follow the Apostle in his own analysis of it.

Let us first approach it in general. Here is something which is not only not believed today, but which is rejected with scorn and utterly ridiculed, and regarded as the funniest of all jokes. The devil! Principalities and powers! Unseen spiritual forces! Your modern man says that this is an insult to human intelligence. 'Fancy,' he says, 'in 1960, with the world as it is, a man really proposing to preach about the devil and unseen spiritual forces! It is an insult to one's intelligence. Why don't you tell us something about how to settle the international problems? Why don't you start an agitation to stop the making of bombs? Why are you not realistic? Why do you refuse to be practical? You are in the realm of folk-lore, you are still manifesting the primitive mind, you are still thinking in terms of fairy-tales. Why don't you face the facts, the stark realities of life as it is today, instead of talking about some unseen spiritual forces and the devil?' 'Ah,' they say, 'all this is behind the times, this is nonsense.' The Apostle's teaching is utterly and completely ridiculed. But what troubles me is that it is being ridiculed not only by the non-Christian world in general, but that it is not receiving much attention from, and not being emphasized by Christian people, including many who are termed evangelical. So many Christians are so much concerned with some particular sin that is getting them down, and so much concerned about personal happiness, that they never consider this great problem. They are so introspective and subjective that they never look at the whole cosmos, the great world problem, this tremendous thing the Apostle puts before us here. To what extent, I ask again, does this teaching concerning the devil and his powers enter into our normal habitual thinking? The Apostle says that we should never relax, never be off our guard, but stand always and be ready and 'at arms' at all times because of the devil and his powers. This entire teaching has been ridiculed.

What is our reply to that? Let me suggest some ideas and lines of thought. This whole matter of believing in the devil and the spiritual powers associated with him, is after all simply the problem of believing in a spiritual realm at all. That is the fundamental question. Do you believe that a spiritual realm exists? There are many who call themselves Christian who obviously do not. They have reduced Christianity to a moral-ethical teaching, and nothing more. To them there is no spiritual realm, no realm which is above us and which influences us. They may say in words that they believe in such a realm, but in their actual lives they do not. They are not aware of its existence. Of course if a man does not believe in God he is quite consistent in refusing to believe in the devil and spiritual powers. If he does not believe in God I would not expect him to believe in the devil. But what I cannot understand is a man who does believe in God but who does not believe in the devil. What I cannot understand is a man who gets up in his church and says, 'I believe in the Holy Ghost' and then regards the devil as a joke! 'I believe in the Holy Spirit', but he does not believe in evil spirits. Such a man is utterly inconsistent. He says he believes in a spiritual realm, but he only believes in one half of it; he does not believe in the other half. What is involved here is our whole attitude towards the spiritual realm that is above us and outside us.

Or let me put the matter in the following way in order that you may see exactly where you stand if you do not believe in the devil and these spiritual powers, or if you are not certain about this. The problem, ultimately, is not just belief in the devil, it is belief in the authority of the Scripture, for that also is closely involved. There are people who do not believe the Bible to be the Word of God, who reject the Virgin Birth, and the miracles, and belief in a substitutionary Atonement, and the personality of the Holy Spirit; and I am not surprised that they reject the devil and the forces of evil. They are educated, they are cultured, they are learned, they are twentieth-century men. They come to this old Book and they say, 'It is an old book and it is a book like every other book. There is much rubbish in it, much error. The writers put in what was believed at the time, but, of course, we know now that that is not true.' So they come to the Book as authorities; the Book is not the authority, they are the authority. Out goes this, out goes that, out goes the Holy Spirit, out goes the devil, and out go many other things. What is left? Simply what *I* can understand and accept, what *I* believe to be true. *I* am the authority, *my* reason is on the throne! So this is not a mere matter of believing in the devil, it involves your whole attitude towards the Scripture. That is so for the reason that this teaching about the devil and his forces is an essential, vital part of the biblical teaching. It is found everywhere from Genesis to Revelation, and especially in Genesis and in Revelation. Our Lord Himself taught it, and if you believe in Him and in His teaching, you have to believe in what He said about the devil and his powers. So we are fundamentally face to face with this question: Do we believe in the Bible as our only revelation of truth, and our only authority, or are we trusting ourselves and our own understanding? Miserable worms that we are, and making such a chaos of our world with our great minds and understanding, who are we to enter into the spiritual realm and to say what is true and what is false? How ridiculous it all is!

But still further! A belief in the devil and his powers is an absolute essential to a belief in the biblical teaching concerning sin and evil. You cannot really believe the biblical doctrine concerning sin unless you believe in the devil and in the principalities and powers associated with him.

Further, a belief in the devil and his forces is absolutely essential to a true understanding of the biblical doctrine of salvation. 'Ah, but,' you say, 'that cannot be. Surely all that is necessary is that I believe Christ died for my sins upon the Cross.' So far you are right, but why did He have to come? What was He really doing on the Cross? According to the Apostle Paul, He was there 'spoiling principalities and powers, making a show of them openly, and triumphing over them in it' (Colossians 2:15). Why did Christ have to come? One of His own answers was this: 'The strong man armed keepeth his goods at peace, but when a stronger than he cometh upon him, he taketh from him all his armour in which he trusted, and divideth his spoils' (Luke

11:21–22). Do not think that you can understand the biblical doctrine of salvation and reject the devil. You cannot! You do not hold the true doctrine of salvation if you do not believe in the devil and his powers. You may only have undergone a little psychological treatment which makes you feel happy because you think your sins are forgiven; but you have not understood the biblical teaching as to why Christ came, and what He had to do, and the fight and the conflict, and the agony in the Garden, and the temptations, and all He endured on the Cross. That has no meaning for you, it cannot have. So you have not got a full Gospel, if you have a Gospel at all.

In conclusion, I assert once more that you simply cannot understand the history recorded in the Bible, the whole history of the world from the dawn of civilization until this present time; you cannot understand modern history and what is happening in the world today, the confusion, the amazing fact of the world as it is in spite of all the advance we have heard so much about; still less can you understand the future, or have any hope with respect to it; unless you have a clear understanding of what the Apostle teaches here about the devil and the principalities and powers, the world rulers of this darkness, the wicked spirits in the heavenlies. You may say that this is depressing. Depressing? I find this the most comforting, cheering, optimistic teaching that is known to me. What is to me depressing is to be confronted by a situation that I do not understand. If I do not understand the situation I feel lost. I was never satisfied with medicating symptoms. I knew the patient might feel a little better, but the question was, What is the matter with the man? And I was ill at ease until I knew. It is a great thing to know the trouble, to make a diagnosis; and the moment you have a correct diagnosis you should feel better and happier because you know what you are dealing with. But, thank God, this Apostolic teaching does not stop merely at the delineation of the character of the problem. It does that in a very realistic manner, but it then leads us on to the source of power and of victory. It gives us a view of history which makes us confident and assured. Though I am fighting against the devil and the principalities and powers, and wrestling against infernal hordes, I can be 'strong in the Lord', and in 'the power of his might'. I can be clothed with the whole armour of

God, I can withstand, and having done all things, still stand, and stand with confidence, knowing that in Him and in the power of His might I am safe, and that His final ultimate victory is always assured.

4

The Enemy Described

Having answered the trivial, foolish, sceptical criticisms of the Apostle's teaching let us proceed to look at the teaching itself, and to consider what it has to tell us in detail. I would remind you again that what we are doing is probably the most practical thing that Christian people can ever do. We are examining the ultimate cause of the present state of the world. Let us look again for a moment at the nature of these forces that are set against us. Our Lord Himself teaches us to do so. In the fourteenth chapter of Luke's Gospel He tells a parable of a king who went to war without really understanding the strength of the enemy, and therefore without sufficient resources, and of how that king was discomfited and compelled to yield (Luke 14:31-33). Unpreparedness is utter folly, according to our Lord, and He applies that parable to His own followers. The same principle applies to us now.

The first thing we have to do is to know something of the strength and the power of the enemy that is set against us. I could illustrate this almost endlessly. The failure to do this, for instance, was the real trouble in the period 1933-1939. There was only one lone voice who kept on warning this country of what was happening in Germany. Nobody would believe it, they did not want to be bothered by hearing about the rearmament and ambitions of Germany. We were having a good time, and wanted to enjoy ourselves. Life was wonderful! We now know that that was how the country reached a condition in which the whole situation became not only precarious but almost lost in

1940. It was all because people would not take the trouble to listen to what was happening in the territory of the enemy. All this is infinitely more important in the spiritual realm; and a man who does not understand the teaching of the Apostle on this matter is either fast asleep in the arms of the devil, or else is an utterly defeated Christian.

Let us look then at these forces and start with the terms that are used. The first is *the devil.* 'Put on the whole armour of God, that ye may be able to stand against the wiles of the devil.' We must start with him because, according to the teaching of the Scripture, he is the chief of all the powers that are set against us. Many names are ascribed to him. Here he is called 'the devil'. He is also called Satan. That is the term that is commonly used in the Old Testament. You will also find it in the New Testament. But there are many other names ascribed to him – 'Beelzebub', 'Belial', 'the evil one', 'the wicked one', 'the strong man armed' and so on. They are used in order that we may understand something about the devil and his nature.

Scripture makes it clear that we must think of the devil in a personal sense. It is wrong to think of him simply as a force or a power. The same error is committed with regard to the Holy Spirit. There are many who do not believe in the Person of the Holy Spirit; they talk about 'It'. But the Holy Spirit is a Person, the Third Person in the Blessed Holy Trinity. The Holy Spirit is not merely a power, not just an influence. Many of our errors in connection with the doctrine of the Spirit and of sanctification arise from a fundamental failure to realize that the Holy Spirit is personal. The result is that people sometimes use illustrations about the work of the Holy Spirit as if He were almost some kind of liquid that can be poured from one vessel into another! But the Holy Spirit is a Person! So is the 'devil'. Hence we have to start by realizing that he has personality, and is a distinct and separate entity. Not only so, we are given to understand very clearly that the devil is a super-human personality, bigger than man, stronger than man, greater than man. Yet, at the same time it is made plain and clear that he is not divine.

Here we draw a very important distinction. There was an ancient heresy which taught more or less that there were two Gods controlling human affairs. It was what was known as dualism or dualistic teaching. There was a great God, the Creator, but there was another God, a kind of 'demiurge' as they called him. Some even taught that he was the actual creator; at any rate he had a great power and control. They said that he was a god over against God. But that is not the teaching of the Bible. The Bible teaches that whereas the devil is super-human he is not divine; he is less than divine, he is a created being. We shall return to this again, but I emphasize this important truth at this point.

Another truth to be emphasized is that which stands out prominently here, namely, the power of the devil. You need to put on the whole armour of God, says the Apostle, that 'you may be able to stand against the wiles of the devil'. Let us remind ourselves of the terms that are used in the Scripture to bring out this element of 'power'. One of them is found in the second chapter of this Epistle, in the second verse, where the devil is referred to as 'the prince of the power of the air' – the leader, the chieftain – 'the spirit that now worketh in the children of disobedience'. The Apostle uses a similar expression concerning him in the second Epistle to the Corinthians, where he talks about 'the god of this world' (4:4). 'If our Gospel be hid,' he says, 'it is hid to them that are lost: in whom the god of this world . . .' The Apostle is not contradicting himself, however; he is not saying that the devil is God. What he is saying is, as we shall see in detail later, that he is, as it were, the god of this world. He is not God, but he is 'the god of this world'. That again gives us some impression of his might, his authority and his power – 'the god of this world'!

Then take another term used by our Lord Himself in the eleventh chapter of Luke's Gospel, 'the strong man armed'. The devil, the one with whom we are confronted, is comparable to a very powerful and strong man armed who 'keepeth his goods in peace' (Luke 11:21–22). It is all suggestive of the devil's tremendous power and authority.

The Apostle Peter describes him in these terms: 'Your adversary the devil, as a roaring lion . . .' (1 Peter 5:8). The lion is the king of the jungle, he is the mightiest of all the animals; and there is nothing that gives us such an impression of strength and force and latent power as a 'roaring lion'. He roars and all creation trembles! Well, says Peter, the devil is like that.

Then there is the designation used in the twelfth chapter of the Book of Revelation: 'A great red dragon!' A dragon again conjures up a picture of might and power. 'A dragon with seven heads and ten horns, and seven crowns upon his heads, and his tail drew the third part of the stars of heaven, and did cast them to the earth' (Revelation 12:3–4). In the same book, chapter 20, we find the dragon termed 'that old serpent, which is the devil, and Satan'.

These descriptions convey ideas not only of subtlety but of strength and of great power. Indeed it is clear from the Bible that the power of the devil is second only to that of the Godhead, undeniably so.

Having glanced in this way at the power of the devil let us go on to consider what he does. What is his purpose? The very words that are used to describe him, and to designate him, answer the question. The meaning of the word 'devil' is 'traducer'. The meaning of the word 'Satan' is 'adversary'. And these are the actual expressions that are used explicitly in the Scripture concerning him. He is called 'the accuser of the brethren'. To accuse is one of his chief activities. He is also referred to as 'your adversary the devil'. He is an adversary who is set against us, an opponent, a foe, the leader of an army set against us. He is also referred to as 'the tempter', for he comes to us to tempt us, to mislead us and delude us. It is all summed up in a statement in the Book of Revelation: 'And the dragon was wroth with the woman, and went to make war with the remnant of her seed' (Revelation 12:17). Similarly in the thirteenth chapter of the same book we read that the devil 'makes war against the saints' (verse 7). How vitally important it is that we should realize all this, that we have an adversary, that there is someone who is always set against us, tempting us, trying to drag us down and to destroy us, someone who is ever ready to accuse us. Such is the teaching of Scripture.

But we must not stop even at that. A great deal is said here about his subtlety – 'the wiles of the devil'. I am not going to deal with that at this point. It is a subject in and of itself. In John's Gospel, chapter 8, he is referred to as 'a liar' and as 'the father of lies' (verse 44). That also is a part of the teaching. Still more significant, in the light of what we have in this twelfth verse of

Ephesians chapter 6, is the fact that the devil, this mighty person, has a kingdom, has a dynasty. He rules and reigns in a certain realm. Our Lord Himself tells us so in the eleventh chapter of Luke's Gospel in the portion already quoted. He said, 'If you say that I am casting out devils by Beelzebub, well then, you are saying that Beelzebub is divided against himself; you are saying that Satan, as it were, is fighting against Satan.' And He argues that if Satan is thus fighting against Satan his kingdom must be divided. 'If Satan also be divided against himself, how shall his kingdom stand? because ye say that I cast out devils through Beelzebub' (verses 17–22).

This is the point of transition to what we are told in the twelfth verse of our Ephesians passage. The devil, this mighty 'prince of the power of the air', this king who has a kingdom, also has servants, emissaries, followers – 'principalities and powers and rulers' against which we wrestle. It is a veritable kingdom of great power with hordes of servants. But what are these? It is interesting to notice that the Apostle uses exactly the same terms in the twenty-first verse of the first chapter of this Epistle, where he shows that he is concerned that we should realize 'the exceeding greatness of God's power toward us who believe, according to the working of his mighty power, which he wrought in Christ, when he raised him from the dead, and set him at his own right hand in the heavenly places, far above all principality and power, and might and dominion, and every name that is named, not only in this world, but also in that which is to come'. 'Principalities and powers' – the very words we have here! Yet clearly and obviously he is not referring to the same powers. The very context makes it clear that in chapter one he is referring to principalities and powers that surround the throne of God. They are described also in chapters 4 and 5 of the Book of Revelation where we read of the beasts and the elders and of myriads of principalities and powers surrounding the throne of God. They are God's agents and emissaries, part of His great eternal Kingdom.

What is being emphasized by the Apostle here is that just as God is surrounded by such powers, so is the devil. The devil is not a solitary power. He has his agents and his agencies. But these are very different from those surrounding the throne of God. They are evil, as we shall see. But the important thing for us to realize is that you and I as Christian people passing through this world of time are being confronted by the devil and all these principalities and powers that are ready to do his behest. As the angels of God are ready to go on their journeys and to minister to our well-being, as the author of the Epistle to the Hebrews reminds us (1:14), so the devil has agents that he can send here and there, hither and thither – 'principalities and powers'. And further, what is emphasized concerning them is their great power and authority. They have a governmental position and they have real authority and power in an executive sense. You may ask, Why does he talk about principalities *and* powers? Why the two words? There is a distinction between them. The idea of 'principality' carries the notion of inherent power. The word 'power' suggests rather the expression, the manifestation of that power. So then, there are these mighty powers which are able to execute the orders of the 'prince of the power of the air', that is, the devil.

Then we come to this next phrase which is so significant today – 'against the rulers of the darkness of this world'. That is the translation given by the Authorised (K.J.) Version. But most scholars would agree that a better translation would be, 'against the world rulers of this darkness'. The term 'world rulers' is designed to bring out the extent and the scope of the power and of the authority. We use this term in a political sense. There have been certain people in the course of history who have stood out as 'world rulers'. It was the ambition of Hitler to be a world ruler. He was not content with merely ruling one country in one continent. Similarly Napoleon had the ambition to become a world ruler, governing the whole world, commanding it, controlling it, determining its affairs and the welfare or ill of its people. The term 'world rulers' as used here is one word in the original. It is a very powerful word which conjures up the notion of power to govern and to rule the whole world.

The word 'world' here has a very special connotation and means the world outside of, or the world not submitting to, the government of God. We use that expression quite commonly in this sense. We say that a man is now in the church whereas formerly he was in 'the world'. Of course a Christian is still in the world in a physical sense; so when you say that a Christian is no longer in 'the world' you are speaking in a spiritual sense. That is the connotation of the word 'world' as used by the Apostle in our text. It conveys this spiritual meaning. It refers to the world apart from God, or the world rebellious against God, the world as organized apart from the laws and the government of God. What the Apostle is saying therefore is that we are confronted and opposed by powers that are really governing and controlling that world, the world as it is in opposition against God, the world outside God and His blessing.

This is surely a most vital matter for us to understand and to grasp and to realize at a time like this. We often say we are 'up against the world, the flesh and the devil'. And by 'the world' we do not mean the material universe. The mountains and the hills and the rivers and the sea are not against us. People *qua* people are not against us: but 'the world' is against us, and the 'world' means that outlook, that whole organization, that tremendous power of evil in which we are living, as it were, and which is everywhere round and about us. Our business is to be 'in the world, but not of it'. These 'powers' are the rulers, the governors, the controllers of that mind, that outlook, which we call 'the world'.

But fortunately for us, the Apostle defines the term still more closely. He says that we are wrestling against the world rulers of 'this darkness'. That again is a most significant expression. The 'world' about which he is writing is a place of 'darkness'. Here once more is the term that is universally employed in the Scriptures to define that mind, that outlook, that way of living that is not governed and controlled by God. We find it in this Epistle in chapter four, where we read in verse seventeen: 'This I say therefore and testify in the Lord, that ye henceforth walk not as other Gentiles walk, in the vanity of their mind, having the understanding darkened'. 'Darkened'! It is in the dark, and therefore it is darkened. In chapter five, verse eight, Paul says the same thing still more specifically: 'Ye were sometimes darkness, but now are ye light in the Lord.' Observe that there he does not merely say that they were once 'in the dark'; he says that the darkness was in them – 'ye were darkness'. It is not merely that they were in a fog, the fog was inside them also. Darkness without and within!

[59]

Such is the state of 'the world'. It is the common description of it everywhere. Look at it, for example, in the Epistle to the Colossians, chapter one, verse thirteen. He is reminding the Colossians of what God has done to them: 'Who hath delivered us from the power of darkness, and hath translated us into the kingdom of his dear Son.' Do you normally, habitually, think of yourself as one who has been delivered from 'the powers of darkness?' What is your view of salvation? What happens when you are converted and become a Christian? 'Ah,' you say, 'my sins are forgiven.' I agree. Thank God that it is so, for otherwise we would be undone. But do you always add this – 'delivered from the power of darkness'? You were once held by that power. You were once the slaves of that power. It is vital that we should realize this.

It is not surprising that the Apostle puts it in this way; and constantly puts it like this, because this was a part of his great commission. Remember how our Lord met him on the road to Damascus, and said to him: 'Rise up, stand upon thy feet: I have appeared unto thee for this purpose, to make thee a minister and a witness of the things which thou hast seen, and of those things in the which I will appear unto thee; delivering thee from the people, and from the Gentiles, unto whom now I send thee.' What for? 'To open their eyes, and to turn them from darkness to light, and from the power of Satan unto God, that they may receive the forgiveness of sins, and inheritance among them which are sanctified by faith that is in me' (Acts 26:16–18). It is the same everywhere.

Is it not strange, Christian people, that we think so little about these things, that this whole aspect of the matter comes so little into our thoughts? It is because we are too subjective. We start with ourselves and we end with ourselves. 'I want peace with God, I want my sins forgiven, I want to feel happy, I want joy in my life, I want this, I want that, I want to overcome temptation . . .!' Why do we not realize that our salvation is always to be thought of in objective, scriptural terms primarily? You may have many experiences, and enjoy what you regard as blessings, but if you do not realize this truth you will still be in bondage and your Christian life will be very poor. As the Scriptures state the case, we have to be delivered from the power of darkness, from the power of the devil, before we can receive forgiveness of sins. That is the first thing according to what our Lord told Paul in His commission on the road to Damascus.

What, then, does the Apostle mean by this 'darkness'? Clearly it means primarily the darkness of ignorance. Ignorance is the main cause of the whole troubled state of the world at this moment. Looking at it in another way you can say that it is blind. It is ignorant of God. The vast majority of the people in the world at this moment are not thinking about God. They boast of their learning, their culture, their sophistication. But the real trouble with an unbeliever is his appalling ignorance, his darkness! For this reason no Christian should ever be troubled to the slightest extent by the pontifical pronouncements made by these supposed great and brilliant philosophers. They are blind, they are ignorant, they do not know. 'The natural man receiveth not the things of the Spirit of God; for they are foolishness unto him' (1 Corinthians 2:14). 'If our Gospel be hid, it is hid to them that are lost, in whom the god of this world hath blinded the minds of them that believe not, lest the light of the glorious Gospel of Christ should shine unto them' (2 Corinthians 4:4). They cannot believe! They are slaves of the devil; the god of this world has blinded them. They are in the dark, they are enshrouded by darkness, and the darkness is in their minds. What a terrible state it is! They know nothing of God.

Furthermore, they know nothing truly even of themselves. They know nothing about the true greatness of man, they know nothing about the soul. They do not believe in the soul or in the spirit in man. They know nothing about the most glorious aspect of man, and the result is that they do not understand life at all. That is why these great thinkers, so-called, are really quite baffled by the state of the world at the present time, and cannot understand it. H. G. Wells taught for a long life-time that if only you educated people they would never fight again, but there he was, trying to write his last book in the early days of the Second World War, in the most educated century of history, and you remember the title he gave it – *Mind at the End of Its Tether*. Of course! Poor man, he could not understand it. This century was meant to be the most glorious century of all. And, of course, it should have been and would have been if he and his sort were right. We are more educated than the men of last century, and they were more educated than their forbears. 'Let knowledge grow from more to more,' said Tennyson. Everything is advancing and going forward, so we must be better! But the facts prove that we are obviously worse. The 'thinkers' do not understand it, they are completely baffled and bewildered, and all because they remain 'in the dark'. We use that expression and say 'the man is hopelessly in the dark about it'; and we try to 'enlighten' him.

Similarly, the world knows nothing about death, and nothing about what lies beyond death. The worldly-wise lie in their beds on Sunday morning reading the Sunday papers and feeling sorry for us. 'Why is it,' they say, 'that in the twentieth century certain people actually go to places of worship still and listen to the exposition of the Scripture?' They tell us they are emancipated; they are intelligent men of the world, men of knowledge and of learning. The tragedy is that they not only know nothing about themselves and about the real meaning of life, they know nothing about death. They do not know that 'it is appointed unto men once to die, but after this the judgment' (Hebrews 9:27). Judgment! They scoff at it; they do not believe it. They scoff at God, they scoff at the Lord Jesus Christ, they scoff at all the saints because they are in the dark, and the darkness is in them. Their ignorance is appalling, and 'the world rulers of this darkness' are gloating over it all, and enjoying it, as they observe these intelligent dupes of theirs, these sophisticated ignoramuses, so utterly and completely blinded and fooled. And these 'world rulers' see to it that the tragedy continues; they are at the back of it all. They are manipulating the Press and all other such agencies. The way in which they do so we shall have to consider later.

The point we are emphasizing here is that they are 'the world rulers of this darkness'. And all that, of course, expresses itself in the kind of life that their victims and dupes live. To find out what that is I refer you to your newspapers. There you will see how this darkened mind expresses itself in practice, in conduct and in behaviour. At the moment it is engaged in fighting a legal action to allow filth to be printed in books. Naturally, it does not put it like that. Instead, pornography is explained to be art, sophistica-

[62]

tion, culture, great literature! That is how the darkness expresses and manifests itself.

'Why is all this?' is the question that any intelligent man should ask. Why do people behave in this way? What is wrong with the nations that they should be building up armaments that are capable of destroying the whole world? What is the cause of the widespread immorality, and the collapse of the sanctities, that we are seeing all around us? Intelligent men ought to ask, What causes all this? But they fail to do so. Otherwise they would discover that there is only one answer. There are unseen 'rulers' who are manipulating world affairs. It is not just 'flesh and blood', it is not just an occasional man who wants to make money out of vice and pornography, it is not just certain people who want to batten on the hire of women's bodies, it is not that men just want to grow rich through owning places of evil and vice. No, they are but the instruments of the 'world rulers of this darkness'. We are not wrestling against men, says Paul, not against 'flesh and blood', but we are wrestling against the unseen powers that are behind it all, the powers that really matter.

Then we come to the last term, 'against spiritual wickedness in high places', as it is found in the Authorized (K.J.) Version. Again we must amend this translation. The original means 'wicked spirits' rather than 'wickedness'. It is 'spiritual forces of wickedness' that the Apostle is describing, not 'spiritual wickedness'. We must avoid thinking of these matters in abstract terms. The Apostle is emphasizing that all these powers are personal. So instead of reading 'spiritual wickedness' we should read 'wicked spirits'. Perhaps the best translation is this, 'we are up against spiritual bands of evil'. Or still better, 'spiritual cohorts of evil'. Cohorts, battalions, legions! That is the thought. There they are, says the Apostle, these myriads of spirits of evil and wickedness. Their nature is evil, their commission is evil, and their work is evil. They are evil in their object and purpose, and in all that they bring to pass.

But according to our English Authorized Version, they are in 'high places'. Again it is interesting to observe the term. Why did the translators say 'high places' here? Exactly the same Greek word in the third verse of the first chapter of this Epistle they translated as 'in the heavenlies'. Let us be fair to the Authorized Version translators. They wanted to give the idea, and rightly so, that the devil and all his cohorts and his legions are not in heaven, surrounding the throne of God. So they hesitated to use the phrase 'in the heavenlies'. And we must show a similar carefulness. We must not think that the devil and the powers associated with him are in the immediate presence of God together with all the holy angels and emissaries and powers and principalities and potentates. Where, then, are they? This has been a matter of great discussion throughout the centuries, and we cannot give a final answer. Some have thought that it means 'in the air'. When we say that we look up 'into the heavens' we mean the sky, the air, the atmosphere immediately above us. So it was believed for centuries that these evil powers are, as it were, between us and God. They are above us, they are in the atmosphere, and they are looking down upon us and controlling us. But that is to materialize it too much. I am not denying that there may be something to be said for it. After all, the devil is 'the prince of the power of the air'.

But the idea meant to be conveyed is surely this; the term used is intended to present a contrast with the earth. We normally speak about 'heaven and earth'. In other words 'the high places' means 'the heavenly places' in contradistinction to earth. 'The heavenlies' really means that the powers which are opposed to us, and against us, and which are making war on us as the saints of God, are not on our earthly level. We must get rid of the notion that we are only wrestling against 'flesh and blood' on earth. Our wrestling is essentially in the spiritual realm, the realm of the heavenlies. It is simply another way of emphasizing what I said earlier, that we must always think of the enemy who is fighting against us as one who is not only personal, with his personal agents, but also as one who lives in the realm of the spirit.

There, then, says the Apostle, is the starting-point, the point of departure, the thing that you have to realize before you go any further at all. 'We wrestle not against flesh and blood.' What then? 'Against the devil', the god of this world, 'against principalities, against powers, against the world rulers of this darkness, against spirits of evil in the heavenly realm.'

Thank God that the Apostle introduces all this by saying, 'Be strong in the Lord, and in the power of his might'. If, after

[64]

considering all this, you feel discouraged, it means that you have not understood it. I am saying that you have to realize that this is the enemy. Yes, but he has already told us, 'Be strong in the Lord, and in the power of his might. Take unto you the whole armour of God.' This is the glory of the Christian position, that though I am confronted by such an enemy I need not be afraid. 'Resist the devil, and he will flee from you.' 'Your adversary, the devil as a roaring lion, walketh about seeking whom he may devour.' What am I to do? Am I hopeless? Do I run away and cry? Not at all! 'Whom resist steadfast in the faith' (1 Peter 5: 8 and 9). 'They overcame him' – the old dragon himself – 'by the blood of the Lamb, and by the word of their testimony' (Revelation 12:11). But do not allow that thought, or the misunderstanding of that thought, to make you feel that you need not be vigilant in respect of the enemy. Remember, says Paul, that you have to stand after every victory. Do not relax, do not go on holiday. There is no holiday in the spiritual realm. Stand, pray, be steadfast, hold on! But as you have to stand you are offered the armour and the ability to 'stand', to 'withstand', and 'having done all, to stand'.

5

The Origin of Evil

We have seen that nothing is more practical from the standpoint of living the Christian life than the teaching of these verses. The Apostle, in the Second Epistle to the Corinthians, says in chapter 2, verse 11: 'We are not ignorant of his devices.' He means, I know something about the wiles of the devil, what he tries to do in a church and among Christian people. And it is because he was not ignorant of the devices of the devil that he was able to instruct and to teach and to help Christian people. That is what he is doing here in this last section of the Epistle to the Ephesians. Another practical reason for considering this teaching is the recrudescence of an interest in spiritism and psychic phenomena. You always get that after wars, and in times of trouble and of difficulty and of crisis. It is becoming increasingly popular today, and it is creeping into the life of the Christian Church. So it is important that we should understand the teaching, that we should recognize spiritism for what it really is, as the work of demons!

I am introducing the subject in this way because I am aware of the fact that this kind of teaching is strange today, not only to the world but even to the Church. That is the supreme tragedy, and it is at the same time the height of the devil's subtlety and ability, that he has so successfully concealed himself, or else transformed himself into 'an angel of light', so that many people no longer believe in the devil at all, and are not aware of his existence. Indeed the majority today regard any consideration of the devil as more or less a joke, and thereby, of course, put themselves into

[66]

a very serious position. Notice what the Apostle Peter has to say about such persons in his Second Epistle and in the · second chapter, beginning at verse 10. He is talking about certain people who have gone astray, 'chiefly them that walk after the flesh in the lust of uncleanness, and despise government. Presumptuous are they, self-willed, they are not afraid to speak evil of dignities. Whereas angels, which are greater in power and might, bring not railing accusation against them before the Lord.' The angels do not speak disparagingly and jocularly about the devil and demons. Though they are much greater than we are, he says, 'they bring not railing accusation against them before the Lord. But these, as natural brute beasts, made to be taken and destroyed, speak evil of the things that they understand not; and shall utterly perish in their own corruption.'

Let me reinforce that with a word from the Epistle of Jude to show the seriousness of this matter, and how there is nothing more monstrous than that people should joke about the devil, and regard as a subject of mirth and jocularity any talk about demons and evil spirits. Jude says, 'Likewise also these filthy dreamers defile the flesh, despise dominion, and speak evil of dignities. Yet Michael the archangel, when contending with the devil he disputed about the body of Moses, durst not bring against him a railing accusation, but said, The Lord rebuke thee. But they speak evil of those things which they know not: but what they know naturally, as brute beasts, in those things they corrupt themselves' (verses 8–10).

In this way we are reminded that we are dealing here not only with a vitally important subject, but with one which we must handle with great caution. We have discovered that there are great powers of evil at work in this world. The next question for our consideration is: Where have these forces come from? How have they ever come into being at all? Or, If we say that these unseen spiritual forces are evil, what is the origin of evil, where has evil come from? That is a great and very important question from the standpoint of our belief in God. Many people today are Atheists; they say that they do not believe in God. That is often the result of this very question – they are troubled by this problem of evil and the origin of evil. So it is very important that as Christian people we should have some understanding of this matter, not only for our own peace of mind, but in order that we may be able to help others.

Or let me put it the other way round. It has often happened that when people have come to understand the true nature of evil they have come to a belief in God. There is, for instance, the case of a philosopher, who was well-known and popular a few years ago, the late Dr Joad. I am not expressing any verdict on his opinions, I am simply reporting that he said in a book that, whereas once he was an atheist, he had now come to believe in God. He said that what had brought him to that belief was the realization, as the result of the Spanish Civil War, and then the Second World War, that there were obviously spiritual forces of evil. He could not explain those events merely in human terms. He came to believe in the whole category and realm of the spirit, and ultimately that brought him to believe in the being of God. As for ourselves, our faith in God is not complete if we do not understand this. We are therefore compelled to meet it and to face it. And, in addition, as I have said, you will never understand the whole course of the history of the world if you do not understand this teaching. You will not understand the past, you will not understand the present, and still less will you have any real hope with regard to the future. Let us then proceed to consider what the Bible tells us about this realm of evil.

What is the origin of the devil, the principalities and powers, the spirits of wickedness in the heavenly places, the world rulers of the darkness of this world? But before we look at the biblical answer to the question, let me remind you that this is a problem that has engaged the minds and the thoughts of men throughout the running centuries. There was a view held for a long time in the ancient world that evil came from a god who was virtually equal to the Lord God Almighty in power and in strength. They said there was a good God, and there was an evil God whom they called a demiurge. They believed that that was the explanation of evil and that these two Gods were equal in their being and in their powers. Many of them believed that it was this evil God that had created this material world. Others believed it was the good God who had created the world but that the other had interfered with it, and so on. Others have believed, and many still believe, in the eternity of evil. They say evil is something that is in the very warp and woof of the whole creation – it is not something that has come into being, it was always there. They do not attempt to explain its origin, they just postulate that evil is something that always has been, something that is eternal in and of itself.

The prevailing view today, however, is, that there is no such thing as evil at all, that what has been called evil is really just the absence of good, or the absence of perfection. This is the view that arises inevitably out of the theory or supposition of evolution. According to this view everything is developing, growing and advancing. But obviously, they say, we have not arrived at absolute perfection yet, and until you arrive at perfection there will be certain defects and blemishes, there will be an element of incompleteness. That is, they say, what has always been called 'evil'. But it was wrong to regard it as positive, it is only negative. The trouble is that things are not what they ought to be, they have not arrived at this ultimate perfection. What has always been called evil is but a lack of qualities rather than a positive entity in and of itself, a mere negative condition rather than a positive one.

If this view is true all we need is great patience. Of course we may need to wait a few million years before this great process terminates in perfection! But in any case it is going to happen, so we must put up with things as they are, and exhort one another to make the best of it while we are here, and consider ourselves unfortunate that we are living now and not in a number of millennia to come. And this, of course, immediately affects one's whole view of man and his ultimate destiny, of life and what can be done with the world at this present time. There, then, are some of the views concerning evil and its origin, found amongst those who do not go to the Bible, and rely upon it, for instruction in these matters.

Now let us turn to the biblical view and be positive. I do not propose to waste your time in refuting those other theories in detail; they are hardly worthy of it, as we shall see as we now look at the biblical teaching. The Bible starts with God: 'In the beginning God.' God over all; God from everlasting to everlasting; God Self-subsistent and existent within Himself; God in His own inscrutable wisdom beginning to create, and first of all creating the hosts of heaven – angelic beings. God created the hosts of heaven for His own purpose, for His own ends, in order that they might serve certain functions, and carry out His behests. The author of the Epistle to the Hebrews says, 'Are they not all ministering spirits?' (Hebrews 1:14), and he is referring to angels. In other words the Bible teaches that God created first and foremost the heavens and these citizens of the heavenly regions who seem to be divided into 'angels and authorities and powers'. These were all made and created by God, and they were all, of course, perfect and complete. That is the starting point. We are not talking about the earth, but about these heavenly realms and regions, and how God created these spiritual entities – angels, principalities, powers. We are not given any details about them, but if you look at the Book of Revelation you will read there – it is all in symbols – about certain beasts and elders and so on. There are clearly gradations in these beings; there are diversities of office which we do not understand perfectly, but we can sum it up thus: angels, principalities, powers – all perfect, all glorious, and all under God, ministering for God and to God. But what happened to them in course of time?

Here, we come to the very essence of the biblical teaching about this whole matter of evil and sin. We start with the person and personality of the devil. It is clear that the devil was originally one of these bright angelic creatures made by God. If you want proof of that you will find it in Isaiah 14:12–17 and Ezekiel 28: 1–19. But it is found also in the Book of Job, the first chapter and the sixth verse: 'Now there was a day when the sons of God came to present themselves before the Lord, and Satan came also among them.' The phrase, 'The sons of God,' in the Old Testament generally stands for the angels, and here we are told that a day came when the angels presented themselves before God, and amongst these sons of God, was Satan, the devil. In the same way Ezekiel 28 and Isaiah 14 compel us to come to the same conclusion. 'Lucifer, son of the morning!' These descriptions, though primarily, perhaps, meant to apply to Tyre and to Babylon, are generally agreed to have a much wider meaning. That is something which is quite customary in prophecy. You start with the immediate, but it is also a foreshadowing of something bigger which is to come. This happens with regard to good as well as evil. There are many prophecies in the Psalms which appear to relate to king David alone, but obviously they go beyond David and point to the Messiah. There are promises made to the Children of Israel which primarily refer clearly to their coming back from the captivity of Babylon; but they are too big for that alone, they are at the same time pictures of the Christian salvation and the salvation of the soul. That is why they are quoted so frequently in the New Testament, to show the fulfilment of prophecy.

It is exactly the same in regard to this matter of evil. In describing the fall of Tyrus or of Babylon the prophets were inspired to suggest something bigger. Tyrus and Babylon are not merely earthly powers that are opposed to God, they are also symbols, as it were, of the power of the devil and his forces. And so what is said about them is really applicable to him. Hence we find that this great power is described as wandering backwards and forwards, and that he was in the Garden of Eden. In other words the impression given is that the devil was one of these great angels, one of these created powers which God brought into being that they might serve Him, and be used to His honour and glory. That is the great original picture.

But something has obviously happened. How do you explain the origin of evil? The answer that is given is that there was what has been described as 'a pre-cosmic Fall'. When I say 'cosmic' I am thinking of this universe that you and I dwell in and inhabit, the universe as we know it. But, according to the Bible, before this cosmos was created there was a tremendous calamity, a fall, a pre-cosmic fall. That is surely what is described in Ezekiel 28 and Isaiah 14. For a reference to the same thing in the New Testament we turn to the First Epistle to Timothy in the third chapter and the sixth verse. The Apostle is telling Timothy not to ordain a novice as an elder or as a bishop. He says: 'Not a novice, lest being lifted up with pride he fall into the condemnation of the devil.' A most significant statement! Take that with the two passages from the prophets and this is the result. Here amidst all these bright angelic beings was this outstanding one, 'Lucifer, son of the morning!' – one of the greatest, ablest, and most powerful of them all. He became ambitious. He became dissatisfied with his position of subservience to God and desired to be as God Himself.

So he rebelled against God, he raised himself up against God in his ambition. 'Lifted up with pride,' as Paul expresses it in writing to Timothy, he withstood God, he became a rebel. And the result of this was that he fell. He was punished by God by being degraded. And not only so, he lost his perfection, and the freedom he had formerly enjoyed.

The great principle which we must lay hold of is that God, in His own inscrutable wisdom, allowed this to happen. Though we cannot understand finally, and must always be careful about speculation, it does not seem to me to be very difficult to understand, if one may speak with reverence, why God allowed the devil to fall. I have reminded you that these angelic beings were created perfect, and anything that is perfect must have complete freedom of will. So obviously these beings had complete 'freedom of will'. Anything that is perfect must be free. Adam was created perfect and was free. Adam had free will. No other man has ever had it since; but Adam had it. And it is this very quality that contains the possibility of rebellion and of falling, and therefore of the origin of evil. Thus it came to pass that this perfect being exercised the freedom of his will in a wrong direction, through pride and being lifted up, and so fell, and came under condemnation and punishment.

But the story does not end there. In addition to doing this himself, it is made clear that the devil at the same time persuaded certain other of these angelic beings and powers and principalities to follow him in the course he had taken. The scriptural warrant for this belief is found, for instance, in the Book of Revelation, chapter 12, verse 4. Remember, however, that it is put there in symbolic form and that it is imagery. John is talking about 'a great dragon', the devil: 'His tail drew the third part of the stars of heaven, and did cast them to the earth.' That is surely a symbolic way of saying that the devil, when he himself fell, dragged down with him the third part of these great powers whom God had created. Again, there is a statement in the Second Epistle of Peter, chapter 2, verse 4: 'For if God spared not the angels that sinned, but cast them down to hell, and delivered them into chains of darkness to be reserved unto judgment.' What I am emphasizing is that some of the angels sinned, and were cast into darkness, to hell, and were delivered into chains of darkness to be reserved unto judgment. You find the same truth in the sixth verse of the Epistle of Jude.

This, then, is the picture that is given, bearing in mind that all this is before the creation of the world. The devil influenced these others and together they rebel against God. And so they fell; they became evil and came under God's condemnation. But they are sufficiently great in power and in number to form and to establish a kingdom, a kingdom of evil, a kingdom of darkness; and the whole ambition and object of all the activities of the devil and his cohorts is to fight against God. The devil, 'lifted up with pride', fell, and ever since, of course, because of his fall, he has been animated by an intense hatred of God. He has only one ambition, namely, to destroy God's works and to produce chaos. God is a God of order. The devil is intent upon producing chaos. Now, we begin to see the relevance of this teaching. The world since those events has always been a place of chaos. We know it as a place of chaos today. In Scripture, and in Scripture alone, do we find the explanation of the matter. These great powers have established a kingdom and now there is a great warfare – God and His bright angelic hosts are fighting against the kingdom of the devil, the kingdom of darkness, and against the forces and spirits of evil that are set against God.

There, in its essence, is the biblical explanation of the origin of evil. It is the result of that tremendous event in the angelic, in the heavenly realm, right above us altogether. I am emphasizing this again for this reason. The whole tragedy of the world today, as I see it, is that we are so utterly earthbound. We start with man, we start with the world, always with ourselves, and especially twentieth-century man. But if you want to understand the twentieth century the first thing you have to do is not only to go back to the beginning of history in Eden, you have to go back into eternity, before the world was ever made; and there you will see this great alignment of forces, good and evil, light and darkness, God and the devil and their forces.

There is one other thing I must mention. It is not quite so clear, and is more speculative; but I refer to it because it may have a very great significance, and it certainly does help one's understanding of certain problems connected with different aspects of the Christian faith. There are those who believe that this great cataclysmic event which took place in that pre-cosmic fall when the devil and the angels fell, involved also an original material creation. This, they argue, is the key to the understanding of the second verse in the Bible. The first two verses of Genesis read thus: 'In the beginning God created the heaven and the earth. And the earth was without form, and void; and darkness was upon the face of the deep.' The word 'deep' there really means 'the chaos'. It is a description of a state of chaos. The idea, the speculation, is that before this cosmos that you and I are aware of, there was an original creation. That first verse in Genesis, it claims, is really a reference to the great original creation. It is a general statement that God has made everything. But it may also include the idea that God made a world, a cosmos, in which these angelic principalities and powers lived and functioned and dwelt. But when some of them fell in their rebellion and pride and dis-obedience, God punished their universe also, and it was reduced to a state of chaos. So that what is described in Genesis 1, verse 2 onwards, is the restoration, the re-creation of this original creation which had got into a state of chaos and of darkness.

This is a matter about which we cannot be certain; it is more or less a speculation; but there is something to be said for it. I cannot imagine God's act of creation passing through a chaotic stage at any point at all. I cannot believe that creation as a work carried out by God was at any stage an abyss, a void, a chaos. That does not fit in with God's work. Everything in creation, in nature, everywhere, at every step and stage, is characterized by that same perfection of form. Inchoate, perhaps, under-developed, not yet perfect; but right at its particular stage. It is never chaotic. The most rudimentary form, the most embryonic form is never chaotic, there is never this sense of void. But we are told that the Spirit 'brooded' upon this chaos, this deep. So that theory may well be true. And if it is true, it provides an answer to those who say that they do not believe the account of creation in Genesis because of the findings of the geologists who, looking at nature and at the material universe, say that there is evidence there that rocks or various formations have existed for long ages. They may be right, they may be wrong. We must not believe everything that even a geologist says! But even granting that they are right, the answer may be that all that they are discovering is the result

[74]

of a great original catastrophe which happened when, with the fall of the angels and of the devil, punishment was meted out upon the whole universe, leading to the chaos that resulted. I do not emphasize this; I put it forward for consideration. However, what we must be clear about is, that before the cosmos as we know it now, there was this tremendous event, the fall of the devil and certain angels, and that the powers and forces of evil result from that fall.

The next step is that God created the world as we now think of it. That is what is described in the first chapter of Genesis. God made all things perfect, as all God's works are perfect, man included. So there was a perfect creation – Paradise! God looked upon it all and saw that 'it was very good', and God was pleased and satisfied with it. There, then, was God's perfect world, and all was harmony and peace, and man living in fellowship with God. But then the question arises, if that was so, why is the world as we see it now? The Bible supplies the answer. God had made a perfect world and He delighted in it. But the forces of evil, the devil and the fallen angels and the principalities and powers, with their evil desires and their unhealthy ambition and their hatred of God, looked upon it and determined to destroy it. So the devil came and tempted the woman, and through the woman the man. In other words, we learn of the fall of man, everything that we find described in the third chapter of the Book of Genesis. Evil did not start in Eden, it was already in existence. The devil, Satan, came in, taking the disguise of a serpent; but it was he who did it. And we see that his object was to mar and ruin God's work. Man, of course, was the main object of attack, because he is the head of creation, and God had made him in His own image. He had made man lord of creation, and the governor of the world. But the devil came in and tempted him; and man succumbed and fell.

The results of the Fall are endless. I am simply concerned to emphasize the one particular aspect for the moment, that by listening to the devil man became the slave of the devil, became a citizen of the devil's kingdom, and under the power of the devil. Hence the devil is described in the Bible as 'the god of this world', 'the prince of the power of the air, the spirit that now worketh in the children of disobedience'. That is the result of man's fall; he has put himself under the power of the devil and his evil agencies. He belongs to the devil. The Bible teaches that clearly in many places. We have referred earlier to the story of Saul of Tarsus meeting our Lord on the road to Damascus and of his being commissioned to do certain work. The Lord said, 'I am sending you to be a minister and a witness unto the people, to open their eyes, and to turn them from darkness to light, and from the power of Satan unto God' (Acts 26:18). The implication is, that by nature, they are under the 'power of Satan'. And so it is not surprising that, when Paul comes to write to the Colossians, he says: 'Who hath delivered us from the power of darkness and hath translated us into the kingdom of his dear Son' (Colossians 1:13). Man is in the kingdom of darkness, the kingdom of the devil; he is under the power of the devil, under the dominion of sin. 'Sin shall not have dominion over you,' says Paul to the Roman Christians (Romans 6:14). The implication is that it had dominion over them before they became Christians.

Or take again our Lord's description already quoted, 'When a strong man armed keepeth his palace, his goods are in peace' (Luke 11:21). That is the Lord Jesus Christ's description of the world apart from Himself. 'The strong man armed' describes the devil. What is the world? His 'palace'! The 'goods' are mankind as the result of sin. So the terrible consequence of the Fall is that man is not free any longer; he is a slave of the devil, he is the 'goods' of the strong man armed, he is under the power and the dominion of Satan and sin and evil. Again, take the Apostle John's description of it in his First Epistle, chapter 5, verse 19: 'We know that we are of God, and the whole world lieth in the evil one.' What a terrible description! The whole world, apart from Christian people, is in the embrace of the wicked one, is in the arms of Satan. He has them in his grip, and he is dominating the whole of their life. That is what the Bible tells us about the origin of evil and of sin. That is why man is as he is – the pre-cosmic fall led to the cosmic fall, the Fall of man!

The result is that the whole course of man's history has been entirely changed. Man, from the moment he fell through listening to Satan, is no longer free. He is the slave of Satan. He is the underling of 'the god of this world'. He is no longer the 'lord of creation'. He is mastered by these things, and in many senses their servant. Though he still has great ability, he is the victim of the very forces he was meant to control and tries to control. 'Ah but,' you say, 'he has split the atom!' I know, but he is the slave of the atomic power, is he not? The whole position has been reversed: man has lost his freedom; he is no longer the lord of creation, he is the slave of the devil and of hell! So that we have to realize that the real problem of the world at any moment can only truly be understood in the light of this great spiritual conflict between God and the devil. The problem confronting us is not simply a matter of what can be done to man by his fellows. That is why neither Acts of Parliament nor international conferences are going to solve our problems. Behind all human affairs are these unseen powers. The ultimate source of trouble is the devil; man is really the instrument that is being used, he is the pawn upon the board, as it were. But behind man are these other forces that are always determined to produce a state of chaos in order to upset God's universe.

So I remind you that the starting point of all our considerations is that 'we wrestle not against flesh and blood'. We can deal with men because they are of like powers with ourselves – 'but we wrestle not against flesh and blood, but against principalities, against powers, against the world rulers of this darkness, against spiritual wickedness in heavenly places'. And the devil is immeasurably more powerful than we are. Read the Old Testament and you will find that he has defeated every saint, every patriarch, every prophet. 'There is none righteous, no, not one; all have sinned and come short of the glory of God.' No man has ever been able to stand successfully against the devil. He is too powerful; he is that bright spirit, 'Lucifer, son of the morning!', great in his power, great in his understanding, great in his authority, great in the forces which he can marshal. And the natural man is helpless in his hands – 'The strong man armed keepeth his goods in peace.'

All this is but the introduction to this subject. We have now seen what is at the back of the world situation and problem, and how it has all come into being. But we shall have to go on to consider what these powers and forces are doing in detail. We shall see how this subtlety and power and understanding and brilliance and authority are actually used in practice against nations and against individuals. We are face to face with the great problem of evil, and of man fighting these powers as he passes through this world.

There, then, is the introduction to it all. You must face the problem of the origin of evil. You do not really think if you have not faced that. We are meant to think, and the Bible encourages us to do so, and helps us to do so. And it has its explanations. We have been looking at the origin of it all. Do not start with man, do not start even with the world. Go back beyond that. The original calamity took place in the heavenly places and the world is but the scene of this mighty battle between God and the devil.

Is this discouraging? I say again that it is far from discouraging. I find it to be most encouraging because now I understand what is happening. But still more, I know that 'the Lord reigneth'. He is 'over all', and He has sent Someone into this world who has been able to master 'the strong man armed' and to 'rob him of his armour'. The Christian is not only aware of the forces arrayed against him, he is one who is able to be 'strong in the Lord, and in the power of his might', one who can 'put on the whole armour of God'. And though he is fighting 'Lucifer, son of the morning', the devil, principalities and powers, he can 'stand', and continue to stand, and be finally 'more than conqueror'. May God give us grace and wisdom to consider these things, to meditate upon them, that we may take unto ourselves 'the whole armour of God, to enable us to stand in the evil day; and having done all, to stand'.

6

The Wiles of the Devil

The important principle which we must always keep in the forefront of our minds is that the only way to understand the long story of the human race is to realize that it is the result of the Fall. That is the only key to history, any sort of history, secular history as well as this more purely spiritual history that we have in the Bible. You cannot understand the history of mankind apart from this great principle. History is the record of the conflict between God and His forces on the one hand and the devil and his forces on the other; and the great controlling principle is of vast importance, not only to an understanding of past history, but to an understanding of what is happening in the world today. Similarly it is the only key to the understanding of the future. At the same time it is the only way in which we can understand our own individual experiences. These are the aspects of the question we must now begin to consider.

Here then is the position by which we are confronted. The devil and all these subsidiary powers and forces that operate at his behest, and under his control and power, have but one central object, and that is, to destroy God's work. The devil – having lifted himself up with pride, having become jealous of God who had made him, and who had given him life and being and authority and power – fell and was punished. Part of the punishment is that he is confined within certain limits, and this stirs up his hatred. And in order to vent his spleen upon God his one great concern is to bring disorder into God's perfect creation. So his main tactic always is to produce confusion, trouble and chaos. Therefore above everything else his supreme ambition is to separate man from God, and to do everything that lies within his power to hinder man from worshipping God, obeying God, and living to the glory of God. Man, after all, is the highest point of God's great work in creation. There is nothing higher than man. Man was made 'the lord of creation', the supreme being, under God, on earth. Therefore, obviously, he is the very special object of the attacks and the onslaughts of the devil. It is not surprising, therefore, that we should find as we look through history and through the teaching we find in the Bible, that the devil has concentrated his attention upon man, and that his object has been to separate man from God and from living the kind of life for which God intended him.

How does the devil pursue this object? how is this work put into operation? According to the teaching that one finds in the various parts of the Bible, it is done partly by the devil himself. But the devil is not omnipresent; he is not everywhere at the same time. Notice the expression that is used in verse 7 of the first chapter of the Book of Job. God asks the devil where he has come from that day when the sons of God were gathered together. His answer was, 'From going to and fro in the earth, and from walking up and down in it.' He is not everywhere. Neither is he omnipotent; so he does not do all this work himself. Part of it is delegated to the fallen angels, and to the spiritual forces the Apostle mentions, the demons, these 'unclean spirits' as they are sometimes described in the Scriptures. In this way the work of the devil is carried on, and there is much evidence in the Scriptures that in it a very elaborate strategy is employed. For instance we read that there are very special occasions when the devil does the work himself. We shall consider an instance where the devil himself tempted king David. He did not send an underling, he went himself. And, of course, we are told that in the case of our Lord it was the devil himself who tempted Him. He did not leave that in the hands of some subsidiary agent.

Let us bear in mind also the great power of the devil and his forces. The Apostle describes him as 'a roaring lion, seeking whom he may devour'. We must never forget that he is described as the 'great dragon'. The power of the devil is alarming. Our Lord says to Peter, 'Satan hath desired to have thee, that he may sift thee like wheat.' These are indications of his tremendous power. But perhaps the ultimate proof of the power, and the confidence, and the ability of the devil, is to be found in the fact that he did not hesitate to tempt and to attack even the Son of God Himself. He approached Him with confidence, with assurance, for he had defeated all others. The greatest saints, the patriarchs of the Old Testament, and prophets, had all been defeated by the wiles of the devil; so he does not hesitate to approach our Lord and to speak as he did, offering to give Him all the kingdoms of the earth if He would but bow down to him and worship him. That is indicative of the great power of the devil.

At the same time let us observe that the devil's power is a limited power. Notice again that in the case of Job the devil, notwithstanding his great authority and power, is clearly still under the supreme authority of God. This is a mystery. No one can pretend to understand it. But it is a part of God's great purpose. As we have seen, in His own inscrutable wisdom, God allowed evil to come in, and in the same way He permits the devil to go on exercising a certain amount of power. He could have destroyed him at the beginning. He has chosen not to do so. But it means that the devil's power is a limited power. It is comforting to remember this fact as we look at the state of the world nowadays, and see that evil seems to be rampant, and God, as it were, seems to be defeated. But it is not so. All that is happening is still under the power of God. 'The Lord reigneth.' We must never forget the permissive will of God. He allows the devil to do certain things. And, indeed, there is very clear teaching in Scripture that God does this at times in order to punish the foolish human race. He as it were abandons them to the devil in order to bring them to their senses. Thus, you see, God can even use the devil, and has often done so, to bring His own purposes to pass, and also to punish His recalcitrant people. There, then, is the general picture of what is taking place.

But let us turn to the particulars, because it is only as we consider them that we shall see the relevance of all this to ourselves, to our personal experiences, and to the whole condition and state of the world in the present day. How does the devil exercise this power?

In what ways is his strategy manifested? It is clear, in the first place, that the devil has a certain amount of power even over nature itself. Once more we turn to an important statement made in the Book of Job. When the devil suggested to God that Job was a good man only because God was blessing him, and that if God ceased to bless him Job would very soon curse Him to His face, God, as it were, said to the devil, 'Very well, all that he has I put in your power; only upon himself put not forth your hand.' Go and do what you like with Job, said God in effect to the devil, but do not touch his person. 'So Satan went forth from the presence of the Lord', and without delay his evil work began. One of Job's servants brought to him a report that his oxen and asses had been stolen and their keepers had been slain. 'While he was yet speaking, there came also another, and said, 'The fire of God' – that is to say, lightning – 'is fallen from heaven, and hath burned up the sheep, and the servants, and consumed them; and I only am escaped alone to tell thee' (Job 1:16). That is clear teaching to the effect that it is within the province and the power of the devil to cause lightning, and to cause destruction as the result of the lightning. But Job's troubles were not yet over. Another servant brought his report: 'Thy sons and daughters were eating and drinking wine in their eldest brother's house, and behold there came a great wind from the wilderness, and smote the four corners of the house, and it fell upon the young men, and they are dead; and I only am escaped alone to tell thee.' Obviously that was a hurricane.

But let us be clear about all this. The Bible does not teach that lightning and hurricanes are always the work of the devil. Let no one jump to the conclusion that those statements in Job are merely the manifestation of the ignorance of an ancient people, and that they did not understand the weather as we do, because they did not have meteorological offices and their reports. The Bible never teaches that most things happen as the result of secondary causes. But as it teaches that God Himself sometimes acts over and above His own laws in miracles, or in sending pestilences or earthquakes, so we are given to understand that the devil at times may have a like power, and that he can send lightning or a hurricane. We must bear in mind, however, that the Bible does not offer this as the universal explanation. But it does tell us that these things may be the result of the special activity of the devil.

In the same way we see that the devil may have power over animals. The behaviour of the Gadarene swine is surely an evidence of the possibility that even animals may be taken hold of and possessed and used in this way as a part of the manifestation of this power of the devil and his cohorts over the very forces of nature itself, and over the animal creation. This is a very sobering thought. It is something that the modern man very rarely thinks about at all. Yet it is perfectly clear in the Scripture. And I suggest that it is something that is confirmed by the reading of history. There are suggestions in the New Testament that there were storms on the Lake of Galilee more than once which seem to be clearly an attempt of the devil to destroy the life of our blessed Lord Himself. That is an aspect of the manifestation of this power.

But let us turn to something which is much more important for us, namely, the manifestation of this subtle, terrible power of the devil over man himself, and first and foremost over man's mind. The devil, we are told everywhere, is subtle; he uses wiles. 'The serpent,' we read in Genesis 3, 'was more subtle than all the beasts of the field.' Subtlety is the great characteristic of the devil. So obviously he uses it in order to trip up and to trap man and to keep him from God and the blessings of God. He uses it most of all by attacking man in the realm of his mind, for the supreme gift in man is the gift of mind. It is a part of man's original endowment, and that which differentiates him from the animal. The animal acts in the main by instinct. But man has this curious power of thinking, objective thinking, of being able to look at himself objectively, and to reason and to argue, to consider, and to be logical. All this is a part of man's original endowment, and is undoubtedly the gift of God to man. And though man has fallen, he remains in certain ways a noble creature; he still has 'mind' and ability. Mind is man's highest gift, and therefore the devil concentrates his attack upon the minds of men.

A general statement concerning this matter is made by the Apostle in chapter two of this Epistle in the second verse: 'Wherein in time past ye walked according to the course of this world, according to the prince of the power of the air, the spirit that now worketh in the children of disobedience.' That is to say, everybody who is born into this world becomes a creature of this world. We are all immediately influenced by the mind and the outlook and the way of the world. By nature, we all walk 'according to the course of this world' and follow the way in which the world thinks and does this and that. We are all born old, as it were. We inherit traditions and habits and customs. Wordsworth had it in mind when he put it in his way: 'Shades of the prison-house begin to close upon the growing boy.' But, much earlier than Wordsworth understood, the shades are there even when he is an infant. They do not begin in boyhood, they were always there. There is 'a mind of the world', there is an outlook of the world, there is a worldly way; and every human being falls into that rut. But what is it that determines the matter? The Apostle answers that it is 'according to', determined by, controlled by, 'the prince of the power of the air, the spirit that now worketh in the children of disobedience'. The devil is controlling this world mind, this world outlook.

He does so in many and varied ways. We are told, for instance, that it is the devil who 'blinds the minds' of men to the truth of God (2 Corinthians 4:4). In that chapter the Apostle, dealing with the preaching of the Gospel, says that it is obvious that everybody does not believe the Gospel. But why is it that some people do not believe the Gospel? The Apostle's answer is, 'If our Gospel be hid, it is hid to them that are lost: in whom the god of this world hath blinded the minds of them which believe not', lest they believe. This is important and significant. The man of the world boasts about his freedom and talks about 'free thought'. It is the supreme achievement of the devil, to persuade man that at the point where he is most muddled and enslaved he is most free! Think of the many thousands, indeed millions, in the world at this moment who are rejoicing in the fact that they are not Christian because of their great minds, great brains and great understandings. How tragic it is! The tragedy of such people is that they have been 'blinded by the god of this world'. He has created this artificial mist, this obscurity; he has put these opacities into their very eyes, and they cannot see. They are 'blinded'. And it is the god of this world, the devil, who has done it.

It is very difficult for us as Christian people to realize as we ought that we should be filled with a sense of great compassion and sorrow for such people. It is difficult for us because of their arrogance and pride. But we should feel sorry for them. They are the dupes, the slaves of the devil; they are blinded by him; they cannot use their minds aright because the devil makes it impossible for them to do so.

The supreme activity of the devil is upon the mind of man. But his work has many other manifestations also. Read the Gospels and you will be amazed at times at the bitterness and the hostility of the Pharisees and others to our blessed Lord. It is not simply that they disagreed with Him, or that they asked Him questions; what you find is that there is a malice, a hatred, a bitterness. It is a part of the activity of the devil upon the minds of men. There is nothing that I know of that is more appalling than the bitter reaction of people to certain aspects of plain Christian truth in the New Testament. They are not content with saying that they cannot accept that truth, that they cannot believe it; they become bitter and display a deep hatred and animosity. Whether they realize it or not, that is the result of the operation of the devil within them. Why the hatred, the passion, the bitterness, the antagonism? It is all indicative of the influence of the devil and his bitter hatred of God. He does not want God to have any glory. And it is always at the points where God has given the greatest indications of His glory in the Scriptures that people are generally most antagonistic. They want to hold on to man and his power, and they therefore hate the thought that God is sovereign in His power over man. There, then, are some indications of the way in which the devil 'blinds' the minds of men and infuriates their spirits.

But, short of that, he does it by insinuating doubts. He did so at the beginning, as told in the story in Genesis 3. He came to Eve and said, 'Hath God said?' Adam and Eve had never questioned God before. But the serpent comes with his wily question, he insinuates a doubt. He does not speak it openly, he plausibly insinuates it. Have you not found that in your own experience? You are in a perfectly happy mood when suddenly a thought comes to you unexpectedly, or a suggestion in something you are reading implies a doubt. It just suggests it to you.

[85]

From the beginning the devil has been tempting man with these doubts, especially with regard to God and His ordering of affairs. There is a striking and dramatic example of this in the case of the Apostle Peter. Peter at Caesarea Philippi, according to the account in Matthew 16, had made his great confession. Our Lord had asked, 'Who do men say that I am?' 'But who say ye that I am?' And Peter said, 'Thou art the Christ, the Son of the living God.' Marvellous! But immediately afterwards our Lord proceeds to tell the apostles about His forthcoming death, and Peter says, 'Be it far from thee, Lord: this shall not happen unto thee'. Our Lord at once rebuked him, saying, 'Get thee behind me, Satan; thou savourest not the things that be of God, but the things that be of men'. You are failing to understand, you are querying my eternal mission. Our Lord had come to die, but Peter queries it, doubts it, and resents it. It is all because of the devil, Satan! 'Get thee behind me, Satan.'

The devil caused Peter to trip at that point. And he attacks us all along this line. He tried to insinuate doubts even into the mind of our blessed Lord Himself. Some of the greatest saints have left on record that he has assailed them with doubts even on their death-beds. That does not mean that they accepted them; what they say is that he tried to make them accept them. We are never promised that he will leave us alone. Do not conclude, then, that because you are assailed by doubts you are not a Christian. It is the devil that is at work. He will hurl doubts at you. The Apostle describes them as 'the fiery darts of the wicked one'. They come at you from every direction. He will suggest all sorts of difficulties and doubts, anything to stop men believing in God. There is nothing more important than that we should differentiate between the temptation to doubt and the act of doubting itself. The devil is constantly trying to insinuate doubts into our minds.

But he has many other wiles that he can use. He tries to overwhelm us with a spirit of fear; and that will often lead to a kind of denial. Look at the case of the Apostle Peter once more, the Peter who says so boldly, 'Though all men forsake thee, I will never forsake thee'. He intends to follow his Lord everywhere. 'Simon, Simon,' says our Lord, 'Satan hath desired to have you, that he may sift you as wheat.' And in a few days you see the bold, impulsive, self-confident Peter denying Christ with oaths and

[86]

cursing, because the spirit of fear, stimulated by the devil, makes him afraid of losing his life. So he denies Him thrice and says that he does not know Him! The devil tries to alarm and to frighten us. When you are most obedient to God he will put up certain possibilities to you, and threaten you with what he terms the evil consequences of your obedience. He does it when people are under conviction of sin. They seem to see the truth plainly and they want to yield to it, but he says, 'Can you not see what it is going to mean to you when you go home? It will cause difficulty there, it will cause unhappiness, it is going to split your family. And then consider what it is going to do to you tomorrow in your office, or in the profession, or in your college.' So he frightens us. This is a part of the work of the devil. You cannot explain these things psychologically. This is not psychology, this is not biology, this is not nature; according to the Scriptures this is the activity of the devil. He has been doing this from the very beginning; and he is doing it very actively still. And so he frightens us from the truth, and introduces this craven spirit of fear. And that, so often, is the precursor of denial of the truth and denial of the Lord.

The devil is also an expert at instigating false teachings. Paul, writing to Timothy, says, 'Now the Spirit speaketh expressly, that in the latter times some shall depart from the faith, giving heed to seducing spirits and doctrines of devils' (1 Timothy 4:1). Have you ever computed the amount of attention and space given in the New Testament to this kind of thing – 'doctrines of devils', 'seducing spirits', 'antichrists', 'the spirit of antichrist'? John's First Epistle and the Book of Revelation have many such expressions. These are just different ways of describing the activities of the devil and of evil spirits who are trying to detract from the glory of the Lord Jesus Christ. 'Prove the spirits,' says John, 'there are many false prophets gone out into the world.' This is the spirit of antichrist. How do you know it? It denies that Jesus Christ has come in the flesh; it creates doubts about His incarnation; it does not believe in the Virgin Birth; it says that He was just a good man, perhaps the greatest man the world has ever known. Where such doubts and denyings are spreading, there we see the work of seducing spirits. They are in the Christian Church, alas, and they have been very active during the past century.

The confusion in the Christian Church today is not merely the result of what is proudly called 'scholarship'. It is the fruit of the activity of the devil. The Apostles were aware of it in the first century. That is why all this boasting about 'modern knowledge' is finally so childish and ridiculous. There is nothing new, ultimately, about the so-called Higher Criticism, which leads men to say that Jesus Christ is only a man, and to deny the Virgin Birth, and the two natures in Him, and the miracles. There were people in the early Church who said it all! John had to write his Gospel and his First Epistle because of that kind of thing. The Apostle Paul long strove against it, as you find in his Epistles to Timothy and in his Epistle to the Colossians. There is nothing new about it, the devil has been engaged in this work from the very beginning. 'Has God said?' '*If* thou be the Son of God'! There is nothing that makes man quite so ridiculous as his pride of intellect. He becomes a fool when he boasts of the modernity of something that is as old as the Fall! Is it not tragic? As he has done from the beginning, the devil introduces the false teachings, and so creates confusion in the Church, and people begin to say, What is Christianity? Is it something that teaches holiness or is it something that permits me to read pornographic literature? Which is it? Far too often in these days, when you look at what the Christian Church is saying, you cannot tell, because she is saying both! That is the work of 'seducing spirits', that is the antichrist. If the devil can only cause confusion in the Church how happy he is! Here are those who claim to be God's people accepting a revelation! But see them, arguing and disagreeing with one another utterly and fundamentally about the very Person of the Lord, and about the great centralities of Christian faith and practice. How the devil must be rejoicing as he sees the way in which those who claim the name of Christ can be so easily seduced and persuaded to teach a lie!

But it does not stop at that. Another way in which the devil comes and causes havoc is by attacking us with evil thoughts. The fact that you are tempted by evil thoughts must not lead you to the conclusion that you are not a Christian. That is what the devil would have you believe, of course. It is his work. I again quote the phrase, 'the fiery darts of the wicked one'. Have we not all experienced them? Even when you may be reading your Bible evil and blasphemous thoughts may come to you. You are not thinking about such things, and you do not want to do so. Where have they come from? What is their origin? Your great psychologists cannot explain it. The only adequate explanation is that the devil hurls them at you. Have you not often found when you wake up in the morning, after you have been fast asleep, that such thoughts immediately come? They are not yours.

This is very comforting and consoling teaching; that is why we are dealing with it in such detail. Had you thought that all this teaching was remote and theoretical? You will find that it provides the greatest comfort. How do you know, you may ask, whether they are your thoughts or the thoughts of the devil? If you hate them and wish that they were not there, then they are not yours; they are the devil's. He attacks us by hurling evil and blasphemous thoughts at us. He insinuates them. And not only evil thoughts but evil imaginations. It is often very difficult to control our mind and thoughts and imaginations. The devil has power to lead them, and especially if you are not aware of it and fail to stop him. And thus he will take you captive, and make you intensely miserable.

I have already mentioned certain fears. I now turn to deal with fears in a more general sense. Go to a pagan country and you will find that it is a country of fears. The inhabitants are afraid of everything, afraid of the dark, afraid of spirits in woods, in trees, in the heavens. A pagan country, which has never known the influence of Christian teaching, is always a country of fears and phobias. That is the tragedy of the world without Christ, it becomes more and more fearful. It is happening increasingly in this country as we go further and further away from God and Christianity. Mascots and interest in astrology return and flourish. All these things are coming back. It is a manifestation of the spirit of fear, people becoming afraid of everything. It is a part of the devil's machinery for keeping us all under his power.

These fears are quite irrational, as can be readily shown. There are certain people whose lives are dominated by fears. Now the thing to do with them, and to help them to do for themselves, is to assist them to consider the utterly irrational character of their fear. For instance, take the case of persons who are afraid as the result of reading about a hurricane or violent storm. Some people are dominated by such a fear. Now they should ask themselves this question: 'Why should I always be drawing the conclusion that the hurricane is only going to attack me? What about all the other people? Why am I not as they are?' and so on. These fears are irrational, and they are the work of the devil.

Some fears are partly temperamental; for we are not all alike; some have strong nerves, some weak. I am not saying that there is anything essentially wrong in the fact that some of us are more fearful than others; but what I am saying is that when you find that you have got a 'spirit of fear', that you are 'dominated' by a fear, you should strive to see that there is this irrational element in it, and that it is beyond the natural. It is something worse than the natural; there is an element of horror about it, and there is no adequate explanation for it. That is always the work of the devil. He keeps people captives by holding them under the dominion of these irrational fears.

Turn now to another category – depression and discouragement. This is one of the most remarkable manifestations of the activity of the devil. He does it with non-Christians as well as with Christians. He depresses the mind. He does it generally by making us concentrate overmuch on ourselves. He keeps us looking at ourselves and examining ourselves, always looking at the past, at something we did in the past which we should not have done. He will keep us looking back until we are utterly depressed. We doubt whether we are forgiven, we doubt whether we are children of God, we feel unworthy, we feel unclean, we feel our lives are a failure. That we become miserable and unhappy, causes the devil to rejoice, for he is able to say, 'There is a typical Christian! that is your Christianity!' Cannot you see that this is an aspect of the wiles of the devil? How wrong it all is! And how we ought to detect it! You have no right to remain in such a depression, because you are assured by God's own word that 'If we confess our sins, he is faithful and just to forgive us our sins, and to cleanse us from all unrighteousness' (1 John 1:9). He is a God who heals the backslider; He is a God who receives back the prodigal son. 'The past shall be forgotten, a present joy be given.' You have no right to look back; you have no right to be perpetually looking within; you have no right to be depressed. If you are depressed, you are merely succumbing to the influence of the evil one. Depression, discouragement, a sense of failure, a sense of utter and complete hopelessness, are generally the result of the devil's activities.

But let us now turn to another manifestation of the devil's activity which is the exact opposite. Pride! Oh, 'the wiles of the devil!' Some would have you believe that the devil always depresses. He can do the exact opposite. He often encourages pride. That was the mechanism he used in the case of Eve, was it not? 'Hath God said?' 'You know,' he said, 'you are much too good to be held down in this way. Why should you not eat of everything in this garden? Why does God place you under a prohibition? What right has He to say that you are not to eat of the fruit of a certain tree?' He played on her pride, and she, being lifted up with pride, fell. So did Adam. Or consider the example of David, as found in 1 Chronicles 21:1. David had had great victories; he had conquered all his enemies. Then you read this: 'And Satan stood up against Israel and provoked David to number Israel.' When you have conquered all your enemies, that is the very moment he comes in and says, 'Well now, just count your great successes, count heads, count the number of your people, the extent of your kingdom.' And so he tempted David on this question of pride, and terrible consequences followed for David and the children of Israel. What a terrible temptation this is! He puffs us up with pride! So the Apostle, in writing to Timothy about the appointment of bishops, elders, presbyters, overseers, says, 'Do not appoint a novice'. He says, Never put a man who has only recently been converted into a high position, 'lest being lifted up with pride he fall into the condemnation of the devil' (1 Timothy 3:6). What tragedies have happened in the life of the Church, and in individual lives, because that exhortation has not been followed! Here is what is now called a 'star turn', a marvellous convert, and the temptation is to put him right into the front at once. The result often is that he is ruined! He becomes proud of his past sin, he begins to boast about his past evil life because it makes him important! Do not promote a novice, says the Apostle, for, if you do, the devil is certain to trap him. Keep to this rule.

Pride manifests itself in many different ways. It makes us over-sensitive; and when we are over-sensitive we are very easily hurt, and we feel hurt. What havoc has been wrought in the Christian church in this way! Pride, as manipulated by the devil, leads to jealousy, to envy, to a sense of grudge because we are not being appreciated, and someone else is being put before us. In this way the devil can upset a church or a community; and he has often done so. His object always is to spoil God's great handiwork, and especially the most glorious thing of all, the grace of God in salvation within the church! All may appear to be brought to ruin, and seemingly the devil has triumphed again. He plays on our pride as well as on our tendency to depression. This passage with which we are dealing is a very practical one, is it not?

'Ah,' you say, 'principalities and powers, the rulers of the darkness of this world, what has all that to do with me?' It has this much to do with you, that most of the unhappiness you have known in your Christian life has been entirely the result of the work of the devil and these other powers; and you did not know it. You thought you had a good case, and a real grudge, did you not? But it was not so. It was simply your ugly pride, your abominable pride, and the devil playing on it like a master pianist, knowing exactly where to put the pressure and where to relax it! Thank God that we have a passage such as this in Ephesians to open our eyes.

And the devil has many other devices. He plays on man's moral nature by tempting him, by rousing lusts and passions and evil desires. And he can work upon our very bodies. In the second chapter of Job, verse seven, we read 'So went Satan forth from the presence of the Lord, and smote Job'. God had given him permission to go further now. Faced with the terrible loss of his sons and his animals Job had stood the test. Then Satan said to God, 'So far I have not touched Job himself. Let me but touch his body, then he will begin to squeal, then he will curse you.' And God replied in effect, 'Go and do it, but touch not his life!' 'So Satan went forth from the presence of the Lord, and smote Job with sore boils from the sole of his foot unto his crown.' 'Ah,' says someone, 'you are teaching now that boils are always the work of the devil.' Not at all! I am simply teaching that they may be! Of course most diseases are due to secondary causes, but they may be directly due to the devil. The devil can cause dumbness, he can cause blindness. There is the woman in Luke 13 of whom we read that she 'had a spirit of infirmity eighteen years, and was bound together, and could in no wise lift up herself'. Notice what our Lord says about her: 'Ought not this woman, being a daughter of Abraham, whom Satan hath bound, lo, these eighteen years, be loosed?' Her condition, He says, was the work of the devil; it was not simply disease. And so you find in 1 Corinthians 5 a reference to 'delivering a man to Satan for the destruction of the flesh'. And you find Paul saying about himself in 2 Corinthians 12:7, 'Lest I should be exalted above measure through the abundance of the revelations, there was given to me a thorn in the flesh, the messenger of Satan to buffet me, lest I should be exalted above measure.' Infirmities, weaknesses, yes, sicknesses and illnesses, *may* be the result of the devil's activity. I am not saying 'always', I am saying they 'may be'. He has this power.

These, therefore, are some of the ways in which he exercises these wiles of his, and is able to bring to pass his evil purpose of causing confusion and chaos in the work of God, and holding men and women captive, and separating them from God and His glory, and the blessings God is ready to give them.

If you recognize these things, you will realize that there is only one thing to do, and that is, 'Be strong in the Lord, and in the power of his might'. And further, 'Take unto you the whole armour of God'. You are facing a most relentless, subtle, intelligent, powerful foe who can attack you from all quarters. There is only one place of safety – 'Put on the whole armour of God, that ye may be able to withstand in the evil day; and having done all, to stand.'

7
The Subtle Foe

We have thus far been considering the power and wiles of our enemy, the devil. Further aspects of this same subject have still to be taken up, but before we do so it may be well to comment on a question which is probably in someone's mind: In the light of Christ's conquest of the devil, and the certainty that he will finally be cast into a lake of destruction, how is it that the powers of darkness are still so determined and active? Why is it that Christians are still engaged in the conflict to which the Apostle is drawing our attention? The answer is that the essential weakness of the devil is that, despite all his cleverness and all his subtlety, he does not realize that he is a defeated foe. He has great knowledge and great power, but he is not aware of the fact that he is hopelessly outclassed. So he still persists with his efforts. He is still trying to defeat God, and as he did not abandon his attacks upon our Lord when he was routed in the temptations in the wilderness but continued attacking, coming back and repeating his onslaughts until the very end, so he continues to this day. The reason is that he is God's adversary! The devil is not so much against us as against God. We are nothing in his sight except that we are God's people. The devil's one consuming passion and ambition is to spoil and destroy the work of God.

For this reason, he tempted Eve in the Garden of Eden, and attempted to ruin God's perfect work. The devil hated it, and he was determined to mar it and to destroy it if he could. That is why he began his warfare, and when our Lord actually lived on earth he brought out all his resources. At that time God was doing the most vital and central thing of all, so the devil brought out all his reserves. If God's work at this point could be destroyed, then the devil's victory would be assured. But he utterly failed to defeat our Lord. The tables were turned upon him completely, as it were, in what happened on the Cross. When he thought that he was finally defeating our Lord, what was really happening was that our Lord was 'putting him' and his forces 'to an open shame, triumphing over them in it'. Having failed there, and still more in the glory of the resurrection, the devil, of course, immediately saw that the only thing left for him to do was to destroy the saving work of our Lord as seen in the establishment and maintenance of the Christian Church. This is the new kingdom that is being formed, this is the new thing through which God is preparing for the final defeat of the devil. So it obviously follows that the devil's particular concern now is to damage and, if he can, destroy, the Church of God, and every single individual member of the Church. The Church, after all, is God's most glorious work: 'She is His new creation, by water and the Word.' This wonderful thing which God is forming, the body of Christ, is more marvellous than the original creation. Naturally the devil is tremendously concerned about the Church, and if he can ruin it or any part of it, he will still have defeated God, and be able to rejoice evermore.

The result is that Christian people are in a very special manner the object of the devil's attack. That is what the Apostle is reminding us of here. Our Lord put the same truth in other words when He says, 'The servant is not above his Lord. If they have called the master of the house Beelzebub, how much more shall they call them of his household?' (Matthew 10:25). He says in effect: You see the treatment I have had in this world, hereafter you will receive similar treatment because you are My people. The world will hate you, because it has hated Me. You belong to Me, and as they have reacted to Me, so they will react to you. It is the devil that makes the world behave in this way.

Our Lord was preparing His immediate disciples and all generations of His people for the hostility of the world. The very fact that we are Christians means that the devil will take a particular interest in us, and will be very specially concerned to defeat us as and where he is able. His object in doing so is thereby to besmirch, as it were, the glory of God, and show the failure of God and of Christ to redeem a people, 'a peculiar people' to Himself.

That being our basic proposition we can go on to a second one, namely, the more Christian we become and are, the more we can expect to be attacked by the devil. That again needs no demonstration. No one has ever been tempted by the devil as our Lord was. He was 'tempted in all points like as we are', but much more so. The devil himself in person always came to Him. Some of these principalities and powers are often sufficient for us, some of the mere underlings, as it were, in the kingdom of evil; but the devil himself, with all his powers fully displayed, always confronted our Lord. So the more we approximate to our Lord the more we are to expect this kind of attack. Hence the Apostle speaks with particular solemnity, and repeats his counsel: 'Finally, my brethren, be strong in the Lord, and in the power of his might'; then again, 'Wherefore take unto you the whole armour of God.' He wants us to realize that conflict faces us. The more Christian we become the more we shall be aware of the conflict. That is the universal testimony of all the saints who have ever lived and adorned the life of the Church. They have all agreed that as they go on in the Christian life the fight against the devil becomes fiercer and hotter. Many tell us in their death-bed scenes that he attacked them even there.

Again, this is the unvarying message of the Bible. The Bible does not teach the type of salvation which says, Come to Christ, believe in Him, all will be well; you will walk down the road with a bright step and everything will be perfect ever afterwards. On the contrary the Scripture warns us that we are entering a life in which we have to put on 'the whole armour of God'.

Whenever I read these verses, or think of them, with this repetition about putting on the whole armour of God, I am reminded of something that happened during the early stages of the last war, in the so-called 'phoney war' stage. The war broke out on the 3rd September 1939, but nothing seemed to happen for months, and some people – superficial optimists, people who did not understand the situation – were almost ready to say, Nothing is going to happen. Indeed, Prime Minister Neville Chamberlain said in the House of Commons, 'Hitler has missed the bus', only a month or two before Hitler really released all his power in the month of May 1940. But my chief reference at this point is to Major-General Sir Ernest Swinton, who used to speak on the radio once each week as a military commentator from September 1939 onwards. Nothing seemed to be happening, no guns were being fired, there had been no clash of arms, no air-raids had taken place, the war seemed dead. But Sir Ernest Swinton kept on saying each week, 'We are fighting for our lives.' He seemed to many to be a pessimist; but he kept on saying it. 'Make no mistake about it,' he used to say, 'we are fighting for our very lives.' And he continued to say it though nothing was happening. The fact was that he knew something about the power and the subtlety of the enemy; he knew what was happening. He knew that this apparent lull was most deceptive, and that if we were wise we would be preparing with all our might and main. He knew that the terrible onslaught was bound to come. And of course it did come!

I ask therefore, Is Christianity a life of ease? Do you simply take your justification and your sanctification by faith and assume that all is well? 'Take unto you the whole armour of God,' says Paul. 'We wrestle not against flesh and blood.' Realize that you are engaged in a terrible warfare, and that because you are a Christian, you will need the whole armour of God, every portion of it, in order that you 'may be able to withstand in the evil day, and having done all things, to stand'. Indeed, the more you advance in the Christian life, the hotter will the fight become. Paul assures us that we are confronted by 'the wiles of the devil', and the terrible power of his forces.

I emphasize that the devil does not use his 'wiles' against the unbeliever, the non-Christian. There is no need for him to do so. There is nothing at all difficult from the devil's standpoint in keeping the person who is not interested in Christ, and who does not believe in Him, in a state of sin. Our Lord Himself has reminded us that 'the strong man armed keepeth his goods in peace'. There is no need for him to be subtle to make worldly, sinful people keep on sinning. There is no need of any subtlety to make people read certain well-known Sunday newspapers, and spend their whole day in doing so. There is no cleverness in that. Everything that is in depraved human nature wants to act

[97]

in that way, and all you have to do is to put the papers in front of them. The same applies in making men live to drink and to dance and to indulge their passions. There is no subtlety there; that is an easy task for the devil. The merest underling can do that, and perhaps even he is not necessary. The lusts that arise in fallen human nature will do that automatically. But the moment we are translated into the kingdom of God, the kingdom of light, the moment we belong to Christ, the devil realizes that the whole position is different; and he now has to produce his 'wiles'. So it is only Christian people who know anything about 'the wiles' of the devil; others remain in ignorance of them.

I suggest, therefore, that a very good test of our standing as Christians is our knowledge of 'the wiles of the devil'. But someone may ask, Why do you spend so much time on this? Why are you making such a big thing of this? Why do you not just say, 'All is well, the devil is defeated, "put on the whole armour of God"?' My reply is that the Apostle warns us most solemnly that we are up against the wiles of the devil. Not only so, but he takes the trouble to tell us in detail about the nature of this armour which we must put on if we are to survive. And I would remind you again that the experience of the saints through the ages teaches us that the greater the saint the more he knows about the wiles of the devil.

There is nothing, I would say, which is more significant about evangelicalism in this present century than the way in which it has largely ignored this teaching concerning the devil and the principalities and powers, and the 'wiles' of the devil. How often have you heard addresses or sermons on this theme in connection with teaching on sanctification? The popular teaching offers to put all right for you at once, and says that there is nothing to worry about. You just 'look to Christ' and all is well. No, says Paul, 'Put on the whole armour of God', in addition to being 'strong in the Lord and the power of his might'. You need the armour, and you will have to make good use of it if you are to stand.

There is no more thorough test of our standing and our position, and our growth as Christians, than our knowledge of, and our awareness of, 'the wiles of the devil'. It is because of the wiles of the devil that we have these New Testament Epistles.

They would never have been written, indeed the Gospels would never have been written, were it not for the wiles of the devil. They were written because the early Christians were in difficulties. Some had fallen into error, had gone astray here or there, and were in some kind of trouble; so these books were written in order to make them and us familiar with 'the wiles of the devil'. They are all given to us partly in order to prepare us for this wily antagonist and all his powers and forces that are arrayed against us. This is the Bible's way of approaching the doctrine of sanctification. To teach sanctification you do not have to go back constantly to Old Testament incidents and spiritualize them, you do not have to take the New Testament miracles and turn them into parables. Not that that is necessarily wrong if you explain clearly what you are doing! What the wise teacher does is to expound the Epistles, and especially this teaching concerning the wiles of the devil. All our problems arise ultimately from that source. What we have to do, therefore, is to understand something about the character of these wiles, and then about the way in which we are to meet them and to counter them, in order that we may resist the devil successfully.

The point I am establishing is that it is not enough just to say, 'Ah, it is all quite simple; you just "look to the Lord" and you will have your victory.' It is not so! The New Testament gives us particular instructions. Any sanctification or holiness teaching that by-passes the detailed teaching of the New Testament Epistles is false teaching; it is not biblical teaching. Ultimately it is some kind of psychology, the teaching of a cult. We have to attend to details because we are told that it is the only way in which we can withstand the devil. We must know something about the nature of his attack.

First of all, ask the question, How does the devil attack us? 'We wrestle not against flesh and blood, but against principalities, against powers, against the rulers of the darkness of this world, against spiritual wickedness in high places.' The first answer is found in the word 'wiles'. Very frequently this word is used in different forms in order to describe the nature of the opposition which is facing us, the character of the attack. The Scriptures go out of their way, as it were, to emphasize them. Go back to

Genesis 3:1. There you read: 'Now the serpent was more subtle than any beast of the field.' Wiles, stratagems, all appear as the result of subtlety. In 2 Corinthians 11:3, the Apostle writes to the Corinthians and explains that he is doing so because 'I fear, lest by any means, as the serpent beguiled Eve through his subtlety, so your minds should be corrupted from the simplicity that is in Christ'. You may think that it ought to be enough to say, 'The moment you believe in Christ and are "in Christ", all is well; all you do is to abide in Christ.' But, unfortunately, the devil and the principalities and powers are at work; and because of this 'subtlety', this 'beguiling', it is necessary that we should know something about it. Listen again to Paul in that same Epistle (2 Corinthians 2:9–11): 'To this end did I write . . . lest Satan should get an advantage of us: for we are not ignorant of his devices' – his planning, his scheming! He will do anything he can to get an advantage over us, says Paul, to get us down, to make us look ridiculous, and to bring God's name into disgrace. 'We are not ignorant of his devices.'

Take another example. Paul, writing in 1 Timothy, chapter 3, about the folly of making novices elders and bishops, says, 'lest he fall into reproach and into the snare of the devil'. Do you know anything about 'snares'? Have you seen men setting traps to catch rabbits, or a snare to catch a bird? The real art in that procedure, of course, is to conceal it. You do not put a trap openly in the middle of a field and leave it there standing in the open. No, you put it amongst some leaves or branches of trees. A person walking along casually would see nothing, and the unthinking rabbit or bird does not see anything. It sees some bits of meat or something to attract it; but it does not see the snare. The whole point of laying a snare is that you camouflage it, you cover it; the procedure has to be subtle. And the Apostle says that the reason why we must not promote a novice is lest he suddenly 'fall into reproach and the snare (the trap) of the devil'.

Again, in 2 Timothy 2:26, Paul is again teaching the Lord's servant how to help people in the Christian life, so he writes, 'And that they may recover themselves out of the snare of the devil, who are taken captive by him at his will'. The devil is always laying traps and snares. They are all about us; and the Apostle says to Timothy, You must be patient, you must show believers

[100]

the dangers, and teach them how to avoid them in order that those who have been snared or trapped by the devil may 'recover themselves', may come out of the trap and recover their freedom.

Our Lord Himself uses a most significant term when He tells us in John 8:44, that 'when the devil speaketh a lie, he speaketh of his own: for he is a liar, and the father of it'. The devil indulges in lies because they are a part of his wiles. He does not speak the truth, he is always prepared to twist the truth, and to speak a lie. His words are intended to trap us and to get us into his clutches. Lying is a prominent part of the wiles of the devil!

Then take again the statement by our Lord found in Matthew 24:24: 'For there shall arise false Christs, and false prophets, and shall show great signs and wonders; insomuch that, if it were possible, they shall deceive the very elect'. That is final! The Lord says that these forces are so subtle and so clever, they will be able to do such marvellous, wonderful things, that even the very elect of God are almost trapped and ensnared by them.

In the same vein the Apostle Paul writes rather sarcastically in the eleventh chapter of 2 Corinthians of 'false apostles', people who set themselves up, calling attention to themselves. He says in effect to the Corinthian church, What is the matter with you, why are you always taken in by these plausible men who come along, men who advertise themselves in a fleshly manner, and set themselves up as authorities? You are always ready to listen to them and to swallow their every word. Oh! how innocent you are of 'the wiles of the devil'. You cannot recognize these 'false prophets', these 'deceitful workers'. They are not straight. They pretend to be Apostles of Christ, and to be concerned only for the glory of God; but there is deceit everywhere. In a very subtle way they are really calling attention to themselves and not to the Lord. Thus does Paul warn them against such people because of the terrible damage they may do.

There is already an example of this very thing in this Epistle to the Ephesians in chapter four, verse fourteen: 'That we henceforth be no more children, tossed to and fro, and carried about with every wind of doctrine, by the sleight of men, and cunning craftiness whereby they lie in wait to deceive'. Paul is there referring to false teachers who are used by the wily devil.

He says that they are 'cunning', and 'crafty', and that they plan to deceive. They are able to do so because of their cleverness and subtlety. But the most remarkable example of this is in 2 Thessalonians 2:8-10: 'And then shall that Wicked be revealed – that "wicked one" – whom the Lord shall consume with the spirit of his mouth, and shall destroy with the brightness of his coming: even him, whose coming is after the working of Satan with all power and signs and lying wonders, and with all deceivableness of unrighteousness in them that perish; because they received not the love of the truth, that they might be saved.' Notice the striking terms. Everywhere Scripture warns us against this 'cunning craftiness' and this 'all deceivableness of unrighteousness' by which we are literally surrounded.

What must be the condition of a Christian who is not aware of all this? Either he must be fast asleep, or he must be the merest babe in Christ. Children are never aware of dangers. It is their ignorance that accounts for this; they are not aware of the dangerous possibilities. The novice does not understand; everything to him is simple and plain sailing. It is only the man who has some experience, who is a little older, who sees these things.

Then take one further word in which the Apostle tells Timothy that he himself, and all who listen to him, have to be prepared for these things. 'Now the Spirit speaketh expressly, that in the latter times . . .' Those times are already here, they have always been here, the very end is only an aggravation of what has been continuing ever since the time when our Lord was here in this world. 'The Spirit speaketh expressly, that in the latter times some shall depart from the faith.' Why? 'Giving heed to seducing spirits.' Are you aware of 'seducing spirits, and doctrines of devils', of some 'speaking lies in hypocrisy; having their conscience seared with a hot iron' – and so on? (1 Timothy 4:1-2).

My last quotation, found in Hebrews 3:13, is a more general one about the character of the sin which results from all this. The Hebrews were in trouble and in difficulties; they were depressed and discouraged, some of them were looking back with longing eyes to the Jewish religion. The author of the Epistle is fearful 'lest any of you be hardened through the deceitfulness of sin.'

I have quoted all these passages of Scripture in order to show how they emphasize constantly this truth concerning 'the wiles of the devil'. I remind you again of the words of Major-General Sir Ernest Swinton: 'We are fighting for our very lives'. 'Judgment must begin at the house of God, and if the righteous scarcely (or with great difficulty) be saved, what shall the end of the ungodly be?' says Peter (1 Peter 4:17, 18). Such is the New Testament teaching. We are fighting for our lives, we are fighting not mere flesh and blood, but the devil with his wiles, and the principalities and powers, rulers of the darkness of this world. All I am asking is, Are we aware of the fight? Are we aware of the conflict? Do we realize that we are in this position?

In the next place I ask a second question: How are these 'wiles' shown or manifested? How can I become aware of the wiles of the devil? How does he employ these wiles? To find an answer, let us first look at what we are told about the devil himself and observe how 'the wiles' are shown in the ways in which he appears. Here is the key to the understanding of this matter. The leading statement concerning this is found in the eleventh chapter of 2 Corinthians from which we have already quoted. In verse thirteen the Apostle says, 'For such are false apostles, deceitful workers, transforming themselves into the apostles of Christ. And no marvel; for Satan himself is transformed into an angel of light. Therefore it is no great thing if his ministers also be transformed as the ministers of righteousness.' Here the interesting and all-important word is 'transformed'. Incidentally, the correct translation in verse fourteen is not 'And no marvel, for Satan himself is transformed', but 'Satan transforms himself into an angel of light'. It is not something that has to be done to him, it is something that he does himself. That gives us the key to the understanding of his activities.

Some of the modern translations of the New Testament are good at this point. They translate this word 'transforms' as 'masquerades'. These people masquerade as the apostles of Christ, and the devil masquerades as an angel of light. The Amplified New Testament, for example, has this translation.

In other words, the idea is that the devil wears a mask, that he is an actor who appears in different characters. He does not always appear in the same manner. If he did so the problem would be less difficult. The picture might well have been in the mind of Paul when he writes of the 'evil day'. There are such things as 'satanic attacks' or onslaughts. These are experiences in the Christian life – and many saints testify to them – when the devil comes as a veritable roaring lion, or to change the comparison, when he comes like a hurricane, a howling wind, with noise and tumult and alarm and terror and destruction in his pathway. He makes a broadside attack upon you, and would sweep you off your feet with terror and alarm. And unless you know something of what the Apostle is writing about here, you will not be able to stand; you will be swept off your feet by him. All the might of his fury, and the vehemence of his bitter antagonism to God will be turned upon you. When you wake up in the morning he will be thundering and roaring at you, and he will follow you through the day. You will say, 'I have never felt like this before. Am I a Christian at all? What is happening to me? I thought I had finished with all that.' The devil will be glaring at you and threatening you; and you will be trembling and feeling almost lost.

But that is only one of his guises, only one of the masks he puts on. That is not how he came to Eve. He 'beguiled' Eve, he enticed her. A roaring lion does not entice anyone. But that mask is now put off, and he comes in the most plausible, pleasing, enticing manner conceivable. He comes as your friend, as someone who is there to help you. Listen to him speaking to Eve: Has God really said you should not eat of this particular tree of the knowledge of good and evil? Ah well, of course, you know why He said that, He wants to keep you down; He does not want you to become what you are really capable of; He knows that if you eat of that tree you will become like Himself; and He does not want that to happen. That is the trouble with God – He always wants to keep everyone down. Do not listen to that, express yourself, stand on your own feet. Thus the devil enticed Eve. He comes sometimes in his most enticing form and as our greatest friend.

Another method he employs is that of insinuation. In this guise he does not say anything directly, he suggests it, he insinuates it. He came to our Lord and said, 'If thou be the Son of God . . .' He is not saying actually in words that He is not the Son of God; but you notice the implication, 'If thou be the Son of God'. In the temptation in the wilderness there is a mixture of enticing and innuendo. So the devil may come to you and say, If you believe that Gospel and become a Christian you will make a fool of yourself; people will laugh at you; you will spoil your career . . . He insinuates these innuendoes. That is a very subtle form of attack which he frequently employs.

But, as the Apostle reminds us, sometimes he discards all these tricks, and the mask he now puts on, or the way in which he masquerades, is that of 'an angel of light'. This time he comes as one who is an authority on the truth; he comes quoting Scripture. The devil has a knowledge of Scripture, and in our Lord's temptations in the wilderness he quoted Scripture to Him, as one who knows it. So he will come to us as one who wishes to enlighten us in the Scriptures. Before, he did his utmost, perhaps, as a 'roaring lion' to keep you out of the Christian life altogether; now he sees that that no longer works with you, so he drops all other methods and comes as an angel of light who offers to lead you into deeper truths which no one has ever seen before. That is what he has always done with all the heretics. He comes to us as one who is anxious that we should get away from externals and come to the really profound things at the centre, which other people have so sadly missed. The men who were troubling Paul, and the church at Corinth, were but the instruments of the devil appearing in that way. They said: 'As for Paul, his presence is weak, and his speech contemptible'. We are amazed, they said in effect, that you have paid so much attention to him. He knows nothing beyond the merest elements and is ignorant of the profound truths. Paul's answer to that was, I taught you the basic elements only because you were carnal, you were babes; you were not fit for more; I knew what I was doing (1 Corinthians 3:1ff). But those other teachers said the exact opposite. They came as 'angels of light' who were going to lead the people straight into the profundities of the truth; they were not going to waste their time in working up slowly to these things, building them up, treating them first as 'infants', then as 'babes', then as 'young men' and so on. They did not do as John did and as Paul always did, and as the Epistle to the Hebrews does (Hebrews

[105]

5:11–14). By one great leap they could lead directly to the whole truth! That is the way in which many heresies have arisen; that is also how most of the cults have originated.

Another guise which the devil adopts, another mask which he puts on – and it is one of the cleverest of all – is that he hides himself altogether, and ridicules the whole notion that there is a devil at all, or any such beings as 'principalities and powers'. Alas! there are not only many people in the world who do not believe in the reality of these things we are considering, but there are many in the Church who do not believe it. There is a proposal on foot at the present time to amend a certain well-known Church Catechism, and to drop mention of the devil altogether.

The devil is at his very cleverest when he persuades people that there is no devil. Concealment is the whole art of angling. One of the first rules in fishing is to keep yourself out of sight, to camouflage yourself. Throw out your line and let it be a long one so that the fish does not see you sitting or standing by. Hide yourself! It is one of the first rules in angling; and the devil is a past master at this. So when he can persuade the Church, especially, that there are no such beings as the devil and principalities and powers and demons, everything is going perfectly well from his standpoint. The Church is drugged and is deluded; she is asleep, and is not aware of the conflict at all.

Lastly, he appears sometimes as a barefaced liar denying the Truth, uttering lies, 'speaking falsehoods'.

In a sense all we have been considering is what I would call a Prolegomenon to Church history, an introduction to the whole history of the Christian Church. Why has the history of the Church been what it is? Why did the Fathers have to call those early Church Councils? Why did they have to draw up their Confessions and their Creeds? They were the answers of the Church to the manifestations of the wiles of the devil which had succeeded because some of God's people had not paid attention to, and had not grasped, the teaching of God's Word.

We shall go on with a further consideration of this; and increasingly we shall apply it to ourselves personally. Meanwhile, if any of you, as the result of the devil's wiles, feel discouraged, depressed, or filled with terror and alarm, you are seriously misunderstanding the Apostle's teaching. True, his wiles exist, but listen, 'Be strong in the Lord, and in the power of his might. Take unto you the whole armour of God.' If you do so, you will have nothing to fear, you will be able to 'withstand in the evil day, and having done all, to stand'.

8

Heresies

We have seen that the devil is never quite so subtle, and never quite so successful, as when he succeeds in persuading people that he does not exist at all! That, as we have suggested, was his supreme masterpiece, and it is certainly a part of our problem at the present time. The tendency now is to say that we must not talk about 'the devil' but only about 'evil'. We must not tell people to 'renounce the works of the devil', we must tell them to 'resist evil'. In other words, the whole tendency today is to say that our fight is only against a principle of evil that is in ourselves and in others, and perhaps in the very environment into which we are born. But it is not considered to be 'consistent with modern knowledge' to believe still in a personal devil. We must not even make that principle of evil positive. What has been called 'evil', we are told, is simply the absence of good qualities rather than something positive in and of itself!

But the whole emphasis of the Apostle here is on the devil as a person. A principle cannot be subtle. It is only a person who can be subtle. 'The wiles of the devil!' The Apostle's whole object is to tell us that we are not fighting merely against flesh and blood, merely against some principle, or absence of principle, which is within us as flesh and blood, as men and women. He goes out of his way to say that it is quite otherwise. In other words what he says is the exact opposite of what is being taught commonly at the present time.

But somebody may ask, 'Does it matter whether you believe

[108]

in a personal devil or not?' The answer is that the Apostle most certainly assures us that we are fighting personalities and 'spirits' of evil, the world 'rulers of this darkness', not the 'darkness', but 'the rulers' of the darkness. His whole object is to get us to see that we must not be deluded in this respect, but realize that there are these spiritual entities, personalities, headed up by the devil himself, who are warring a terrible, subtle, vicious warfare against God and all His people. This is not a matter of opinion, it is not just a matter of accommodating our teaching to suit the modern mind and modern knowledge and understanding; if you do not believe in the person of the devil you are rejecting not only the teaching of the Apostle Paul but you are rejecting the teaching of the Lord Jesus Christ Himself!

The problem that arises here primarily is the problem of revelation. Was the Apostle Paul just a creature of his age, or was he given this revelation by the Lord Jesus Christ through the Spirit? Was our Lord Himself but a creature of His age? He obviously believed in a personal devil, and in these powers. He addressed demons as persons, saying 'Come out'. You cannot say that to a principle! You cannot dismiss the devil, as it were, in that way; you are denying at the same time the Lord Jesus Christ Himself. You are saying that you are in a superior position to Him, that your knowledge is greater, that you have greater understanding. You are involved in the whole question of revelation and of authority.

This digression is important, for the business of preaching is to relate the teaching of the Scriptures to what is happening in our own day; and if this teaching in Ephesians is true there is nothing more dangerous than to substitute for a personal devil a principle of evil! The whole of our faith is ultimately involved in the matter. The trouble with the critics is that they really do not believe in the spiritual realm. Many of them are equally doubtful, as I have shown, of the Person of the Holy Spirit. He is just a principle, a power, an influence. There is, in fact, nowadays, a fundamental lack of belief in the spiritual realm and the reality of these spiritual personalities. Never was there a time when it was more necessary that we should consider carefully what the Apostle has to teach us, and what all parts of the Bible teach us, concerning 'the wiles of the devil'.

Having looked at the wiles in general we must now become more particular in our approach. Here, again, I would sub-divide our treatment of this matter into two main sections. First, we must consider the devil's activity in general, and then his activity in detail, for it is quite clear that there are certain general activities of the devil described in the Scriptures, and which are seen very clearly in the history of the Church throughout the centuries, and in the Church today. These in turn can be sub-divided into strategy and tactics. It is the same classification as is used in military warfare.

We start with these generalities, these matters of broad strategy. There have been certain movements initiated by the devil which have affected the life of the whole Church, and which in turn have affected the lives of individual believers in the Church. We are, indeed, involved in these very things at the present time. 'To be forewarned is to be forearmed.' Let us use again the analogy of international problems. The last War came upon this country suddenly and unexpectedly because people would not face the facts, because we were nearly all believers in, and supporters of appeasement, surrendering this and that, saying that war could not happen again, and that two World Wars do not occur within a quarter of a century! This country kept on refusing to face the plain facts of the international situation. Men wanted to be happy and to enjoy themselves, and dismissed the man who kept on warning us as a 'warmonger', a 'difficult person' with whom nobody could work, an 'individualist'. Precisely the same, it seems to me, is happening in the realm of the spiritual today. People say, 'Do not be negative; let us be positive; let us just preach the simple gospel'. But the Bible is full of negatives, full of warnings, ever showing us these terrible possibilities. If you find in yourself a dislike of the warnings of the Scripture and of this negative teaching, it is obvious that you have been duped by the wiles of the devil. You have not realized the situation in which you are placed.

The movements to which I am referring can be best classified and considered along the following lines. We start with Heresies within the Church, which have been caused and produced by the devil and his powers. I am not concerned to go into the detail of heresies; I am simply concerned to emphasize the fact of heresies, the fact of movements within the life of the Church that have so often led to terrible trouble and produced a state of chaos.

A heresy is 'a denial of or a doubt concerning any defined, established Christian doctrine'. There is a difference between heresy and apostasy. Apostasy means 'a departure from the Christian truth'. It may be a total renunciation or denial of it, or it may be a misrepresentation of it to such an extent that it becomes a denial of the whole truth. But a heresy is more limited in its scope. To be guilty of heresy, and to be a heretic, means that in the main you hold to the doctrines of the Christian faith, but that you tend to go wrong on some particular doctrine or aspect of the faith. The New Testament itself shows us clearly that this tendency to heresy had already begun even in the days of the early Church. Have you not noticed in the New Testament Epistles the frequent references to these things? There is scarcely one of them that does not include mention of some particular heresy that was creeping in, and tending to threaten the life of some particular church. It is seen in this Epistle to the Ephesians; it is still more plain, perhaps, in the Epistle to the Colossians where heretical tendencies were entering through philosophy and other agencies. It is found likewise in the Epistles to Timothy.

Incipient heresy can be detected from the very earliest days. There is an enemy who comes and sows tares. I am not applying that parable in detail, I am using it as an illustration to show the kind of thing we are considering. The enemy's object, of course, is to disturb the life of the Church, to shake the confidence of Christian people, to spoil God's work in Christ. The Epistles were in a sense written to counteract these evils. The threat was already there in many different forms, for before the New Testament closes, all the major heresies were beginning to show their heads in the Early Church.

But from the second century of the Christian era the evil becomes still more evident and obvious. The simple fact is that for several centuries the Christian Church was literally fighting for her very life. With the conversion, and the coming in, of those who were trained in Greek philosophy and teaching, all kinds of dangers immediately arose, and the danger became so great as to threaten the whole life of the Church. People who called themselves Christians, and moved in the realm of the

Church, began to propagate teachings that were denials of Christian truth. The threat became so great that the leaders of the Churches held certain great Councils in order to define the Christian faith. Their object was to pinpoint heresies, and to protect the people from believing them. Such confusion had come in that people did not know what was right and what was wrong. So the leaders met together in these great Councils, and promulgated their famous Creeds, such as The Athanasian Creed, The Nicene Creed, and The Apostles' Creed.

These Creeds were attempts on the part of the Church to define, and to lay down, what is true and what is not true. And in this way they were able to brand certain teachers as heretics, and to exclude them from the life of the Christian Church. The confusion that led to the drawing up of the Creeds was a great manifestation of the wiles of the devil. And today there are many people who recite these Creeds in their churches every Sunday, and then in conversation tell you that what you believe does not matter at all – 'believe anything you like!' But the Creeds are a permanent reminder to us of the wiles of the devil in this respect.

During the great period of the Protestant Reformation likewise the different sections of the Reformed Church drew up their Confessions of Faith, such as the Belgic Confession, the Augsburg Confession, the Heidelberg Catechism, and in this country the Thirty-Nine Articles of the Church of England. In the next century Protestant theologians meeting in Westminster Abbey in London in and after 1643, eventually produced 'The Westminster Confession of Faith'. What was their purpose? I ask the question because we are living in an age when many say, 'Of course, these things do not matter at all, they have no relevance to us'. I am trying to show their vast importance, their extreme relevance at this present time. Confessions were drawn up for the same reason as held good during the earlier centuries. Church leaders, led by the Holy Spirit, and enlightened by Him, saw very clearly that they must, as their first duty, lay down clearly and on paper what is true and what is not true. In part they had to define their faith over against Roman Catholicism. And not only so, but also over against certain heresies that were tending to rise even amongst themselves. So they drew up their great 'Confessions' – which in a sense are nothing but the Creeds once more – in order to give the people light and guidance and instruction with respect to what they should believe.

Is there someone who feels at this point, 'Well, really, what has all this to do with me? I am an ordinary person, I am a member of the Church and life is very difficult. What has all this to say to me?' Or there may be someone who is recovering after illness and who says 'Well, I was hoping to have a word of comfort, something to strengthen me along the way, something to make me feel a little happier; what has all this about Creeds and Confessions and the wiles of the devil to do with me?' If you feel like that, the truth is that the devil has defeated you. The Apostle Paul says, 'Be not deceived: evil communications corrupt good manners' (1 Corinthians 15:33). He means that wrong teaching is desperately dangerous. He is there dealing with the great question of the resurrection, he is concerned with that one doctrine, and he says, Make no mistake about this; it is not a matter of indifference as to whether you believe in the literal physical resurrection or not. 'Ah but,' you say, 'I am a practical man of affairs, I am not interested in doctrine, I am not a theologian, I have no time for these things. All I want is something to help me to live my daily life.' But according to the Apostle you cannot divorce these things, 'Evil communications' – wrong teaching, wrong thinking, wrong belief – 'corrupt good manners'. It will affect the whole of your life.

One of the first things you are to learn in this Christian life and warfare is that, if you go wrong in your doctrine, you will go wrong in all aspects of your life. You will probably go wrong in your practice and behaviour; and you will certainly go wrong in your experience. Why is it that people are defeated by the things that happen to them? Why is it that some people are completely cast down if they are taken ill, or if someone who is dear to them is taken ill? They were wonderful Christians when all was going well; the sun was shining, the family was well, everything was perfect, and you would have thought that they were the best Christians in the country. But suddenly there is an illness and they seem to be shattered, they do not know what to do or where to turn, and they begin to doubt God. They say, 'We were living the Christian life, and we were praying to God, and our lives had been committed to God; but look at what is happening. Why should this happen *to us*?' They begin to doubt God and all His gracious dealings with them. Do such people need 'a bit of comfort'? Do they need the church simply as a kind of soporific or tranquillizer? Do they only need something which will make them feel a little happier, and lift the burden a little while they are in the church?

Their real trouble is that they lack an understanding of the Christian faith. They have an utterly inadequate notion of what Christianity means. Their idea of Christianity was: 'Believe in Christ and you will never have another trouble or problem; God will bless you, nothing will ever go wrong with you'; whereas the Scripture itself teaches that 'through much tribulation we must enter into the kingdom of God' (Acts 14:22), or as the Apostle expresses it elsewhere, 'In nothing be terrified by your adversaries: which is to them an evident token of perdition, but to you of salvation, and that of God. For unto you it is given in the behalf of Christ, not only to believe on him, but also to suffer for his sake' (Philippians 1:28–29). Our Lord says, 'In the world ye shall have tribulation: but be of good cheer, I have overcome the world' (John 16:33). There is nothing which is so wrong, and so utterly false, as to fail to see the primary importance of true doctrine. Looking back over my experience as a pastor for some thirty-four years, I can testify without the slightest hesitation that the people I have found most frequently in trouble in their spiritual experience have been those who have lacked understanding. You cannot divorce these things. You will go wrong in the realms of practical living and experience if you have not a true understanding. If you drop off into some heresy, if you go wrong at some point, if you believe, for instance – I give one example in passing – 'that healing is in the atonement', that it is never God's will that any of His children should be ill, that it is always God's will that all His children should be healthy, and that no Christian should ever die from a disease . . .; if you believe that, and then find yourself, or someone who is dear to you, dying of some incurable disease, you will be miserable and unhappy. Probably you will be told by certain people, 'There is something wrong with your faith, you are failing somewhere, you are not really trusting as you should be', and you will be

cast into the depth of despair and misery and unhappiness. You
will be depressed in your spiritual life, and you will be looking
here and there for comfort. Such a person's condition is due to
error or heresy concerning a primary central doctrine. He or she
has insinuated something into the Christian faith that does not
truly belong to it.

Nothing is more urgently relevant, whether we think of ourselves in particular or the Church in general, than that we should
be aware of heresy. Take the New Testament, take the history
of the Christian Church, or take individual Christian experience,
and you will see that true doctrine is always urgently relevant.
It is of supreme importance for the whole life of the Church.
The Holy Spirit is the power in the Church, and the Holy Spirit
will never honour anything except His own Word. It is the
Holy Spirit who has given this Word. He is its Author. It is not
of men! Nor is the Bible the product of 'flesh and blood'. The
Apostle Paul was not simply giving expression to contemporary
teaching or his own thoughts. He says, 'I received it by revelation'. It was given to him, given to him by the Lord, the risen
Lord, through the Holy Spirit. So I am arguing that the Holy
Spirit will honour nothing but His own Word. Therefore if we
do not believe and accept His Word, or if in any way we deviate
from it, we have no right to expect the blessing of the Holy
Spirit. The Holy Spirit will honour truth, and will honour
nothing else. Whatever else we may do, if we do not honour this
truth He will not honour us.

This is surely one of the major problems in the Church at
the present moment. Everyone is aware of the fact that the
Church is lacking in power. The leaders are trying to seek the
cause of this in order that they may discover how to remedy it;
and apparently, they are all jumping to one conclusion, namely,
that the cause of our lack of power is found in our divisions.
So we must all come together. That is the argument. The divided
Church is the cause of the trouble, and so the argument follows
that if only we all come together we shall be blessed, we shall
obtain the missing power, and tremendous things will happen.
But how are we to come together? One believes this, another
believes that. The main trouble, we are told, is that some put
far too much emphasis on what one believes. Surely, they say,

we ought to recognize that the one thing that matters is that there are great common enemies against us, for example, Communism, so we must all come together, all who call themselves Christian in any shape or form. We are all one; why divide about these things? We must all come and stand together as Christians, and then we shall have power.

We read about these things constantly in the newspapers. Some are rejoicing because Protestantism and Roman Catholicism are drawing nearer together. 'What does the past matter?' they say, 'Let us have the right spirit, let us come together, all of us, and not be concerned about these particularities.' I have but one comment to make about this matter, and I regret to have to make it. To me, all such talk is just a denial of the plain teaching of the New Testament, a denial of the Creeds and the Confessions and the Protestant Reformation! It is carnal thinking, in addition to being a denial of the truth. According to the teaching of the Bible, one thing only matters, and that is the truth. The Holy Spirit will honour nothing but the truth, His own truth. But that, He will honour.

To me the most marvellous thing of all is that, the moment you come to such a conclusion, you realize that in a sense nothing else matters. Numbers certainly do not matter. But today the prevailing argument is the one that exalts numbers. If only we all got together and formed a mammoth World Church! Some would even extend that idea further and bring in everyone who believes anyhow in God. They talk about the 'insights' of Mohammedanism and Hinduism and Confucianism, and dream of all who believe in God uniting against a godless, atheistic Communism. The present, they say, is no time to be dividing on these small, irrelevant differences of belief, the result of which is that we are dividing our forces and become ineffective. I can only comment: What a tragic fallacy! What a tragic failure to understand the basic elementary teaching we are given here in Ephesians about the wiles of the devil!

To explain this matter further I use an analogy which seems to me to be an apposite one at the present time. I am not concerned about its political aspect; but look at the condition of the Labour Party in this country at the present time. People say, 'There is no Opposition today, there is no "Her Majesty's

Opposition".' This is due, they say, to the fact that the Party's members are all divided into groups and factions. They argue with one another, and they will carry no weight until they settle their internal differences and all speak with one voice. Now, when you are talking about a political party, that is absolutely right. Political parties can do nothing unless they have a majority. Political parties function in terms of majority rule. However right what they believe may be, if they cannot command the votes they will not be able to form the Government; in fact, governmentally they will be paralysed. Obviously they must get together and try to achieve unity so that they will command votes and increase the possibility of forming a government.

But this argument is not only wrong, it is dangerously wrong, if you relate it to the realm of the Christian faith. The whole Bible testifies against it. The glories of Church history protest loudly against it. The Christian position is entirely different. Here, you do not begin by counting heads, you are not concerned primarily about numbers and masses. You do not think in that way. You are in an entirely different realm. Here, the one thing you think of primarily is your relationship to God! Over against the modern faith in numbers we must say with an American of the last century, William Lloyd Garrison, 'One with God is a majority'. God has come in, the everlasting, the almighty, the eternal God! It is the power of God that matters. And the moment you realize that, the question of numbers, as regards men, is comparatively irrelevant and unimportant.

Nothing matters in the spiritual realm except truth, the truth given by the Holy Spirit, the truth that can be honoured by the Holy Spirit. Is there anything more glorious in the whole of the Old Testament than the way in which this great principle stands out? God often used individual men, or but two or three, against hordes and masses. Is there anything more exhilarating than the doctrine of the remnant? While the majority had gone wrong, the ones and the twos saw the truth. Take a man like Jeremiah. All the false prophets were against him. There is a man who had to stand alone. Poor Jeremiah – how he hated it and disliked it! He did not like being unpopular, he did not like standing on his own, and being ridiculed and laughed at, and spat upon, as it were; but he had the truth of God, and so he endured it all. He decided at times to say nothing, but the word was like fire in his bones, and he had to go on speaking it. Obloquy and abuse were heaped upon him, but it did not matter; he was God's spokesman and God's representative. Similarly Moses had to stand alone when he came down from the Mount where he had met God. To stand in isolation from one's fellows, but with God, is the great doctrine of the Old Testament in many ways. And it is emphasized in the New Testament also.

Is it not amazing that people should forget the Scriptures and past history? Look at the Early Christian Church. From the standpoint of the modern argument the position was ridiculous. The Son of God goes back to heaven and leaves His cause in the hands of twelve men! Who are they? No one had ever heard of them. We are told about the authorities of Jerusalem that they noticed that they were 'ignorant and un-lettered men'. Incidentally, they added that they had been 'with Jesus'. They did not see the significance of that fellowship. What they saw was ignorant and unlettered men, and only a handful of them at that! A mere handful of men in a great pagan world with all the Jews against them, and all the auth-orities! Everything on earth was against them.

I do not understand that mentality in the Christian Church today which says that we must all come together and sink our differences; and that what we believe does not matter. It is a denial of the Book of the Acts of the Apostles, and of the story of the twelve ignorant, untutored and unlettered men who knew whom and what they believed, and who had the power of the Spirit upon them, and who 'turned the world upside-down'. This is surely one of the central messages of the Bible. The great concern of the New Testament Epistles is not about the size of the Church, it is about the purity of the Church. The Apostles never said to the first Christians, 'You are antagonizing people by emphasizing doctrine. Say more about the love of God and less about the wrath of God. They do not even like the Cross, and they cannot abide the story of the resurrection! Drop that talk about the wrath of God and Christ's ethical teaching!' Not so do the Apostles speak!

There is an exclusiveness in the New Testament that is quite amazing. The Apostle Paul writing to the Galatians says, 'Though we, or an angel from heaven, preach any other gospel unto you than that which we have preached, let him be accursed' (Galatians 1:8). 'My Gospel!', says Paul writing to Timothy. He denounces other teachers. So many of these modern preachers are much nicer people than the Apostle Paul! They never say a word against anyone at all, they praise everybody, and they are praised by everybody. They are never 'negative'! They never define what they believe and what they do not believe. They are said to be 'full of love'. I am not misjudging them when I say that that is not the explanation. The explanation is that they do not 'contend for the truth', they are innocent concerning the 'wiles of the devil'. It is not for us to decide what to leave out and what to drop for the sake of unity. My business is to expound this truth, to declare it – come what may! We must not be interested primarily in numbers, we must be interested in the truth of God. Why are many today denying the glory of the Protestant Reformation? Martin Luther – one man, standing against the whole Church – would be dismissed today as 'just an individualist who never co-operates'. But he stood up and said in effect, 'I am right, you are all wrong!'

Without realizing it the moderns are dismissing Luther as a fool, and as an arrogant fool, because he stood alone. But why did he stand alone? There is only one answer. He stood alone because he had seen the truth of God, and had known and experienced the blessed liberation it brings. He had seen the light and had also been awakened to 'the wiles of the devil'. When a man sees this truth he has no choice. He does not force himself to stand alone. He does not even want to do so; but he can do no other. As Luther said, 'Here I stand, I can do no other, so help me God!' And God did help him. Of course He did! God will always honour His truth and the man who stands for it. Of course such a man will meet criticism and sarcasm and derision; much mud will be thrown upon him. But that does not matter. The man who continues to stand, and who is ready to die for the truth of God, will have 'the peace of God that passeth all understanding' in his heart and mind. He will say with the Apostle Paul, 'I can do all things through Christ which strengtheneth me'. He will 'know both how to be abased, and how to abound; how to be full, and how to be empty'. He will be able to hold on his way quietly, steadily, knowing that God will vindicate His own truth sooner or later. As an individual he may be spat upon and trampled upon, or even be put to a cruel death. But God's truth 'goes marching on!' It will be vindicated, it will be honoured by the Spirit; and he knows that ultimately, beyond this temporary, passing world, he will hear the most glorious words a man can ever hear, 'Well done, thou good and faithful servant'. There is nothing beyond that – to have the Almighty God and our blessed Lord looking down upon us and in effect saying, 'While you were in the midst of all the confusion, you preached the truth; you stood for it in spite of everything – Well done!'

Heresies always result from the wiles of the devil, the efforts of the principalities and powers. Are your eyes open to it? Do you realize the relevance of all this to you as a member of the Christian Church? Are you being carried away by this loose, general, sentimental talk? God forbid that any of us should ever say that it matters not what you believe as long as you are a Christian. May God open our eyes, and having given us to see the truth, then enable us 'to be strong in the Lord and in the power of his might'. 'Take unto you the whole armour of God, that ye may be able to stand against the wiles of the devil.'

9
Cults

We now move on to consider under this section of the general manifestations of the wiles of the devil the question of the cults. I am not proposing to consider the so-called 'great world religions', Mohammedanism, Buddhism, Confucianism, and others, my reason being that, in reality, they do not belong to this subject. The Apostle Paul is here particularly concerned about the wiles of the devil as manifested against Christian people. These other religions are not in any way connected with or related to Christianity. They are, of course, a manifestation of the activity of the devil in general, but not this particular activity about which the Apostle is concerned here. The devil doubtless persuades people to believe in those so-called religions and thereby keeps them from God and from Christ. But what the Apostle is concerned about here are the subtle temptations that come to those who are already believers.

Doubtless many nominal Christians, and many who think they are Christians, and who have been brought up in the Christian Church, have turned to one or other of the world religions. Many such in this country have turned to Buddhism in this present century. I am not considering them. The Apostle is concerned about true Christian people, those who are born again and who know it. We are to investigate the way in which the devil comes to truly Christian people, and with all his subtlety, and manifesting all his wiles, he presents to them something that at first appears to be Christianity, but which in reality is not Christianity at all.

We give attention therefore to the question of the cults. A cult according to the *Shorter Oxford Dictionary* is 'devotion to a particular person or thing as paid by a body of professed adherents'. It may be devotion, you notice, paid to a particular person. We shall see that that is always important with respect to these particular teachings. There are a large number of cults – Christian Science, Theosophy, Jehovah's Witnesses, Christadelphianism, Positive Thinking, The Unity School of Christianity, Anthroposophy, The Science of Thought, Mormonism, and various others. In addition, there are various forms of psychological teaching and thinking which are also cults, but they do not always carry a particular name. Sometimes they are taught from so-called Christian pulpits. They may use Christian terminology, as they all tend to do, but they have nothing to do with Christianity as found and expounded in the Scriptures.

Cults are also found in various forms of mysticism. There is, of course, a true Christian mysticism, exemplified in the Apostle Paul, for Christian mysticism stresses that a man is not only concerned to acquire an intellectual grasp and understanding of the truth, but, in addition, he is concerned to have a living and vital relationship with God and with the Lord Jesus Christ. True mysticism emphasizes the living, experimental, experiential aspect of the Christian faith and the Christian position. If our so-called faith does not lead to any kind of experience, then I doubt whether it is Christian at all! Our faith must be living, real, and experimental. The danger is that the devil may come in at this point and turn true Christian mysticism into something that ceases to be Christian. In other words I am venturing the assertion, which I can prove, that mysticism's greatest danger is to by-pass essential Christianity; which is as much as to say that the mystical system and method becomes so important that the Lord Jesus Christ Himself becomes comparatively unimportant. There are also various types of non-Christian mysticism, some with an admixture of Eastern philosophy which tends to be popular. The Yogi philosophy, I gather from some of the journals, is becoming increasingly popular in this way; and there are people who are turning to it and becoming its devotees.

If you are anxious to know about the cults in detail, there are many books that can help you to do so. A paperback entitled

Some Modern Faiths has been written by Maurice C. Burrell and J. Stafford Wright. There is a larger book by J. Oswald Sanders with the title *Heresies and Cults* (a revised and enlarged edition of his *Heresies Ancient and Modern*), and another entitled *Some Modern Substitutes for Religion*. *Religious Fanaticism* is a valuable work by Ray Strachey, who was a grand-daughter of Mrs Hannah Whitall Smith, one of the founders of the Keswick Convention. It is a most interesting book dealing with freak religious movements in the United States of America in the last century. They were all cults of various types. More learned, and more solid, are the two volumes on 'Perfectionism' by B. B. Warfield. And there are other works of value.

The history of the past demonstrates clearly that there are certain times when the cults become an exceptional danger. This is always the case in times of crisis and of trouble, times of war or the threat of war. There is no difficulty in understanding why this is so from the mere standpoint of psychology. Whenever men are hard pressed or in trouble, they always want to find relief, help, comfort and guidance. That provides the opportunity for the wiles of the devil in the form of cults. This happens also, of course, in times of bereavement, sorrow, or ill-health, or in the event of some mishap in life, or some business anxiety or worry, or anything that makes life difficult for men and women.

Under such conditions the cults tend to flourish and to thrive. There has never been a time, perhaps, in the long history of the world when the cults have had a greater opportunity to flourish than this present time. We have had two World Wars, the whole state of the world since the last war has been unsettled and uncertain, and there is the horrible threat of yet another World War over us the whole time. Life has become difficult and involved, perplexing and trying, the very situation in which the devil puts forward these counterfeits. Therefore it behoves God's people at the present to be clear about these things. I have no intention of dealing with these cults one by one, for that would not be profitable. I shall deal with them in general, because there are certain principles that are common to them all, and we shall find in them a fundamental pattern, despite all the variations that are found in them. Therefore if we grasp the central controlling principles it should be a comparatively easy matter to apply them to the various cults as they happen to confront us individually.

The fundamental pattern common to all is an indication of the hand of the devil. His master hand is to be seen always if you look for it in the background. The devil is not only the great antagonist of God, he counterfeits the work of God. There is nothing more wonderful about God's work than the way in which we can trace a common fundamental pattern in it. We see it in nature, we see it in God's work of providence. In all aspects of the Christian life there is always evidence of a fundamental plan. That plan constitutes theology. And the same is true of the counterfeit, for the devil also tends to do everything in the same way. He does not always use the same colour, nor always exactly the same shape, but there is invariably the same fundamental plan and pattern.

What, then, are these common characteristics? First and foremost, all these cults sound like Christianity. Of course, if they did not, there would be no danger, there would be no subtlety. If they were obvious, patent, open contradictions no one would ever fall into the snare. But the fact is that, if you look at them very generally, and if you are uncritical, you will feel that they appear remarkably like Christianity. Indeed they very often use Christian terms and terminology. They talk about Christ, and about the various blessings that come to men through Him, and so on. And the unwary feel that this must be Christianity. They use the Christian terminology but they evacuate it of its New Testament sense and meaning. But the terms are still there; and the uninitiated, the tyros, are completely deceived. 'This is Christian', they say. 'Christian Science! – it must be Christian, it says it is Christian, and we must accept it as such', and so on!

Another general characteristic is that all the cults offer us very great blessings. Here, again, is a part of the secret of their success. But I must add that they not only offer blessings; they seem to be offering us blessings of a much more wonderful order than the Christian Church is able to do. The Christian Church by contrast seems slow and jaded, and uninteresting and unexciting. If this were not characteristic of the cults they would never succeed at all. They know how to present their case. The devil is a master, an expert! No other creature power in the universe knows so well how to pack the parcel, and to wrap it up in attractive paper and trimmings and adornments, as does the devil. This is an essential part of the manifestation of his 'wiles'.

A certain important point is overlooked in some of the books I have mentioned, even in their titles. We must make a clear distinction between heresies and cults, for cults are not to be regarded as heresies, and for the plain reason that, by definition, a heretic is a man who is a professed Christian but who goes wrong with regard to some particular doctrine; whereas the essential point about the cults is that they are not Christian at all, but counterfeits of Christianity.

For the same reason there is obviously a difference between schism and a cult, and between apostasy and a cult. In the case of apostasy we have seen that the general body of Christian doctrine was held but that there were certain things added which rendered it null and void. But in the case of the cults this general body of doctrine is not held at all; the cults do not represent Christianity on any showing or in any way. By definition they are not Christian at all.

Another general characteristic of all the cults is that their devotees are always sincere. It is a great mistake to think otherwise. One of their troubles, very generally, is that they have 'zeal without knowledge'; they are so sincere that they refuse to think and are carried away. Furthermore they are enthusiastic, they are zealous, they are active workers. Have we Christian people not often been shamed by the way in which they show their zeal? They give up their Saturday afternoons and visit our houses selling books; they walk about the streets with placards, and engage in numerous other activities. Then, too, they are ready to make sacrifices. These characteristics are not confined to the cults. They are found in Communism – the same zeal, the same sincerity, the same enthusiasm. They are also found in many of the false religions. They always give the impression of something marvellous and wonderful that captivates the whole person. They demand a kind of totalitarian allegiance because of their wonderful character and the results which they yield.

Turning now to criticism and evaluation, what are the characteristics which enable us to differentiate between the cults and our Christian faith? The following are some of the tests which can

be applied to any and all of the cults. First, take the question of
their origin. When you are confronted by a new teaching the
first questions to ask are, Where has it come from? how did it
start? why is there such a teaching at all? If you read the history
of past centuries you find that these cults were then non-existent.
You will generally find that they began in the last century. You
will also generally find that they started in the United States of
America. Last century, suddenly, these new teachings appeared.
What happened? Again, speaking generally, they started as the
result of so-called 'revelations' that were given to their founders.
It is also curiously true of most of the cults, not of all but of most
of them, that these revelations were given to women. The claim
is that suddenly at a given point this person was given a revelation
direct from God, and a movement and cult has arisen as the result
of that happening.

So the person of the founder, the person to whom the revelation came, is very important. That is why I like the definition I
have already quoted which says a cult reveals 'devotion to a
particular person'. The founder is always of very great importance
in all these cults – must be, because it is through him or her that
the members claim the authority based on the revelation. Other
people have not had the revelation; it is the founder who has
received it. Therefore the teaching of the founder is usually
important.

In one case at least, you will find that cult members claim not
only that their founder had a revelation but that he even discovered in a marvellous manner various documents which are
claimed to have been written either by God Himself or by angels.
I refer to Mormonism whose founder asserted that he had found
documents written on pages of gold! Strangely enough, although
these documents were supposed to have been written centuries
earlier, they were in fact written in the linguistic idiom of the
United States of America round about the 'thirties of the last
century! The main point, however, is that Mormons claim that
the Book of Mormon was sent down from heaven and written,
not on ordinary papyrus or paper, but on 'pages of gold!' Not
ordinary paper, but gold! Joseph Smith suddenly finds them.
They had been awaiting discovery for hundreds of years, but this
man was led miraculously to them and directed to make them

known! Thus was Mormonism launched into the world. It well illustrates what I mean when I emphasize the 'wiles of the devil' and the way in which the packet is presented.

Heresies do not start in any such manner. In the case of a heresy a man who has been a keen student of the Scriptures, and perhaps a preacher of them, gradually begins to go astray in his interpretation. He does not claim a revelation, it is a matter of interpretation. We must thus differentiate between heresies and the cults. It is very rarely that the heretic has claimed this direct illumination or revelation from heaven. He claims that his teaching is the result of his study of the Scriptures and that he has worked it out. But in the case of the cult there is always this dramatic, unusual element of a divine revelation. It is a part of the exaggerated claims which the cults always make. 'Ordinary Christians' they say, 'simply expound the Scriptures; anyone can do that. But the man (or woman) I am following had a revelation from heaven in a most amazing manner; therefore he (she) is the person to listen to.' It is unusual, it is extraordinary, the element of the miraculous seems to come in. And, of course, that is what always gives the teaching such a great impetus.

That leads to the second point, namely, that the cults always √ recognize, and are governed by, an authority additional to the Bible. In the case of Christian Science it is the book by Mrs. Eddy, *Science and Health*. It was given to her by a 'revelation'; therefore it must be authoritative! What adds to the difficulty in handling this matter is that some cultists say that they believe the Bible, whereas some do not, and ignore it altogether. Most of them do not ignore the Bible, they claim rather to be keen Bible students. But they always claim to have an authority additional to the Bible, and that authority derives from the founder – either the writings of the founder, or the recorded aphorisms and statements of the founder. There is a kind of corpus of truth and of doctrine additional to the Bible.

In the case of what is known as Seventh Day Adventism – and here there may be doubt as to whether we are dealing with a cult or a heresy – the authority is that of a woman, Mrs. Ellen G. White, who claimed to have had a revelation. The writings and the sayings of Mrs. White are fundamental and controlling. I am aware that there is a movement at the present time among

Seventh Day Adventists to try to depreciate the influence of Mrs. White; nevertheless it has been there from the beginning, and, in a sense, it is basic to their whole position.

Cults either ignore the Bible altogether, or they say, 'Ah yes, the Bible gives us the truth, but if you really want to understand the Bible you must interpret it in the light of this revelation which has come to us'. In speaking thus, of course, they resemble Roman Catholicism which also claims this extra authority, this extra understanding, this further revelation. And in practice, whatever lip-service they may pay to the Scriptures, the real authority is this other, this extra, this new, this direct revelation that has been given.

Any teaching that confronts you must be examined in terms of this second principle. Where exactly does the Bible come in? what is their view of the Bible? Often you will find that they by-pass it altogether, as if it had never been written. The new revelation is ultimately their authority. It can be illustrated, perhaps, through the Bible; but it is this that matters. It does not come out of the Bible, it is not based upon it, it is not an exposition of, an exegesis of the Bible. It is always this other 'revelation' and the Bible is given a subsidiary place.

That, in turn, brings us to the next general canon of criticism, namely, that these cults invariably go astray with respect to certain essential doctrines. If you take the cardinal, fundamental doctrines of the Scriptures and test the particular cult or teaching in their light, you will find that it is always in error, and always goes astray, and always denies the vital Truth. They do not all go wrong at the same place, but that does not save them. There are certain absolutes, and to go wrong on any absolute is to put yourself outside Christianity. Some of these cults are even wrong about the doctrine of God Himself. God becomes a mere force to some of them. Many of them do not believe in the account of the creation, and God as the Creator, at all. They believe in Him as a great life force, but not as a personal being. He is but a force, a power, an influence. That is not true of all, but it is true of several of them. But it is when you come to the Person and work of the Lord Jesus Christ that you will find most easily and obviously how they go astray. Most of the cults are not only uncertain but are in complete error about the Person of the Lord

Jesus Christ. With few exceptions they are Unitarian; they do not believe in His full and proper Deity. They do not really believe in the Incarnation and the marvel of the two natures in one Person. To them He is just a man, the supreme scientist, or the supreme religious genius, the great teacher. The glory of what we read concerning Him in the Bible is generally absent. They have little or no appreciation of His work, and especially His work of atonement, as I shall explain later.

In regard to the doctrine of the Holy Spirit you will find the same lack. Generally they ignore Him altogether. If He is mentioned, He does not come in as a Person. The cults are not interested in, or concerned about, the doctrine of the Trinity; it is not essential to their position. They operate on another level. They have their formula, and to them that is the only thing that matters. But in the Bible the Trinitarian position is seen to be essential – God the Father, God the Son, God the Holy Ghost. The greatest marvel and wonder in connection with our salvation is the participation in it of the Three blessed Persons of the Holy Trinity. But in the cults the Three Persons may be denied, or any one of them may be denied. Generally speaking, the Holy Spirit does not appear at all.

Moreover, as I have already indicated, many of the cults are very shaky about the whole question of creation. Indeed some of them appear to flourish because they *are* altogether wrong about creation and about the material universe. Christian Science really flourishes because it says that there is no such thing as matter; and because there is no such thing as matter there can be no such thing as disease, and, therefore, there can be no such thing as pain. It is because it utters such folly with regard to such subjects, leave alone its utter wrongness about the Person of the Lord Jesus Christ, whose Name it uses, that we assert that its use of the term 'Christian' is a lie and a fraud. For the same reason its supposed cures have nothing to do with 'science' and are purely psychological.

Another doctrine which is most important when cultic matters are evaluated is the biblical doctrine of sin. The absence of a belief in sin is the hall-mark of the cults. That is what I meant earlier when I said that cults are often preached from so-called Christian pulpits. Certain men have become very popular through preaching that there is no such thing as sin, that it is very wrong to talk about sin, and that the Church, by preaching a doctrine of sin, has kept the people from truth. Instead of a belief in sin, they say, you must believe in yourself. 'Positive thinking', as it is termed, is very popular in America today, and it is being preached in this country also. It sounds so marvellous – 'There is no such thing as sin; you must not speak against yourself, you must not look down on yourself. Believe in yourself; you are wonderful if only you realized it! What the Bible calls sin is an insult to mankind; we now understand all these things psychologically.'

None of the cults likes the doctrine of sin; and, of course, for the very good reason that you are never going to be popular if you preach the biblical doctrine of sin. But the cults must be popular, otherwise they cannot succeed. God is not in them, so something has to keep them going. The men and women who keep them going, do so by pandering to people, pleasing them and praising them.

It is exactly the same with regard to the doctrine of salvation. Obviously if the cults do not believe in sin you would not expect them to be right about salvation. They do not believe that the Son of God came from heaven to earth in order to take sin upon Himself and to bear its punishment. They do not believe Paul when he says that 'He hath made him to be sin for us, who knew no sin, that we might be made the righteousness of God in him' (2 Corinthians 5:21). They do not believe Peter when he says, 'Who his own self bare our sins in his own body on the tree, that we, being dead to sins, should live unto righteousness, by whose stripes ye were healed' (1 Peter 2:24). They do not believe in a substitutionary atonement. You never hear them talking about it, it has no place in their method of salvation. But the Bible shows it to be absolutely essential! The Apostle Paul, in going to Corinth, says, 'I determined not to know anything among you, save Jesus Christ and him crucified' (1 Corinthians 2:2); and yet the cults flourish without mentioning 'Jesus Christ, and him crucified'! They do not believe in sin, they do not believe in God's way of salvation. They deny the most glorious element in the Christian faith, namely, that the Son of God was made a sin-offering, that God laid our iniquities upon Him. You never hear that from them; it is not essential to their position, you can be right without it. They by-pass the Cross and for that reason we brand them as counterfeits and shams, and as a manifestation of the 'wiles of the devil'. Anything that is in error about salvation, and especially about the cruciality of the Cross, is not Christian, it is just a cult. However much it may bandy about the name of Christ and Christian terminology, and talk about love, it is an utter denial of the truth, it is the counterfeit of the devil.

Lastly, you will find that it is always wise to test the cults on the matter of prayer; because they do not really believe in prayer. This is not surprising in view of their wrongness about sin and salvation, and the blessed Persons of the Holy Trinity, and our whole relationship to them. They do not know anything about prayer. What they know is their own formula. They know nothing about a soul agonizing in prayer before God. They regard that as terrible! They know nothing about 'waiting upon God', struggling in prayer, striving to lay hold upon God! It is not there at all. And, as I say, it is not surprising. So it is always well to test a cult on this very practical matter of prayer. Do they really believe in prayer, or merely in something that at first sounds like prayer, but which on analysis turns out not to be prayer at all, but something very different?

This distinction was brought home to me once when I heard a man preaching on the subject of prayer. He had announced the title of his sermon. (It is not difficult to find titles for your sermons if you are not expository; it is very difficult if you are expository.) The title was this: 'Five minutes a day for health's sake'. That is prayer! He was really teaching a form of Couéism, a man talking to himself, self-suggestion, and thinking beautiful thoughts. That was supposed to be prayer! Such men believe also in thought transference, and teach that if you think beautiful thoughts about another person it will help that person to become beautiful; or if you think healing thoughts about the person who is ill, and if a large number do so together, such thoughts somehow help to heal that sick person. This semi-magical element is a curious admixture of oriental philosophy, magic, and mysticism. The idea is that if a number of people think healing thoughts together, somehow these thoughts are transferred through the ether, so the person who is ill will gradually be healed by the healing thoughts. And this is put in terms of prayer. God is not really addressed at all. You are addressing your thoughts to the person who is ill, or the person who is in trouble, or the person who does not like you; it is your directing of your thoughts that matters. The activity is not on the part of God; it is your own activity. But it is called prayer. That is where we see 'the wiles of the devil'. All these things are presented to us in Christian terminology; but the moment you examine them you discover, as I am showing, that they are entirely evacuated of any true and real Christian content or meaning.

Thus we have glanced at three big, broad tests by which we can, and always should, examine any one of these cults that may be presented to us. God give us grace and wisdom! Oh the cleverness, the subtlety of it all! The devil, as 'an angel of light', puts his clever, subtle counterfeit before us with the end and object of destroying our souls and robbing us of the glories of salvation in the Son of God. Is it surprising that the Apostle says, 'Be strong in the Lord, and in the power of his might. Take unto you the whole armour of God, that ye may be able to stand against the wiles of the devil'?

10

Counterfeits

There is one further general point about the cults which needs to be emphasized. Individually, the cults are a striking criticism of the Christian Church, for if the Christian Church were functioning as she should be, the cults would never have an opportunity at all. Hence the appearance of cults is a condemnation of the Christian Church and a mark of her failure. People are looking for satisfaction, for power, and for certainty. They are in a difficult world, they have their personal problems as well as the more general problems, and they are baffled and bewildered; and they are looking round for something which is authoritative and able to help them. Many of them say that, having looked to the Christian Church, and having failed to find satisfaction there, they have been driven to turn elsewhere. If they have heard nothing but the liberal-modernistic misrepresentation of the Gospel, it is not at all surprising that they have turned to the cults; for there is no salvation in such preaching. It is simply a kind of moralism which tells men to live a better life and to pull themselves together, to do this or that which they have already failed to do. People do not want exhortation; they want something which can deliver them. But modernistic-liberal teaching cannot deliver anyone; it never did, it never can. There is no power in it, it is just ethics and morality.

But let us be absolutely honest and confess that a dead orthodoxy is equally useless and valueless. If the people outside see church members who are perfectly orthodox but always miserable, always moaning, always complaining about their sins and their

[133]

failures, and who look wretched and unhappy, again it is not surprising that they turn to the cults. They are already miserable themselves and they do not want to be made more miserable; they do not merely want to be told how difficult life is and how everybody fails. So a dead orthodoxy, likewise, has caused many to turn to the cults. They have an instinctive feeling that there is life and power available; and, not finding it in the Christian Church, they turn elsewhere for the satisfaction of their needs.

All this makes it all the more urgent for us to apply various tests to these agencies which seem to be offering people just what they need. Now it is obvious that the mere test of doing good is not sufficient. People say, 'But surely you cannot be opposed to such-and-such a cult. Look at the good it is doing.' The argument is that anything that does good must be of God, and Christians should welcome it. Anything that makes us feel better must be good; anything that changes us from a life of failure to a life of success must be right; anything that helps us to give up certain sins or certain bad practices that have ruined our lives must be right and must be of God. And Christianity surely, the argument runs, must not be opposed to these things. Anything that improves men individually or collectively, and gives them a sense of release and of liberty, of happiness and of power, must surely be of God, and must come under the general umbrella and heading of Christianity.

Our answer to such an assertion is that it is just at this point that the devil's wiles become most evident. There are many agencies in the world which do not believe in God at all, which ridicule Christianity, but which, nevertheless, can produce apparently good results. They can make people feel very happy, they can give them release and deliverance from worry and anxiety. Couéism can do so. Couéism has nothing at all to do with Christianity, but we cannot dispute the fact that it has helped many people and still does so. Such is the relationship between mind and matter, that if you keep on saying to yourself, 'Every day and in every way I am feeling better and better', you probably will feel better. Not only so; the psychotherapists can produce similar results, and are doing so. They can help to deliver people from certain fears and phobias. Indeed there are even physical treatments that can do this.

We face, then, the question: Are these agencies Christian because they appear to do good? I answer: The moment you say that anything that does good must of necessity be Christian, and must of necessity be true, you have already capitulated to the devil. Such tests are not sufficient. The general tests of doing good and making people feel happier and better can indeed even be dangerous. The tests we apply must never be merely utilitarian. We must have other tests which are objective, and which are based upon certain specific standards.

According to the whole teaching of the Bible what matters finally and supremely is not how you and I feel, but our relationship to God. In our Lord's parable of the Pharisee and the publican who went up into the temple to pray, the Pharisee had no problems, no complaints, he was indeed in such a happy state that he could say to God, 'God, I thank thee that I am not as other men are, and especially as this publican. I fast twice in the week, I give a tenth of my goods to the poor . . .' (Luke 18:10–14). He was a good and moral man, a religious man, doing a lot of good, helping other people, a man without worries or troubles, who thought all was well. But our Lord said that that man did not go down to his house justified. This is a very subtle matter; it is where the wiles of the devil come in. What matters is not how you and I feel, but our relationship to God. Any agency that makes me feel satisfied when my relationship to God is not right, is of the devil, and is my greatest danger. It may have done me good, it may do good to society, and it may be a very good thing in a social sense, but it is not therefore necessarily Christian. The Apostle's great concern, and it must be our great concern also, is that we are to be specifically and definitely Christian.

But there are further tests. Of particular interest and importance is the examination of the way in which, according to the cults, the blessing will come to you. They offer you all that you need – peace, happiness, release, guidance, healing. It may be any one of these things or all of them together. Having applied your doctrinal tests in an objective manner, proceed to apply this further test: How do they tell you the blessing will come to you, and in what way do they claim that the blessing has already come to them? You will invariably find that the blessing offered is never based upon exposition of the New Testament; it comes when you accept a given formula, or if you practise the method that is suggested to you. It is always an idea or a formula or a method. This idea came suddenly to the founder in a vision, or in some other way, and from that one idea he elaborates his system. The teaching is never based upon the Scripture because they never obtained it from the Scripture. It has always reached them in some other way, as we saw in discussing the origins. They may try to support their teaching by quoting texts of Scripture at random, but the cult is not founded upon or derived originally from the Scripture.

Here, we see the obvious contrast to Christianity. Read the works of any of the great teachers in the Christian Church throughout the centuries and you will find that in the main they have always derived from an exposition of the Scripture. The great Confessions of the Faith, and the Creeds, are always sub-stantiated by scriptural quotations. They always refer you to certain Scriptures. In other words they are synopses of the doctrine taught in the Bible. But it is not so with the cults; there is none of this direct relationship to the Scriptures. The thing of importance in their eyes is their particular 'formula'.

It follows from this, that in its teaching each cult gives nothing but a constant repetition of its one formula. The stress is always upon one idea, one formula, and nothing else. Such teaching as the cults have always lacks variety; it always lacks the element of largeness and of greatness, the sense of vastness and of glory which you invariably find when you come to the Bible itself. The Bible is a very large book, a long book. Take the Epistles, how expansive they are! They open out vistas, they stimulate the imagination, and lead us into ever expanding realms. There is always growth and development. But that is never the case with the cults. The formula dominates and pervades all; there is nothing great and glorious and wonderful; and there is no room for growth and development.

Another aspect of this selfsame point is that it is nearly always true to say of these cults that the teaching ultimately depends upon the 'personal testimony' of the people who have belonged to it before you. They do not expound the Scriptures and teach the doctrine concerning God the Father, God the Son, and God the Holy Ghost, and salvation by divine grace. They talk about

[136]

themselves and their own experiences. They tell you about their former lives and what they once were; then they tell you of 'what happened to them, with the implication that if you only accept the formula it will happen to you also. The methodology of the cult is entirely different from the Christian method; it is not scriptural in any respect. It is merely the formula, plus the personal testimony of what happened to someone as the result of accepting and applying the formula in his or her own life. If you go and do likewise, the same result will follow.

Unfortunately there are some evangelical Christians today who imitate the methodology of the cults, and who thereby do a great disservice to the Christian cause. We are to preach 'Christ Jesus as Lord', as did the Apostle Paul. We are to give an exposition of the truth of God. We are not to be entirely subjective, starting with ourselves and ending with ourselves, and recommending Christianity simply because it does various things. That is the method of the cults, but it is not the Christian method. Unlike the cults, we are to present objective truth, and to expound the New Testament message.

But let us turn to a second point and show that not only is the teaching of the cults not based upon the New Testament teaching, it is even unlike the New Testament teaching in certain respects. Firstly, the formula or the practical teaching which they give is never the outworking of, or a deduction from, the doctrine of the New Testament. Invariably the cults start on the practical level. 'Those people in the churches,' they say, 'preach doctrine; always doctrine, remote from life, something entirely intellectual. It doesn't help you. What you need is practical help.' But to start on the practical level is always dangerous because you will have no standard of judgment. The moment you start with the pragmatic, the utilitarian, you are already defeated by the devil. The New Testament never starts with the practical. How often does that need to be said? Look at this Epistle to the Ephesians. Take the first verse in chapter four: 'I, therefore, the prisoner of the Lord, beseech you that ye walk worthy of the vocation wherewith ye are called'. That is very practical; but you notice that it is at the beginning of chapter four, halfway through the Epistle. The Apostle has already written three chapters, in which the message was not practical. It was pure doctrine, great, glorious doctrine! The Apostle never deals with the practical until he has first laid down the doctrine. The New Testament always introduces the practical with the word 'Therefore'. What you do in practice should always be a deduction from what you believe; and if you reverse that order you are in deadly danger. If you have not got a 'therefore' in your system which comes out of your doctrine, what you have is a cult, and not the New Testament teaching, not Christianity. But you will find that the cults always start on the practical level. What they have is never a deduction from doctrine, but something which 'works' in practice, the idea that came suddenly to the founder, the formula that he or she elaborated. It is never a deduction; and because it is not, it is not Christianity.

Secondly, you will find that the cults never give the impression that what is going to happen to you is the result of the Holy Spirit working in you. Speaking generally, they do not mention the Holy Spirit. But the essence of Christianity is that the Holy Spirit is given to us, and is within us, whether we are conscious of Him always or not. He is ever stimulating us, working in us, pointing us to the teaching, enabling us to put it into practice and to understand it, and so on. But that is never the case with the cults. They just come to you as you are and say, 'You can start now, here it is, you do this'. It is just a simple application of the formula. The impression is never given that it is something that 'God worketh in us both to will and to do'. We are never told, as in Christian teaching, 'Work out your own salvation with fear and trembling, for it is God that worketh in you both to will and to do of his good pleasure' (Philippians 2:12, 13).

That in turn brings us to the third point. We are reminded of it in the verse I have just quoted from Philippians 2 – 'fear and trembling'. There is never much fear and trembling among the cults: but there is much glibness, and a great deal of self-satisfaction, almost a boastfulness. I regret to say this, but it is the truth; there is not much humility seen in the devotees of the cults. They have arrived, they have 'got it'. But Paul says, 'Work out your own salvation with fear and trembling'. They say, 'There is nothing to fear. I was once very different, but look at me now, all is well. Wonderful!' Full of boasting and, almost,

[138]

arrogance! It is the antithesis of what you find in true Christianity.

Then let us go on to another characteristic. You will always find that the cults make much of the point that this formula, this method of theirs, is 'quite simple'. Its glory is its simplicity. 'Marvellous! wonderful!' they say. 'Look at those people working their way laboriously through the New Testament Epistles and spending so much time on them. It is such utter nonsense. We can give you what you need; do not bother to go through your New Testament. Take this formula, apply this idea.' The cults have all the characteristics of the patent medicine, the quack remedy. The great feature of the quack remedy, as is emphasized by the advertisers, is that it is always simple, never involved. It is always going to save you a lot of trouble. Here it is; it is a wonderful remedy; it is all-inclusive, it will cure all ailments. Just this one thing, and you do not need anything else! The cults in the same way claim to cover all your problems. Whatever the aches and pains of your soul, take their remedy and all will be well!

Nothing is more characteristic of the cults than this confidence, this salesmanship, and especially this all-inclusive claim. Indeed some of them not only claim that they can solve all the problems of the individual, but that they can solve the whole problem of the world and of politics quite easily. But the Bible does not speak in that way. If you read, for instance, what the Apostle Paul says in 2 Corinthians, chapter 4, you will find the picture of a man who is very different from the devotees of the cults. He writes, 'We have this treasure in earthen vessels, that the excellency of the power may be of God, and not of us. We are troubled on every side, yet not distressed; we are perplexed, but not in despair; persecuted, but not forsaken; cast down, but not destroyed; always bearing about in the body the dying of the Lord Jesus, that the life also of Jesus might be made manifest in our body.' In other words there is none of this cheeriness, brightness, supreme confidence and self-satisfaction. The Apostle is triumphing gloriously! Yes, but as a Christian; and there is a note of seriousness and of urgency, a realization of the immensity of the problem and the need of care and wariness. That is the typical New Testament teaching. But there is in these cults always an element of what I am constrained to describe as 'childishness'. It is a kind of wishful thinking – no problems recognized, everything dismissed, everything solved. 'It is all so simple,' they say. Indeed, any teaching, though it may be given by evangelical Christians, which keeps on saying that it is 'quite simple' – that your sanctification, for instance, is 'quite simple' – without any problem, savours more of the cults than of Christianity. The Apostle Paul never used such an expression. His method is what you find in this Epistle to the Ephesians in chapters 4, 5, and 6. He blends his doctrine and his application, he 'works it out', and emphasizes the seriousness of the situation. It is not easy. 'We wrestle not against flesh and blood.' We are fighting against these terrible powers; and any notion that it is all 'quite simple' is false to New Testament teaching.

Another great characteristic of the cults is that they offer you the cure, the blessing, 'at once'. It is the 'short cut' method always; that is why it wins adherents. But it is not Bible teaching. The New Testament tells the convert: 'You have become a Christian, you are converted; thank God'. But do not run away with the notion that henceforward your whole life will just be a case of 'They all lived happily ever after'. The New Testament says that you must not think in those terms. It says that you are in a very difficult world, a sinful world, a world that is dominated by the devil and his cohorts – these principalities and powers! It tells you that you will often find it difficult just to stand on your feet at all. Indeed you will need 'the whole armour of God', you will need to be 'strengthened with might by his Spirit in the inner man', you will need to be 'strong in the Lord, and in the power of his might'. Then you will be able to stand, but only then. 'Quit you like men: be strong!' says the New Testament.

'Ah well,' says the typical, lazy modern man, 'I do not want that. I thought Christianity was something that solved all my problems and put everything right at once. I thought that I had to do nothing; but now you are telling me that I have to struggle and fight, watch, pray, fast, sweat. I do not want that, I want something that really solves my problem.' At that point the cults come along and say, 'Quite right. Of course! That other teaching is all nonsense; it is not Christianity at all; we can introduce you to real Christianity. Believe our teaching, apply our formula, and immediately all will be well.' The cults do not talk about 'growth in grace, and in the knowledge of the Lord'; they do not talk about 'work out your own salvation with fear and trembling'; and there is no process of mortification of the body and of the flesh. It is immediate arrival at perfection; and all you have to do is to keep yourself there. All problems have gone, there is no struggle left, there is no difficulty to solve; it has all been done and done at once. Short cuts!

Anything that offers a spiritual short cut – and I do not care whether it calls itself evangelical Christianity or not – is not the Christianity of the Bible. There are no short cuts here. New Testament Christianity is the outworking of the mighty doctrine of Christ and His apostles, which a man believes by the power of the Spirit, the Spirit working in him. It is watching, it is praying, it is 'mortifying the deeds of the body', it is 'a keeping under of the body', it is pummelling it, as Paul expresses it in 1 Corinthians 9:27, 'hitting it until it is black and blue'. That is Christianity in New Testament terms; and it is in entire contrast to the cults which do it all 'so simply', and do it all 'at once'.

Let us next look at the nature of the blessing which is offered. This is another excellent way of discriminating between the cults and Christianity. You will find invariably that the cults always start with *you*. In a sense I have already been saying as much, and inevitably so because the cult starts on the practical level. It always starts with *you*. It approaches you and tells you that it can do this, that and the other for you. What do you need? What is your trouble? What is the matter with you? What are you looking for? Are you over-anxious and burdened and worried? Do you find it difficult to sleep at night? Do you find it difficult to relax from your business or your profession? Are you looking for peace? Are you looking for guidance, because you do not quite know what to do? Are you dithering? If only you could have something that gives infallible guidance always, how wonderful it would be! 'Very well,' says the cult, 'come with us for we can help you. Do you want consolation? Are you bereaved and sorrowing, have you lost some dear one, and is your whole life ruined? Would you like, perhaps, to be in touch with your loved one who has gone?' That is how they come! Or, 'Is it your trouble that you are being defeated by some particular thing that keeps on cropping up in your life? Is there some practice or habit or sin that is getting you down, and do you want to be rid of it?' Thus do the cults come to you at the point of your need, and they come to you as friends claiming that they have the very remedy you need just where you are, direct and immediate. Sometimes it is health, physical healing and its concomitants. That, then, is the nature of the blessing offered; it starts with us, it is something for us, it is something that we need immediately. It can solve these problems which are worrying and perplexing us, and of which we are so acutely aware.

But the Gospel method is quite different. The first thing in the Gospel is the knowledge of God. That is the great message of the Bible from beginning to end. Why did the Son of God come into this world? The answer is, according to Peter, 'to bring us to God' (1 Peter 3:18). Or as Paul states it, 'God, who commanded the light to shine out of darkness, hath shined in our hearts, to give the light of the knowledge of the glory of God in the face of Jesus Christ' (2 Corinthians 4:6). It does not start with my aches and pains, my guidance, my worry. No, but to know God! If I am right there, these other things will be resolved. We do not start and stop with them, and leave out God altogether. We start with God. The whole object of Christianity is to bring us to a knowledge of God as God, and a knowledge of the Lord Jesus Christ. 'This is life eternal.' What? That I no longer worry or that I have got rid of that thing that gets me down? No! – 'that they might know thee, the only true God, and Jesus Christ whom thou hast sent' (John 17:3). The knowledge of God, and the knowledge of the Lord Jesus Christ through the Spirit, is the beginning. What follows? A knowledge of God's great plan and purpose for man and the world, an understanding of the whole of history, and the course of the universe, and the end of time! That is Christianity. But these cults never mention such things. Holiness! Here is another vital biblical emphasis. Not simply that I stop doing this or that particular thing; no, but that, positively, I am made holy. There are men who never drink, never gamble, never commit adultery, never smoke, never go to a cinema; but they are not of necessity holy; they may be simply self-satisfied little Pharisees! Holiness is not negative; it is positive; it is to be like God. 'Be ye holy, for I am holy', says the Lord. They know

[142]

nothing about that, they never mention it. Holiness does not simply mean getting victory over particular sins. It is to be like God who is himself holy.

Again, Christianity gives very great prominence to what it calls 'the hope of glory'. I know that this is ridiculed today; but it is New Testament Christianity. The New Testament attaches much greater significance to the world that is to come than it does to this world. 'Our citizenship is in heaven!' And it tells us about the glory to come; the cults never do so. They only propose to help you while you are here in this life. *You – you* are at the centre. You start talking about yourself, and you will always be giving your experience. Not a word about the hope of glory, not a word about heaven and that great regeneration which is to come, 'the new heavens and the new earth, wherein dwelleth righteousness'. As I have said already, in the cults there is nothing vast, grand, glorious and immense, leading a man ever onwards and forwards and thrilling him to the depths. Just this little circle in which you always go round and round repeating the same thing constantly! The type of blessing that is given is altogether and entirely different from that given by the Gospel.

My last word on this matter is a kind of summing up of all I have been saying. But I want to emphasize it above everything, because this is my reason for abominating the cults. And we must hate them, because they not only fail to pass the acid tests, but they are found to be actually opposed to that which is indicated by the acid tests. The test of all tests is the Person and the work of the Lord Jesus Christ. Any movement or teaching that does not make the Lord Jesus Christ and His death upon the Cross, and His glorious Resurrection, an absolute necessity, and absolutely central, is not Christian, but a manifestation of 'the wiles of the devil'. In other words, any teaching or movement which says that you can have this or that blessing without first of all believing in the Lord Jesus Christ as the Son of God, as the Saviour of your soul, and as your Lord, without whom you have nothing, is a denial of Christianity. If your cult or teaching, or whatever it is, can include Jews, Mohammedans, anyone, and give them the 'blessing' without their acknowledging and confessing that He, and He alone, is the Son of God, and that He, and He alone, can save because He died for our sins, it is not Christian.

Any blessing that you may get apart from the Gospel of Christ is a denial of Christianity; and you must reject it. You must do so, because the biblical teaching is that there is no knowledge of God apart from the Lord Jesus Christ. 'No man hath seen God at any time; the only begotten Son which is in the bosom of the Father, he hath declared him' (John 1:18). You can learn certain things about God through nature and history and providence; but you will never know God truly in those ways. Indeed I go further; there is no access to God except through the Lord Jesus Christ. Any man who tells you that he can find God, and have access to God, other than in and through the Lord Jesus Christ, and Him crucified, is denying New Testament Christianity, however much good he may appear to do, because Christ Himself said, 'I am the way, the truth, and the life; no man cometh unto the Father but by me' (John 14:6). That is absolute and categorical. There is no access to God, there is no knowledge of God as Saviour and Deliverer except in and through the Lord Jesus Christ. Or, as the author of the Epistle to the Hebrews states it, 'Having therefore, brethren, boldness to enter the holiest of all by the blood of Jesus' (Hebrews 10:19). A movement that by-passes this truth, and that says the blood of Christ is not necessary, is antichrist. It is opposed to God and His Christ, let it do as much good as it may. That is 'the wiles of the devil' and 'an angel of light', doing good and deluding people. There is no entry into the holiest of all except 'by the blood of Jesus'. Even though it be under the auspices of the Christian Church, and call itself Christian, or whatever it may call itself, any teaching which says you can get to God, and know God, and be blessed of God, apart from the blood of Christ, is a denial of this central teaching, and is therefore an insult to God and His dear and blessed Son.

Or let me put it in this way: Any teaching that tells you that you can have any blessing apart from Christ is a denial of this selfsame truth, because every blessing that comes to us from God comes in and through the Lord Jesus Christ. Notice how Paul writes to the Colossians: 'That their hearts might be comforted, being knit together in love, and unto all riches of the full assurance of understanding, to the acknowledgment of the mystery of God, and of the Father, and of Christ; in whom are hid all the treasures of wisdom and knowledge' (Colossians 2:3). He says again: 'Beware lest any man spoil you through philosophy and vain deceit, after the tradition of men, after the rudiments of the world, and not after Christ; for in him dwelleth all the fulness of the Godhead bodily' (Colossians 2:9). Every blessing that ever comes to man comes solely in and through the Lord Jesus Christ, and any blessing that is offered you apart from Him and His death and His blood is ultimately a denial of the faith.

This is why I speak with passion, as we all should. It is an insult to Him, it is an insult to His all-sufficiency. There is no need of the cults because everything they offer, and more, is given in Christ. They have no right to exist. They are an insult to Him, their very existence is an insult to Him. There is nothing He cannot give. He is 'the Alpha and the Omega, the beginning and the end'; He is 'the first and last'; He is 'the all in all', and 'we are complete in Him'. A man who tells me that Christ is not enough, that he needs some other formula in addition, is insulting Christ, is denying Him. Christ has everything, because He is everything. The Apostle tells us: 'I know both how to be abased, and how to abound; everywhere and in all things I am instructed both to be full and to be hungry, both to abound and to suffer need. I can do all things through Christ which strengtheneth me' (Philippians 4:12, 13). Or again, 'In nothing be anxious; but in everything by prayer and supplication with thanksgiving, let your requests be made known unto God. And the peace of God, which passeth all understanding, shall keep your hearts and minds through Christ Jesus' (Philippians 4:6, 7). If you are even considering the cults and wondering whether they can help you, you have already denied Christ. There is nothing that He cannot give you, He is everything, He is all and in all. Charles Wesley was constantly saying this:

> *Thou, O Christ, art all I want;*
> *More than all in Thee I find.*

And yet people are turning to the cults. Here is Charles Wesley again –

Thou hidden Source of calm repose:
Thou all-sufficient Love divine;
My help and refuge from my foes;
Secure I am if Thou art mine:
And lo! from sin and grief and shame,
I hide me, Jesus, in Thy name.

Thy mighty name salvation is,
And keeps my happy soul above;
Comfort it brings, and power, and peace,
And joy and everlasting love:
To me, with Thy dear name, are given
Pardon, and holiness, and heaven.

Jesus, my All in all Thou art,
My rest in toil, mine ease in pain;
The medicine of my broken heart;
In war my peace; in loss my gain;
My smile beneath the tyrant's frown;
In shame, my glory and my crown:

In want, my plentiful supply;
In weakness, mine almighty power;
In bonds, my perfect liberty;
My light in Satan's darkest hour;
My help and stay whene'er I call;
My life in death, my heaven, my all!

If you feel that He is not enough, and that you must turn to the cults for help or aid or assistance; if you say that He needs any help or assistance, you are denying Him, you are insulting Him. It is 'the wiles of the devil'. This faith, which has supported and strengthened and blessed the saints throughout the running centuries, and which has stood every conceivable test, is enough. You need not turn to some new-fangled idea that only began last century or this century. Go back to the 'Old, Old Story', which is ever new and ever true. Come back to the fount and the source of every blessing; come back to the everlasting God and His Son, our glorious Saviour, the Lord Jesus Christ, and the Spirit will enter you, and your every need will be supplied. But only in that way!

11

Watchfulness

We come now to the more particular, the more personal, and the more individual activities of the devil. Here we are dealing with something that can happen to individuals in the Church while the Church herself may be more or less healthy. There is almost no limit to the ways in which the devil, in his desire to spoil the work of God in Christ, attacks God's people. He does so on the big scale, he does so in individual instances. He does not care how it is done, as long as he brings any individual Christian, or any group of Christians, into a state of bondage and of unhappiness, and thereby mars their testimony to the exceeding riches of God's grace in and through His dear Son.

This subject of 'the wiles of the devil', as they are experienced by us as individual Christians, is one that has often been dealt with in literature. Take, for instance, such a famous book as John Bunyan's *Pilgrim's Progress*. He pictures there how, first of all, a man is convicted of his sin and escapes from the City of Destruction and is in great trouble until his burden rolls away at the Cross of Christ. But his troubles do not end then; the rest of the story is nothing but a very graphic and wonderfully pictorial account of the wiles of the devil. Bunyan wrote it in order that he might help struggling pilgrims who are exposed to these wiles as they go through this journey called life. His *Holy War* is a similar treatise, and likewise the whole of his teaching in respect of 'Mansoul'. This was Bunyan's way – and a very helpful way it is – of introducing people by means of allegories to the wiles of the devil, in order that, being forewarned, they should be forearmed.

[148]

The same is true in regard to many other Puritan writings of three hundred years ago. One such famous book, by Richard Sibbes, is called *The Soul's Conflict*, and another, *The Bruised Reed*. Robert Bolton wrote a book entitled *Comforting Afflicted Consciences*. Many of the writings and sermons of that great century of preachers were devoted to this subject of the wiles of the devil as they are manifested in the lives of individual Christian believers.

And at this point one must add truthfully, that you find the same tendency in Roman Catholic literature. Whatever their deficiencies, and we shall be looking at them, they are quite clear about the devil and his wiles. Hence they have always had large numbers of so-called Manuals of Devotion, the object of which has been to help members of their Church to deal with the various problems that arise. Furthermore, their whole system of casuistry in many ways also deals with this particular problem. Thus there has been in the past a great and wealthy literature dealing with this subject, showing thereby how, in the subsequent history of the Christian Church, the thing against which the Apostle warns these Ephesians has been a constantly recurring problem.

On the other hand, it has been a very striking fact concerning Christian life and witness since about 1880 – and I am referring particularly to evangelical Christian life – that very little of this kind of literature has been produced. Why is it that that which was so characteristic of the Puritan era and which produced those books which were used and read so much by all who came under the powerful influence of the Evangelical Revival of the eighteenth century, and which continued to be read until about 1860 or 1880, suddenly came to a stop? Books which had been reprinted constantly were no longer reprinted, neither were they replaced by any others. No one seemed to be concerned about this conflict against the 'principalities and powers', about how to stand against 'the wiles of the devil'.

It seems to me that there is only one explanation for the decline of interest in this subject. It is that there has been a type of holiness teaching, a teaching concerning sanctification, which has left no room for this aspect of truth. Such teaching has been based on one principle only, which it has continued to repeat, claiming that it alone can solve all the problems. The whole of the

Christian life has been reduced to just 'surrendering to' and 'abiding in' Christ. The apostolic teaching concerning the fight against the devil has scarcely been given any consideration whatsoever. This same omission, it seems to me, supplies an explanation, in certain ways, of the present state of the Christian Church with its superficial spirituality. It represents a failure to realize the true nature of the Christian life, the conflict in which we are placed, and the absolute necessity, therefore, of being clothed with the mighty power of the Lord Himself, and of putting on piece by piece the 'whole armour of God'.

I recall vividly something which was said to me about the year 1941. A friend of mine told me that his wife – both of them were fine evangelicals – had been reading a most extraordinary book which had amused her very much. She thought it was fantastic and almost ridiculous. It happened to be *The Screwtape Letters* by C. S. Lewis. Here were two evangelical people who had become such strangers to the teaching about the wiles of the devil that when they read a book dealing with that very subject they regarded it as a joke. They were amazed at what seemed to them to be a caricature of the Christian life. They thought that its author had written it solely to amuse and to entertain. But C. S. Lewis had undergone a certain experience himself, and was well-read, especially in allegorical literature, including Bunyan; and he had come to see the significance of this aspect of the Christian life. He had seen that it is a vital and essential part of the Christian's life while he is in this world. But we have become such strangers to it that his book was regarded as mere entertainment. We thus see the urgency of paying close heed to this aspect of Christian truth.

First of all we must make a general approach to the subject in order that we may see how the devil in all his wiliness and subtlety is able to attack us as believers along certain lines. There are certain great watchwords in the New Testament that serve as a perfect introduction to our theme, and that should open our eyes to the whole character of the devil's wiles. The first is 'Watch' – 'Watch ye'. Our Lord used that word frequently, as also did the Apostles. Paul in writing to the Corinthians says, 'Watch ye, stand fast in the faith, quit you like men, be strong' (1 Corinthians

16:13). 'Watch' at once suggests that there is a very subtle enemy. Any army engaged in warfare always has to put its sentries, its watchmen, in position, for one never knows what the enemy is about to do. You must not assume that, because it is night, he intends to do nothing; he may take advantage of the cover of the darkness. So an army posts sentinels who must march backwards and forwards. It is necessary to watch in all directions day and night without intermission. In the same way failure on our part to watch, to be aware of this and that, gives the devil a wonderful opening. Many people are defeated by the wiles of the devil simply because they never talk about the devil. They do not watch. They say, 'I have been saved, all is well; I am in Christ, I am resting on Him, there is no need to watch, He is looking after me, all I have to do is to keep my eyes on Him'. They are not watching the enemy, they are not being wary about the wiles of the devil, they do not realize that we are in a great warfare. It is just a question of 'resting', every problem is solved, there is nothing more to do. And the result is, of course, that, failing to heed the constantly repeated New Testament exhortation to 'watch', they are caught and defeated.

The next exhortation refers to the Word itself. The Apostle Paul is very careful to tell Timothy, who was such an easy prey to the devil in certain respects, to 'pay attention to reading', not to forget the Scriptures 'which can make thee wise unto salvation'. (2 Timothy 3:15). There is the constant exhortation to read the Scriptures. Indeed every one of these New Testament Epistles was written because of this very conflict, and in order to help people to detect and frustrate the wiles of the devil. So if we neglect the reading of the Word we shall certainly be defeated by him. It is one of the ways, the best way of all perhaps, of watching. In the Bible we are given teaching which warns us about the various ways in which the devil can come to us. There we have an authoritative account of his machinations, his wiles and his subtlety, and the more you know about those things the more easily and quickly you will be able to detect him in his first moves, and be able to stand against him. So the reading of the Word is essential, and Christian people who do not show diligence in that reading are specially liable to be trapped by the wiles of the devil.

In the Word we learn about the heresies we have been considering, and the causes of schism, and all the other evils which the devil promotes. We are also given detailed instruction as to what he seeks to do to us one by one in a more personal manner. We are told to 'prove all things', not to believe every spirit but to 'try the spirits'. We shall never be able to do that if we do not know the Word and its teaching. So by encouraging us not to read the Word of God the devil comes in all his wiliness. Incidentally it is a very interesting point to notice about *The Screwtape Letters* that C. S. Lewis does not deal with this question of not reading the Word. That is a significant point which reveals a real defect in his teaching. The chief of the evil spirits of whom Lewis writes does not give any instruction to his underlings to prevent the believers from reading the Bible. But this is one of our main weapons, as we shall see later.

Another New Testament exhortation concerns praying. 'Watch and pray, lest ye enter into temptation', says the Lord. Again, He says that 'men ought always to pray and not to faint' (Luke 18:1). If you do not pray you will faint. The Apostle Paul says, 'Pray without ceasing'. Never stop praying, always be praying. He says it is the only way in which you can keep going. We find it here also in Ephesians, chapter 6, at the end of this particular section we are considering. 'Praying always with all prayer and supplication in the Spirit, and watching thereunto with all perseverance and supplication for all saints.' It is surely obvious that the New Testament tells us that we must pray to this extent, and that to neglect prayer exposes us immediately to all the wiles and subtleties of the devil. Our Lord Himself spent much of His time in prayer. He did so to fortify Himself, to have communion with God, and to be given light and instruction, and to be blessed in His own spirit. And so we get this constant injunction and exhortation to be 'instant in prayer', in season and out of season. The neglect of it at once exposes us to the wiles of the devil.

The last thing I would mention is 'self examination'. 'Examine your own selves', says the Apostle; 'Examine yourselves whether ye be in the faith; prove your own selves' (2 Corinthians 13:5). His exhortation is addressed to believers. But that has fallen out of practice. We do not believe in self-examination any longer. We say, 'You must not look at yourself; look to the Lord. If

[152]

you look at yourself you make yourself miserable. Look to the Lord, always be looking out of yourself.' And as we shall see, the neglect of self-examination is probably one of the greatest causes of defeat in the Christian life.

If the devil can discourage our watching, all is going to be well from his standpoint. If he causes us to neglect the reading and studying of the Word, and the understanding of the Word, it will suit him admirably. If he causes us to neglect praying we shall faint, and in that condition become an easy and obvious prey. The neglect of self-examination led to the ill state of the church at Laodicea. They thought that they were doing well and were rich. But actually they were 'wretched, and miserable, and poor, and blind, and naked'. They had not examined themselves, they did not know that they were blind, they did not realize that they were naked. There is nothing more terrible than the neglect of self-examination. So the devil in his wiles comes to us and does his utmost to discourage us at every one of these special points.

The questions we should therefore ask ourselves are: How do we emerge in the light of this examination? Are we watching, and watching unto prayer? Are we diligent in our reading of the Bible? Are we examining ourselves? Do we ever take a kind of spiritual stock-taking to discover where we are? Any teaching, or any view that we may hold, that discourages any one of these activities, or leads to a superficial performance of any one of them, is a manifestation of the wiles of the devil. If you really believe that just to read a few verses and a short comment on them in a matter of five minutes, and to have a brief word of prayer, is adequate for your day, then I say that you do not know anything about the wiles of the devil. That is not the New Testament method; that has not been the verdict of the saints throughout the centuries. But a superficial spirituality imagines that that is enough – 'I have read my portion and had my "quiet time", all is well, I must go on' – not aware of any stagnation in the soul, not aware of a lack of growth, not aware of an appalling superficiality. That type of life is a glaring illustration of the success of the wiles of the devil! He has come as an angel of light saying, 'That is enough, just a little; other people do not read at all, you are really very good, there are many nominal Christians who never read the Scriptures at all. You are a Scripture reader;

all is well with you.' And because you have read just a few verses he has persuaded you that you have read the Scriptures truly, and that you know the Word of God! Anything that encourages a superficial performance of any of these things is always a manifestation of the wiles of the devil.

But let us move on to consider the routes along which the devil attacks. This is, after all, a matter of strategy. There is nothing more important in a war than to consider the routes of attack. The French before the last war foolishly stopped their Maginot Line at Sedan, and neglected their defences from that point along the Belgian border to the sea, not realizing that the Germans had always come through north of that point and were always likely to do so. If we neglect a study of the routes of attack it is obvious that we are likely to be defeated.

The devil has certain routes which he follows very regularly. Clever though he is, he lacks originality in this respect. First, the mind is the chief route, because in many ways it is the most important one. If he can deceive us there, we shall be wrong everywhere, because the highest thing in man is his mind.

Then, too, he comes along the line of experience. That is another great realm of our life, where we are not so much concerned with intellectual understanding and formulation of truth, but with the more experimental aspect. A goodly proportion of our lives is lived in the realm of experience – feelings, sensations, sensibilities, desires, moods, states. This is more elemental than the mind, and we should always be struggling to attain a mastery over it by using the mind and the understanding. It is our failure to do so that accounts for so many of our troubles. So the devil attacks us along the line of our experiences.

A third line is the realm of practice – our behaviour, our conduct, the things we do, and the things we refrain from doing. And what we actually do in practice depends very largely upon mind and experience.

It is of vital importance for us to realize that the devil attacks us along these three lines. He does not confine himself to one route. We must not assume that he is always going to come in the same way. If you are only preparing to resist him in one way he will certainly come some other way. If, as it were, you are guarding

your front door, he will come in at the back door; if you think
you have got rid of him through the windows in the front, he
will be in through the windows at the back. He comes from every
conceivable direction. It is not surprising that the Apostle says,
'We wrestle not against flesh and blood, but against principalities'
– not one, but myriads of them – 'against powers' – almost an
endless number – 'against the rulers of the darkness of this world,
against spiritual wickedness in high places'! These expressions
explain why I have been at such pains to give a description of
what the Bible tells us about the character of this enemy, the
number of emissaries, the agencies, the forms, the guises, the
different appearances; they almost baffle description. And they
can attack us at any point and in any way. The three main routes
I have given can be subdivided almost endlessly.

In the next place, it is interesting to observe how the devil uses
these three main lines of attack, and again a broad classification
is possible. Firstly, he produces a lack of balance between these
three aspects of our life; and secondly, taking them individually,
he makes us give either too much or too little attention to each
one of them. Of course the devil varies the detail of the
mechanism. His mode of attack reminds me of some of the locks
you can buy to save your car from theft or robbery. One firm has
devised safety locks which have up to 3,000 possible combina-
tions. Similarly, while with the devil there is one underlying
principle, as it were, the variations within that principle can be
almost endless.

We start with the first of the lines of attack – the wiles of the
devil as they are displayed in producing a lack of balance in the
Christian life as between the mind and the experience and the
practice. There is no more frequent or fruitful manifestation of
the wiles of the devil than this. Indeed, in dealing with the
heresies and with apostasy and schism and the cults, we have seen
that each is ultimately due to a one-sided emphasis somewhere or
somehow. The cults thrive on the desire for experience. Many
of the schisms have been due to a lack of balance in the matter
of the mind and of the intellect. So the devil pays particular
attention to this aspect; his desire is to produce imbalance.

The question of balance is of great importance in every realm of the Christian life. Even physically it is important to determine the right amount of time and attention to give to the mind and to the body. Neglect your body and eventually your mind will not function so well. Or take the question of diet which is so popular today. It is important to have a balanced diet – not too much of any one ingredient, but all ingredients in the right proportions – if you want to be really healthy. The same balance holds good in other directions. When you are defending your country, you must know how much to put into your army, how much into your navy, how much into your air-force; and the need for constant change must be kept in view. But you must always maintain an over-all balance between the various services. The same holds good in the Christian life, as the devil very well knows, and he tries to get us to become imbalanced.

The Christian life can be compared to a three-legged stool. The three legs have to be of the same length if you are to keep your balance and to sit comfortably. There are some who are persuaded to give exclusive attention to the mind, to knowledge only. We call them intellectuals; they are interested in ideas. Nothing matters to them but knowledge, and they spend their time reading and studying and gathering a great amount of knowledge. Feelings and emotions they tend to despise. They are men of mind and knowledge and understanding, and they discount the experimental aspect. As regards practice they do not deny that practice is important, but they are too busy reading to be very much concerned about it.

The devil has wrought havoc in the Church in general, as well as in individual lives, many times throughout the centuries by producing a kind of scholasticism. It is interesting to draw a graph of the history of the Church. Perhaps a great revival starts, an outpouring of the Spirit of God, with great light and understanding, marvellous experiences and practice following. Then it is likely that certain excesses tend to come in, so the authorities very rightly begin to say, 'Now we must have teaching; we must control this development; we must have the mind enlightened'. So they put great emphasis upon teaching. And, oftentimes, in less than a hundred years you will find a dry-as-dust and utterly dead orthodox scholasticism which spends the whole of its time in debating minutiae and refinements. A perfect system has been produced, all intellect, all mind; the great living doctrines have been hardened into a kind of sterile scholasticism which is utterly valueless. There may be much boasting about orthodoxy; but the system is dead; conversions are never seen; Christians are not built up, and moved, by the truth; the whole has become purely a matter of the mind.

This is a very real danger, and it is a danger for each one of us. There are many whose view of Christianity is purely intellectual. Such was the case with Lord Melbourne, Queen Victoria's first Prime Minister, who said on one occasion, 'Things are coming to a pretty pass if religion is going to start being personal'. That is a typical attitude. Going to church is a part of the social round; it is right, of course, to worship God; but you must not become personal about these things. And, of course, the same outlook is seen in the eighteenth century. The chief charge that was brought against Whitefield and the Wesleys and others of the Methodists was the charge of enthusiasm. The authorities argued that Christianity is the most dignified, the most orderly thing in the world, and that these Methodists were getting much too excited about their religion, and giving way to an undesirable enthusiasm. So they tried to stop the preaching of those men of God who were filled with the Spirit. Now that can happen to any one of us, and it tends to happen to some of us particularly. We tend to become all intellect, to become spiritual tadpoles – all head, no real body, and entirely lacking in the symmetry which should ever characterize the Christian life.

The next danger is that some people put the whole emphasis upon experience; they are interested only in emotions and feelings. 'Look at those people,' they say, 'they seem to have heads full of knowledge, but they are useless. They never seem to feel anything; they are always talking about doctrines, but they talk about them as if they were talking about geometry. They are not moved by them. Why don't they shout out sometimes? Why don't they let themselves go? Why don't they feel something?' Such people think that a meeting is of no value unless it has given vent to shouting and exclamation, a kind of riot of the emotions. The answer is, that emotion is a vital part of Christian faith; but emotionalism is not. The devil always tries to make us over-react. The first group are so afraid of emotionalism that they crush

[157]

emotion altogether, and the third group we shall consider tend to do the same. But this second group think of Christianity solely in terms of what they feel – sensations and sensibilities. They are not interested in exposition, they do not want understanding. But if they are made to feel something and have a thrill, then they pronounce it wonderful. They look for feelings only, and they judge everything solely by that standard. And, alas, that tendency is often encouraged; things are done deliberately to work up feeling – singing, hand-clapping, shouting, affecting illustrations moving the emotions directly, pressure on the emotions. In these ways the devil comes in and causes Christian people to lose their balance. How often it has happened! We are all liable to imbalance – some of us more than others!

The third line is the realm of practice. Here we are dealing with practical persons who are not interested in theology and doctrine, and who are very suspicious of emotional people. They are hard-headed men who say that what is needed is that we do something. 'With the world as it is,' they say, 'what are you doing about it? You may have your theories, if you like, but I am concerned to do something to put things right.' So the whole of their emphasis falls on practice, on conduct, on behaviour and morality. They have no liking at all for reading and the study of doctrine, or for people who get excited. The man who really matters in life is the man who 'gets things done', a man of his word, an honest man, a good man, a moral man, a man who does good. 'What is the point of preaching about high doctrines while so many problems are pressing round and about us, statesmen failing us, the clash of nations and the trouble within nations? Why don't you do something?' they ask. So they spend their time in 'doing things' and imagine that that is the sum total of Christianity.

These, then, are the ways in which the devil by his wiles comes in and upsets the balance. The Scriptures are always characterized by balance. Make an analysis of any one of the New Testament Epistles, and you find that they generally start with a preliminary salutation which is affectionate and full of love. This is followed by an exposition of doctrine reminding the readers of different aspects of the truth. Then you meet the word 'therefore', and application and practice follow. The regularity with which this occurs is very striking. It is the great characteristic of the biblical teaching. Every side and aspect and part of man is catered for. So if we are lacking in this balance we do not conform to the biblical pattern.

Another serious result following from this lack of balance is that it shows that the person concerned has completely failed to see the inevitable relationship between the three aspects and is therefore wrong about the three. If you have the true view of the truth, you must feel it. If you do not feel it you have not got the true view. Do you really believe that Jesus Christ is the Son of God, and that He gave His body to be broken and His blood to be shed that you might be forgiven? You say that that is your belief, and that you believe in the substitutionary view of the atonement, that the Son of God loved you to that extent. If you say that you have not felt anything as the result of so believing, I say that you have not believed it, you have not seen it, for 'Love so amazing, so divine, demands my soul, my life, my all'!

What happens to me as I 'survey the wondrous Cross'? Do I sit in a state of calm intellectualism, unmoved? Surely, if I have truly realized its meaning, I say rather –

> *My richest gain I count but loss,*
> *And pour contempt on all my pride.*

If you have really seen this truth you are moved to the depth of your being. And not only so, you resolve to do something about it.

> *Love so amazing, so divine,*
> *Demands my soul, my life, my all.*

If you believe that Christ died in that way in order to save you from sin, can you go on sinning? It is not logical, apart from anything else. So there is no value in saying that you believe this great truth if your feelings are not engaged, if you are not moved emotionally, and if you are not moved also to action. Lack of balance indicates a complete failure to see the inevitable relationship between the three.

But still more serious, it implies a failure to submit ourselves to God's way of dealing with man and delivering him. God's way is to deal with the whole man, and that is where Christianity differs from the cults. The cults never deal with the whole man;

they only deal with parts of him; everything false only deals with a part. The glory of the Christian way, and the most thorough test therefore as to whether you believe the true Gospel or not, is that it takes up the whole of you; the whole man is involved. If it does not, there is something wrong; the devil has defeated you with his wiles. So if a man says to me, 'I am not interested in my feelings', all I say to him is, 'Very well, what you think of as your salvation is yours only; it is not God's'. God is as much concerned to save your feelings as He is to save your mind. Again, if a man says, 'I cannot be bothered about what I do in practice', I give him a similar reply. 'Our old man was crucified with him,' says Paul to the Romans (6:6). What for? 'That the body of sin might be destroyed, that henceforth we should not serve sin.' On the other hand, if a man says, 'I am not interested at all in theology and doctrines, and in painfully working through these Epistles', I say to him, 'You may not be, but all I have to say to you is that you are dismissing and despising and rejecting what God has provided for you. You have no right to say that you are not interested in acquiring an understanding of His Word. God has given you a mind, and if you are not using your mind and disciplining yourself to study the Scripture, and to read every-thing you can that will help you to understand the Scripture, you are refusing and spurning God's own gift, you are insulting Him.' It is God's way of salvation to save the whole man, and not simply parts of man. We have no right to pick and choose. God's way of salvation in Christ takes up the intellect, the heart (emotions), the will, the understanding, the sensibilities, the experience, the practice, everything – the whole man, even the body eventually! And if we pick and choose we are insulting God and throwing back into His face one of His gifts, and one aspect or another of His great salvation.

Finally, this lack of balance means that we are bringing the Gospel and the Name of God Himself somehow or other into disrepute. God's purpose is to produce new men, made in the image of Christ, and having the balance that His Word shows between the mind and experience and practice. We are meant to be like Him, to conform to His image; and if we are lop-sided, imbalanced, truncated Christians, we are bringing God's work in Christ into disrepute, we are failing to glorify Him as we ought.

'Glorify him' says the Apostle Paul, 'with your mind and with your body: whatsoever ye do in word or deed, do all things to the glory of God.' Eating and drinking, and all else is to be done to the glory of God. The whole man, the entire personality, is to be devoted to His service. And if we fail in this matter we are not only succumbing to the wiles of the devil, we are detracting from the glory of God and of the Lord Jesus Christ.

There is nothing more marvellous, I repeat, about this salvation than its perfect balance. The Christian is a man who knows in whom he has believed; he is able to give 'a reason for the hope that is in him'. He rejoices in the truth, he rejoices in the Lord Jesus Christ with 'a joy unspeakable and full of glory'. And at the same time he does his utmost to be holy, because God is holy. He has had a vision of the everlasting glory ahead of him, and 'he that hath this hope in him, purifieth himself, even as he is pure' (1 John 3:3). Hence it must of necessity be one of the main objectives of the devil to upset the balance, and to make us concentrate on one aspect only, to the exclusion of the others. The true way is to be altogether 'ever, only, all for Thee'.

12

'Philosophy and Vain Deceit'

The Christian life at the beginning is essentially simple, but the moment you come into it you begin to see that there are complexities, not because of the life itself, but because of what we are considering in these verses. There is an essential simplicity in Christ, as the Apostle Paul reminds the Corinthians (2 Corinthians 11:3). But the devil is always concerned to turn that 'simplicity which is in Christ' into something involved and complex and difficult. Hence the Apostle warns us here in these solemn and moving words to be always on our guard, and above everything, to realize something of the character and the quality of this most powerful adversary who is set against us. We have already seen how important it is for us to maintain a true balance, lest we become eccentric Christians. We turn now to a consideration of the particular attacks which come along the route of the mind.

The gift of mind, the gift of apprehension, the gift of understanding is the greatest of all God's gifts to man. The ability which man has of contemplating himself and of thinking in an abstract manner is the one thing that above all else marks him out from the animals. But because of man's fallen condition, it has become his greatest danger. The devil, therefore, has always been particularly active in attacking mankind along this route of the mind, the intellect and the understanding; and the Scriptures have much teaching with regard to this particular matter. We shall deal later with his more direct attacks upon the feelings and the will.

Obviously, in this first group we are dealing in particular with intelligent people. The more intelligent people are the more exposed they are to the attacks which we are about to consider. We are here dealing with men and women who are anxious to learn and to know the truth. There are people who do not want to learn, who are not interested in knowledge, who say that they are just practical people. There are others who live on their feelings, and who imagine that, unless they have a riot of feelings nothing has happened. What we shall be saying does not apply to them. They are already deeply enmeshed in the wiles of the devil. People who refuse to think and to use their minds in connection with their Christian faith are in the most dangerous condition possible. They are obvious prey for the next cult that gains currency, or the latest excitement. But if we are aware of this, and are concerned, therefore, about knowledge and understanding and apprehension of truth, then there are certain special temptations and dangers to which we are exposed. I call attention to some of them which I have picked out of the Scriptures themselves.

We begin with the wiles of the devil as manifested through what the Apostle calls 'philosophy and vain deceit'; 'Beware lest any man spoil you through philosophy and vain deceit, after the tradition of men, after the rudiments of the world, and not after Christ' (Colossians 2:8). It is generally agreed that this was the heresy peculiar to Colosse. It is quite clear that the members of the Christian church at Colosse were highly intelligent and intellectual people, and therefore they were particularly subject to temptation along this line. But it was not confined to them. In the First Epistle of Paul to Timothy prominence is given to this same subject, both in the first chapter, and also in the last chapter where the Apostle talks about 'science (learning) falsely so called'. Indeed this theme is found in many of the New Testament Epistles, as in 2 Corinthians, where Paul says that he is much concerned 'lest, by any means, as the serpent beguiled Eve through his subtlety, so your minds should be corrupted from the simplicity that is in Christ' (11:3). Emphasis upon the intellect was characteristic of the Greek mentality. The Greeks were a highly able and intelligent people. The Apostle does not have to

[163]

write in this way to the Galatians. They were a much more primitive people, a people who lived much more on their emotions and feelings. So he does not have to write about this intellectual danger to them; but he does to these others. It is most interesting to trace this particular danger in the various Epistles.

Here, then, was a danger that had already arisen in the earliest days of the Christian Church; and I would hazard the opinion that it is, of all dangers, perhaps the greatest at this present moment in the life of the Christian Church. Beyond any doubt, in the last analysis the greatest single enemy of the Christian faith and the Christian truth is philosophy. This is the case because philosophy implies a final confidence in human reason, in the power of man's mind, in man's ability to arrive at truth, to comprehend it, and to encompass it. The ultimate problem is always the problem of authority. What is the ultimate authority with respect to truth? This is absolutely fundamental. According to the teaching of the Bible from beginning to end our supreme authority is God's revelation. Here is the great watershed that determines a man's whole position in these matters. We are either trusting entirely and exclusively to the revelation which God has been graciously pleased to give; or else ultimately we are trusting to our own ability, our own knowledge, our own understanding.

It is precisely at this point that the wiles of the devil prove so deceptive. Christians face the danger of being governed by what is called modern knowledge, modern thought, and especially today, 'science', and not only scientific knowledge, but any kind of knowledge. The Greeks stood for this above all other nations. They were famous for their philosophers who had lived and had taught before our Lord ever came into this world – Plato, Socrates, Aristotle and the rest. They represented the great flowering period of the human mind and intellect, and were trying to understand the meaning of life and of the whole universe. They had a feeling that there was a power behind it all; they believed in various gods, and they were trying to please and placate these gods. It was at Athens, the greatest centre of Greek culture, that the Apostle Paul found an altar bearing the inscription, 'To the Unknown God'. They were trying to find that God by the processes of reason and of thought and of meditation. That is, essentially, philosophy.

The Bible starts, however, on the supposition that man, because he is fallen and sinful and finite, can never arrive at that knowledge. That is the first postulate of the Christian message – 'The world by wisdom knew not God' (1 Corinthians 1:21). At its best and highest, in the flowering period of Greek philosophy, it failed. But it was when the world by wisdom knew not God that 'it pleased God by the foolishness of preaching (or the foolishness of the thing preached) to save them that believe'. There is thus an absolute distinction. The Gospel starts on this basis, that we are completely helpless in this matter of getting to know God, that we are incapable of arriving at truth, but that God in His infinite kindness has been pleased to reveal it, and that all we have to do – to use the words of our Lord – is 'to become as little children'. 'Except ye be converted, and become as little children, ye shall not enter into the kingdom of heaven' (Matthew 18:3). Or, to use the language of the Apostle Paul, 'If any man seemeth to be wise in this world, let him become a fool, that he may be wise' (1 Corinthians 3:18). In other words, if a man wants to be wise in this ultimate sense he has to stop being a philosopher! The philosopher is 'the wise man'. So if any man really wants to be wise, says Paul, let him become a fool in order that he may be made wise. To 'become a fool' means that you say, 'Very well, I admit I cannot do it, my mind is insufficient, modern knowledge does not help me. I am absolutely shut in to the revelation that God has given.'

To reach that point is to arrive at the beginning of Christianity. 'But,' says someone, 'that is obscurantism, that is to commit intellectual suicide.' Not at all! It means that man, using his reason, comes to the inevitable conclusion that his reason is not sufficient. That is my paraphrase of the immortal statement of Blaise Pascal, a brilliant mathematician and scientist, who said, 'It is the supreme achievement of reason to show that there is a limit to reason'. The main trouble today is that men do not see the limit to reason; they are still trying to understand by their own abilities. Christianity begins for me when I come to the end of my reason; when my reason, as it were, dictates to me that I must look to and believe and accept the divine revelation. I confess that I do not know, that I cannot understand. I become 'as a little child', and I look up into the face of Him who is 'the Way, the Truth, and the

Life'. That is the beginning of Christianity! But from the moment you enter it in that way you begin to use your understanding, and it grows and develops, and there is literally no end to it.

Such is the basic Christian position; and no man can become a Christian unless he passes that way, for there is no other way. But – and this is what the Apostle is telling us – the moment we become Christians in that way, the devil will begin to attack us. He will say to us, 'You are quite correct; that is the right way to become a Christian'. He had been saying the exact opposite before, of course; but now having seen that he has failed, and that we have become Christians by the grace of God, he takes a new line altogether, and he says, 'Yes, you are quite right; that is, of course, the way to begin; you must be "given something". But now, having entered on such a life, surely you can no longer believe the Bible as it is. You see, the Bible was written long ages ago; its last book was written nearly two thousand years ago, some of it is much older and goes back through many centuries. It was quite up-to-date when it was written and, of course, the New Testament is invaluable, but it is written in an ancient idiom, and no one understands these terms any longer. Not only so, there is a great deal of knowledge available now which people of the early centuries did not possess. If you really want to be a modern up-to-date twentieth-century Christian you have got to pay attention to modern knowledge, the discoveries of science, and so on. The science of biology, for instance, has taught us the fact of evolution, that man was not created as the Bible tells us, but has gradually evolved. And various other discoveries have been made. The newspapers tell about cave paintings 60,000 years old, or even older than that. Anthropology has added much to knowledge; so humans are now in an entirely different position. Of course, you must still believe in the Lord Jesus Christ, but...'

Now the moment you submit to the devil's 'but' you have already succumbed to his wiles. That is, I believe, one of the greatest dangers confronting the Christian Church. I fear that it is true to say that it is the greatest danger confronting evangelical people at this present moment. There is in the United States of America what they call 'The New Evangelicalism', which, as I understand it, is nothing but a manifestation of this very thing.

They say Evangelicalism must be brought up-to-date; it has been too negative and obscurantist; it has not been paying sufficient attention to science and to learning; it has lost intellectual respectability. One finds increasingly that Christians are not hesitating to accept as basic and reliable certain extra-scriptural statements and authorities. The question of the relationship of the Bible and religion to modern scientific knowledge is a very difficult and complex one; but it need not be as complex as the devil is making it at the present time. The following is the position as I understand it. As long as science deals with facts we should accept it; but the moment it begins to deal with theories, put up all the queries that you can think of. The essence of the modern problem is that the devil is clouding the issue by confusing theories and facts. Evolution is nothing but a theory; it is not a proved fact. So when men talk about evolution, they are not being scientific, they are speaking as philosophers. It is pure speculation. I am asserting that we must never accept speculation or supposition as one of our basic authorities. Or, to state the matter in a different way, the great basic truths I must take and accept only from the Bible. In other words, when I am considering the whole nature of 'man', I must take my knowledge of man from the Bible. When I am considering the doctrine of sin, I must take it from the Bible. I must not take it from the theory of evolution. The Bible tells me that man was made perfect and subsequently fell. Whatever theory may be put before me, I will not believe any other view of man's present condition, because I know that it is wrong. The Bible is God's revelation! The whole of the Christian salvation depends upon this essential fact. I cannot go on saying that I believe the Christian doctrine of salvation if I cease to believe in the fall of man because of the theory of evolution.

It is a principal part of the devil's subtlety to try to change my authority. He suggests that I should no longer believe in the Fall and in the biblical doctrine of sin because 'Science teaches . . .'. And if I dally with his suggestion, at that moment I have gone outside the realm of revelation, and am saying that man with his reason and ability, and his power to investigate and to collate facts, is able to lay down postulates with regard to fundamental truth. But the Bible starts by telling me that he cannot do so,

that that is the very thing that man has failed to do, that he is
blinded by the god of this world, and does not know himself
because he does not know God. So I must never behave in
that way.

The fact of the matter is that there is no new knowledge which
in any way makes the slightest difference to the basic postulates
of the Christian faith and message. Hence we must 'beware of
philosophy and vain deceit'. The Apostle Paul tells us in the first
chapter of his First Epistle to the Corinthians that he preaches
the Cross of Christ, though 'not with wisdom of words, lest the
cross of Christ should be made of none effect' (verse 17). A man
may start by believing in the Cross of Christ, but if he brings in
philosophy and becomes influenced by it, he will end by saying
something different, and so make the Cross of Christ 'of none
effect'. He will end with something which is entirely and radically
different from his original belief and position. The New Testament
Epistles had to be written because of that possibility. Some of the
clever philosophers were saying, 'It is quite right and proper to
be a Christian; but if you really want to understand the truth, do
not take it as Paul put it in its crudeness, talking materialistically,
as he did, about Christ's blood, and about the justice and the
righteousness of God. The Cross is something very beautiful if
you but see it truly.' And so they evaporated the glory of the
Cross into some beautiful philosophical thought; and for that
reason the Apostle calls it 'philosophy and vain deceit'.

We can sum it up by saying that we must not base the view we
hold, or the position in which we stand, so far as it involves our
relationship to God, upon anything except the revelation that is
given in the Bible. The moment we accept any extra-biblical
authority we have already succumbed to the wiles of the devil.
Let us be wary; let us be careful. The devil comes in and says,
'Do you really want people to listen to your message? If you do,
you must start by realizing that you are preaching in the mid-
twentieth century and not in the first century. If you think that
modern, educated, enlightened people will believe that old
simple Gospel as it was preached by the Lord Jesus Christ
Himself and by Paul, you are making a terrible mistake. They will
not listen to you, they will ridicule it. So,' he continues, 'you
must present it in such a way that they can accept it. You must

not offend their susceptibilities, you must not make your message an offence to their knowledge and to their intellectual understanding.'

That, I maintain, is of the very devil. If we really believe the message of the Bible we have got to say, This is the truth of God! It is, and always has been, offensive to the natural man. It was offensive to men in Paul's time. The Greek philosophers, when they listened to Paul, said that he was a fool, a 'babbler'. His message was 'folly' to them. 'The natural man receiveth not the things of the Spirit of God, for they are foolishness unto him; neither can he know them, because they are spiritually discerned' (i Corinthians 2:14). They were already saying it was folly even then; men will always go on saying it is folly. But let them say what they will, my business is to preach the truth of God; and the Holy Spirit will honour that truth. It can even convince intellectuals. It has done so, it is still doing so.

The moment I begin to use 'enticing words of man's wisdom' and to bring in my modern knowledge, and base part of my position upon modern discovery, I have already abandoned the true position, and my only real authority. There is no difficulty about this the moment you know anything about science and its speculations, and observe the way in which it is always changing. At the present time we have two scientists in Cambridge fighting one another about the origin of life. That is excellent! It just shows the hollowness of basing our position on 'science'. How can you base your ultimate position upon what any man may say? He is not only finite, but also blind and sinful. In the Bible, and in it alone, is the true authority; scientific theories come and go, but biblical truth goes on. It is the truth once and for ever 'delivered to the saints', and there is no other truth. 'Beware of philosophy and vain deceit.'

Furthermore, let us take note that the desire to be philosophical and to have understanding is liable to come into our minds in another way. It does not always come in the open way which I have been indicating, as a sort of fundamental controlling influence upon my basic thought, but sometimes – and this is a much more common way – as a desire to understand everything connected with the divine revelation. We have all fallen to this

temptation. We say, 'But I cannot understand how this or that
. . . I cannot understand how one death can cover all – I don't
see that. I don't see how the righteousness of Christ . . . I cannot
follow it. I . . .' This desire for understanding is another aspect of
'philosophy and vain deceit'. The natural mind always craves to
understand everything. The philosopher is a man who claims
that he has it in him to comprehend, to encompass all truth; and
he invariably wants to have a system which will cover everything.
It must always be complete, there must be nothing left which he
cannot explain. Now that desire is in every one of us. We are all
philosophers by nature; and there are many who are kept out of
the Christian life simply because 'I don't understand this, I don't
understand that'. But even after you have come into the Christian
life the devil will come and will worry you with this temptation,
and make you say, 'But I cannot follow this, I cannot see how . . .'
We have to be content with what has been laid down once and for
ever in Deuteronomy 29:29: 'The secret things belong unto
the Lord our God: but those things which are revealed belong
unto us and to our children for ever, that we may do all the words
of this law'. There is no advance on that! There are 'secret things',
and there are things which God has been pleased to reveal;
and you and I have to be content with the things that have been
revealed, and not even attempt to try to get an understanding of
the things that are 'secret'. This is one of the most important
rules in the Christian life.

Let us look at the matter in terms of a statement of the
Apostle to the Corinthians: 'Let no man deceive himself. If any
man among you seemeth to be wise in this world, let him become
a fool, that he may be wise' (1 Corinthians 3:18). This is a basic
rule. In other words, you and I have to come to this position
and say: Because this is the truth of God, by definition there
will be things about it that I cannot understand. Paul himself
stands back and says, 'Great is the mystery of godliness! God was
manifest in the flesh' (1 Timothy 3:16). Notice his words –
'Great is the *mystery* of godliness'. Who can understand that?
'Ah but,' people say, 'I don't understand how there can be two
natures in one Person!' Of course you cannot! How foolish you
are, ever to have thought that you could! Fancy pitting your
little mind and brain, and your ignorance, against the mystery

of godliness! 'I cannot understand!' Of course you cannot understand. What you have to do is to understand yourself first, for the moment you understand yourself you will not try to understand mysteries, you will realize that by definition it is impossible, for they elude understanding. Is it possible for a finite mind to encompass the Infinite? Philosophy should never be allowed to insinuate itself into these matters; it should be entirely excluded.

I have no doubt whatsoever in my own mind that the Christian Church is as she is today, very largely because for the last hundred years so much time has been given in the theological colleges and seminaries to the teaching of philosophy. It is the greatest enemy of the Christian truth. If a man by means of philosophy becomes a Christian, how unfair and unequal it would be! There would be no point in sending foreign missionaries to the heart of central Africa. How could they possibly preach the Gospel to people who know nothing, who cannot even read and who cannot think? The whole position is idiotic. No, when we come to the Gospel we are all one. The greatest philosopher is as much 'a fool' as the most ignorant, illiterate pagan.

This is basic Christianity. Thank God that it is so, otherwise it would not be God's way of salvation; it would be unequal, it would be unfair. When you come to listen to the Gospel you have to start by saying, 'God in His amazing love and grace has been graciously pleased to reveal these things; I am going to rejoice in them. I cannot understand them, they are so glorious; that is why I cannot understand, and I am not even going to try to do so.' So in the future, when someone comes to you and says, 'What I cannot understand is this! Can you explain it to me?' you must not be afraid to say, 'Of course I cannot, I myself do not know'. There are many things we do not know. Take the early chapters of Genesis. There are things there about which I am not clear. I do not understand them. But that does not worry me; I am not meant to know them. All I know is, as the author of the Epistle to the Hebrews states it in his eleventh chapter, verse 3: 'Through faith we understand that the worlds were framed by the word of God, so that things which are seen were not made of things which do appear'. That is the truth concerning creation, and I do not know anything beyond what I am told there. There are many gaps in my knowledge; that does not worry me. I am content with the knowledge that God is, and that God is the Creator. 'In the beginning God created the heaven and the earth,' and he created 'all that in them is.' God 'made man in his own image' – that I am certain of! There is no question but that man is a unique creation, 'in the image of God'. Why then is he as he is today? Man rebelled and fell – that I am certain of! Now there are many things that I am not certain of when it comes to details. Do not be worried; just say, 'I do not know'. One day I shall be given the full and final revelation in the glory; but while I am in this world, I say, 'The secret things belong unto the Lord our God: but those things which are revealed belong unto us'.

Never go beyond the knowledge of what has been revealed, and never give the slightest encouragement to the desire to understand what you are never meant to understand. Take again that question, 'How can there be two natures in one Person?' Or the questions, 'Where is the soul in man? What is the relationship between the soul and the body?' We simply do not know the answers! And yet we know that we have a soul! We cannot understand these things, they are mysteries. What is astonishing to me is that men and women do not see that the more knowledge grows the greater becomes the mystery of it all. Look at the atom. 'Ah,' men say, 'we have split the atom, we now understand.' Do we understand how this almost inconceivable power is held in that minute thing in such tremendous tension? Of course we cannot understand it. It is a great and a wonderful mystery. The more knowledge advances the greater does the mystery become. Let us then be content with what has been revealed and resist the subtle temptation of the devil along that second line.

But we move on to consider a third question. There is always the danger that the devil will come to us and try to persuade us that the knowledge which we have received from the Scripture needs to be supplemented a little. Here again I refer to that statement in which the Apostle warns Timothy to be very careful about this very thing. 'O Timothy, keep that which is committed to thy trust, avoiding profane and vain babblings'. What a wonderful description of the writings and speeches of the philosophers! 'Profane and vain babblings!' – 'and oppositions of science falsely so called' (1 Timothy 6:20). This does not mean 'science' in our modern sense but the 'knowledge' that was in opposition to the Gospel. 'Timothy,' says Paul in effect, 'there is only one way to keep yourself free from these vain babblings and this knowledge. Hold on to that which has been committed to thy trust, keep it, guard it, never look outside it, keep yourself rigidly there. These other people have gone after philosophy and they have "erred concerning the faith".' He had previously told Timothy about some who had already made 'ship-wreck' of their faith (1:19) by embracing the peculiar heresy against which the Apostle was warning Timothy himself, and exhorting him to warn others; it was a kind of admixture of philosophy and mysticism.

Next to philosophy, mysticism is surely the chief danger. Mysticism is a manifestation of, and the result of, the desire for 'immediacy', 'an immediate knowledge'. There is something right in that, because we are meant to know God; but it is because we are meant to know God that the devil introduces mysticism. It teaches that it is possible to have an immediate and direct knowledge of God in a much easier manner than that which is taught in the Scripture. We touched upon that when dealing with the cults, which are all based on that idea. But apart from the cults there are various movements in the Church that go under the name of 'Mysticism'. Put simply, mysticism teaches that God is in you, God is in every one, and that if you want to know God, all you have to do is to concentrate on this one thing, shut out everything else, and sink into yourself. You will go through a kind of negative phase and die completely to yourself, and then you will come to the point of illumination. And so you have 'the mystical way', so called, and the various steps on the mystical way. This type of teaching has been threatening Christianity from the very beginning. It was threatening the Christians who were under the pastoral care of Timothy; it was threatening Christians at Colosse. It was a curious admixture of mysticism and speculation, and elements borrowed from Judaistic teaching and 'mystery religions'.

[173]

Perhaps the most perfect example we have had of this very thing in England during the present century was William Ralph Inge, once Dean of St Paul's. He was famous as a philosopher, but he was also very much interested in mysticism – the two things often go together. This is so because when you get into trouble with your thinking and cannot reason any further, you can leap into mysticism and then get direct knowledge. Both are wrong because they both by-pass the Scriptures. You will never arrive at a knowledge of God by sinking into yourself. There is no ultimate knowledge of God apart from the Lord Jesus Christ and the full and the perfect revelation that is in Him. Hold fast the Head, says the New Testament, 'in whom dwelleth all the fulness of the Godhead bodily' (Colossians 2:9). There is no direct way to God apart from Him. You cannot by-pass this great doctrine. Beware then of 'philosophy and vain deceit', this attempt to short-cut the New Testament, and to arrive by some mystical procedure at this wonderful, immediate, direct knowledge and experience of God. It is an aspect of 'philosophy and vain deceit'.

There is nothing that is attacking the Church in a more subtle manner than 'philosophy and vain deceit' at the present time. It insinuates itself in a most specious way in most modern books on religion. This is where things went wrong in the last century. Whenever the Christian Church is afraid of 'being a fool for Christ's sake' she has already gone wrong. This change for the worse took place about the period 1850–1870. There had been the great Evangelical Awakening in the eighteenth century. It was mainly among poor people, the masses, the working people who were in a state of ignorance. And the churches that emerged out of that awakening consisted of such people. They were dismissed, of course, and laughed at by people like Lord Chesterfield and various other intellectuals. The great thinkers and philosophers and cultured people of the eighteenth century called it 'enthusiasm', and despised it. That is how it started, and while it kept to that it was very powerful. But as the last century advanced things began to change. The despised people, and especially their descendants, became 'respectable'; their children had more education, and they began to say, 'We must have a cultured ministry. We can no longer proclaim that simple unvarnished Gospel, we must have it illustrated by quotations from Greek philosophy, the Latin classics, and so on.' So the Church began to turn to knowledge, culture, and philosophy. Mid-Victorianism is mainly responsible for the present state of the Christian Church. It sold the pass. The Church wanted to be intellectually respectable, she wanted to be able to parade her fine understanding of things before the world. But the moment she does that she has sold everything. We are to be 'fools for Christ's sake'. If you believe the Christian Gospel people will say to you, 'What, do you still believe that? Do you still believe in sin? Psychology has explained that long ago.' They will laugh at you. 'Do you still believe the Bible? Do you still take that as your ultimate authority? Do you really say that you put the Bible before all that has been discovered in the last 2,000 years about these very things?' And if you do not say unashamedly, 'Yes – because it is still the Truth, and the only Truth', you have already succumbed to 'philosophy and vain deceit'. We are meant to be 'fools for Christ's sake'. 'God forbid that I should glory, save in the cross of our Lord Jesus Christ, by whom the world is crucified unto me and I unto the world' (Galatians 6:14). God forbid that I should glory in anything else! 'Ah,' people say, 'but we want interesting sermons; we like to hear about how science is now explaining the miracles and making it more easy to understand the Bible.' God forbid that I should ever do such a thing! If you think it is more easy to believe in miracles now than it was 2,000 years ago you still do not believe in miracles! You will never understand miracles; by definition they are beyond understanding. Nothing is needed in addition to the Bible, we must never add any plus to it. This is everything, this is all, this is complete. This is God's revelation; and I must reject anything that offers itself to me as an addition, or a kind of supplement to it. It is as up-to-date now as it was at the beginning; and it will always be up-to-date. I do not covet anything different. I do not know as much as the Apostle Paul knew about God and about Christ; neither do your modern philosophers. Therefore, I propose to go on listening to him and not to them. Reject everything else. All that Paul taught had been given to him, it was a revelation that he had 'received'; and we are entirely shut up to it. So we must shut our eyes to every form of 'philosophy and vain deceit'. That is one of the ways of 'taking unto you the whole armour of God'. It is just one of the ways of having 'your loins girt about with the truth'. May God give us wisdom to gird ourselves with the truth that we may be able to withstand all 'the wiles of the devil'.

13

'Knowledge Puffeth Up!'

In attacking the minds of Christians the devil employs another method which is similar to the one already mentioned, yet essentially different. It is possible for a believer who has avoided the danger of introducing philosophy and imposing it upon the Bible, and who sincerely recognizes the Bible as his sole authority, and desires to submit himself wholeheartedly to its evident meaning – it is still possible for such a man to go astray by becoming purely theoretical in his attitude towards this precious knowledge. It can happen to all, but I emphasize again that it is the particular danger of those who have keen minds, and who desire to understand and to grow in knowledge. The devil, knowing us as he does, always suits the particular form of temptation to our exact mentality. At this point I am not referring to people who do not read the Scriptures, or indeed little else, and who say, 'I am interested in nothing but my experience'. The devil does not trouble such people in this way, but to those who truly long to grow and develop, he comes and says, 'Of course, you are quite right; what you need, and what everyone else needs, is more and more of this knowledge'. But he presses the thought so far that in the end they get into a condition in which their whole relationship to truth is purely theoretical and academic. And this involves the terrible danger of becoming more concerned about, and more interested in, our intellectual knowledge of Christian truth than in our knowledge of the Lord Jesus Christ Himself; and if the devil with all his wiles can beguile us into this condition he is more than satisfied.

In other words, it is the failure to realize that the ultimate end of all knowledge is to bring us to a knowledge of the Person Himself. We are not to stop at knowledge concerning Him, precious though that is, and vital.

We must always guard against the terrible danger of believing the doctrines concerning God and the Lord Jesus Christ and the Holy Spirit without having a simple faith in the Three blessed Persons. The great doctrines are in Scripture, and it is essential that we should know them. I cannot put too much emphasis upon the value of such knowledge. But the devil comes and tries to press us to the point at which we are only interested in the doctrines and have lost the Persons, and we are left with nothing but a body of theoretical truth. In that condition we virtually turn Christian doctrine into a body of philosophy, and our relationship to divine Persons may be entirely dormant. This is, of course, another manifestation of that lack of balance which we were considering earlier, the danger of becoming increasingly intellectual and theoretical, the danger of becoming entirely objective, so that we approach all this great and glorious truth in the same way as we would approach any other truth or teaching.

This, alas, can be illustrated very easily from the long history of the Church; it has happened so often! After periods of revival, often there have followed periods of a dry arid scholasticism in which people were mainly interested in a theoretical understanding of the truth. God had been lost and the Lord Jesus Christ was not known personally. Unfortunately there are indications of this in the Church at the present time. It is possible for us to have such an exclusively intellectual interest in the truth that we even stop praying. I have known of certain very orthodox branches of the Christian Church in which they do not hold prayer meetings at all, and in which they have ceased to be evangelistic in their preaching. It is all 'teaching', nothing but teaching. A real concern for souls has gone, and even a realization of the absolute need of 'prayer without ceasing' has disappeared. Those caught in this snare are living entirely in the realm of the intellect, and their whole interest in the truth is purely theoretical, as if Christianity were but a matter of believing and accepting a number of propositions.

From time to time this terrible danger has afflicted every branch of the Church in one way or another, and it has produced various reactions in the history of the Church. There is no doubt, for instance, that Monasticism, and the idea that a man must get apart, and go out of the world, and become a monk or a hermit or an anchorite, arose as a reaction against this danger of a barren intellectualism. Suddenly a man realized that he had nothing but a theoretical interest in truth, that it was purely a matter of the mind, with no effect on his life. So he felt that there was only one thing to do; he must get right away from the world and concentrate on the cultivation of his spiritual life. Mysticism arises in much the same manner. Monks and mystics went from one extreme to the other. All extremes are bad; and that of becoming too theoretical and abstract is one of them.

To be very practical, I am prepared to assert that the moment you begin to find yourself regarding Christian truth as merely a subject for study you have already succumbed to the devil. This is the peculiar danger confronting certain types of persons who regard the Bible as just a text-book. I am always unhappy when a man comes to me and says, 'I am a great Bible student'. I believe, of course, that all Christians should study the Bible, but not in that way. Every man should come to the Bible because it is the bread of life, food for the soul, something which is essential to our well-being. But when a man says in a glib way, 'I am a Bible student', it suggests to me that it is more than likely that he has nothing but a purely theoretical and academic approach to truth. That, in and of itself, may be a snare of the devil. And when in addition you enter for examinations on scriptural knowledge it becomes even worse.

I am almost prepared to say that it is sinful to have examinations on biblical knowledge, because you are thereby encouraging this purely theoretical approach. Do I know the books of the Bible? Do I know how to analyse them and their contents? And do I stop at that? That is not the way to approach the Bible. This is God's Word which is meant to feed the whole soul; and its teaching must always be applied. We must never stop at the theoretical and the intellectual level.

It follows, of necessity, that this danger is peculiarly that of preachers – a man like myself – and theological students. All of us who handle God's Word and teach it are exposed to a very great danger. I would say once more what I am profoundly convinced is a terrifying truth, confirmed by my experience more and more, that to be a preacher, an expositor of God's Book, is one of the most dangerous things in the world. There is only one thing I know of that is more dangerous than to be what we call a 'full-time' preacher, and that is to be a lay-preacher, for the latter does not have to face the difficulties of the preacher, the pastor who has to live with the people to whom he is preaching. The lay preacher is in a much more dangerous position because he has the privilege and the power without responsibility. He lacks the restraints that tend to keep the pastor in order. I am not minimizing the dangers confronting the pastor-preacher, or the student, I am simply emphasizing that it is even greater in the other case. The danger confronting the pastor-preacher is the danger of a professionalism which leads to a theoretical, academic approach. The Bible becomes but a book in which a man searches for and finds texts for sermons. So he begins to read his Bible in that way, always looking for a new sermon or for a text. God have mercy upon the man who gets into that state! That is an utter abuse of the Bible.

This not only applies to the preacher and the teacher; it applies also to all who listen to preaching. You can listen in a theoretical manner. You can listen as an 'expert'. You can listen as a sermon-taster, as an expert on preaching. The moment we are in that condition, on the one side or the other, we are obviously succumbing to the wiles of the devil.

We are really dealing with the danger of ceasing to come under the power of the truth. The moment you cease to be under its power you have already become a victim of the devil. I must apply that to myself as a preacher. If I can study the Bible without being searched and examined and humbled, without being lifted up and made to praise God, and to feel as much of the desire to sing when I am alone in my study as when I am standing in a pulpit, I am in a bad state. This is the truth of God, it is the power of God, and we should always feel something of that power.

This applies also to listening to the truth. If you are able to attend churches and go away without having felt the power of the truth, then either you or the preacher is failing miserably. If it is all merely a matter of intellectual entertainment, giving and receiving a certain amount of knowledge, seeing some error exposed, and hearing a portion of Scripture analysed and explained, and the truth set forth – if it stops there and does not come to you in such a way as to make you feel uncomfortable; if it does not make you realize your deficiencies, your unworthiness, your failures; if it does not expose hidden, secret things in your heart; if it does not make you feel that you have got to pull yourself together, and to do something about yourself; if it does not ever move you and thrill you and make you feel like shouting in praise, well then, you are in a dangerous state.

And into such a state the devil will try to bring you. 'Ah yes', he will say, 'the more you know the better, study with all your energy and ability.' But if you do so in the wrong way you will become one-sided, intellectual and theoretical, and never feel truth's power. Anyone in that state should repent and realize that he is in one of the most dangerous conditions imaginable. If you can listen to God's truth without being terrified at times, then there is something wrong with you. If you have got into an unfeeling state you need again to come under the power of conviction of sin and to be made to wonder whether you are a Christian at all. If you can handle biblical truth lightly and in a detached manner, in a purely objective way, saying, 'I was saved years ago, I am a Bible student now, I am interested in high doctrine or prophetic problems', you had better examine the foundations again, for you are in one of the most dangerous states the soul can ever know.

The next matter I mention, and it follows from the former, is intellectual pride. It is not exactly the same as the former, but the former tends to lead to it. Intellectual pride is a condition of mind and soul which the Bible calls being 'puffed-up.' Paul says in 1 Corinthians 8:1 – 'Knowledge puffeth up.' All kinds of knowledge tend to puff us up. But biblical knowledge in particular tends to do so. A man becomes proud of his knowledge and of his understanding; he becomes an authority; and, in turn, of course, he despises others. That was one of the great troubles in Corinth. The strong brother despised the weaker brother – that ignorant fellow who does not 'know' anything! The strong, enlightened, knowledgeable persons were despising the other brethren for whom Christ had died. The apostle does not spare these 'strong' brethren; he deals with them severely. 'Knowledge,' he says, 'puffeth up, but love (charity) builds up.'

The terrible temptation to become proud of our knowledge of the Bible, proud of our knowledge of doctrine, is ever present. And while in that state it is clear that we are not in contact with divine Persons. No one can be proud in the presence of God, no one who really knows the Lord Jesus Christ can be puffed-up. As the Apostle says, 'We know nothing yet as we ought to know'. At best we only see 'as in a glass darkly', in this life and world. We have nothing of which we can be proud. As James puts it, 'Be not many masters, my brethren' (James 3:1). Be careful, he says, that you are not setting up the standard for your own judgment. If you set yourself up as an authority, well, expect to be judged as an authority. If you say, 'I know all about it', you will be examined on that very basis. Any pride or self-satisfaction in the presence of God is quite unthinkable. We know nothing yet as we ought, we are but beginners, paddlers on the very edge of this mighty, boundless ocean of truth. Let us beware of intellectual pride; it was the cause of the original sin, and it has been the besetting sin of God's people ever since. 'He that glorieth, let him glory in the Lord' – not in his knowledge of the doctrine, not in his knowledge about the Lord. Let him glory in the Lord Himself, and in nothing else (1 Corinthians 1:31).

Another danger – again one which is dealt with in many places in the New Testament – is the danger that, having started in the Spirit, we go back to the flesh. This is the great theme of the Epistle to the Galatians, summed up in the words 'Are ye so foolish? having begun in the Spirit, are ye now made perfect by the flesh?' (Galatians 3:3). The Apostle was writing to Christian believers, and this is one of 'the wiles of the devil' with regard to a believer. It is the danger that, having started

[182]

by seeing clearly that justification is by faith only, and that everything in the Christian life is by faith, you can unconsciously begin to slip back to reliance on your own works in some shape or form. It is a very subtle temptation. Even Peter tended to succumb to it as the result of a fear of brethren who had come down from Jerusalem, and at Antioch the Apostle Paul had to 'withstand him to the face', as he reminds us in the second chapter of Galatians. It is the danger of going back from the true position. Having seen at the time of your conversion that salvation is entirely of faith and trust, you shortly begin to rely upon your good works and activities, on what you are, or on your understanding; and at that point you bring in these fatal additions. Any kind of addition is always and inevitably wrong. In the Galatian case it was circumcision as the result of the teaching of the Judaisers. But however the temptation to turn aside may arise, it is essential to remember that we cannot perfect the work of grace on the flesh level; everything must be on the level of the Spirit; and it is always by faith. Everything is ultimately by faith and on the ground of faith; and we must not fall back from that basic truth. So we have to examine ourselves in this respect. Do we realize that on our deathbed we shall be utterly, entirely and absolutely dependent upon the Lord Jesus Christ and His perfect work? All our righteousnesses are 'as filthy rags'; we must rely solely upon Him. Do all you can, gain all the knowledge you can, work as much as you can, but never rely upon any of these things. We must rely solely and entirely upon Him.

Another aspect of this subject is the danger of being obsessed by one aspect of the truth. I use the term 'obsessed' deliberately; because while it falls short of a psychopathic obsession in a strict medical sense, there is no doubt about the reality of the obsession which the devil produces in certain people. He does so when he fixes their attention upon one aspect of the truth only. The truth is very large and comprehensive. It is one of the glories of the truth that it is so vast and profound in its height and depth and breadth and length. But the devil persuades a man to fix on one thing only, and as he goes through the Bible he sees nothing else. He sees it always speaking about it, always writing about it, always underlining it, always putting it forward. To such a man there is nothing in the Bible but this one thing. His obsession is a clear manifestation of the success of 'the wiles of the devil'.

It is very interesting to listen to what people say and to note how they introduce themselves. How men betray themselves by what they say unconsciously, and reveal their different obsessions! Some people seem to think that the Gospel is nothing but a message about physical healing. They rarely talk about anything else; to them nothing matters but this one thing. Others are obsessed – and I use the term deliberately – by the question of sanctification. Nothing else interests them. They have lost the balance of truth completely, they are always preaching their particular theory of sanctification. They have long since ceased to evangelize, for their pet theory monopolizes their attention. We should not form movements with respect to particular doctrines; to attempt to do so is to lose balance. Many people attend meetings and gatherings because they are anxious to be delivered from some particular sin; what many of them really need is to be converted! They do not even know the doctrine of justification! There should always be a balance, a fulness of doctrine, 'the whole counsel of God', and not just one particular aspect. There are no 'specialists' in the spiritual realm, and the moment a man claims to be such he has become 'obsessed'. It matters not what the particular doctrine may be; whenever it becomes an obsession it is wrong. If you are more interested in one particular doctrine than you are in your knowledge of God and of the Lord Jesus Christ, you have got truth out of focus, you are an obsessed person spiritually. The narrower your circle the more expert you can become in it. The extent and the range of knowledge is smaller; hence you seem to know all about it, and to know much more than others. So it immediately leads to a state of spiritual pride. May God keep us from becoming 'obsessed' Christians, harping always on one note, never leaving it out, always obtruding it.

Another group misled by the 'wiles of the devil' consists of those who are in danger of becoming interested in externals only. There are many such people. The devil comes to a good man, a man who is very much concerned to know about the truth, and fixes his attention on one particular matter such as church government. There are people who talk about nothing else but church government. In their view all that needs to happen to revive the Church today is to have a different form of church government – as if that were central! So they become interested in the mere machinery of the matter, or in some particular tradition. There are people who get very excited about denominational allegiance. Quite often they do not even know why they belong to a certain denomination, except that they happen to have been born into it, for their parents belonged to it before them. They know no more than that; but they will fight to the last ditch for their denomination and their group. That is sheer traditionalism, and the devil readily makes use of it. How many people there are who are more interested in church alignment or denominationalism than in the Lord Himself and in the salvation that flows to us through Him!

Then there are those who become interested in history only. Nothing is more fascinating than history; and yet if you simply become an historian, or are animated by nothing but an antiquarian interest in Christian matters, the devil has you safely asleep. It is good to read about the great saints of the past, but beware lest you live on their experiences and do not have the same experience yourself. In other words, when you read the experiences of great saints of God always asked the question: Do I know this? Have I got that? Can I speak in this manner? If not, why not? The devil will encourage you to garner knowledge, and will persuade you that, because you enjoy reading about these things, you are in the same position as such men.

All these things are seen clearly in the history of the early Church. The Jews who had become Christians were in a very difficult position. They had behind them the great tradition of Judaism and the Old Testament teaching and doctrine. But Gentiles also had become Christians. It was very difficult for the Jew to realize that the man who had just come in from paganism was really in exactly the same position as himself. That was what was happening in Galatia and in other places; certain Jews could not shed that which they had been brought up to believe. But we must never allow traditionalism to govern us. That does not mean that we despise the past – of course not! Let us learn from it, but let us not become slaves to it. Thank God for every good custom and tradition, but the moment I worship tradition I am in a dangerous state. We must be guided by the truth of the New Testament, and not governed by tradition, however old and venerable it may be. This tendency is obvious in the life of the Church today amid all the talk about union and ecumenicity. Why are there so many denominations? The answer is that they are held by tradition, and nothing else. They are agreed about doctrine, or the irrelevance of doctrine! And the same temptation can befall those of us who are evangelicals. We must beware of traditions that do not really belong to the vitals and essentials of the Christian life, but are the mere accidents of history or of circumstances.

Of all the tragedies the devil produces in his wiles, side-tracking people and taking them off at a tangent, there is no more pathetic condition than that of the spiritual crank. The devil uses his wiles to rob such people of the riches of the Christian life and its glorious experiences. Not only so, but through these people he does great harm to the cause of God, because they make it appear to be ridiculous. Any man with a modicum of common sense and of intelligence can see that at a glance. So the devil pays special attention to this type of thing. I am sorry to have to say it, but among other things I am referring to some of the many vagaries with respect to 'prophetic teaching'. Some people become sheer cranks over this. They take up one particular matter, and emphasize it as if it were everything. They are always talking about it, they see nothing else, they are interested in nothing else. Prophetic teaching – what is going to happen, as related to what has happened – fills their vision. Circumstances and actual events often compel them to change their teaching because what they have asserted does not come to pass. Then they take up another line. And on and on it goes; and the whole question of prophecy is brought into disrepute and ridiculed before the eyes of the public. There are different emphases, of course, but they all have this particular general emphasis that prophecy is everything to them.

[186]

We should all be interested in prophetic teaching because it is so definite a part of biblical teaching; but I have no doubt that it is the side-tracks and vagaries and eccentricities which have been so evident in the last one hundred years in prophetic teaching, that have led many people in the Church today to avoid prophetic subjects. They do not want to become cranks, and the result is that they evade the prophetic teaching altogether. That is equally bad, of course. The devil comes saying, 'Ah, quite right, prophecy! especially today; look at the facts'. Our friends do not realize that he has so spoken throughout the centuries. They say, 'We must be in the last times'. But certain people said that quite as confidently two hundred years ago and more. They have been saying it throughout the centuries. 'But, ah, look . . .' I agree, but others have said that, and we may be wrong also. The danger is to particularize overmuch and go off at a tangent; and the moment you go off at a tangent you have left the great circle of truth.

Another example of this is the interest in biblical numbers. I have seen many people completely side-tracked by Numerics. It is a very interesting subject. There is deep meaning in the numbers that are used in the Bible – no question about that! But what the devil does is to encourage this interest unduly. Christians read many books about it, and in the end they are able to prove almost anything. They put down certain numbers corresponding to certain particular letters, and they make their additions and their subtractions, and spend the whole of their time in playing with biblical numbers. It is a very real snare.

Let me add one other example – and it is strictly contemporary – an interest in different translations of the Bible. I am referring to the type of man you may have known as a non-Christian. You saw his conversion, and you watched him beginning to grow in the Christian life. He came under certain influences and then you observe that when he writes to you he now adopts a new method. He ends his letter – or perhaps he introduces it as a postscript – with a quotation of Scripture; but in the brackets that follow you find 'Weymouth', or 'Way', or 'Moffatt', or 'Phillips', or N.E.B. or R.S.V. and so on. Speaking generally, I do not hesitate to assert that this is a manifestation of 'the wiles of the devil'. The man has become interested in the Scriptures, and whenever you meet him he says, 'Have you seen the latest new translation?', 'Have you heard of this or that version?'

I once knew a good Christian man who had carried over from his old unregenerate life into the new regenerate life a habit of this kind. The man of the world meets another man of the world, and he says, 'Have you heard this one?' and then tells him a story. This particular man no longer liked worldly stories, but he would come to you and say, 'Have you heard this one?', and would then quote a special translation of some particular verse of Scripture. He lived on that kind of thing; for he still had that kind of mind and mentality. Often, also, such persons are interested in the exact meaning of some word they have just discovered, and this has changed everything for them. They wax eloquent about it, and are tremendously moved by their discovery; it never occurs to them that this obviously cannot be as important as they imagine. They fall into the real danger of turning the Bible into a sort of Quiz book; it becomes a mere collection of spiritual crossword puzzles, and you spend your time playing with words and phrases and translations, and with the mechanics of translation. At that point you have lost the truth, you have become interested merely in the superficialities and the externals.

I have seen many a fine Christian taken right off on to a side track, a siding, by these things. He ceases to do any Christian work, ceases to have any concern about the souls of the lost. Indeed he even seems to be no longer concerned about knowing the Lord and enjoying fellowship with Him; his whole interest is in one or other of these side issues. There is nothing more barren, more arid. Some of the driest periods in Church history have been due to it. God preserve us from these things!

My last division under this heading of the intellectual, and the approach through the mind, is the whole problem connected with doubts. The devil can be very subtle at this point, he can plague a man with doubts. He succeeds by suggesting to him that the doubts are his personal doubts, and that doubts are always and invariably sinful. This is very subtle. What the devil does is to conceal himself and to make the man think that the doubts are arising in himself and in his own mind; whereas what is actually happening is that he is hurling at him what the Apostle later calls his 'fiery darts'. He hurls doubts at us all, but because some do not understand that they are from the devil, and imagine that they are from themselves, they condemn themselves and feel that the doubts are sinful. They begin to doubt whether they are Christians at all; and the devil gets them into bondage and into a state of terrible unhappiness and misery.

There is nothing sinful in and of itself in being assailed by doubts. Some of the greatest saints have been attacked by doubts hurled at them by the enemy right to the end of their lives. That is not sin. They hated the doubts, and they rejected them. That was the proof that they were not theirs. It is when a man begins to accept them and to agree with them that they become his. But the devil, of course, tries to confuse the issue at that point.

Indeed I have been tempted sometimes to say that the man who is assailed by doubts in that way by the devil is probably in a safer and healthier condition than the kind of person who says, 'I have never had a single doubt worrying me since I was converted'. There is surely something suspect about this second type of person, because as certainly as a man is a Christian the devil will attack him with these very wiles, and with all his subtlety.

Doubts may come at you from every direction, most of all perhaps when you are reading the Scriptures or when you are praying. But do not allow him to persuade you that they are *your* doubts. If you hate them, if you reject them, and if you, like Luther, feel like rising up and throwing that inkpot at him who is besieging and attacking you, there is no sin involved at all. It is the devil tempting you. He went to the Son of God and said, 'If thou be the Son of God'. And surely he attacked Him in the same way on the Cross, saying, 'If God were your Father, would He allow you to be subjected to this?', and so on. We shall deal with that later, but it had to be mentioned at this particular point.

These, then, are some of the ways in which the devil in all his subtlety, and with his wiles, attacks and besieges the individual soul. Realize that you are confronted by such an enemy. Take unto you, therefore, 'the whole armour of God'. You will need every bit of it. We are told what it is in its various portions. Put it all on, be fully clothed with it. Leave no unguarded places, for the devil may come from anywhere. It is only as we are 'strong in the Lord, and in the power of his might', and clothed with this whole armour, that we shall be able to withstand the wiles of the devil.

14

Faith and Experience

We have been considering the attacks of the enemy upon the minds of believers, and the way in which he does so, producing an arid, barren intellectualism, or pride of intellect and understanding, and especially in the matter of heresies. We have looked at some of the heresies; others will come before us as we proceed. At this point I shall leave the wiles of the devil as they are manifested in the attacks upon the minds of believers, and shall proceed to the second main section, in which we shall look at the way in which the devil attacks us in the realm of experience.

It is very difficult to draw an exact line between these various categories. Where does the mind end and where does experience begin? Obviously they are closely related; but we must draw some sort of line, otherwise we shall be in a state of confusion. I shall draw a line, therefore, between the attacks which are more directly and particularly upon the mind, and various other attacks which are more subjective and in the realm of experience. Christians often get into difficulties in the realm of experience because they have a faulty understanding of the truth. All these things are interrelated: 'Evil communications corrupt good manners'. 'As a man thinks, so is he.' And, clearly, if there is any defect in the intellectual understanding and apprehension of the truth, there will inevitably follow some sort of trouble in the realm of experience. So one often finds in pastoral experience that many of the experimental troubles which torment people, and about which they come to talk to a pastor or a minister, are the result of either faulty understanding or some wrong teaching at one point or another. Here then is one difficulty, that of drawing an exact line.

Another difficulty is that it is much more difficult to recognize the wiles of the devil in this matter of experience than in the attacks upon the mind. He is subtle everywhere; but as we make a comparison between the two it will be fairly obvious that in the realm of experience he is particularly subtle because it is so subjective. When we are dealing with doctrine and heresies, we are, after all, dealing with something outside ourselves, and we have the Scriptures and the Creeds and the Confessions, and books which have been written in exposition of the truth, to help us. The theme is outside us and objective. But in the realm of experience we are dealing with something which is almost entirely subjective, and concerned with our feelings, our emotions, our states, our moods. Obviously, therefore, analysis is bound to be exceedingly difficult.

To use a comparison, it is generally easier for us to deal with some purely theoretical, academic problem than to deal with the problem of our own health, for instance. Because we are the sufferers, because we have the aches or pains, or some difficulty in our constitution, it is more difficult for us than for someone looking on to be exactly aware of what is happening. We are an interested party, we are experiencing the sensations. That makes it much more difficult than when we are dealing with something entirely outside ourselves. We all tend to be on the defensive, we all tend to put ourselves in the right always; and to that extent the devil has his opportunity. We are not on guard as we are with objective truth. It concerns us personally, so we protect ourselves, and guard ourselves; and as a result it is much more difficult for us to recognize what is happening to us. Is not that our common experience? Whenever there is any trouble or quarrel or dispute, it is always due to someone else, is it not? We are never in the wrong; we are always right, it is always the other person who is at fault! The devil with his wiles and in his subtlety blinds us. Self-interest, self-concern and self-protection come in. The result is that we cannot exercise such a good and objective judgment as we can with regard to matters that are outside us.

As in the case of the mind, and as with regard to practice, one great characteristic of the devil's activity in subjective matters is that he always creates confusion. He gets us into a state of confusion and of muddle. Another characteristic is that he always tends to drive us from one extreme to the other. In correcting one thing, we are so prone to over-correct that we tend to fall into the opposite error, which is quite as bad as the first which we were correcting, and the result is a state of confusion.

To put the matter very simply and practically, we are dealing with the ups and downs of Christian experience, and especially with the fact that there are so many Christian people who are not happy. Indeed some are quite miserable; they are always in some kind of perplexity and unhappiness, carrying a burden, worrying over a problem in the realm of their experience. All this is the result of 'the wiles of the devil'. There is no other adequate explanation of it. Why are we not all rejoicing in this great and glorious salvation, and praising God with the whole of our being? There is only one answer, 'the wiles of the devil'. Somewhere or other in the realm of experience he has caused confusion, and we do not know where we stand. The result is that our testimony is greatly marred.

We start our examination of this theme by looking at the whole question of the place of experience in the Christian life. Two main difficulties and problems present themselves to us. The first is that some Christians put the entire emphasis upon experience; nothing matters to these people but the experimental, the experiential aspect. They are not interested in truth, or in definitions; they say that nothing matters but that a man should be able to say, 'Whereas I was once blind, now I see'. Unless a man can testify to a great change in his life they feel that he has nothing. It is the only test they apply. They are always talking about it. They tell us about what happened to them, and say that the same can and should happen to us, and so on. They are not concerned to examine what has produced the change; they are not interested in the fact that there are many agencies that can produce change. The experience is the one thing that matters, nothing else counts at all.

This extreme view can take a variety of forms; for instance, that which we find in the fourth chapter of the Book of Job. Eliphaz the Temanite is a fine illustration of the type of man to whom experiences are the one thing that matters. Job was in terrible trouble, suffering from that skin condition and in an agony. His children had been killed by a hurricane, his animals had been stolen by the Sabeans and the Chaldeans. While he was thus afflicted one of his friends named Eliphaz comes to him and this is how he speaks; 'Now a thing was secretly brought to me, and mine ear received a little thereof. In thoughts from the visions of the night, when deep sleep falleth on men, fear came upon me, and trembling, which made all my bones to shake. Then a spirit passed before my face; the hair of my flesh stood up: it stood still, but I could not discern the form thereof: an image was before mine eyes, there was silence, and I heard a voice saying . . .' In other words he was saying to Job something like this: 'Listen to me, I know what I am talking about. I am a man who has had an experience, I have seen a vision'. There are persons of a certain type who are always talking about strange, remarkable experiences, visions, ecstasies and various things that have happened to them. The experiences are their authority, and on them everything is based. They are always saying, 'Listen to me, this is what has happened to me, and I am speaking, therefore, with this unusual authority'. And, of course, the devil encourages them also, not only to talk about it constantly, but to seek further experiences along the same line. There are certain persons whom the devil attacks along this line. He knows they are interested in it perhaps because of their natural temperament, or because they have become interested in psychic phenomena, or because of something in their background, some confusion in their reading or in their teaching. The devil therefore presses and encourages them with the result that they are always seeking these unusual and exceptional experiences.

We believe, of course, that experience is absolutely essential to a Christian man. But we are dealing at this point with people who live on experiences and who base everything upon them, and who are interested in nothing else. Some of them live on past experiences. I have known many such Christian people, and they have always struck me as being very sad and pathetic. There are not many of them left now, but at one time I used to meet quite a number. Whenever I met them, or whenever I was preaching in their district and they came to speak to me at the end of a service, I knew that in a few moments they would be telling me about the things that had happened to them in the Welsh Revival of 1904 and 1905. Always! They were living on those experiences, always talking about them, always looking backwards. That was *the* thing, the one thing – as if nothing had happened to them since then. They never told me about the things that had happened to them subsequent to 1905, but always of the amazing things that had happened during the time of revival. Amazing things indeed they were, and they are things about which we should speak; but we should not live on them.

I knew a minister whose whole ministry was ruined by this fault. During that same revival this man had had very remarkable and astonishing experiences from God; there was no question about that. He had been used in a very remarkable manner. But the revival ended, as all revivals end, and the poor man, instead of understanding the position, and proceeding with his work of expounding the Scriptures and preaching the Gospel in the power of the Spirit, was still expecting the unusual experiences to continue. But they did not come. During the revival this man never had to prepare messages, words were given to him, and there was great freedom and power. But when the revival ended that had also ended. But he still did not prepare, he was still expecting the unusual; and it did not happen. So he became depressed and spent about forty years of his life in a state of barrenness, unhappiness and uselessness. When he talked about the revival experiences he became a transformed man, his eyes flashed and he spoke with animation. But normally he was hypochondriacal, unhappy, miserable, and utterly ineffective in his ministry. This is but an illustration of the kind of thing to which I am referring. The devil has ruined many a Christian life through encouraging people to live on experiences – seeking them, looking for them, always talking about them, looking back upon them, relying upon them. And so he nullifies their value as living Christian witnesses.

There are many Christians who at once recognize that particular fallacy, indeed they recognize it so clearly that the devil in his subtlety drives them right over to the opposite extreme. They become people who are not interested in experience at all. To them, experience, and the emphasis upon experience, is something they almost despise. They look at the Christians who are always talking about their experiences, and they ask, 'What do *they* know about the truth?' Then they begin to expatiate about the truth; nothing matters to them but the truth only. Notice where the devil comes in. The truth is essential, absolutely vital, but if a person says that truth alone is essential he is as wrong as those who say that nothing but experience is essential. In this way the devil uses this big question of the whole place of experience in the Christian life and causes unutterable confusion. The trouble with the people in the second group is that they talk much about the truth but very often they have never felt its power. 'Having a form of godliness' says the Apostle, 'but denying the power thereof' (2 Timothy 3:5). They have never felt the power of the truth, they have never been mastered by it. They have had a purely intellectual interest in it. The truth they talk so much about has never changed their lives; it has never made a vital difference to them. This is surely as wrong as the 'experience only' position. One says 'Nothing matters but experience'; the other says 'the one thing that matters is, Have you got this insight and understanding, this grasp of the truth?' The second group look at Christianity objectively only, the first, subjectively only.

As I state the matter in this way it appears to be obvious. But is it equally obvious in practice? What do we really know about Christian truth in experience? Are we what we are because of our belief of this truth? Has this truth mastered us, has it gripped us? Does this truth really control us? Let us make no mistake about this; the truth of God is something that is to be experienced. It is not a philosophical system, it is not a mere ethical teaching. The whole object and end of the Christian religion is to bring us to a knowledge of God; and God is not some kind of philosophic 'X'. He is not an abstraction, a mere postulate in philosophy. God is! He is a Personal Deity. And He is to be known.

The Apostle John, the last of the Apostles, writing a letter as an old man, says, 'That which was from the beginning, which we have heard, which we have seen with our eyes, which we have looked upon, and our hands have handled, of the Word of life' (1 John 1:1). He says in effect, This is not philosophy, this is not mysticism; this is concrete, a living Person, God in the flesh! We have touched Him, our hands have handled the Word of life; 'the life was manifested, and we have seen it, and bear witness, and show unto you that eternal life, which was with the Father, and was manifested unto us. That which we have seen and heard declare we unto you.' He declares it to them, not because it is a glorious, grand system of truth, superior to everything else, but because it is such an amazing 'body of theology' that it is thrilling to contemplate. 'That which we have seen and heard declare we unto you, that ye also may have fellowship with us.' What is this 'fellowship with us'? 'Truly our fellowship is with the Father, and with his Son Jesus Christ.' Elsewhere he writes, 'This is life eternal, that they might know thee, the only true God, and Jesus Christ whom thou hast sent' (John 17:3). It does not mean to know *about* Him. The devils know about Him and they tremble (James 2:19). It is the knowledge of experience, it is the knowledge of fellowship, it is the knowledge born of intimacy.

The devil, I repeat, causes unutterable confusion at this most central point. The essence of the Christian position is experience – experience of God! It is not a mere intellectual awareness or apprehension of truth. That can be of the devil. If it does not bring me to the knowledge of the Father, and of His Son, it is of no value to me. But let me remember, on the other side, that it is equally important that my experience should be an experience of the Father and of His Son. There are cults that can change your life, cults that can deliver you from things that defeat you, cults that can give you happiness. Psychotherapy also can do so, and many other agencies, even an operation on your brain. We must have a test. If the experience is not an experience of the living God through His Son who has come to live and to die and rise again in order to give it; if it is not through the Holy Spirit, it is not a true Christian experience.

The devil comes, and in his wiliness deludes us. A man says to me, 'I have had an experience, my life is changed, something marvellous has happened to me'. I tell him that it is good that he is a better man than before, but what I ask him to tell me is, Why are you a better man? We must test the experience on both sides. Without experience there is nothing. There is no value in having a head full of knowledge if it has not mastered you, if it has not given you a knowledge of God. The end and object of all knowledge is to bring us to an experimental knowledge of the living God, and of His Son Jesus Christ. Do we know the power of the truth? Have we a living experience of God and of His Son? Is God real to us?

This is precisely where the devil comes in with his wiles on one side or the other. Let us be clear about it. Experience is essential and is vital. The Christian is a new man; he is unlike everyone else. But he is a new man as the result of the grace of God in and through our Lord and Saviour Jesus Christ. If you have had an experience but you still remain without a belief in God, it is not a true experience. If you rely upon an experience, but do not believe in the Lord Jesus Christ in His full Deity and in all His glory and in His atoning work, it is not a true experience of the Father, and of the Son, in the fellowship of the blessed Holy Spirit.

Let us now go on to consider the place of feelings. Feelings are a part of experience, but they are not identical with it. Experience is greater than feeling. It includes the whole aspect of fellowship and of communion. Feeling is a particular aspect of experience. Here, too, the devil causes endless confusion, and, once again, in the same way, by either overdoing the importance of feeling or else dismissing it and despising it.

Some people live on their feelings, and overdo this element of feelings altogether; nothing interests them but feelings. That is their one criterion in judging a meeting. If they have not wept, nothing has happened, and it is of no value at all. Of course this question of feeling can take many forms. It is not always weeping, it is sometimes excitement, almost hysteria. If these people have not been lifted up right out of themselves, and almost lost control of themselves, they feel that nothing has happened. That is their one test of the operation of the Holy Spirit.

Some people live on emotionalism or on sentimentalism. As they believe that nothing matters except this kind of riot or excitement of the emotions, they will, of course, do everything they can to encourage it; and quite often it is deliberately worked up. There are services in which people clap their hands and shout and sing and repeat certain types of choruses – it is done deliberately to work up excitement. And the more excited they get, and the more emotional they become, the more wonderful, they think, the blessing of the Spirit has been. It is mere emotionalism.

Another aspect of the same thing is sentimentalism. Many of us know something about this, perhaps from experience. I certainly remember a stage in my own experience when at a Communion Service I used to see certain older people weeping as they took the Communion; and I felt that that was the one thing that mattered in the Communion Service. And because I could not weep I was in great trouble, and I would do anything to try to make myself weep, feeling that until I had wept in taking the Communion I had never taken it truly! Later I came to analyse what it was that made many of these good people weep, and I came to the conclusion that with many of them it was artificially produced. They deliberately did this, they made themselves do it.

But then the devil comes and makes such sentimentalism appear to us to be ridiculous, and so we go right over to the other extreme and take up the position in which we say that this kind of manifestation of feeling is not only a weakness but may indeed be altogether wrong. Certain people are so afraid of emotionalism that they have driven emotion right out of their lives altogether; their attitude is that nothing matters but what a man believes. It is adherence to the truth that counts. They have never felt anything, and they do not want to feel. Indeed some of them go so far as to say that you need not devote any attention at all to feelings.

About the year 1760 a man called Sandeman began to teach unusual doctrine and got quite a following. His teaching was that feelings do not matter at all. Many Christian people, he alleged, were miserable and unhappy, because they were looking inwards for some feeling or some experience. But that, he said, was wrong. Does not Paul teach in Romans 10 saying, 'What saith the Scripture? The word is nigh thee, even in thy mouth, and in thy heart; that is, the word of faith, which we preach; that if thou shalt confess with thy mouth the Lord Jesus, and shalt

[199]

believe in thine heart that God hath raised him from the dead, thou shalt be saved. For with the heart man believeth unto righteousness; and with the mouth confession is made unto salvation' (verses 8–10). From these verses he elaborated a teaching that says that it does not matter whether you have felt anything or not; the one question is 'Do you confess with your mouth the Lord Jesus?' If you do, all is well.

This teaching became known as Sandemanianism. I have a feeling that it is very rife at the present time. It is the teaching of those who say, 'Do not bother about your feelings. Do you believe? If you do, all is well.' The result is that there are many supposed Christians who have never felt the power of the truth at all. 'Take it by faith', they have been told. And they have done so, as they think. They have assented to a proposition. But they have never felt anything. They have never known sorrow for sin, they have never known what it is to grieve over their inward corruptions, they have never known what it is to be melted by the sight of the glory of the Lord and of His wonderful truth. They have been told not to worry about their feelings. They have never been moved by the truth. They do not even know what it is to rejoice in it. They simply 'believe' it, and therefore think they have become Christians, and must just go on in that way. They put a certain amount of discipline into their lives, and that is all. Thus the wiles of the devil come in.

There are certain fundamental Christian postulates; one is that man, the whole man, is to be involved in the Christian faith. That is the glory of the faith. Mind and heart and will are all to be engaged; and if they are not all engaged there is something seriously wrong. The truth is not only to be looked at and appreciated intellectually; if a man really sees it, he must feel something; the heart must inevitably be engaged and involved as well as the mind. Similarly, belief must lead to practice and action. John in his First Epistle writes: 'These things write we unto you, that your joy may be full' (1 John 1:4). Not only experience, but an experience of joy! 'Rejoice in the Lord alway,' says the Apostle Paul, 'and again I say, Rejoice' (Philippians 4:4). It is inconceivable that a man should really perceive the truth of this Gospel and feel nothing. It is impossible that this amazing message that tells us that God, before time, planned this scheme of salvation, that the Son came in the fulness of the time, humbled Himself, divested Himself of the signs of His glory, should leave us unmoved. You say, 'I believe in the Incarnation'. But how do you say that? Look at His life during the years of His public ministry. Listen to His incomparable teaching, look at Him staggering up Golgotha, look at Him upon the Cross. 'Ah yes,' you say, 'I believe in the Cross, I believe that Christ died for me and my sin, I believe in the substitutionary doctrine of the atonement.' If you can say that dispassionately you have never seen it; you know nothing about it!

> *When I survey the wondrous Cross,*
> *On which the Prince of glory died,*
> *My richest gain I count but loss,*
> *And pour contempt on all my pride.*
>
> *Love so amazing, so divine,*
> *Demands my soul, my life, my all.*

Anyone who has truly believed these glorious truths must feel as Isaac Watts did when he wrote these words.

Furthermore, it is a part of this message to say that 'the love of God is shed abroad in our hearts by the Holy Ghost which is given unto us' (Romans 5:5). In the Bible there is constant evidence of the most profound emotion. Take the Psalms: 'The Lord is my Shepherd; I shall not want'. 'Yea, though I walk through the valley of the shadow of death, I will fear no evil.' Read some of Isaiah's magnificent passages, chapters 40, 53 and 61 for example, and you will find the same emotion. Isaiah is obviously moved to the depth of his being by the glory and the grandeur of the truth – 'Comfort ye, comfort ye my people, saith your God', and so on. When you come to the New Testament you again find emotion. Take a passage like the 8th chapter of Paul's Epistle to the Romans, with its moving periods, its mighty eloquence. The Apostle is moved to the very depth of his being. 'We are led as sheep to the slaughter,' he says. 'Nevertheless,' he goes on to add, 'I am persuaded that neither death, nor life, nor angels, nor principalities, nor powers, nor things present, nor things to come, nor height, nor depth, nor any other creature shall be able to separate us from the love of God, which

[201]

is in Christ Jesus our Lord.' The Apostle Paul had a giant intellect, but he is so carried away at times that he breaks the rules of grammar and style! Some of the pedants who are trying to translate him today accuse him of being guilty of what they call inconcinnity and anacoluthia – inelegancies of style and incomplete sentences. The explanation is that the Apostle was moved and carried away by the truth! Indeed we are told that he wept many tears as he was talking to Christians about matters of the faith (Acts 20:19). But this is not confined to the Bible; look at our hymn-books! What was it that enabled these men to write their hymns? What led them to do so? There is only one answer – they were moved by the truth, they felt the truth, they were disturbed by the truth. It is something that is found endlessly in the experiences of the saints of God throughout the centuries.

But someone may say, 'I recognize the value of what you are saying, but on the other hand I am afraid of emotionalism'. That is the problem for many with regard to experience and with regard to feeling. They see certain excesses and they dislike them. On the other hand they recognize that coldness and lifelessness must be wrong. How can one tell the difference between these things? What is the difference between emotionalism or sentimentalism on the one hand and true emotion on the other? No one wants to defend emotionalism or sentimentalism. Let us consider the difference between the true and the false. In the first place emotionalism is generally worked up. In some shape or form it is artificially produced. Its second characteristic is that it always lacks the element of understanding. It is always a direct assault upon the emotions, it by-passes truth. Emotionalists care little about the source of the feeling as long as they get it. Hand-clapping, tambourines, anything may be used to work up the feelings and make a person lose himself. The swaying of the body also in rhythmic fashion may be used. It is always produced in a way that by-passes the understanding. The third characteristic of emotionalism is that the element of excitement, of rowdiness, of excess is present. Emotionalism is always characterized by this element of riot and excess.

Another most important fact about emotionalism is that it always leaves you exhausted. It tires you, it takes energy out of you. It is the same as alcoholic drink which seems to fill a man with energy, but which in actual fact is sapping his energy, and leaves him with a horrible tiredness, weariness, and exhaustion. Finally, it never affects the life and the living in a good sense. Obviously it cannot do so, for it is not based on truth. Men may have wonderful experiences, and riots of the emotions; but their lives often indicate something very different.

Sentimentalism is a little more subtle. Sentimentalists are always ready to denounce emotionalists, but I suggest that sentimentalism is nothing but polite emotionalism. That is the only difference. It is the difference, as it were, between emotionalism in rags and emotionalism in evening dress. Sentimentalism is very polite. For an illustration of the difference between sentimentalism and true emotion, I suggest you read the works of J. M. Barrie, and compare them with Shakespeare. Barrie was an arch-sentimentalist, Shakespeare produces and stimulates true emotion. Sentimentalism is not a riot of the emotions; it is too polite for that. It only tickles the emotions. It does not really move; it just tickles.

Sentimentalism is the result of emphasizing and concentrating upon the presentation of the truth rather than upon the truth itself. For example, if a man when preaching tells an affecting story you feel something. It was not the truth that made you feel, it was the story, the illustration. That is typical of sentimentalism. It is never gripped by truth, but it is very much interested in the form in which the truth is conveyed; in other words, in the mechanism, in the presentation. Hymn tunes of a certain type often lead to sentimentalism. People feel that they are moved; but it may be nothing but sentimentalism. Perhaps it was only the tune, or perhaps the beauty of the words of the hymn. It was not the truth itself. We must beware of this false element. Its next characteristic is its superficiality; it is genteel, it is polite. A sentimentalist is always in perfect control of himself; but he allows something to happen just on the surface of his life and no more. The result is that he is always pleased with himself. He is glad to find that he can still feel; and that gives him a sense of satisfaction. He mistakes this superficial, genteel feeling for true emotion. Lastly, it never has a real effect upon the life. It may well lead a man to do something that will salve his conscience, or make him feel a little happier. He has had this superficial feeling and he does something as the result of it. But he has not been gripped by truth, he does not know what it is to be mastered by the glory of the Lord. He is but salving his conscience, he is putting himself right with himself. In this sentimental mood he has done a good deed, or a kind act; and probably, as he is doing so, he is evading the truth itself, he is covering over something.

What is true emotion as contrasted with both emotionalism and sentimentalism? It is never artificially or lightly produced. Man cannot create emotion; it is too deep for that. It is always the result of an understanding of truth itself. True emotion always results from a recognition of the truth; and the result is that it is characterized by depth. There is also an element of nobility in it, and of wonder and amazement. You never find that in emotionalism, which is all excitement, frothy, voluble, on the surface. Neither does emotion have the politeness of the mere sentimentalist. There is something deep, as expressed by Wordsworth –

> 'To me the meanest flower that blows can give
> Thoughts that do often lie too deep for tears.'

Emotion is profound, is noble; there is always in it an element of wonder, surprise, amazement. The whole person is gripped and moved in the manner I have illustrated out of the Scripture.

Another very valuable test is that true emotion is always energizing. It is like an electric battery which gives you power and it moves you and stimulates you. It has not the excess, the riot of emotionalism; it is not the mere playing with emotion that characterizes sentimentalism; but is the result of the energy and power of the Holy Spirit. It means that the whole man is galvanized by the life of God.

The result is that true emotion always leads to action, and always makes a real difference. If you think you have felt something in a service now and again, and you desire to know whether it is true emotion or not, the time for testing it is not while you are still in the building; it is the day after. You can experience emotionalism and sentimentalism in a meeting; but if it is a true emotion as the result of seeing something of the truth, or a glimpse of God, or the Lord Jesus Christ, and some recognition of the glory of it all, it will continue. It will move you to action. It will master you, guide you, direct you; it will be with you;

it will have energized you, it will have been productive. It is comparable to what the Apostle in writing to the Galatians calls 'the fruit of the Spirit'; and it is glorious abiding fruit.

God give us wisdom to see these things, that we may recognize that the wiles of the devil may so manipulate them as to spoil our Christian life subjectively, and also our witness and testimony before others! Thank God we are reminded that we can be 'strong in the Lord, and in the power of his might', and that we can 'take unto ourselves the whole armour of God'.

15

Physical, Psychological, Spiritual

As we have been examining the wiles of the devil it has become increasingly clear that the devil is the great counterfeiter of God and His works, and that he has a fundamental method. God Himself always works on a fundamental plan, as is evident in creation and in nature. There are variations, of course, in the application and operation, but there is an essential plan. The same is the case with the wiles of the devil. His particular use of this plan can vary so much that at times it is almost impossible to recognize it; but if you take the trouble, you will always find that it is there. It is good and right, therefore, that we should keep our eye on this fundamental plan.

We now turn to consider 'the wiles of the devil' as they are to be seen in the confusion he creates between the physical, the psychological and spiritual realms. 'What has this got to do with me?' says someone. The answer is that this is a subject which is, perhaps, one of the most practical we can ever consider. This is a realm in which the activities of the devil are particularly frequent and most damaging. We are strange creatures, made up of body, mind, and spirit; these are interrelated and react upon one another. Many of our troubles in life are due to this fact, and to our failure to realize the place, function, and sphere of each one of these realms. The devil, of course, takes full advantage of this, and attacks along this line. Let it be clear that we are dealing with Christian people. It is to them only that the exhortation to 'put on the whole armour of God' is addressed.

[206]

It is extremely difficult to define the limits of these three realms; or, to put it in another way, difficulty arises because of the border-line cases, which are not easy to classify. Hence this subject has been largely neglected, and helpful books – and they are few in number – are only to be found in a certain type of Roman Catholic literature or in Puritan literature. The Roman Catholics who developed an elaborate system of teaching on the theme, have what they call Manuals on the Devout Life. As for the Puritans, three hundred years ago they were real experts in this matter. They were primarily interested in the pastoral side of their work, and as you read their fine, voluminous works you will find that they are concerned with unravelling the problems and the difficulties of the Christian life. They not only stand comparison with the Roman Catholic writers, they are altogether superior because they are more biblical. I am thinking, not only of such great theological writers as Dr. John Owen, but this is equally true of John Bunyan, whose *Grace Abounding*, *Pilgrim's Progress*, and *Holy War* are really intended to do this very thing. Bunyan was aware in his own experience, and in his knowledge of the experience of others, that the wiles of the devil are continually being manifested with regard to the believer; so while in prison for twelve years in Bedford, he made use of his time in writing his great works in allegorical form to help Christian people to do the very thing we are exhorted by the Apostle to do in this Epistle to the Ephesians. Bunyan's works are a profound analysis of the wiles of the devil.

But it is interesting to observe that from about the end of the seventeenth century, roughly, this matter has been sadly neglected. The explanation is that during the eighteenth and most of the nineteenth century Christians had the Puritan writings. They were constantly being reprinted and read, so there was no need for fresh literature. But from about the middle of the last century onwards these great writings have been regarded as 'literature' and are no longer read to the same extent. A lighter and superficial view has become prevalent concerning evangelism, sanctification and the whole of the Christian life. It is a view which does not even recognize the problem; and the result is that this most vital and central aspect of our Christian experience has scarcely been written of at all. This is, surely, a most significant fact. In other words, the condition of the Church is what it is today – and I am including the evangelical section – very largely because of ignorance of the 'wiles of the devil'. A 'patent remedy' type of evangelism and teaching concerning sanctification, which is not scriptural, and has not even begun to realize the nature of the Christian life, and the strength and subtlety of the enemy that is set against us, has been in control. The wiles of the devil necessitate, not only the work of the preacher, but the work of the pastor, and this has been largely forgotten, so that much damage has been done to individual souls.

I wish I had kept a record of my experience in this respect. So often Christian people have come to me in trouble and have told me their story. They had got into difficulties as the result of the wiles of the devil, and they have gone to some well-known leader in their particular circle; but far from being helped they were made to feel much worse, for all that happened was that they were told by some 'bouncing' type of Christian leader to pull themselves together, to shake themselves, and not to give way to that which troubled them. In other words the leader who was consulted knew nothing about the wiles of the devil. Many Christian people, in fact, are in utter ignorance concerning this realm where the borderlines between the physical, psychological and spiritual meet. They not only are not able to help others, they have often done them great harm. Frequently I have found that such leaders had treated those whose trouble was obviously mainly physical or psychological, in a purely spiritual manner; and if you do so, you not only do not help, you aggravate the problem. Nothing is more important, therefore, than that we should look at this subtle, difficult and involved matter. All I can do here is to give some general headings and propositions.

First let us look at the mistake of regarding the physical or psychological as spiritual. Sometimes Christian people are in great trouble because they mistake what is nothing but a purely physical condition for a spiritual condition. Remember, we are body, soul and spirit. Christians may be taken ill with some diseased condition and may not even be aware of it. All that they know is that they do not feel as they used to feel. A kind of lethargy overtakes them, they do not enjoy reading the Bible as they used to do, they cannot pray as they used to do, they are in a depressed condition. They cannot understand themselves, and the devil comes to them and suggests that it is because they are slipping in a spiritual sense. Perhaps he even raises the question as to whether they have ever been spiritual at all, and thus torments them and worries them and agitates them. They are not able to concentrate as they did formerly, and they feel that they cannot be as active as they used to be. The devil comes in and suggests that God is somehow displeased with them, that they are being punished, and so on. So they find themselves in an agony of soul. An example will help.

I remember on one occasion, some twenty-five years ago, receiving a letter from a lady, asking me to try to help her, and to listen to her story. She said that she had been experiencing the kind of thing I have been describing – this kind of lethargy, her interest not as great as it once was, inability to do things. She was in a spiritual agony feeling that things had gone seriously wrong. She had heard of a certain well-known preacher who claimed to be an expert in matters psychological and spiritual, and she had written to him; and for many months he had been treating her by correspondence. But the lady, far from getting better, was getting worse. When I met her one glance told me that she was suffering from a disease known as pernicious anaemia. As the result of her anaemia she had lost her energy and her power of concentration. A person cannot have pernicious anaemia and still feel bright and energetic and keen and enthusiastic. Now if you try to help a Christian who is suffering from pernicious anaemia, and not being medically treated for it, by merely telling her to pull herself together and to try to think beautiful and positive thoughts, not only are you not helping her, you are being cruel to her, you are aggravating the problem. All she needed, of course, was the recognized treatment for pernicious anaemia; and she made a complete recovery in every way. That is an example of confusion as between the physical and the spiritual, and regarding something that is essentially a physical condition and problem as if it were a spiritual problem. Ignorance underlies this confusion, but the devil takes advantage.

This confusion can happen also purely as the result of overwork and over-tiredness. How often have I met this! A man does not realize that he is doing too much in a profession, or in a business; but as a Christian he feels that he should be doing much active Christian work. So when he finishes his regular work he has some Christian engagement every night of the week, and does not get home until a late hour. In addition he has certain work which he may have to take home from the office, and which he does after he gets home in a tired condition. He has been following this course for months, perhaps years. The first thing he becomes aware of is that he does not enjoy reading the Scriptures as he used to do, he does not pray as he used to do, he cannot think as he used to do, he seems to be losing interest; and the devil comes in at once and attacks him on the spiritual level. The man's immediate reaction is to engage in still more Christian work. He is determined to show that he is not slipping spiritually, so he adds to his burden; and on and on he goes. Many such people have come to me to consult me in a purely spiritual manner, outlining their spiritual problem in an agony of soul; and I, appearing to be very carnal and materialistic in my outlook, have just advised them to go for a holiday and to take a rest, and when they come back to try to use a little common sense, to realize that there is a limit to what the body can stand, and that the nervous system must not be overstretched perpetually, and cannot stand up to such a strain. This condition is purely physical; but the devil presents it as a purely spiritual problem; and so the soul is in an agony. The only spiritual element that is involved is that the man has not understood, as he should have done, that he has a body, and that he is to respect it and not abuse it!

The same applies, of course, to old age. Many Christians get into trouble along that line as they get older, and their faculties naturally and inevitably begin to fail. They say, 'I am not as I once was, I seem to be losing something, I am slipping'. It may be spiritual; all I am suggesting is that *sometimes* it is purely physical; and we must be very careful, therefore, lest we condemn one another unfairly, and do great harm to one another in our ignorance. It is important that, as Christians, we should realize that we are still in the body, that we carry the body with us, and that the interactions of these various parts are very intimate and very important.

The second error is the mistaking of the psychological for the spiritual. Under the heading of psychological I am including temperament, natural make-up that makes us what we are. There are different types of personality. We are not all alike, and we are not meant to be alike. But there are many who fail to realize this, and they fall into the error of thinking that the moment you become a Christian you should be identical with all other Christians. This is one of the most fruitful fields for the mani- festation of the wiles of the devil. We must approach this problem, I repeat, by realizing that we all have different types of personality, that that is how God made us. Secondly, we have to realize that when we are converted, when we are born again, our temperament remains exactly what it was before. A man's temperament is not changed when he is converted. If you imagine that when the Apostle Paul says, 'If any man be in Christ, he is a new creature; old things are passed away; behold, all things are become new' (2 Corinthians 5:17) he means that every Christian is identical with every other Christian, you are completely wrong. The fundamental elements in our personality and temperament are not changed by conversion and by re-birth. The 'new man' means the new disposition, the new understanding, the new orientation, but the man himself, psychologically, is essentially what he was before.

Certain people, by birth, by nature, and by temperament, belong to a depressed type; some are mercurial; others are phlegmatic. Some people are lively and animated, some are very slow. You are aware of these differences as you encounter them. There are differences also between nationalities. It is simply a fact that some people are born with a depressed and melancholic type of temperament. I came across an interesting statement con- cerning this recently in a letter written by William Cowper, the poet, to his friend William Unwin, about the Rev William Bull, who was for many years a congregational minister in Newport Pagnell. Cowper living a short distance away at Olney became a great friend of Bull. Soon after they met, Cowper wrote to Unwin about him. He said that Bull was a man who had a marvellous imagination, and that when his imagination ran freely his conversation was most scintillating, brilliant, interesting and entertaining. But, he added, on the other hand, that he

[211]

seemed to have 'a delicate sort of melancholy in his disposition, not less agreeable in its way'. Cowper goes on to philosophize and says, 'Every scene of life has two sides – a dark and a bright one'. And then he makes this statement: 'The mind that has an equal mixture of melancholy and vivacity is best of all qualified for the contemplation of either'. That is, to me, a most important and significant statement. Every scene in life has the two sides, there is the dark side and the bright; therefore the best type of nature, says William Cowper, is the man who has that sort of mind which is an equal mixture of melancholia and vivacity. Not only vivacity, not only melancholia, but a man who partakes of both. The Rev William Bull had a little of each of them, and as you read his biography it is very interesting to see how the melancholic side took charge now and again, and poor William Bull was in great trouble about the condition of his soul. He did not realize what was true about himself. Cowper, looking at Bull, could see it in his friend, but, as I am about to show, could not see it in himself. Thus both of them were strongly attacked by the devil and found themselves in trouble. William Bull did not realize the truth about his own temperament; hence at times he attributed what was purely temperamental to that which is spiritual.

I do not hesitate to speculate that this was probably the greatest problem that the mighty Apostle Paul ever had to face, because he conforms, beyond any doubt, to that description of the highest type of personality and character as defined by William Cowper. We see in him vivacity, enthusiasm, eloquence. And how he gets carried away! But then he has indicated clearly in passages in 2 Corinthians, chapter 7, and 2 Corinthians, chapter 12, that he was often tempted by depression. 'Without were fightings, within were fears.' He was a sensitive man, a highly-strung man, a man who could be depressed. He was hurt by the Corinthians – demanding, expecting love of them, but not always getting it; and depressed when he did not get it.

He was once Saul of Tarsus but when he became the Apostle of Christ, his temperament had not changed. As a persecutor of the Church he was violent beyond all others. Paul was always at the top in every sphere of activity; as a student at the feet of Gamaliel he was always head of the list. He tells us that, as regards conformity to details of the law, he surpassed all his contemporaries and countrymen; in his zeal he persecuted the Church beyond all others. When he became an Apostle, the same characteristics still show themselves. He did not suddenly become a quiet preacher. He preached with all the intensity of his mighty emotional nature. He weeps, he tells us; and at times had fears within, and was cast down. The man's temperament is exactly what it was; the zeal with which he persecuted is the same zeal with which he now preaches. The temperament remains a constant. But it is very difficult at times to remember this. And so, when for some reason or another – partly physical perhaps, or perhaps due to overwork – the vivacious side slows down, and the melancholic side tends to take over, we imagine that we are in bad and sad spiritual condition.

To deal with this we have first to recognize the fact. We have to get to know ourselves, for, if you do not know yourself, the devil will very soon get you into trouble along this line. You have got to know your temperament and the sort of person you are. And having acquired that knowledge, you have always to be on guard and to watch. You have to realize that there are these differences, and that the devil is always ready to attack you in respect of them. Above all – and this is to me the important rule – you have to realize that, although you still have the same temperament that you always had, as a Christian you must not become its victim.

The natural man is the victim of, and controlled by, his temperament. That is why, so often, others find it difficult to live with him. He cannot control his temper; he forgives and forgets in a moment, and does not realize the damage he has done during his bouts of passion. As for the Christian, his temperament is not changed; but he can control his temperament, and should control his temperament, and must control his temperament. He recognizes what it is; therefore he watches it and is on guard against it. He does not allow the devil to come in and make him think that his problems are always purely spiritual. So you must not be a victim of your temperament, and must be careful of the wiles of the devil at this particular point.

We can go one step further and assert that sometimes the problem is not merely a matter of temperament but becomes actually a case of psychological disease. William Cowper is perhaps the classic instance of this. He was subject to, and suffered from periodic attacks of melancholia, a psychological condition. But he did not know his condition. We learn from the hymn in which he asks, 'Where is the blessedness I knew when first I saw the Lord?' that he thought his problem was spiritual. He was in an agony of soul, and felt at times that God had deserted him. It was entirely due to this diseased condition of his mind.

There have been many similar cases. Thomas Shepard, a great Puritan in the United States of America three hundred years ago, undoubtedly suffered from the same condition. He did not know it, and he used to lash himself about his spiritual condition, when it is quite clear that he was suffering one of his periodic attacks of depression. I do not elaborate, because at that point the sufferer really needs the expert help of someone who understands a little about all this, a wise physician, for the trouble may be purely medical. I only say that it is important to draw these distinctions, to recognize them, and to make sure that you are not allowing the devil to get you into an agony concerning your spiritual condition when it can all be explained in terms of the physical or the psychological.

But if there are some who are in trouble because they mistake the physical and the psychological for the spiritual, there are others who do the exact opposite and mistake the spiritual for the physical. Unfortunately this is becoming more and more common in Christian circles. I am dealing now with the tendency to evade spiritual problems by explaining them away in terms of the psychological or the purely physical. What amazes me most of all is that it has become rampant in the evangelical section of the Church. Psychology and psychiatry have had a great vogue among evangelical people in the last thirty years. Articles have appeared in certain religious periodicals along these lines and many are thinking in these terms.

Let me illustrate by telling a story. One Sunday night about fifteen years ago a young man came in to see me at the close of a service, looking very agitated and distressed. He said, 'I wonder whether you can help me. Can you recommend to me a Christian psychologist?' I asked him, 'Why do you need to see a psychologist?' He then told me his story. He had been a baker in the West of England. An evangelist had been in his town on a ten days' mission, and this young man, having a good voice, had become the soloist in the mission. At its close the evangelist turned to him and said, 'Have you ever thought of going in for full-time work? You have got a gift, you know.' 'But I cannot speak,' said the man. 'Ah,' said the evangelist, 'you only need a little bit of training; with that voice of yours you would make a fine evangelist.' So he told him that he could have training at a college which had recently been opened for that very purpose, and strongly recommended him to go there. So the young man had gone to the college. He said to me, 'I discovered in the first week that I could never do it. I could not follow the lectures. I had never been taught how to take notes. I left school at a very early age, I really could not do it.' However, he thought he must not give in, and so he persisted. But by the second week he was quite certain that he was making a big mistake, and that he would never be able to pass the examinations and become an evangelist. So he went to see the Principal of the College and told him all this, and that he felt he would like to resign and go back to his work. The first thing the Principal said to him was, 'You need to see a psychologist'. So the young man had come to see me, wanting to know if I could recommend him to a Christian psychologist! My reply to the young man was this: 'My dear friend, you do not need to see a psychologist. If ever you needed to see one, it was when you went to the College. But by now you have come to yourself. Go back to your work as a baker and go on bearing your Christian witness and testimony as you have been doing in the past.' But the Principal's advice had been, 'You need to see a psychologist'. He thought that the young man was not balanced, and was unstable and changeable. He could not see that the young man had been given the wrong advice at the beginning. There was no psychological problem at all. It was a pure matter of spiritual understanding, indeed common sense. The young man should never have been taken out of his bakery. That was his work, that was his realm. He was, and would continue to be a fine Christian as a baker. The young man went home, and immediately got rid of all his troubles.

That was not by any means an uncommon experience. People

come and say, 'I would like to see a psychologist, can you recommend someone?' whereas, quite often, indeed generally, the problem is a purely spiritual one.

Sometimes the trouble is that the troubled ones have never been Christians at all. They think they have been converted, for they have 'taken a decision', and they have been told that they are Christians. But shortly they are in trouble, and a little conversation reveals that they have never really been Christians. They were either pressed to a decision, or they had some emotional experience which they mistook for conversion. But the good people who have been trying to help them regard them as Christians and have talked to them solely about sanctification, whereas they should have been talking to them about justification. If you talk to a man about sanctification only, when his great need is to be shown the way of justification, you will aggravate his troubles, and he will be in unutterable confusion. Make certain that these people are truly Christians. Make certain that they have a foundation, for if there is not a foundation, you cannot build on it.

Furthermore, you will find, very often, that even if such persons are Christians, their real trouble is that they have a very incomplete understanding of the truth. They have had an experience, but they have not been taught much, they have remained where they were as babes in Christ. Inevitably they get into trouble through the sheer lack of knowledge and of instruction. They need both, so do not send them to the psychologist; teach them the doctrines of the Bible, and you will find that what appeared at first sight to be a great psychological problem vanishes and disappears in a most amazing manner. Instruction in the way of righteousness, a grasp of the plan of salvation, an understanding of the doctrines, gives them complete deliverance. They have been turning in on themselves in this purely subjective, unhealthy state – always looking in and analysing – and all they need is to come to an understanding of the truth.

Sometimes the trouble is due entirely to a lack of self-discipline. Christian people have come to me and said, 'I need to see a psychologist, can you recommend one who is a Christian?' I say, 'What is the trouble?' 'Temper,' they say, 'I cannot control my temper.' What has happened is that the devil has said to them, 'The trouble with you is that you are a psychological case; you must go and have psychological treatment', whereas their problem is a purely spiritual one. (I am dealing, remember, with Christians.) When I am asked such a question I say, 'No, I recommend no Christian psychologist to you'. 'Well,' they ask, 'what do you tell me to do?' I say, 'Control your temper!' 'It is very difficult,' they say. 'Of course it is difficult,' I reply, 'have we not all got our difficulties? You are simply trying to get out of it by saying "I am a psychological case. I am not just an ordinary person with a bad temper. I must get some psychological help". In the meantime the devil is rejoicing because you have regarded what is a purely spiritual problem as if it were psychological. My friend, as a Christian you have no right to lose your temper. The New Testament Epistles tell you not to do so. Control yourself, "Let not the sun go down upon your wrath". Control your tongue. What a practical book the New Testament is! You need not rush off to the psychologist, medical or ministerial, or to the latest vogue; read your New Testament, discipline and control yourself.'

People come to me about other sins in exactly the same way. They say, 'I must be a psychological case, I am always falling to my particular sin. The temptation to it makes me tremble. Do you think I need some psychological help?' I reply, 'The Bible tells you that what you need is to "fight the good fight of faith" in a spiritual manner.' The whole tendency to evade the spiritual in terms of the psychological is rampant at the present time.

We turn next to the tendency to explain away sin altogether. The Wolfenden Report on homosexuality did just that! Moral perverts, we are told, are psychological cases and you must regard them as such. Then there is what is called today 'diminished responsibility'. Everything is being explained away in terms of diseased conditions or psychological states. But sin and disobedience cannot be explained away in these terms. It is a terrible and a horrible danger.

Finally, I call attention to the failure to apply the truth to our every condition. I remember a person coming to me because she said she had a horror and a phobia of thunder and lightning. She had suffered from it for twenty-three years, but now the thing had become acute, for the reason that she now practically never attended a place of worship, because of her fear. She would set out from her home to go to a service, and she would suddenly see a cloud. She would begin to think that it would soon become a thunder-cloud and that there would be a storm of thunder and lightning. She was so much afraid that she might break down in the Chapel and create a scene that she went home so as not to disgrace the Christian cause. She had been treated psychologically for her fears and had been given all sorts of advice, and had prayed for years that she might be delivered from them. It seemed to me that there was only one thing for this lady to do. It was to realize that she was a child of God, no more and no less a child of God than all the other Christians whom she knew. Why should she be more concerned about her life and her possible death in a thunderstorm than anyone else? If she were struck by lightning, would she cease to be a child of God? I told her to think, not about thunder and lightning, but about God as her Father, about His care for His children, and that she was disgracing God. What she must seek was not to be delivered from this particular fear, but to be a good Christian, a noble disciple, and to be worthy of God in every way. She must stop thinking psychologically, and think in a spiritual manner.

Some Christians suffer from claustrophobia, others from agoraphobia, others are frightened by storms, gales, and so on. The devil will try to get you to think that this is a purely psychological matter, and that you need psychological treatment. 'Resist him, steadfast in the faith,' and 'put on the whole armour of God'. Say, 'No! I am a child of God, and whatever happens to me I am in God's hands, and God will allow no harm to come to me ultimately. He has said, "I will never leave thee, nor forsake thee", so I must not give way to these fears. I am not going to fall back on the other kind of aid. I believe in the living God who is my Father in Christ Jesus.' You must apply your faith, you must face this thing and see that it is of the devil, and resist it, standing on your faith and applying the truth to your every need.

Two striking biblical examples illustrate my point. The first is in the Book of Ezra. Ezra and his people were about to return to Jerusalem from captivity in Chaldea, a long and dangerous journey. They were on the verge of asking king Artaxerxes for protection, when we find Ezra saying, 'For I was ashamed to require of the king a band of soldiers and horsemen to help us against the enemy in the way: because we had spoken to the king, saying, The hand of our God is upon all them for good that seek him' (Ezra 8:22). 'We cannot go back on that,' said Ezra in effect. We are certainly in a dangerous position and it is very alarming; but if we ask the king for a band of troops to protect us, we shall be letting God down. We have told the king that God protects His people; and on God's help we must rely.' 'So we fasted,' says the Book of Ezra, 'and besought our God for this: and he was intreated of us.' All was well.

The case of Nehemiah had similar features. The position was urgent, it was acute. The enemies were many and active. A false friend came to Nehemiah and said, 'You and I had better go and hide in the temple, then we shall be safe'. Nehemiah gave this immortal answer, 'Should such a man as I flee? And who is there that, being as I am, would go into the temple to save his life? I will not go in' (Nehemiah 6:11). That is the complete answer – 'Should such a man as I flee?' – a man of God, a child of God! Am I willing to escape into the temple in order to save my life? No! I prefer to die in open battle that God may be glorified in and through me. It is inconceivable; a man such as I must never flee. And you must use that way of thinking, whatever the particular form in which the enemy is attacking you at this moment. Do not flee at once to a psychologist! You are a Christian, and God can deal with your problems. Do not explain away spiritual problems in terms of the psychological or the physical only. The two extremes are wrong, both those of the first group and those of the second. The devil comes along all lines. Realize the truth about yourself, and 'take unto you the whole armour of God'. Such is the Christian teaching. It is true for you. Whatever comes to meet you, fight as a Christian, stand as a man, and 'having done all things, to stand'. 'Such a man as I.' Say that to yourself; and you will find that your problems will soon be solved. You will not need to escape in any one of the various directions that the devil in his subtlety and his wiles will be so ready to suggest to you. Thank God, I say once more, that we can 'be strong in the Lord, and in the power of his might'. Thank God for the Word, the understanding, the instruction, the enlightenment, the knowledge. Get hold of it, apply it, practise it in every realm and department of your life; and the wiles of the devil will not be able to confound you.

16

True and False Assurance

We now move on to the consideration of another aspect of the way in which the devil exercises his wiles with respect to our experience. I refer to troubles in connection with assurance of salvation, and we shall find that the wiles are manifested along exactly the same lines as we have already seen. The devil's method is always to produce confusion. He does that, as we have seen, by driving us from one extreme to another. We shall see this again exemplified as we now consider the question of the devil's attack upon our assurance of salvation.

All Christian people are meant to have assurance of salvation. God has not only provided a way whereby we can be saved, and not only saved us, but He lets us know that He has done so. This is a glorious aspect of the Christian life. The Christian is not meant to remain in doubt and uncertainty.

There are sections of the Church which dispute the doctrine of assurance. The Roman Catholic Church deliberately discourages it. Obviously, were she not to do so, there would not be so much need for the priesthood, and for the power of the Church and her authorities. She deliberately keeps her people in uncertainty about their condition in this life and in the next. So the Romanist has to go to the priest and confess; he needs indulgences; he prays for the dead, and so on. But that is a gross and a terrible travesty of the New Testament teaching.

In a sense, the New Testament teaching is more concerned about this great matter of assurance than about anything else. It is the theme of many of the Epistles. As just one example, take John's First Epistle: 'These things have I written unto you that believe on the name of the Son of God; that ye may know that ye have eternal life, and that ye may believe on the name of the Son of God' (1 John 5:13). We are meant to have assurance, we are meant to know certainty.

This is so for obvious reasons. It is God's will for us to be able to pray with confidence and with assurance. The prayer of the Christian believer is not meant to be uncertain. He is not vaguely seeking and groping after God. In the Epistle to the Hebrews you will find that one of its greatest themes is just this matter of assurance in prayer. 'Let us therefore,' says the author, 'come boldly unto the throne of grace' – 'boldly', with confidence, with assurance – 'that we may obtain mercy, and find grace to help in time of need' (Hebrews 4:16). He speaks similarly in chapter 10: 'Having, therefore, brethren, boldness to enter into the holiest by the blood of Jesus, by a new and living way, which he hath consecrated for us, through the veil, that is to say, his flesh; and having an high priest over the house of God; let us draw near with a true heart in full assurance of faith, having our hearts sprinkled from an evil conscience, and our bodies washed with pure water' (Hebrews 10:19–22). That is the way to pray. The Christian is meant to pray with confidence, and with full assurance of faith. He is a child going to his Father, not uncertainly, not hesitatingly, but with boldness, with this great assurance and confidence.

In addition the Christian is meant to know peace and joy. Take again that First Epistle of John, at the very beginning in the first chapter. He says, 'These things write we unto you, that your joy may be full' (verse 4). Here is the old Apostle at the end of his very long life, writing in the knowledge that he will shortly die, and considering the welfare of the Christians whom he is leaving behind in the world. He says that he is writing to them in order that they may have fellowship with him, which fellowship is indeed with the Father, and with His Son. But he writes to them, not only that they may have this fellowship, but also that their joy might be full. Even in a world like this their joy is meant to be 'full'. The Apostle Paul writes in a similar way to the Philippians: 'Rejoice in the Lord alway: and again I say, Rejoice'

(4:4). That is meant to be the experience of Christian people; not only saved, but knowing that we are saved, realizing it, and rejoicing in it 'with joy unspeakable and full of glory' (1 Peter 1:8).

This being the case, it is not surprising that the devil pays particular attention to this aspect of the Christian's experience. Anyone who has any pastoral experience will know that a greater number of problems arise just at this point than perhaps in any other connection. The devil has a wonderful field here, and he makes full use of it in the exercise of his wiles. That is why so much of the New Testament is devoted to this particular question. The apostles were anxious that these Christian people should be enjoying the fruits of this great salvation. But the early Christians were often in trouble, and they therefore needed these exhortations. These great expositions of doctrine followed by the exhortations are all designed to give the assurance and joy of salvation – peace and joy and happiness in Christ Jesus.

The space given to this subject in the New Testament is proof positive, in and of itself, of the wiles of the devil in this respect. From first to last his aim is to rob Christians of this glorious aspect of their salvation. The New Testament, however, comes to their aid, and teaches them how to counter and defeat the devil. They are even given the promise that Satan will shortly be bruised under their feet (Romans 16:20).

There are certain books which deal with the theme of assurance in a particularly helpful manner. Possibly the greatest of them is *A Treatise concerning Religious Affections*, written by Jonathan Edwards, the great American divine of two hundred years ago. It is one of the most masterly analyses of the true and the false in this matter of peace and assurance that has ever been written; it is incomparable. Another is by Richard Sibbes, one of the Puritans of three hundred years ago, who was known in London, where he preached, as 'The heavenly Doctor Sibbes'. They applied that term to him, not only because he seemed to have an unusual knowledge of the glories that await us, but also because he was such a wonderful physician of the soul. He published a book of sermons called *The Soul's Conflict*. It has been a healing balm to many a distressed soul. Sibbes has another book called *The Bruised Reed,* along the same lines: all his works are designed to comfort and to strengthen God's people. Indeed most of the

[223]

Puritans were experts on this very subject. They were always applying scriptural cordials, spiritual balms, to the wounded, to the grieved soul. For example, listen to these words from another great Puritan, Thomas Brooks:

'Such is Satan's envy and enmity against a Christian's joy and comfort, that he cannot but act to the utmost of his line to keep poor souls in doubt and darkness. Satan knows that assurance is a pearl of that price that will make the soul happy for ever; he knows that assurance makes a Christian's wilderness to be a paradise; he knows that assurance begets in Christians the most noble and generous spirits; he knows that assurance is that which will make men strong to do exploits, to shake his tottering kingdom about his ears; and therefore he is very studious and industrious to keep souls off from assurance, as he was to cast Adam out of paradise.'*

How then does the devil deal with us in this matter? How does he exercise his wiles in connection with this whole question of assurance? The first thing he does is to try to give us a false assurance, a false rest, a false peace, and a false joy. Obviously if he can delude any of us with the counterfeit, he is going to keep the true from us; and that is one of his favourite wiles. He comes to the Christian and offers him something which appears on the surface to be true Christian peace and joy and happiness and rest; but on closer analysis in the light of the Scripture, and in experience itself, eventually it turns out to be nothing but a horrid counterfeit, something false and spurious.

An example of this is found in the Book of Revelation, concerning the church of the Laodiceans: 'Unto the angel of the church of the Laodiceans write; These things saith the Amen, the faithful and true witness, the beginning of the creation of God; I know thy works, that thou art neither cold nor hot: I would thou wert cold or hot. So then because thou art lukewarm, and neither cold nor hot, I will spue thee out of my mouth. Because thou sayest, I am rich, and increased with goods, and have need of nothing; and knowest not that thou art wretched, and miserable, and poor, and blind, and naked' (3:14–17). You cannot

* Thomas Brooks, in *Heaven on Earth*. Banner of Truth, 1961 reprint p. 130.

better that description of a church, or body of Christian people, who have succumbed to the wiles of the devil in this particular respect. They were perfectly self-satisfied, and felt they were rich; everything seemed to them to be going well; they needed nothing at all; and yet they were in a terrible and tragic condition.

Clearly the church at Corinth was also subject to this same temptation. The Apostle, addressing them in the first Epistle, chapter 5, says: 'It is reported commonly that there is fornication among you, and such fornication as is not so much as named among the Gentiles, that one should have his father's wife. And ye are puffed up, and have not rather mourned, that he that hath done this deed might be taken away from among you.' They were 'puffed up' in spite of this; everything seemed to them to be in order; there was no trouble. They had a false peace, a false rest, a false joy. There is a hint of the same thing in the Second Epistle to the Corinthians, where Paul urges them: 'Examine yourselves, whether ye be in the faith; prove your own selves' (13:5). Obviously the Apostle would not have used such language were it not that he had grave reasons for thinking that there was something seriously wrong with the life of that church.

What is the cause of the condition in which a Christian believer, a professor of the Christian faith, is of the opinion that all is well, and seems to have a great and wonderful assurance? One of the chief causes is that somehow or other he has been ushered into the Christian life too precipitately. This condition is commonest in people whose conversion has been forced. It is the result of a mere intellectual assent to truth without the knowledge of the power of the truth. There is a type of evangelism which urges people to say, 'Here it is, this is what Scripture says. Are you prepared to say you agree to it?' 'Yes!' 'Very good, you are a Christian, all is well.' Now there is a sense in which that can be correct as a statement of justification by faith, but there is another sense in which it can be the greatest of all dangers. The mere repetition of statements and of formulae does not necessarily prove that we are Christians. 'The devils also believe, and tremble' (James 2:19). There were people in the early Church who had once made all the correct affirmations. Consider what John tells us in the First Epistle. There were certain people, he says, who had 'gone out from among us', and by going out they had given proof positive that they 'were not all of us', that is to say, 'they were not really of us' (1 John 2:19). But they had been in the Church, and they would never have been accepted in the early Church, which was very careful about these matters, unless they had subscribed to the truth. They had agreed with all the statements, and yet they had 'gone out', proving, says John, that they were never truly Christian at all. But at first they gave every outward appearance of being right. All their statements were correct; they seemed to be perfectly orthodox, and for a while they seemed to rejoice in it. A similar state of things is mentioned in the early verses of the sixth chapter of the Epistle to the Hebrews, where we find people not only saying the right things, but also 'tasting of the heavenly gift, and the powers of the world to come'; and yet the writer shows quite clearly that they had never been regenerate. But they gave the appearance of being Christian. Undoubtedly the most prolific cause of this happening is that men and women are hurried and forced to confess to the truth before they really possess it, and before it becomes a part of them.

Let us, then, examine the characteristics of this dangerous condition in order that we may avoid it. In the first place, what is wrong with such a person is that there has really been no radical change in the life; indeed, no new life. There has been a modification of the old life, but that alone does not make a Christian. A Christian is not a man who has modified his old life; he is a man who is born again, and has new life. There is a new principle in him, a new dynamic, a new disposition placed there by the Spirit of God. That is what makes a man a Christian!

The danger arises because the change can be counterfeited, can be simulated, as an artificial flower is sometimes almost indistinguishable from a living flower. For some reason or another a man may have become unhappy in his life, and his conscience may be worrying him. He comes across the Christian message and he adopts it. He puts a curb upon what was wrong in his life, and conforms to a new pattern and a new way of life. He does it all by an effort of the will. And that can be done up to a certain point; there is nothing to stop it. Moral men live by the use of their will-power and their understanding. So a man may modify his life to such a considerable extent that, looking at it casually, you would say that he is an exceptionally fine Christian. Yet that man may not be a Christian at all!

The difference between the true and the false is the difference between having a principle of life within you at the centre which controls everything, on the one hand, and just adding something to what you have, or producing a modification of what you are on the surface, and on the surface only, on the other hand. It is a difficult and a subtle matter; but we are dealing with 'the wiles of the devil' who of all the manufacturers of artificial products is the greatest artist and the greatest expert; and he has caused endless confusion in the Church throughout the centuries by doing this very thing. He has confused individuals in the same way.

The vital question we must ask ourselves, therefore, is: Am I aware of something entirely new within me? Am I aware of being controlled and mastered by something, or rather by Someone, not myself? Can I say in any degree, 'I live, yet not I, but Christ liveth in me'? Am I aware of the divine Person that is in me? Can I say, 'And the life I now live in the flesh, I live by the faith of the Son of God, who loved me and gave himself for me' (Galatians 2:20)? Are you aware of the fact that something has been done to you? Not that you have done something, not that you have been modifying what you were, or what you had, or what you have. Are you aware that, down in the depth of your being, God has done something, and has put something into you? Can you say, 'We are his workmanship, created anew in Christ Jesus' (Ephesians 2:10)? Can you say, I am an 'epistle of Christ, written not with ink, but with the spirit of the living God; not in tables of stone, but in fleshy tables of the heart' (2 Corinthians 3:2, 3)? This is the one differentiating criterion. And if a man is honest with himself he is able to tell the difference.

Another test arises from the fact that the person whose profession of Christ is false and spurious is never troubled about himself in any way. Like those in the church of Laodicea, he is full, rich, having everything, never unhappy about himself at all, never having any question about himself, never disturbed about himself. This is a very searching test. The devil always makes one blunder, which is always the blunder made by the forger or by the manufacturer of the counterfeit; he overdoes things. The kind of person who has been rushed into a false 'conversion', and who has a false peace and a false joy, never has any problems or difficulties at all, and cannot understand all this of which we are speaking. William Cowper's hymn containing the lines, 'Where is the blessedness I knew, When first I saw the Lord?' is meaningless to them. It is all foreign to them, indeed it is ridiculous to some of them, and they cannot understand why people should ever have written such books as *The Soul's Conflict* and *A Treatise concerning Religious Affections*, or some of Bunyan's works. They do not understand because they have never met with problems that faced the pilgrims in *Pilgrim's Progress*. 'Ah,' they say, 'from the moment I believed I have never had any trouble.' They have never been aware of any difficulty. They have never been troubled by the consciousness of a sinful nature; they do not know what it is to feel that there is 'another law in their members' dragging them down. They are never in any difficulty about themselves.

There is nothing more alarming than this kind of 'Euphoria', as it is called in medical terms. There are certain diseases which give a kind of euphoria; the person does not know that he is ill, he feels remarkably well. That is the characteristic of some diseases, and it is certainly the characteristic of this particular spiritual disease. The false and spurious type are remarkably happy and well; they have never felt so well; never were things so good with them; never has any trouble come to them at all. In other words they are very unlike the Apostle Paul and the writers of the New Testament, who were aware of problems within themselves, and especially in the body. The Apostle Paul had to 'keep under his body', but these people never have any such trouble; they do not understand the Apostle's language. It has all been wonderful ever since they believed. It is a contrast not only to the New Testament teaching, but to the experiences of God's saints throughout the centuries, who have had great troubles in their fight against 'the world, the flesh and the devil'. The presence or absence of spiritual problems is a very good and subtle test therefore.

Another manifestation of their spurious Christianity is that these people always have a great dislike of self-examination. They tell us that we must not engage in it; it is a 'looking in'; and if we indulge in it we are simply going to make ourselves miserable. They say, 'Look to the Lord; look out, don't look in at all, never examine yourself in any way'. A violent objection to self-examination is always a sure indication that the experience is false and spurious, because the New Testament is full of exhortations to us to examine ourselves, to prove our own selves, to make certain of our position. We are constantly being warned against the false – false spirits, false apostles, and falseness in ourselves. But the deceived ones dislike such warnings, for they have a feeling that if they start examining themselves they are going to be made miserable. It is like a man who is ill and who will not go to see a doctor. 'Ah no,' he says, 'if I go to the doctor he will make me stay in bed, or he will suggest an operation.' So instead he tries to persuade himself that all is well. What utter folly that is, in every realm! It happens very often in the spiritual realm. In other words, the trouble with this kind of person is that he or she is always too healthy – no difficulties, no problems, no doubts! They say, 'What are all these morbid people talking or writing about? They talk nonsense; there is something wrong, they are not healthy-minded.' I answer, that if a person thinks or says such things he or she is contradicting the teaching of the New Testament.

The next test is the presence of some form of Antinomianism; which means that the life of these people does not correspond to their great claims. They claim to be rejoicing in their salvation, without troubles, without problems. All is peace and joy; all is well. Surely we are entitled to expect an unusual type of spiritual behaviour from such persons. If people are in such a relationship to God that there are no difficulties or problems, you have a right to expect them to be exceptionally shining and glorious examples of self-control and of self-discipline. In every respect they should be models of what the Christian man ought to be. But you will generally find that the very opposite is the case. There are obvious, glaring defects in their lives; they do not correspond to what they claim to be.

In other words the false is always lacking in the marks and the characteristics of the true. The man who has true peace and joy and a real assurance is never glib, is never light-hearted. There was no man, possibly, who had a greater assurance of salvation

[229]

than the Apostle Paul; but he is never glib, never light-hearted. Can you imagine his being frivolous? Can you imagine his saying these things with a swagger? Never! Indeed in his Epistles, and especially when he writes to young men like Timothy and Titus, he says that even the young men are to be 'grave', and 'sober', and serious. That, of course, should be obvious because the truth itself is so great and glorious. It concerns our relationship to God. A man who is glib in his talk about God is virtually telling us that he knows nothing about God. Job is one who fell into that trap for a while. But when he came back to God the first thing he did was to put his hand upon his mouth, and to say, I spoke foolishly. His wife had spoken still more foolishly. Ignorant woman that she was, she did not know what she was talking about. There is never any glibness or light-heartedness about the true Christian who has a real and a genuine assurance.

Again, the true, as distinct from the false, is always filled with a sense of wonder and of amazement and of surprise. In other words the true Christian does not say, 'Of course I am saved!' He says, 'It is an amazing thing that I should be saved at all. How did the Almighty God ever bring Himself to look upon me?' 'I,' says Paul, 'am the least of the apostles, that am not worthy to be called an apostle, because I persecuted the church of God.' 'Last of all he (Christ) was seen of me also, as of one born out of due time.' 'The Son of God, who loved me' – even me! – 'and gave himself for me.' Paul cannot get over this; he is amazed at it, he is astonished at it. And anyone who realizes something of what salvation means must be filled with this same astonishment. There is none of the light-hearted glibness which says, 'I am saved and all is well'. On the contrary, the one truly saved says, 'A most astounding thing has happened; the great and eternal and almighty God in His holiness has found a way to forgive me'. That is how Charles Wesley felt when he wrote:

> *And can it be, that I should gain*
> *An interest in the Saviour's blood?*
> *Died He for me, who caused His pain?*
> *For me, who Him to death pursued?*
> *Amazing love! how can it be*
> *That Thou, my God, shouldst die for me?*

And Isaac Watts thus describes his experience:

> *When I survey the wondrous Cross,*
> *On which the Prince of glory died,*
> *My richest gain I count but loss,*
> *And pour contempt on all my pride.*

And if, in your peace and joy and rest, there is not this element of astonishment and amazement that you are what you are, you should examine yourself and look at the very foundation again.

The next characteristic of the person truly saved always is – humility! What a neglected grace is this grace of humility! We are living in an age which believes in the cult of personality – self-confidence, assurance. It is the antithesis of the New Testament which teaches 'Blessed are the meek' and 'Blessed are the poor in spirit'. Listen to the words used of our Lord Himself: 'The bruised reed he will not break; the smoking flax he will not quench.' He, the Son of God, 'humbled himself'. See it also in His followers. Look at it in many mighty men, with their genius, their flaming intellects, their wonderful understanding. Look at it in the Apostle Paul. Examine the lives of the saints of the centuries and you will find that all the churches are agreed about this, the church of Rome included. There is no greater 'mark' of the true saint than humility. So if there is not this element in our peace and joy; if, on the contrary, it is characterized by boastfulness and self-confidence and glibness, it is not genuine. Indeed, it is the horrible counterfeit, the artifice the devil manufactures.

By way of a final test, the true stands in complete contrast with the Laodicean characteristics – resting upon your oars, self-satisfied, and feeling you have nothing to do but to maintain what you are. Rather is it described in the words, 'Blessed are they that do hunger and thirst after righteousness: for they shall be filled'. The more a man has, the more he realizes what he has not got, and the more he desires to have. This is always the hallmark of the true Christian – a sense of dissatisfaction with what he has. He is not satisfied, he always wants more. The classic account of such an experience is found in the writings of the Apostle Paul. If ever there was a man in the Christian Church who had a right to be satisfied with himself it was Paul – in understanding, in knowledge, in ability to expound, in experiences that had been given to him. Yet he speaks thus: 'Brethren, I count not myself to have apprehended: but this one thing I do, forgetting those things which are behind, and reaching forth unto those things which are before, I press toward the mark for the prize of the high calling of God in Christ Jesus' (Philippians 3:13, 14). Here we find the characteristic of the true saint. He is not self-satisfied and content, and resting on what he is or has. He thanks God for what He has given him, but he can see the vast ocean spreading away endlessly beyond horizons that he cannot even imagine, and feels he is but a little child paddling on the edge of it all. So he wants to press on and to press forward. His ambition is, 'That I may know him, and the power of his resurrection, and the fellowship of his sufferings, being made conformable unto his death' (Philippians 3:10). 'Not as though I had already attained, but I follow after', always 'pressing toward the mark', going on, conscious of deficiencies and unworthiness, realizing how much more there is to possess.

But the people with the false peace know nothing about this; their belief is that really there is nothing to be added; they have got everything, they have arrived. Is it not obvious that this is nothing but the horrible, ugly, foul counterfeit of the evil one?

The first thing then that the devil tries to do is to keep us from a true assurance, and from a real peace and joy and rest, by offering us and giving us the counterfeit. And as long as we have the false we will not seek anything else. The Laodiceans were not seeking anything; that is why the Apostle as the messenger of Christ has to speak to them in such strong language. 'I counsel thee', 'I urge upon you', 'I plead with you', 'Do it at once'. 'You must buy this gold, you must find new raiment, you are altogether wrong; you have no idea of your condition. I urge you, I counsel you . . .'

But the devil does not leave it at that. He first tries to get us into this state of quiescence, into this drugged condition, by giving us the counterfeit; but if he fails in this respect, he has not finished; he then changes his tactics completely. He turns from one extreme to its exact opposite, he will change his tactics, he will change his colours as a chameleon, he will spare no effort in order to bring down God's people.

At this point he begins to appear as 'the accuser of the

brethren', as 'our adversary the devil'. Having tried to make people think that they are wonderful Christians, he turns right round and says that they are not Christians at all. He now sifts you, and tries you and examines you; he who before discouraged you from self-examination will now begin to examine you, and will force upon you a self-examination which is so extreme that you will doubt whether you have ever been a Christian at all. He will shake you, he will try to bring you right down; he will try to move the foundation under your feet. He becomes 'the accuser of the brethren', 'the adversary'.

As we begin to consider this aspect of the wiles of the devil, we remind ourselves that there is one thing, thank God, which the devil cannot do; he cannot rob us of our salvation. That is an utter impossibility. We are in the hands of God, we are 'His workmanship', 'no man (or devil) shall be able to pluck us out of his hands'. If we are not clear about this doctrine, we are already defeated by the devil. The devil can never rob anyone of his salvation! If he could, he would do so and no one would be saved. The devil is 'the strong man armed', as our Lord says in the figure he uses in the Gospels. And as 'the strong man armed', he keeps 'his goods in peace' and men cannot get out of his clutches. 'But when a stronger than he shall come upon him, and overcome him, he taketh from him all his armour wherein he trusted' and sets the goods at liberty. If that were not true there would never have been a Christian, there would be no such thing as a saved, redeemed person. We, all of us, have to be taken out of the clutches of the devil. The Lord Jesus Christ has done that, and the devil can never get us back. If he could, we would all go back. But he cannot. The Apostle John is very explicit about this – and it is a most comforting thought – in his First Epistle, chapter 5. In verse 18 we read, 'We know that whosoever is born of God sinneth not' – he does not go on sinning, he does not remain in the realm and the territory and the dominion of sin – 'but he that is begotten of God keepeth himself, and that wicked one toucheth him not'. He cannot clutch him, he cannot hold him! 'And we know that we are of God, and the whole world lieth in the wicked one.'

This is the comfort, the final comfort; this is a vital part of the whole armour of God. The devil can never rob us of our salvation; he can rob us of the peace that accompanies salvation; he can take from us the rest that is meant to be the portion of the people of God. And it is precisely at this point that he exercises all his ingenuity and manifests his subtle wiles. He knows he cannot get us back into his kingdom, so there is only one thing to do. 'Very well,' he says, 'they belong to the Lord and not to me. What I will do is to make them miserable, I will make them wretched, I will rob them of the joy of what He has done for them'. So he begins to exercise his wiles.

If you are in any doubt as to the wiles of the devil in this respect ask yourself certain questions. Are you enjoying assurance of salvation at this moment? Can you say of yourself what the Apostle Peter says to those unknown Christians in the first century: 'Whom having not seen, ye love; in whom, though now ye see him not, yet believing, ye rejoice with joy unspeakable and full of glory' (1 Peter 1:8)? Is that true of you? Peter was not writing about himself, he was not writing about the other Apostles. He was writing about unnamed Christians, 'strangers scattered abroad'. He did not know their names. All he knew was that they were Christians, and because they were Christians, his words were true of them. Are they true of us? Is your joy 'full', as John says it should be, and as it might be? If it is not, it is because of the wiles of the devil. You can be a Christian and yet lack assurance. You are saved, but you may not know it, because of the wiles of the devil. He can rob you of the joy, the happiness, and the power of salvation. He cannot rob you of the salvation. Often he has brought the Christians into a state of misery, as if they were not Christians at all, by his horrible wiles!

17

Attacks Upon Assurance (1)

In considering the devil's attacks upon us in the realm of assurance of salvation we have seen how he sometimes tries to delude us by giving us a false, spurious counterfeit sense of assurance. We now move on to look at the way in which he tries to shake our assurance in various ways. We laid down a proposition which is most important, namely, that the devil cannot rob us of our salvation, try as he will. But while he cannot rob us of the salvation itself he can most certainly rob us of the joy of salvation, that is, of the enjoyment of the salvation. Hence it is possible for us to be Christians and yet not to be really happy. It is the explanation of the so-called miserable Christian. There are people who say that there is no such thing as a miserable Christian. The simple answer is that there is; and it is the wiles of the devil that produce such a condition. It therefore behoves us to examine this matter.

The first way we must consider is the one I have already hinted at in passing; the devil causes us to query the very possibility of assurance. There are many claiming to be Christians who have never had assurance of salvation because they do not even believe in the possibility of it; they say that it cannot happen. The Roman Catholic Church, for instance, denies the possibility of attaining real assurance, as I mentioned very briefly in the previous chapter. She says that no person can be assured that he is going to heaven while in this life and world. It is part of her misunderstanding of the Gospel and it fits perfectly into her whole complicated system. It means that the church member is always dependent upon the priesthood, that he has always to confess his sins to priests. The confessional is brought in, and all that accompanies that, and indulgences, prayers for the dead, and so on. It means, also, that we need the help of the saints and therefore pray to them. Even when he dies his fate is still uncertain. He has to go to a place called Purgatory, and while there prayers by the Church on earth have to be offered for him, candles have to be lit, and payment has to be made to the Church. Of course, you are assured that ultimately the Church will arrange final salvation, but uncertainty as to salvation continues while you are in this world. The entire teaching and practice of Rome does away with the doctrine of assurance. It is, indeed, the key to the understanding of that utter travesty of the Christian Church as she is depicted in the New Testament. It is obvious that if you believe that kind of teaching you will never have assurance; and the result is that you will always be more or less unhappy and miserable.

But this teaching, unfortunately, is not confined to the Roman Catholic Church; there are Protestants, and some of them very good Protestants, who tend to hold the same teaching. They do so for the reason that they regard assurance as presumption. They say, 'Who am I to say that I am a child of God, and that I am saved? I am so unworthy, I am aware of so much blackness and evil in myself. Surely,' they say, 'this is presumption.' I have known some very godly people, some of them very active workers in the Christian Church, who have been in this position. They have regarded it as almost sinful to claim assurance of salvation. I have known devout Christians who regarded the claim to assurance of salvation as the hall-mark of superficiality and ignorance of doctrine. For different reasons the Barthian teaching is also opposed to the teaching of assurance.

If the devil can succeed in making us think along these lines, he has obviously already achieved his end and object, and he will easily keep us in a fearful, unhappy state – sometimes up, sometimes down, probably more down than up, and almost afraid to be happy. Indeed, he can press this point, and has done so very often, to this extent, that in a sense your only assurance of salvation lies in the fact that you are miserable! I am not exaggerating. I could give chapter and verse for it. There have been sections of the Church that have been so much afraid of false joy that they have gone to the other extreme and, as I say – ridiculous though it is and sounds – they have a kind of contentment only when they have felt utterly miserable and complete failures.

The answer to such ideas is the teaching of the New Testament itself which exhorts us to gain assurance. John says to us in his First Epistle, chapter 5, verse 13: 'These things have I written unto you that believe on the name of the Son of God; that ye may know that ye have eternal life'. That you *may know* it! The Apostle Paul exhorts: 'Rejoice in the Lord alway: and again I say, Rejoice'. We are not meant to rejoice in ourselves, and if we look inwards we cannot do so. We are to 'rejoice in the Lord'. Ultimately this is a matter of understanding clearly the doctrine of justification by faith alone. It is the bringing in of works in some shape or form that accounts for this failure to realize that the Christian is meant to rejoice. As a well-known hymn of Isaac Watts puts it so well:

> *The men of grace have found*
> *Glory begun below;*
> *Celestial fruit on earthly ground*
> *From faith and hope may grow.*

We are meant to be a rejoicing people as we are 'marching to Zion', but if we give the impression that to be Christian is to be miserable, despondent and unhappy, we shall not succeed in attracting other people to the Lord Jesus Christ and to God. So the devil naturally makes great use of this wrong teaching, and he does so especially with the most conscientious people, for they are the very people who are afraid of making a false claim and of bringing the Gospel into disrepute. 'What if I should say that I am saved,' they say, 'and then someone sees something wrong in me?' But that is an altogether false argument. The Apostle describes the members of the church, even at Corinth, as 'saints'. And they were! They had been separated unto God, and were His children, though they were guilty of some very grievous sins. We must beware therefore of the snare of the devil at this point and not allow him to entrap us and bring us into a state of confusion.

A second stratagem or manifestation of the devil's wiles is that he tries to persuade us to believe the exact opposite of what we have just been considering, namely, that you cannot be a Christian at all if you do not have assurance of salvation. Again we see that the devil's method, his principle of operation, is always the same; it is to take Christians from one extreme right over to the other. The devil is always to be found at the extremes. So when we have escaped from his suggestion that assurance of salvation is impossible, he now argues on this other side and says, 'If you have not got assurance you are not a Christian at all!'

Here is a matter concerning which we have to be very careful. Even the Protestant Reformers, one feels, fell into this trap to a certain extent and at certain points. It is not at all difficult to understand why they did so. It was, of course, their reaction against the Roman Catholic teaching to which I have been referring. They were anxious to bring out the faith principle, and the fact that justification is by faith only. They said that a person does not have to wait until he is absolutely perfect before he knows that he is a child of God, and that he is saved. Consider the case of Martin Luther. As a monk he was unhappy, because he felt that he was not good enough; he could not be sure that he was a Christian until he had got rid of every sin; indeed, until he had not only ceased to commit acts of sin, but until the very desire for sin had left him. The Roman Catholic Church had taught him that he must be completely sanctified, absolutely perfect, before he was entitled to this assurance. But, suddenly, the Holy Spirit opened his eyes to this glorious New Testament teaching, 'The just shall live by faith.' He saw that this righteousness of God is given through faith, and that it is something which can be received immediately. At once he was liberated, and simultaneously he rejoiced in the assurance of salvation.

It was not surprising, therefore, that he, and the other Protestant fathers who followed him, should have gone so far as to say that faith always includes knowledge, that you really cannot have faith without assurance, that you cannot truly see this and believe it, without automatically rejoicing in it and being absolutely certain of it. But in saying that they went too far. Of the two, of course, it is much better than the Roman Catholic teaching, because it does bring out this vital element of justification. But it goes too far, and thereby has often been the means of causing great unhappiness and uncertainty, not to say misery, in the minds and hearts of many Christian people.

We can prove that that early Protestant teaching was wrong by quoting again 1 John 5:13: 'These things have I written unto you that believe on the name of the Son of God; that (in order that) ye may know that ye have eternal life, and that ye may believe on the name of the Son of God'. John was writing to believers; but they were lacking in assurance. He writes in order that they may have it. And, of course, the whole of the Epistle to the Hebrews is in a sense written with the same end and object in view. In other words we must be clear that it is possible for one to be a true believer and yet, for various reasons, to lack assurance of salvation.

This happens generally because of defective teaching, or because the devil has persuaded us in some way or another to be looking too much inwardly at ourselves. We are taught to examine ourselves; but if we do so excessively we shall be cast down in misery and unhappiness. We must therefore avoid the two extremes of no self-examination and too much self-examination. It is a clear understanding of the doctrine of justification by faith only that should lead to assurance of salvation. 'Therefore,' says the Apostle in Romans 5:1, 'being justified by faith (or 'having been justified by faith') we have peace with God.' Even if you adopt the alternative translation, 'let us have peace with God', it still leads to the same result. One translation says you have peace, the other says you should have it, but both show that a clear understanding of justification should lead to assurance and to rejoicing.

It is possible to be a Christian without assurance, without the certain knowledge of salvation. 'Well, then,' you ask, 'how may I know whether I am a Christian at all?' The answer is that if you know that you are a sinner; if you have ceased to rely upon your own works; if you are looking only to the Lord Jesus Christ and His perfect work on your behalf – in His life, in His death upon the Cross, in His resurrection and ascension – if you are not looking at all to yourself; if you have 'no confidence in the flesh'; if your only hope is in Him, and you are trusting in and relying utterly upon Him; then you are a Christian. What you need is instruction, by which your eyes will be opened fully to the truth. You can be a Christian without assurance; but you should have assurance, and you should not rest content without it. You should realize that you are a very defective Christian without it, defective from your own experimental standpoint, still more defective from the standpoint of your witness and your testimony. We are meant to be a rejoicing people, and we have no right to be anything else. I am not saying that you are not a Christian if you are not rejoicing; but I am saying that you should rejoice, and that you should deal with yourself until you do rejoice. Get a clear understanding of the doctrine of justification by faith only.

Another way in which the devil attacks our assurance is by making us look back. How often are Christian people robbed of their joy and their assurance by the devil persuading them to look at the past, to some skeleton in the cupboard! There is nothing he does so frequently as this. There is nothing, therefore, that one has to do so frequently as a pastor or physician of souls as to exhort people to let the dead past bury its dead and to remind them of the necessity of 'forgetting the things that are behind'!

The devil comes to a man who has only become a Christian, perhaps, late on in life, and says, 'It is too late! You are a coward, you are a cad, you have had your fill of the world's pleasures, and now when you are beginning to be afraid of the fact that you are getting old and are facing dying, you turn to God and to Christ. You are a coward! No (he says) it cannot happen in that way, God is a just and a righteous God and He cannot allow you to live in the world until the last minute and then turn . . . Too late, my friend.'

Or perhaps the devil makes you think of the years you have wasted. You have spent long years living the life of the world in godlessness and irreligion, and you cannot forgive yourself for such waste. You see it now. But there it is, facts are facts. The devil can make you so utterly miserable in that way that you will be quite dejected. You will lose all the joy of your salvation because of the years that you have mis-spent. They have gone, irretrievably, and you cannot get them back. Then the devil says further: 'If you had not wasted them think what you might be now!'

[240]

Is it not extraordinary that we can be deluded and trapped in this manner by the devil? Do you not know something of this? 'Think,' he says, 'of what you might be now if only you had become a Christian in your adolescence when you were young! But you have allowed the opportunities to slip, you have come in late. You might by now have been a shining, glorious, wonderful saint. But you have missed the opportunity.'

Another way in which he puts the same point is by saying, 'Think of the good you could have done. If only you had become a Christian when you were young you might have been a foreign missionary, a great church might have come into being as the result of your activities, you might have given great gifts to various causes. The whole story might have been so different, and you would have been a Christian noted for your wonderful achievements.' The devil so holds us face to face with these vain regrets that he can cast us down into the very depths of despondency and almost despair. He will try to keep you looking at your past in all these ways – vain regrets, the opportunities that have gone, that are never to come back again!

What do you say to him in reply? How do you meet him? When we come to the positive exposition of 'the whole armour of God' we shall of course deal with this more fully.* Let me anticipate to this extent, to give immediate relief to any burdened unhappy souls who have been looking back across wasted years, a wasted life, and wasted opportunities. In the Name of God I say to you, realize that it is always the devil who makes you look back, and the reason he does so is that he wants to spoil the present and the future. He knows that as long as you are looking back you will have no pleasure in the present, you will not be doing your work properly in the present, and you will not be able to do your work in the future. Regrets are useless. You cannot undo the past; there is nothing you can do about it. If you had no other reason for not looking back, that should be enough. Do not waste your time, but realize that it is the devil attacking you. To be downcast because of your past means that you are downcast in the present; and as 'the joy of the Lord is our strength' it is obvious that, while you are unhappy, you cannot be functioning properly. So for that reason alone, refuse to look back.

* This will be done in a subsequent volume.

But let me give you better cause for encouragement. The devil says, 'It is all wasted, irretrievable, you will never have an opportunity again. The years have gone and gone for ever, life has been a sheer waste.' Turn to him and say, 'I remember the words of my Lord who said that you are "a liar, and the father of lies", "a liar from the beginning", and I see that you are still a liar, for what you are saying is not true. God says to me: "I will restore to you the years that the locust hath eaten" (Joel 2:25). Thank God I agree.' The word of God is the only word in the universe that can speak to you in this way. And God *can* do it! Do you realize that in the hand of God you can do more in five minutes than you could have done in fifty years on your own? Do not listen to the devil. The past is not altogether hopeless, it must not mortgage the present or the future. God delivers you, makes you a new creation; you are a new man in a new world. Leave the past. Never look at it again. It is always the devil that makes you look back. Refuse it, set your face steadfastly towards the future, that glorious future that is before you!

I must remind you also of the way in which the devil sometimes raises up some past sin, and so holds it before you that you cannot get away from it. Whichever way you look it is there – that thing, one sin perhaps, that you committed in the past!

One brief illustration will demonstrate the point I am trying to establish. I remember very well the case of a man who became a Christian at the age of seventy-seven. He had lived a very evil and violent and godless life. But at the age of seventy-seven, in a very wonderful way, this man was converted, and the time came for him to have his first Communion. He had never been at a Communion Service in his life before, and this to him was the greatest moment of his life. Having seen the way of salvation, having understood justification by faith only, the old man had come to see that all his sins had been forgiven, blotted out as a thick cloud, and that God had cast them into the sea of His forgetfulness. He was truly rejoicing in his salvation in a most wonderful manner. Then came the Sunday night, the first Communion Service in which he partook. I shall never forget his face and the sight of the joy and the tears mingling together! He was really having a foretaste of heaven, and we were all rejoicing with the man. The next morning, Monday morning, there was a loud

[242]

knock at our door before we had even got out of bed. On going downstairs we found this poor old man standing at the door heartbroken, utterly wretched, weeping uncontrollably, utterly disconsolate. Having got him into the house, and having questioned him, I discovered the cause of his trouble. He had gone home from the service with friends rejoicing, and had gone to bed, and was lying on his back and on the point of going to sleep, when suddenly it came to mind that thirty years before, in a public-house and during a discussion about religion, he had said, and had repeated with oaths and cursing many times, that Jesus Christ – forgive the expression — was a bastard! He had not thought about that during the thirty years at all, he had probably said the same thing many times. Such was the position. He had been converted, had become a Christian rejoicing in his salvation, had taken his first Communion, and was at the very height of his enjoyment and happiness. Then, in bed, happier than he had ever been in his life, suddenly this thought and memory came back to him. Where did it come from? There is only one answer; it was one of 'the wiles of the devil', one of 'the fiery darts of the wicked one'. He threw one of those darts at this poor old man, knowing that he was rejoicing. He resurrected a sin of thirty years before and hurled it at him: 'Who are you to take Communion? Who are you to call yourself a Christian? How can you be a Christian?' And he had spent the whole night in agony and torment; sleep was impossible. He was down in the depths of the lowest hell; he had never been so low nor so unhappy and so miserable.

'But,' you ask, 'how could that have happened? You say the man had seen the doctrine of justification by faith only?' That is the kind of thing a superficial Christian says who does not know about 'the wiles of the devil': 'Once saved, always happy': 'I believed and put my name on a card'. 'Happy – perfectly happy – ever afterwards; no more troubles.' It is just not true! We are confronted by a most subtle adversary and foe. He knows exactly how to trip us and how to catch us. When nothing else seems to work he will take up one thing, perhaps, as in the case of the old man, out of a life which had been altogether evil, utterly profane and violent and foul. He picks out one thing, the most sensitive thing of all to hurt a Christian now, namely, the fact that he should have ever used such an expression about the Son of God who loved him and died for him. But with that he accused the man and robbed him of his assurance and joy.

The only way to deal with such a situation – and thank God for this! – is that it does not matter what you may have said in the past; what matters is what you say now. How often I have had to say that to people! 'But you know,' they say, 'I said this, and I argued like that.' 'My dear friend,' I say, 'I do not care what you have done in the past, the question is, What do you think of the Son of God *now*?' I pointed out to my old friend that his very distress was the proof that he was a Christian. If he had not been a Christian he would still be saying the same things, and thinking it was rather clever to do so. His distress was proof of the fact that he was a Christian. If he could have cut his tongue out he would have done so. He would have done anything to erase that terrible statement. The devil had made another mistake. You can turn the tables on him, and send him fleeing away from you, if you 'stand steadfast in the faith'. If you love the Lord and desire to know Him, I say in the Name of God, that it does not matter what you may have said or done in the past. It is what you are saying now that matters. Have nothing whatsoever to do with the past.

Another group of troubles arises as the result of variations in our experience. Here again is a most fruitful line which the devil frequently adopts. A man becomes a Christian and is full of rejoicing and of praise and of thanksgiving. But later he begins to notice that he does not feel things as he used to do, does not seem to enjoy them as he did at first. At first everything was wonderful – Bible reading, prayer, fellowship of Christian people, activities, everything. But now he begins to notice that this is no longer the case. He does not have the feelings he once had; he has not got the enjoyment, and he is aware of a curious dryness. He seems to be walking in a darkness like that which the prophet Isaiah describes in chapter 50 and verse 10, 'The child of God walking in darkness', and he feels that he has lost something, and that he cannot get it back. He begins to say, ' "Where is the blessedness I knew when first I saw the Lord?", because it seems to have gone.' Then the next step is, 'Well, I wonder whether I am a Christian at all. Surely if a man is truly a Christian he cannot pass through this sort of phase; things ought to be getting better and better, but I seem to be worse rather than better. Am I a Christian, have I ever been a Christian? Was it some false or spurious experience that I had? Was it a psychological something that happened to me? Is it really possible that I am not a Christian after all?'

I am sure that you will recognize the experience of many who have been Christians for any length of time when I put this case before you. Have you known the wiles of the devil at this point? If you have not, then I say that you had better make sure that you really are a Christian. If you know no variations in your experience I take leave to put the question as to whether you are a Christian at all. As I was indicating in a previous study, that is the effect of the teaching of the cults. The cults always claim too much. The Christian does know variations in his experience. When a man becomes a Christian he is not suddenly lifted from the ground right up to the heavens, to spend the rest of his life in orbit up there. That is not true. There are variations. Are you the same two days running?

To illustrate what I mean I use an illustration from the realm of preaching. I will let you into a secret! To me, the most wonderful thing about preaching is that I have no idea whatsoever as to what is going to happen in a service as I walk up the pulpit steps. It is very difficult for us to realize that variations occur, and the devil attacks us at that point. We always want to be in the heights; but it is not so, there are variations.

These variations are partly due to the physical element in us, a consideration that we must not exclude. Though you are a Christian you are still in the body, and you cannot separate and divorce yourself from your body. Many of the saints have had to face this problem. The physical element and the psychological element both tend to impinge upon the spiritual. As we have seen, they can take advantage of variations in our experience; and the Christian is unhappy and cast down and wonders whether he has ever been a Christian at all. The fact is that the devil persuades us to pay too much attention to our states and moods and feelings, instead of to our relationship to the Lord Jesus Christ, and thus prevents us from experiencing the enjoyment of salvation.

A simple illustration will help at this point. The Christian has

[245]

a heart which beats, and that beat comes through to the pulse. If it is too rapid, or too slow, there is something wrong with you. The pulse beat is therefore important. But if you spend the whole of your time in counting your pulse you will not do anything else. Now there are many Christians who are doing just that. They spend the whole of their time taking their spiritual pulse-rate, or taking their temperature. They are not quite sure that they are well, so they get the thermometer, and also feel their pulse. Many Christians have spent the whole of their Christian lives in that condition, persuaded to do so by 'the wiles of the devil'. 'Of course I want to be a healthy Christian, I want to be well,' they say. Yes, but when you become so greatly concerned about your health that you make yourself ill you have obviously lost the right balance. The question of balance is all-important. The light-hearted, glib Christian, and the morbid, ultra-sensitive, over-careful, hypochondriacal Christian are both wrong; and there are many such. So the solution to the problem is just to realize that, whenever you are miserable and unhappy, you should question yourself and say, 'What am I unhappy about?' You will probably find that you are unhappy because you are not enjoying your relationship to Him as you should, and as you need to, and that makes you query whether you are in the relationship at all. Whatever I may feel, it is the relationship that matters; and my feelings do not make the slightest difference to the relationship, thank God!

I am reminded of the illustration the Scottish evangelist John McNeil used to employ in order to make this point clear. He was a travelling evangelist who would be away from home perhaps two or three years at a time, going round the world holding meetings. Then he would come home for a rest. He wanted to get people to see the difference between the relationship and the enjoyment of the relationship. He imagined himself arriving home on one occasion in a very tired and weary condition after he had been working very hard, and his wife and his seven or eight children meeting him. He pictured himself turning to his wife and saying, 'Mary, who are these?' She replied, 'Well, John, they are your children.' And he, tired and exhausted, said, 'You know, Mary, I do not know what it is, but I somehow do not realize, I do not feel that they are my children'. Then his wife replied, saying, 'It does not matter whether you feel it or not, John, you are their father!' Remember the story and apply it when you say, 'I do not feel now as I used to feel'. Thank God that if your name is written in the Lamb's Book of Life it is there whatever you may feel. That is the thing that matters! Listen –

> *Twixt gleams of joy and clouds of doubt*
> *Our feelings come and go;*
> *Our best estate is tossed about*
> *In ceaseless ebb and flow:*
> *No mood of feeling, form of thought,*
> *Is constant for a day;*
> *But Thou, O Lord, Thou changest not,*
> *The same Thou art alway.*
>
> *I grasp Thy strength, make it mine own,*
> *My heart with peace is blest;*
> *I lose my hold, and then comes down*
> *Darkness, and cold unrest.*
> *Let me no more my comfort draw*
> *From my frail hold of Thee;*
> *In this alone rejoice with awe –*
> *Thy mighty grasp of me.*

I may feel that I have lost Him, but He will never leave me. 'I will never leave thee, nor forsake thee.' 'I will never let thee go.' 'O Love that wilt not let me go.' Rest on it, whatever your feelings may be. He will never let you go. He cannot deny Himself and you are His, and you are His for ever.

> *Let me no more my comfort draw*
> *From my frail hold of Thee;*
> *In this alone rejoice with awe –*
> *Thy mighty grasp of me.*

Do not forget the addition – 'with awe'. It is amazing, it is wonderful, it is not to be trifled with, it is not to be played with. It must not lead me to say, 'Well, I can do what I like, I can sin as much as I like, I am saved once and for ever, always saved, though I . . .' No, no! 'Rejoice with awe – Thy mighty grasp of me.'

So when the devil comes to you and tries to shake you because of your varying feelings and moods and states, tell him that you are not saved by your feelings, but saved by Christ, and that you are relying on Him, and on Him alone. Do that, and you will find that your feelings will come back; they will be restored to you. As long as you rely on Him, 'His mighty grasp of you', you will be able to defeat the wiles of the devil and rejoice again with a 'joy unspeakable and full of glory'.

18

Attacks Upon Assurance (2)

Another very fruitful source of trouble in the life of Christian people is the devil's misinterpretation of God's dealings with us. There is much teaching concerning this in all parts of the Scriptures. It is particularly likely to occur in connection with chastisements – God punishing us in various ways – or, short of that, in our difficulty to understand the occasional withdrawals of God's smile from us.

This is something which all Christians must surely recognize. The classic example of it is the case of Job, a devout man of God. But God allowed the devil to try him, to test him and to tempt him. To that end God withdrew from him certain blessings which he had formerly enjoyed. He was not able to find God as he had done formerly, while certain painful things were allowed to happen to him. The whole Book of Job is a great treatise on this subject of God's dealings with us.

Job, in his multiplied afflictions, at times succumbed to the wiles of the devil. He was encouraged to do so by the friends who visited him – 'Job's comforters', as they are called. They made things much worse because they were, quite unconsciously, and without desiring it, being used as tools of the devil. Their interpretation of Job's circumstances was quite wrong. They played the devil's game and made Job think that his trials were happening to him because he had been presumptuous, proud, self-satisfied, and guilty, perhaps, of some secret sin. The devil used them, as he often uses such people still, to depress one of God's children.

In the New Testament the great treatise on this subject is the Epistle to the Hebrews. The main trouble of the Christians to whom it was addressed was that they could not understand the things that were happening to them. That is really the background to the Epistle. They needed to be reminded of the fulness of the Christian faith and the pre-eminence of Christ because they were becoming uncertain of the Christian faith and were looking back at their old Jewish religion. They could not understand why they were suffering persecution, why they were being robbed and misunderstood, and why they were undergoing hardship. The devil had come in and was creating doubt in their minds.

Job and Hebrews are two great books in the Bible that are devoted to this subject; and in various ways you find the same theme in many other places. Our Lord Himself at the end of His life was very careful to warn His disciples about trials to come. He said, 'In the world ye shall have tribulation'. He warns them to expect tribulations and troubles. And yet, in spite of such words, we are all ready to listen to the devil and to succumb to his wiles. What he does is to tempt us to doubt God's love to us. He says, 'What kind of a God is this that allows you to suffer in this way?' You are familiar with the argument, no doubt. 'If God be God, and if He is a God of love, why is this happening to me?' And the temptation is the stronger when he contrasts what is happening to you with what is not happening to certain other worldly, godless people.

The same temptation to doubt God is also the great theme of the seventy-third Psalm: 'Verily I have cleansed my heart in vain' (verse 13). Look at those other people, 'their eyes stand out with fatness: they have more than heart could wish' (verse 7). But as for me, I am always suffering, I am always in trouble. What kind of love is it that allows this to happen to His children? The devil comes and shakes the Christian along that line so that he begins to doubt and to query the love of God and the kindness and the mercy and the compassion of God.

If the devil does not do that, or if you can answer him at that point, and can show him that this is not inconsistent with God's character as love, then he says, 'Well, there is only one conclusion to draw, and that is that you are obviously not a Christian. If you say that God is still a God of love, well then, the explanation must be that you are not a Christian at all, for if you were a Christian you would not be treated in this manner. What earthly parent would treat his child as God is treating you? No, you are not a child of God at all; you thought you were a Christian, but it is quite clear that you are not a Christian at all.' It is in this way that the devil reduces many Christian people to a state of un-happiness, uncertainty, and insecurity, simply by misrepresenting God's dealings with us.

To state the matter in a different way, the devil succeeds in making us misunderstand completely one of the profoundest and most wonderful aspects of Christian teaching. I can sum it up in two statements. One is in the Epistle to the Romans, chapter 8, verse 17: 'If (we are) children (of God), then (we are) heirs; heirs of God, and joint-heirs with Christ'. Then the Apostle im-mediately adds, 'if so be that we suffer with him, that we may be also glorified together'. Paul is reminding Christians that they are children of God and that they have great security. Then there follows from verse 18 what is perhaps the richest of all teachings on the association of glory and suffering. There is nothing more profound in the whole realm and range of Scripture.

The same teaching is equally clear in the twelfth chapter of the Epistle to the Hebrews and summed up in the sentence, 'Whom the Lord loveth he chasteneth, and scourgeth every son whom he receiveth' (verse 6). That is the only reply to the wiles of the devil at this point; and using it we should never succumb to this particular temptation. To do so is to fail to see one of the most beautiful and glorious aspects of our position as Christians; it is to fail to see that God is our Father, who is concerned that we should grow and develop. How childish we are! No child ever likes discipline and chastisement and punishment. (Incidentally, one great trouble in this country today, increasingly, is that the Government has also become childish and does not believe in punishment – hence the increasing problem of juvenile de-linquency.) He always wants to be picked up and carried. Why should he walk when he can be carried? He always wants things that he likes; sweets are much nicer than food, and it is a cruel parent that makes a child eat solid food; and so on! That is the typical childish attitude.

It is the same in the spiritual realm. But any father worthy of the name desires that his child should grow and develop, and therefore he takes measures to see that this will take place. The Scriptures have been provided for our growth; here is food, here is instruction, here is spiritual exercise; but if you do not take it, if you do not use it, God has other methods, and He uses them in love. God is determined that we shall grow. He insists upon our growing; and if we are not prepared to submit to discipline and to grow in the normal and the prescribed manner, God is not at a loss to know what to do. Some of His methods are these very things that trouble us so much, and cause us to listen to the wiles of the devil. God does not always want to carry us as children, as it were. He wants us to stand and to be men; He wants us to become adult; He wants us to grow and to develop.

One of His ways of producing this result is to withhold things from us for a while. When everything comes easily we make no effort; it is just a matter of enjoyment. But when we begin to encounter difficulties and problems we are forced to think; we begin to read the Scriptures and to pray as we have never prayed before. This is one way in which God teaches us to 'grow in grace and in the knowledge of the Lord'. He withholds Himself. God often acts like a human parent. The argument in Hebrews, chapter 12, reads as follows: 'If ye be without chastisement, whereof all are partakers, then are ye bastards, and not sons. Furthermore, we have had fathers of our flesh which corrected us, and we gave them reverence: shall we not much rather be in subjection unto the Father of spirits, and live? For they verily for a few days chastened us after their own pleasure; but he for our profit, that we might be partakers of his holiness.'

We have to apply all this. When you are chastised, or when God's smile seems to be withdrawn, when you are passing through deep waters, realize that His object is to test you, to train you, to make you grow and to develop. The time to be troubled, says the author of the Epistle to the Hebrews, is not when you are having a hard time, but when you never have a hard time and find everything going smoothly, with never any ripple on the surface. Adversity has always been a great means of instruction. It is God's gymnasium for training the muscles and developing the vigour and the power of His people. So do not whimper and cry when you are sent to the gymnasium, but thank God for it. It is not pleasant at the time, 'but afterward it yieldeth the peaceable fruit of righteousness to them that are exercised thereby' (Hebrews 12:11).

Another of God's reasons for treating us thus at times is in order that He may reveal more of Himself to us. It sounds contradictory that God should withhold Himself in order to reveal more of Himself to us! Yet the assertion is precisely true. At first we know very little about God. We know something of His love and mercy and compassion in Christ and His forgiveness. But that is only the beginning. There are depths in God's love and compassion, His concern and solicitude for His people, of which the beginner, the child in Christ, knows nothing, and it is only as you pass through the dark waters of adversity that you get to know these everlasting resources. The saints bear a universal testimony to this. God's people, looking back, have always thanked God for trials and adversity, because it was through them that they really began to know God.

Again, this truth is illuminated by the human analogy. It is as you experience human love that you get to know more and more about it. The people who think that the beginning of love is everything know nothing about love. Love grows and develops and expands. And this is infinitely more true in the case of the love of God. You know little about God's patience, long-suffering, tenderness and compassion, until suddenly everything seems to go against you to drive you to despair, and then you gradually begin to know God in a new way. You then realize why an unexpected trial happened to you. It was to enlarge your knowledge, to expand your horizon, and to lead you on into the profundities and the depths of God's own glorious character.

Furthermore, adversity is one of God's ways of preparing us for the glory which is to come. 'If so be that we suffer with him, that we may be also glorified together'. 'It is through much tribulation,' says a word in the Scriptures, 'that we enter into the kingdom of God' (Acts 14:22). We are in a preparatory school at the moment. This is not *the* life, it is only the preparation. It is the glory that awaits us that is really *the* life, and for that we are being prepared. That glory is pure, it is holy. There is no sin in heaven; there is no evil there. Do you think that, as you are, you are fit to go to heaven? Of course you are not! Many people would be bored if they were suddenly transported to heaven, because they would no longer have any of the things on which they have lived here. On what do we live? Are we ready for this glory, for heaven, for holiness, for the sight of God? Certainly not! We need to be prepared for it, and adversity is God's way of preparing us for it. And if we will not listen to His Word and apply it, He will sometimes use the chisel on us, and chisel off some of the rough, hard corners.

We have to be humbled. So He puts us in the fire of affliction, in the crucible of purification. He has only one object, to get rid of the dross and to refine the gold. But in our childishness we listen to the devil, and we grumble and complain. 'Why is this happening to me? I am trying to be a good Christian; look at those other people.' I trust that we shall never speak in that way again, thus falling victim to the wiles of the devil. Cannot you see that in all this, God, as your Father, is manifesting His love to you, and revealing His great and gracious and glorious purpose with respect to you? He intends to make you perfect, 'without spot, or wrinkle, or any such thing'. He has first to rid you of very much rubbish. So let us learn to say with Richard Keen –

> *When through fiery trials thy pathway shall lie,*
> *His grace all-sufficient shall be thy supply;*
> *The flame shall not hurt thee, I only design,*
> *Thy dross to consume and thy gold to refine.*

In other words, when troubles are happening to you; when you are tempest-tossed, and do not understand it, and the devil comes with his suggestions; then fall back on something you are absolutely certain of, namely, His unchanging grace. God has given you the final proof that He is your Father, and that He has loved you with an everlasting love. It is all in Jesus Christ and Him crucified, the 'Rock of Ages'. Hide yourself in Him, and stand, saying, 'He that spared not his own Son, but delivered him up for us all, how shall he not with him also freely give us all things?' (Romans 8:32).

If recently you have been giving way to a miserable self-pity, feel ashamed of yourself and realize that it is nothing but childishness. See God's grand plan for you, and yield yourself to

His gracious, loving purposes. 'Whom the Lord loveth he chasteneth, and scourgeth every son whom he receiveth. If ye be without chastisement, of which all are partakers, then are ye bastards, and not sons' (Hebrews 12:6, 8).

The next matter we must consider is the way in which the devil frequently shakes the confidence and assurance of Christian people when they fall into sin. Suppose that a Christian man falls into sin. As the result of listening to the devil, he immediately begins to feel utterly hopeless, and to doubt whether he has ever been a Christian at all. He queries his whole relationship to God. Indeed he goes further and feels that he has no right to ask for forgiveness. Of course, before conversion it was different; he had never been a Christian, he was ignorant. But now that he is a Christian and has fallen into sin, how can he ask for forgiveness? He has no right to do so. So the devil comes and exercises his wiles, and the sinning Christian is soon in the depths of despair, miserable and unhappy, feeling that he has lost everything.

In this case the Christian's trouble results from his failure to do what the Apostle tells us in detail to do: 'Take unto you the whole armour of God'. That means, among other things, that your loins must be 'girt about with truth'. Take the truth and say to the devil, 'Let us examine what you are saying'. Certain fallacies must be exposed. The first is that, according to the devil's argument, every Christian is perfect and sinless. In effect, that is what he has been saying. You have fallen into sin, and because you have fallen into sin he makes you doubt whether you are a Christian. There is only one conclusion to be drawn, namely, that every Christian is completely perfect and sinless. Sinless perfection! And unless you are in a state of sinless perfection you are not a Christian at all. But Scripture makes no such claim for the Christian this side of glory and this must be your reply to the devil.

That is really enough in and of itself. But, in addition, a man who feels that, because he has fallen into sin, he forfeits his standing in Christ, and has no hope at all, is clearly confused on the whole matter of justification by faith only. Obviously he is going back to 'works'. He feels that, because he has committed this one act of sin, he is no longer justified, he is no longer right with God. So he is no longer standing in the position of faith; he no longer accepts justification; for him it has become justification by faith plus works. The moment a man so speaks, he has gone back 'under the law', he is back under works again, and he will be miserable and unhappy as long as he remains there. On your deathbed your only hope will be that you are justified by faith only, faith in 'Jesus Christ and him crucified'. If you think you will be able to rest at that moment on the excellent work you have done, and on all your excellencies as a Christian, you will have a very rude awakening. In the light of eternity it will be just nothing. Once more the devil has over-reached himself, as he always does in these matters; he has made an attack upon the whole doctrine of justification by faith only.

Or we may look at the problem in the following way. The trouble at this point is that the Christian has temporarily lost hold of the wonderful teaching of the Scripture which emphasizes that what happens to us in our justification is not only that we are forgiven, but that we are brought into a new relationship with God. This is the fundamental postulate. Once more we see, then, that it is a superficial understanding of the doctrines of the Scripture that accounts for most of our troubles. If you think of salvation as a matter of forgiveness you will soon be in trouble when you fall into sin again. You must realize that when you believe the Gospel, and are justified by faith only, a tremendous change in your position takes place. Previously you were 'under law', you were 'in Adam', you were a 'natural man', you were alienated from God, you were an enemy of God, you did not belong to God's family. But when you become a Christian you are not only forgiven – thank God that is true! — but there is something infinitely greater, namely, there is a change in your whole position. You have been 'translated from the kingdom of darkness into the kingdom of God's dear Son'; you have been 'born again'; you have been 'made a partaker of the divine nature', you have been adopted into the family of God, you are a member of the household of God. You are 'in Christ', you are joined to Christ, you are a part of Him. As you were 'in Adam', you are now 'in Christ'; you are a child of God, and if a child, 'then an heir of God, and joint-heir with Christ'. Such is your new and eternal position.

[256]

It is because we do not hold on to this aspect of truth that the devil can shake us. He says, 'But you have fallen into sin, so you cannot be a Christian'. To which the right reply is, 'My actions do not affect the relationship'. Look at a simple human illustration again. Is there not all the difference in the world between offending against the law of England and offending against your father or mother? One relationship is that of law, the other is a relationship of love. When you offend against your father or mother you do not change the relationship, you do not cease to be their child. That was the fundamental fallacy of the Prodigal Son. He deserved to fall into that fallacy because of the way he behaved; but he was quite wrong. He goes back to his father and says, 'Father, I have sinned against heaven and in thy sight and am no more worthy to be called thy son'. He was about to add what he had decided to say when he was in the far country, 'Make me as one of thy hired servants'; but the father interrupted him, smothered him with his love, embraced him, kissed him, and said, 'Bring forth the best robe', 'kill the fatted calf', 'let me have the ring'. The father is really saying, in effect: 'My dear boy, I know you have been a fool, I know you have been prodigal, I know you have made a mess of your life, you have squandered all the goods which I gave you, and you are down in the depths and the dregs; there is nothing to be said for you. Nevertheless, you are still my son!' A son does not break the relationship even though he behaves like a fool. 'This my son,' says the father, 'has come back.' The foolish elder brother could not understand it, he thought that the sinful life of his brother had broken the relationship, and he wanted him to be regarded as a servant. But he is still a son!

Thank God, sin and failure and transgression do not affect the relationship; and therefore when the devil comes and suggests that you are not a Christian because you have sinned, answer him by saying, 'I agree that I have sinned, but I am still a child of God'. The relationship is not changed. In other words you must never go back to the question of justification because you have sinned. To do so is to fall immediately into the snare of the devil. He will always try to take you back to the beginning. The answer to him, quite simply, is that a believer is justified by faith once and for ever. You do not have to be re-justified every time you sin and repent. No, justification is once and for ever – 'being justified by faith'. It is an act in the past; the Apostle uses the aorist tense; justification can never be repeated and does not need to be. You are justified only once. And now your sin and your failure is in the realm of the family, it is in the realm of your relationship to the Father; and nothing can break that relationship. So answer the wiles of the devil in that way.

Perhaps another kind of illustration will help. Imagine a man who is anxious to climb to the top of a mountain. He starts from ground level and continues to climb until he has reached a point two-thirds of the way up to the summit. Suddenly in making a further effort he falls, and slips back, say, twenty yards. But that does not mean that he the man is down at the bottom of the mountain again. What would you think of a man who said, 'I was two-thirds of the way up to the summit; but I have fallen, and so I have to go all the way back again to the bottom and start climbing once more'. That would be sheer folly. That, then, is the way in which you should think and argue when you find yourself confronted by the wiles of the devil. The man who has fallen two-thirds of the way up to the summit of a mountain gets up from where he is, and goes on. He does not go down to the bottom again. It is precisely the same in the spiritual realm.

You may think that this is dangerous doctrine. That is the charge that has always been brought against it. When the Apostle Paul included it in his Epistle to the Romans the legalist Jews began to say at once, 'Shall we therefore continue in sin, that grace may abound? (Romans 6:1). 'He seems to be saying,' they alleged, 'that where sin abounded, grace did much more abound. Very well, then; you may sin as much as you like; you may fall as often as you like; you may do anything you like; you are saved, all is well with you.' But if you draw that conclusion you are simply saying that you know nothing about love. A man who knows anything about love is much more afraid of wounding love than he is of breaking a law. Love is much more wonderful than law; it is much more delicate, it is much more sensitive. Hence a man is more careful in the realm of his family than he is in the realm of external law. Multiply that by infinity, and you have the Christian looking into the face of his Father. He does not trade upon his Father's love; but he has got to realize

[258]

the position; and he has got to be able to answer the devil.

Sin does not change my relationship to God. I am no longer sinning against law. 'I am dead to the law', I have finished with the law; the law and its terrors have no more to do with me. But what happens is that I am now sinning against the love of Christ, 'who loved me and gave himself for me'. I am a cad now, I am sinning against the One who has loved me even unto death. That is fundamentally more terrible. But it does not change my relationship, thank God; I do not go back and consider whether I am justified or not; I do not go back and say I need to be justified again – if I do so I have entirely succumbed to the devil.

Never allow the devil to raise with you again the question of your justification. The Apostle John expresses this in his First Epistle: 'If we confess our sins, he is faithful' – He would be going back on His own character if He did not forgive us – 'he is faithful and just to forgive us our sins, and to cleanse us from all unrighteousness' (1 John 1:9). We are not sinless and perfect in this world, we cannot be; and therefore, if we think we are, there is something wrong with our doctrine. But John safeguards his doctrine against the error of the foolish, who veer off at a tangent as such people are always ready to do. He tells Christians that he is writing to them that they may not fall into sin, but that, if any Christian does sin he is not to feel that he has ceased to be a Christian; let him realize rather that 'we have an advocate with the Father, Jesus Christ the righteous: and he is the propitiation for our sins: and not for ours only, but also for the sins of the whole world'. Never allow the devil to make you go back to the question of justification. If you have truly believed in Christ and are justified by faith, that is once and for ever, never to be repeated. Fall as a child before God, confess your sins, and He will forgive you your sins, and cleanse you from all unrighteousness.

A third matter which has often tripped people is a special sin called 'the sin against the Holy Ghost'. It is something with which the devil often trips Christian people. He does so in terms of the teaching of our Lord where He says, 'Wherefore I say unto you, All manner of sin and blasphemy shall be forgiven unto men: but the blasphemy against the Holy Ghost shall not be forgiven unto men. And whosoever speaketh a word against the Son of man, it shall be forgiven him: but whosoever speaketh against the Holy Ghost, it shall not be forgiven him, neither in this world, neither in the world to come' (Matthew 12:31). The other Scripture which is so frequently used by the devil is in the sixth chapter of the Epistle to the Hebrews: 'It is impossible for those who were once enlightened, and have tasted of the heavenly gift, and were made partakers of the Holy Ghost, and have tasted the good word of God, and the powers of the world to come, if they shall fall away, to renew them again unto repentance; seeing they crucify to themselves the Son of God afresh, and put him to an open shame' (verses 4–6). The devil comes to you and tells you that you are guilty of that, that you have gone back, that you have sinned against the light, that you have sinned as a believer, that you have therefore sinned against the Holy Ghost; and there is no possible return. Scripture says so. You are hopelessly lost; nothing can be done about you at all; there is no place of repentance for you. Hebrews 10 gives similar warning (verses 26–31).

The answer as regards these two scriptures can be summarized in the following way. There is nothing in them which says that the people described were regenerate. It is possible to have many experiences of the Holy Ghost without being regenerate. In every great revival of religion there have been people who, as it were, have been swept along by the tide. They appeared to be Christians and spoke as such, but they showed afterwards that they had never been Christians at all. There are people of whom John says again in his First Epistle: 'They were among us, but they went out from us – and thereby have proved that they never really were of us' (1 John 2:19). They appeared to be Christians, but there is nothing to say that they were ever regenerate.

The truth is, that what these portions of Scripture deal with is not the question of a man falling into sin, but with a man denying, renouncing and repudiating the whole of the Christian faith; a man denying the Lord Jesus Christ and His atoning and sacrificial death; a man making fun of the blood of Christ and delighting to do so. The people dealt with in these passages were deliberately ridiculing, laughing at, denouncing the entire Christian message, saying it was of no value, turning their backs upon it, returning to Judaism and feeling very proud of themselves as they did so.

[260]

In the same way, in Matthew 12 and its parallels, you find exactly the same thing. What is this sin, this blasphemy against the Holy Ghost, that our Lord speaks of? It is to ridicule the work of the Spirit. Not just to fall into sin, but to ridicule the entire work of the Spirit, to ridicule the spiritual realm, to say that Christ is doing His work by means of Beelzebub. It was the condition of the Pharisees, with their proud and arrogant denial, refusal and rejection of the truth as it is in Christ Jesus.

In the light of these considerations we can draw the following conclusions. If you are troubled by the thought that you have sinned against the Holy Ghost, it follows automatically that you are not guilty of it, simply because you are troubled about it. In Hebrews 6 and 10, and Matthew 12, people are proudly and arrogantly rejecting and denying the truth; they want to have nothing more to do with it because they think they have something better. They are not worried about having sinned against the Holy Ghost; they do not believe in the Holy Ghost; He is the very One they are denying. So if you are worried about this matter, it is proof positive in itself that you are not guilty of this sin, but stand in marked contrast with those who are guilty of it.

Again: Are you troubled about your lack of faith, and your lack of love to the Lord? Are you troubled that you are a poor Christian, and on those grounds have drawn the deduction that you are not a Christian at all, and that you have sinned against the Holy Ghost? Again it follows automatically that you are not guilty of the blasphemy against the Holy Ghost, because those who are guilty are not troubled about their lack of faith, and lack of love; they dismiss the whole thing with disdain. They are arrogantly and proudly rejecting it and spitting upon it. So if you are aware that you are lacking in it, you stand clearly contrasted with such people.

Finally: Can you say honestly that your greatest desire is to have greater faith, to know more of God and His love, to love God and the Lord Jesus Christ more, and to serve Them more truly and more whole-heartedly? If you can so speak, then you are the exact opposite of the people who are guilty of blasphemy against the Holy Ghost. They do not want to know the Lord, they arrogantly deny Him; they do not want to love Him more; they regard Him as someone who is to be dismissed, someone who is childish in all His teaching. 'The blood of Christ!' – they treat it with disdain, they are not interested, they do not want it. But if this is your fervent desire; if you can say 'Lord, it is my chief complaint that my love is weak and faint', well then, far from being guilty of the sin of blasphemy against the Holy Ghost, you are proving that you are a child of God. Any desire after God and the Lord Jesus Christ and the Holy Ghost; any longing, any hungering and thirsting after righteousness; any desire to be loved and to show love more and more; is an absolute proof of a new nature, and that you are a child of God, and an heir of heaven. It is the exact opposite of the blasphemy against the Holy Ghost.

Is it not becoming more and more obvious that we must take unto us the whole armour of God and leave no unguarded place? Be fully armed. 'Be strong in the Lord and in the power of his might. Take unto you the whole armour of God, that you may be able to stand against the wiles of the devil.' Thank God, it is possible; we can conquer him, defeat him, resist him, and cause him to flee from us.

One of the best and quickest ways of doing so is to join old John Newton in offering the prayer:

> *Be Thou my shield and hiding-place,*
> *That, sheltered near Thy side,*
> *I may my fierce accuser face,*
> *And tell him Thou hast died.*

19

Quenching the Spirit (1)

As we continue our study of how to stand against the wiles of the devil we do so now in terms of the words that are to be found in the First Epistle to the Thessalonians, chapter 5, verse 19: 'Quench not the Spirit'.

The wiles of the devil, as we have already seen, are manifested in a great variety of ways, but there is none that is more often employed than that which aims at defeating the work of the Holy Spirit in us.

The Christian Church as we know her, and as she has been known traditionally throughout the centuries, really came into being and began her work on the day of Pentecost as recorded in Acts 2. There was, of course, the Church under the old dispensation – 'the Church in the wilderness', as Stephen described it in his oration recorded in the seventh chapter of the Acts of the Apostles – but the kingdom of God has taken this particular form of the Church, the Christian Church, since that day of Pentecost. The apostles and certain others were gathered together in an upper room. Our Lord had told them to continue in prayer; He told them that they were not yet ready for their task, they lacked the power, they lacked the ability, they lacked the understanding; but He said, 'ye shall receive power'. So He told them to wait until the gift of the Holy Ghost should come upon them. Then on the morning of the day of Pentecost they were all gathered together, and of one accord, when 'Suddenly there came a sound from heaven as of a rushing mighty wind, and it filled all the house where they were sitting. And there appeared unto them cloven tongues like as of fire, and it sat upon each of them. And they were all filled with the Holy Ghost, and began to speak with other tongues.' The vital fact is that 'they were all filled with the Holy Ghost'. It is from that moment, as it were, that the Church, the Christian Church as such, really began to function. The account which we have of the early Church in the New Testament, in the Book of Acts and in these various Epistles, is nothing but an account of the Holy Spirit presiding over the life of the Christian Church. The first Christians lived under the power, and influence, and leadership of the Holy Spirit. We find phrases in the Book of the Acts such as, 'It seemed good unto us, and to the Holy Ghost'. We read of the Apostle Paul that he and his companions 'assayed (attempted) to go into Bithynia: but the Spirit suffered them not'. Then they wanted to preach in Asia, and again the Spirit restrained and prevented them. You cannot read the New Testament without feeling that the life of the Church was lived in and under the power of the Holy Ghost. Our Lord had predicted and promised this. He had said in effect: 'Do not be upset because I am going to leave you; I am not going to leave you comfortless orphans, I will send you another Comforter, the Holy Ghost'. And so He told them something about what the ministry of the Holy Ghost would be. He promised this; and the promise was fulfilled on the day of Pentecost.

The chief work of the Holy Ghost is to glorify the Lord Jesus Christ. Our Lord said, 'He shall not speak of himself, he shall glorify me; he shall bring to your remembrance whatsoever I have said unto you'. His chief function is to glorify and to manifest the Son of God, the Saviour, the Redeemer, the Lord of glory. His other function, and it is subsidiary to that great central function, is to 'mediate' and to 'apply to us' the great salvation which our blessed Lord and Saviour had worked out while He was here in the days of His flesh. He did so by obeying the law actively and positively in His life of obedience, then passively by submitting Himself to the punishment of our sins upon the Cross, and by conquering death and the grave. He thereby completed the work necessary for our salvation, our reconciliation to God. Apart from that work no salvation was possible; He had to come. 'The Son of man is come to seek and to save that which was lost.' 'As the serpent was lifted up in the wilderness,' He said, 'even so must the Son of man be lifted up.' By His coming, His incarnation, His perfect spotless life, His atoning sacrificial death, His resurrection and ascension, He has opened up the way of salvation. Now the Holy Spirit was sent in order to apply this to us. It is He who now brings this completed, perfect salvation into our lives and into our experience. He convicts us, quickens us, enables us to believe and gives us faith, produces the new nature, the rebirth in us, leads us and guides us in the process of sanctification and in many other ways.

This, then, being the work of the Spirit, it obviously becomes a very important target for the wiles of the devil. The devil has only one central purpose, namely, to mar, and if he can to ruin, the work of God. That is what he did at the beginning in the Fall. God having made everything perfect, the devil came in and spoiled it; and now in this new creation, in this new beginning and the start of the new humanity in the Lord Jesus Christ, the Son of God, who is 'the firstborn among many brethren', the devil tries to do similar work. His object is to mar and to ruin this second, this new humanity, as he had ruined the first. Our problem as Christians is not 'flesh and blood' – in ourselves or in anyone else; the problem is not man. If the problem were merely man we would be more or less competent to deal with it. But 'we wrestle not against flesh and blood, but against principalities, against powers, against the world rulers of this darkness' that we see round and about us, 'against spiritual wickedness in high (heavenly) places'. And the whole object of these powers is to mar the great salvation which the Son of God has achieved, and which He is working out through the Spirit in the Church, in you and me, in all who have ever belonged to the Christian Church. It is not surprising, then, that the devil has paid particular attention to this aspect of our life, our relationship to the Holy Spirit. The whole history of the Church shows this, and our individual experiences illustrate it endlessly.

As we have seen repeatedly, the devil has fundamentally only one method. He can vary his technique but the technique is relatively unimportant; it is the method that really matters. He can put on different guises, and change like a chameleon. But the thing that is fundamental is that he always tries to drive us from one extreme to the other.

One method he employs is to drive people to excesses with regard to the Spirit and the doctrine of the Spirit. He comes to us and he says, 'Yes, when the Holy Spirit came upon the Church, they were speaking with other tongues, and working miracles. You are all meant to be like that, and like that always.' So he presses this; as an 'angel of light' he preaches the doctrine of the Spirit to us; and he suggests to us that unless we are constantly in a state of rapture we are not Christians at all. Much attention is given to this in the New Testament Epistles.

The Epistle which deals with this matter most extensively is the First Epistle to the Corinthians, and especially chapters 12, 13 and 14. The Apostle Paul deals with the confusion in the Church at Corinth which had arisen because the devil had succeeded in driving them to excesses. But, of course, confusion is not confined to the members of the Church at Corinth; there are hints of it in other Epistles. And the subsequent history of the Church shows the same very clearly. There was much trouble in this respect during the Commonwealth under Cromwell. Certain sections of the Puritan movement were attacked by the devil along this line. Such people as the Fifth Monarchy men, and the people who came to be known as Quakers, are all illustrations of this. Their teaching, in general, was that nothing matters but what they called the Inner Light, the Spirit in you. Under the influence of the wiles of the devil, they tended to be carried off to such extremes that they lived solely on their feelings, on their impulses, on what they called their 'leadings', on impressions on their spirits. They say, 'I suddenly felt; I was suddenly led; an impression was made upon my mind'. Such people tend to live entirely and only in the realm of the subjective aspect of the Christian faith. They are not much interested in the written Word, the Scriptures. Their emphasis falls upon the Spirit, and they assert that He is ever in them to direct and guide them. They live entirely in the subjective realm, paying great attention to moods and feelings and states and impressions.

This is a vital, essential aspect of the Christian life; but the devil tends to drive some of us so far along that line that they tend to ignore the written Word. Some of the Quakers of three hundred years ago did not hesitate to say that they neither needed the Word, nor cared what it said. The Author of the Word was in them Himself. What need had they to go to a Word which had been written centuries before, when the Author Himself was speaking to them as He had spoken to the writers of the New Testament? Thereby, of course, they denied the uniqueness of the Apostles, the uniqueness of the prophets, the doctrine of the inspiration of the Scriptures itself, and caused great confusion to themselves and to others.

There is a tendency for certain churches and individuals to fall into this same error at the present time. The result is that they tend to lose any sense of discrimination. They act solely on impulses, feelings, leadings, and impressions. They are generally very honest and sincere people. The devil does not try this line of attack on anyone but the most sincere people, the people who are most anxious to be spiritual and to please God. They do not discriminate, they act immediately, they are certain; they do not realize that the Word tells them to 'prove' the spirits, to 'test' the spirits, to examine them. 1 Thessalonians 5:19 is followed by, 'Despise not prophesyings. Prove all things.' 'All things' means all the impressions that come to the spirit, whether to yourself or to another. Test them. Do not accept them simply because someone gets up and says, 'I am filled with the Spirit; you are bound to believe what I am saying'. Do not take what he says at its face value; test him, prove him, try him. There are antichrists, there are false spirits. These people turn a deaf ear to such warnings; the devil has pressed them so far that they are sure their guidance is infallible, and that if it is a strong impression it cannot be wrong. The result is, as I say, disorder and confusion.

The Apostle has prepared us to deal with such problems and persons. He says in writing to the Corinthians in the fourteenth chapter of the First Epistle, verse 33, 'God is not the author of confusion, but of peace'. These people introduce confusion, they all speak at the same time. They were doing so in Corinth, several of them giving prophecies at the same time, several speaking in tongues together. And the Apostle has to say to them that if a stranger came along he would think them all mad. They claimed that the Spirit had moved them; but, says Paul, remember that 'the spirits of the prophets are subject to the prophets'. Christians must control themselves, and they do so if they are guided by the teaching of the Word.

[267]

It is not a sign of high spirituality when there is shouting and high excitement and hand clapping. 'God is not the author of confusion, but of peace, as in all the churches of the saints' (1 Corinthians 14:33). And so he ends that great 14th chapter by saying, 'Let all things be done decently and in order'. If ever anyone knew what it was to be filled with the Spirit it was the Apostle Paul. He says to these Corinthians, 'If it is a question of speaking in tongues, I can speak in tongues more than all of you. If you want a competition in that', says Paul, 'you are already beaten, I have gone beyond you all.' 'Yet' he says, 'I had rather speak five words with my understanding, that by my voice I might teach others also, than ten thousand words in an unknown tongue' (verses 18 and 19). In other words, 'God is not the author of confusion'. 'Everything,' he says, 'must be done decently and in order.'

One of the manifestations of the devil's wiles, therefore, is to press a genuine experience so far that it leads to excess, disorder, confusion and great harm to the Christian cause. Extravagant claims are made which are later found not to be true at all; statements are made which cannot be substantiated, professions are made which are not proved in the life. And the result is that Christianity, and the great salvation, are brought into disrepute among the masses of the people.

The second line of attack, however, is the most urgently important one for us. There are sections of the Church that need to attend to all that I have said; but, speaking generally, that is not the main message needed by the Christian Church today. The message needed today, on the contrary, is 'Quench not the Spirit'. The devil says, 'Of course, what you have just been saying is right'. And most Christian people would say, 'Certainly, quite right, "let everything be done decently, and in order". None of this shouting, this excitement, this ebullience! "God is not the author of confusion, but of peace".' They are so sure of that that the devil drives them right over to the other extreme, and so it becomes necessary to say to them, 'Quench not the Spirit'. There is nothing in the world comparable to the Bible for balance. This perfect balance is the glory of true Christianity. 'God is not the author of confusion.' 'Quench not the Spirit.' 'Despise not

prophesyings. Prove all things. Hold fast that which is good'
(1 Thessalonians 5:19–21). The quenching of the Spirit is the
commoner source of trouble at the present time. I do not hesitate
to assert that the state of the Christian Church today is mainly
due to it. And in so saying, I include the Evangelical section of
the Church as well as that which is not Evangelical.

'On what grounds do you make that assertion?' asks someone.
I answer: Read the New Testament description of the individual
Christian, then its description of the Christian Church, and having
done so, compare yourself and the Church today with what you
have read. Is it necessary to write the First Epistle to the
Corinthians to the Church today? Is there any need to control
excesses in the realm of the Spirit? I have only to ask the question
for us to see that undoubtedly the great sin today is that of
'quenching the Spirit'.

But not only compare and contrast the Church, and the
individual Christian, today with what you find delineated in the
New Testament; take the Church and the individual Christian and
compare and contrast the present picture with what has been seen
so many times in the subsequent history of the Church in periods
of reformation and revival. Read the accounts of some of the
little groups that were in existence even before the Protestant
Reformation – the early Waldensians in Northern Italy, the
'Brethren of the Common Life' and others, the followers of John
Huss and of John Wycliffe. Read their story and you will find a
return to the New Testament pattern and picture. Then read
about the great Reformers and the Reformed Church in this and
in other lands in the sixteenth century. Go on then to the
seventeenth century and read about the Puritans. Turn to the
eighteenth century and the early Methodists, whether they were
followers of Whitefield or of Wesley. There you see the Christian
Church as she is seen in the New Testament, and as she is meant
to be. Contrast them with what is so often true, and so generally
to be seen, at this present time.

The cause of the contrast is undoubtedly the 'quenching of the
Spirit'. In various ways we are guilty of quenching the Spirit. The
Church is meant to be as she is depicted in the New Testament;
and we must never be satisfied with anything different, either
individually or in a corporate sense.

[269]

One way in which the Church quenches the Spirit is that she so often fails to recognize the truth concerning Him, His personality and His indwelling of us. There are many today who even deny the Person of the Holy Spirit; they refer to the Holy Spirit as 'It', as if He were but an influence. I am troubled by the translation of the words we are considering as they appear in the New English Bible. It reads, 'Do not stifle inspiration'. The Spirit Himself is not mentioned. The change is not due to the translators' expert knowledge of Greek. The Greek text has 'the Spirit', *the* Spirit; and not 'stifling' but 'quenching'. Why talk about 'inspiration' when the Apostle wrote 'the Spirit' – the Spirit Himself? This is indicative of the attitude today towards the Holy Spirit. Our Lord, when He talks about the Holy Spirit, talks about 'He' and 'Him'. 'When He is come.' 'Another Comforter.' Not merely an influence! How we detract from the glory of this great salvation! The Three Persons in the blessed Holy Trinity are concerned about us. Not 'inspiration', but the blessed Spirit Himself. The Father, who is over all, sent His Son, His only begotten Son; and then the Father and the Son sent the Third Person, the blessed Holy Spirit. How can we avoid being guilty of quenching the Spirit if we are not clear about His Person? He is co-equal with the Father and with the Son: 'God in Three Persons; blessed Trinity'. We must not detract from the glory of the Third Person. He is not just an influence, not some 'It'; He is indeed God the Holy Ghost.

What our Lord was saying in John chapter 14 can be expressed thus: Just as I am now looking at you and speaking to you, and you know that I am with you, so the Spirit is going to be with you; He is going to dwell within you. Not only so; He says 'The Father and I will come. We will take up our abode in you and dwell in you.' That is the teaching of the New Testament with regard to this matter. The Holy Ghost not only came *upon* the Church on the day of Pentecost, He dwells *within us* as believers. The Apostle states that plainly to the Corinthians. 'What? know ye not that your body is the temple of the Holy Ghost which is in you, which ye have of God, and ye are not your own? For ye are bought with a price: therefore glorify God in your body, and in your spirit, which are God's' (1 Corinthians 6:19). The Holy Spirit dwells within us, and He is in the Church. In the Epistle to the Ephesians we find the following at the end of the second chapter: 'Ye are no more strangers and foreigners, but fellow-citizens with the saints, and of the household of God; and are built upon the foundation of the apostles and prophets, Jesus Christ himself being the chief corner stone; in whom all the building fitly framed together groweth unto an holy temple in the Lord: in whom we also are builded together for an habitation of God through the Spirit'. That is the Church!

We can be guilty of quenching the Spirit without realizing it, simply by not knowing that He dwells in the midst in the Church, and that the Church is 'a habitation of God through the Spirit'. But He Himself dwells in every one of us; our bodies we must always think of as 'the temples of the Holy Ghost'. We should overcome sin by reminding ourselves that He is within us, tabernacling in these bodies of ours. Is that always in the forefront of our minds? If not, we are guilty of quenching the Spirit. We must be reminding ourselves of this constantly. 'What? know ye not?' Say that to yourself, speak to yourself, preach to yourself; remind yourself of the indwelling of the blessed Holy Spirit.

But, more particularly, we quench the Spirit by not allowing Him to work in us as we ought. This is what is brought out by the word *quench*. It is not 'stifle'; it is stronger – *Quench*! Quenching immediately conjures up the image of fire. That is why the Apostle used the word translated 'quench'; it brings us at once to the notion of fire. You 'quench' a fire; so what he is really saying is, Do not quench the fire of the Spirit that is within you. Of all the images used with respect to the Holy Spirit there is none used more frequently than that of fire. John the Baptist used the word quite dramatically. Some of the people, having heard his preaching, said, 'Is not this the Christ?' John overheard them and said, 'I am not the Christ. I indeed baptize you with water; but one mightier than I cometh, the latchet of whose shoes I am not worthy to unloose: he shall baptize you with the Holy Ghost, and with fire: whose fan is in his hand, and he will throughly purge his floor, and will gather the wheat into his garner; but the chaff he will burn with fire unquenchable' (Luke 3:16 and 17). On the day of Pentecost, when the Spirit came, He descended in the form of 'cloven tongues as of fire'. Indeed there is already an adumbration of this in the Old Testament, where the Holy Spirit is referred to as 'the spirit of burning' (Isaiah 4:4). This is the emblem that is used in order to bring to us the truth concerning the Spirit. Here the Apostle puts it negatively, 'Do not quench the Spirit'. We are also told not to 'grieve' the Spirit. That is not the same as to quench the Spirit. Grieving the Spirit has a much more direct reference to the Person Himself; quenching is more related to His influence, and to His effect upon us. Of course, by quenching Him we also grieve Him, but here we are dealing with the quenching.

As Christians we are meant to be living a 'life in the Spirit'. We are no longer 'in the flesh', we are 'in the Spirit'. The Christian life is a 'life in the Spirit'. We are meant to be 'filled with the Spirit' (Ephesians 5:18). The normal Christian life is to be a life filled with the Spirit. It is a spiritual life, governed, controlled, guided by the blessed Holy Spirit. The devil's chief desire and object is to prevent our living that life, and he is so successful that the average man in the world looking at the Christian Church says, 'Of course I am not a Christian; what need is there to be a Christian? I cannot see much difference between a Christian and a man who is not a Christian. Indeed,' he adds, 'I know many more moral people doing good work outside the Church than there are inside the Church.' It is because Christians are not showing the power of this life in the Spirit that the masses are outside the Church today. To evangelize successfully the Church must become a spiritual Church. Then she will challenge the world; but not until then. The devil's chief aim is to persuade us to quench the Spirit; and, alas, he is very successful.

We can know whether we are quenching the Spirit or not by considering what the Spirit does as fire. First of all He gives light and understanding. The Apostle prayed for the Ephesians that the Spirit might do this very thing for them: 'That the God of our Lord Jesus Christ, the Father of glory, may give unto you the spirit of wisdom and revelation in the knowledge of him: the eyes of your understanding being enlightened; that ye may know . . .' (Chapter 1:17-18). The Spirit gives understanding and knowledge; He explains the mysteries of the faith, giving us an understanding of the doctrine of salvation, that we may know these things clearly and apprehend them and lay hold on them. But the Apostle continues, 'That ye may know what is the hope of his calling, and what the riches of the glory of his inheritance in the saints, and what is the exceeding greatness of His power to us-ward who believe. (verses 18–19). Later in chapter 3 we find him saying that he bows his knees before this God who is the Father of all fatherhood, praying that we may ultimately come 'to know the love of Christ, which passeth knowledge, and be filled with all the fulness of God' (verse 19).

Do we know these things? Are we clear about the way of salvation? Can you explain it to another? Do you understand the teaching of these Epistles? Or are you like so many modern Christians who say, 'Of course, I have no time for these things, I am too busy'. The Spirit is here to enlighten us, to open our eyes, to make these things plain and clear, to get rid of all confusion in understanding and knowledge and apprehension. Look at the Apostles themselves before and after the day of Pentecost. Before, they were confused, they did not understand. But the fire came, and immediately Peter preaches and expounds the Scriptures: he has knowledge, understanding, comprehension. This is typical of the Spirit's work.

Another thing I want to emphasize is the warmth of the fire. Do not quench the fire, do not quench the Spirit. In other words you must not be a cold Christian. Christianity means warmth, it means a glow. Paul has to write even to a man like Timothy, and say, 'Stir up the gift that is in thee', which might better be translated, 'Fan into flame the fire'. Stir up the embers, 'maintain the glow', as someone translates it. Now that is Christianity – warmth, fire! Do not quench it! You cannot think of a fire without thinking of heat being radiated, and you and I as Christians are meant to be like that. 'Yes, of course,' you say, 'but if you have true scholarship you will not be animated; you will be dignified, you will read a great treatise quietly and without passion.' Out with the suggestion! That is quenching the Spirit! The Apostle Paul breaks some of the rules of grammar; he interrupts his own argument. It is because of the fire! We are so decorous, we are so controlled, we do everything with such decency and order that there is no life, there is no warmth, there is no power! But that is not New Testament Christianity; and that is why so many people are outside the Church. Does your faith melt and move your heart? Does it get rid of the ice that is in you, the coldness in your heart, and the stiffness? The essence of New Testament Christianity is this warmth that is invariably the result of the presence of the Spirit. Do you not feel that as you read that most lyrical of books, the Acts of the Apostles? Live in that book, I exhort you; it is a tonic, the greatest tonic I know of in the realm of the Spirit. The Christian spirit is a warm spirit. I am not thinking of some artificial appearance which looks like fire. People try to make electric fires look as if they are coal fires, but it is not the same thing. I am talking about FIRE and not mere appearance.

The Spirit not only gives warmth, but with warmth He also gives assurance. A true Christian, filled with the Spirit, knows that his sins are forgiven, and that he is a child of God. 'The Spirit beareth witness with our spirit, that we are the children of God.' He has 'the Spirit of adoption, whereby we cry, Abba, Father.' He knows it, he is certain of it. He knows God's love to him. The Apostle in writing to the Romans says, 'The love of God is shed abroad in our hearts by the Holy Ghost which is given unto us' (8:5). 'Shed abroad!' Not a little trickle, but an outpouring, a great profusion. As He was 'poured forth' upon the Church on the day of Pentecost, so is He poured forth into our hearts, bringing the love of God. Is that love in your heart? If not you are somehow quenching the Spirit. The Christian is a man who knows that God loves him. He is amazed at it, but he knows it; he is melted by it, he is moved by it.

Not only so; he knows that he is a child of God and that he is a special object of God's care. God pours His love upon him and into him. And the result of this is that he in turn loves God, and he loves the Lord Jesus Christ. You cannot have the fire of the Spirit within you without loving God. You not only believe in God, you love Him; you not only believe in the Lord Jesus Christ, you love Him; and you are grieved at the fact that your love is not greater than it is. 'Whom having not seen.' The Apostle Peter says to Christians, 'Whom having not seen, ye love; in whom, though now ye see him not, yet believing, ye rejoice with joy unspeakable and full of glory' (1 Peter 1:8). Is that true of us? Do we know something of this 'joy unspeakable and full of glory'? Do we really love Him? I am not talking about merely saying so, I mean, Do you feel it? Is your heart moved

[274]

and melted and drawn out to Him? That is how we are meant to be – 'Be not filled with wine, wherein is excess; but be filled with the Spirit'. And this is the result of it.

That in turn leads to gratitude, the desire to praise Him and to magnify Him, to live to His glory. That is truly to be a citizen of the Kingdom of God. Paul, writing to the Romans, says, 'The kingdom of God is not meat and drink, but righteousness, and peace, and joy in the Holy Ghost' (Romans 14:17). 'Rejoice in the Lord alway: and again I say, Rejoice', says the Apostle, to the Philippians (4:4). When the Spirit comes there is warmth; we are melted, we are moved, we love. The fruit of the Spirit begins to manifest itself, and it is 'love, joy, peace, long-suffering, gentleness, goodness, meekness, faith, and temperance'.

We should all be as a burning fire. There should be this flame within us burning out the dross, but above all filling us and inflaming us with a great love to Him. We should begin to pray with Charles Wesley –

> *Enlarge, inflame, and fill my heart*
> *With boundless charity divine.*

God forbid that any of us should be allowing the devil to persuade us to quench the Spirit in any manner! Do you know anything of this fire? If you do not, confess it to God and acknowledge it. Repent, and ask Him to send the Spirit and His love into you until you are melted and moved, until you are filled with His love divine, and know His love to you, and rejoice in it as His child, and look forward to the hope of the coming glory. 'Quench not the Spirit', but rather 'be filled with the Spirit' and 'rejoice in Christ Jesus'.

> *Spirit of God, descend upon my heart;*
> *Wean it from earth; through all its pulses move;*
> *Stoop to my weakness, mighty as Thou art,*
> *And make me love Thee as I ought to love.*
>
> *Teach me to love Thee as Thine angels love,*
> *One holy passion filling all my frame –*
> *The baptism of the heaven-descended Dove,*
> *My heart an altar, and Thy love the flame.*

20

Quenching the Spirit (2)

A further test which we can apply to ourselves in order to discover whether we are guilty of 'quenching the Spirit' suggests itself immediately when we remember that the Spirit is represented by the emblem of fire. It is the one mentioned by John the Baptist. He said, 'I indeed baptize you with water, but one mightier than I cometh, the latchet of whose shoes I am not worthy to unloose: He shall baptize you with the Holy Ghost, and with fire' (Luke 3:16). Fire is characterized not only by heat and light but also by power. It advances, and destroys wherever it goes. Similarly, power is a characteristic of the Holy Spirit.

Are we, then, aware of the power of the Spirit within us? If not we are quenching the Spirit. An extraordinary paradox is involved in this matter. The Spirit is the Spirit of God, and is all-powerful; and yet it is possible for us to 'quench' the Spirit, to 'resist' the Spirit, to 'grieve' the Spirit. It is a great mystery, but it is true. You cannot reconcile these things ultimately, but the teaching is quite plain. In spite of His almighty power He comes also as a dove – the gentle dove who can be offended.

How do we know whether the Spirit is working in us powerfully? One test is found in the Epistle to the Philippians, 'Wherefore, my beloved, as ye have always obeyed, not as in my presence only, but now much more in my absence, work out your own salvation with fear and trembling. For it is God which worketh in you both to will and to do of his good pleasure' (Philippians 2: 12–13). God works in every Christian by and through the Holy

Spirit – the fire, the power. He prompts us, He urges us, He leads us. As Paul expresses it in Romans 8:14: 'As many as are led by the Spirit of God, they are the sons of God'. The Spirit produces a kind of disturbance within us, 'moving', 'urging', 'prompting'; we are aware of a power dealing with us, a power other than ourselves.

Another test is that the Spirit always leads to life and vigour and liveliness. The truly spiritual man, the Christian filled with the Spirit, is never a man who has to drag himself and force himself to do things. There is a power in him, a vigour and a liveliness, because the Spirit is a life-giving Spirit. The contrast drawn in the Scripture between the non-Christian and the Christian is that between someone who is 'dead in trepasses and sins', and someone who is 'alive from the dead', who has been 'born again'. The non-Christian is dead, is lifeless, he knows nothing about God, nothing about the life of the soul, nothing about a spiritual energy. He does not live, he only exists. That is the tragedy of the world today. Worldly people talk about life, about 'seeing life'. But it is not life, it is mere existence. There is no life apart from God the Spirit.

Everyone who is a Christian, filled with the Spirit, knows about this vigour, this liveliness; so he does not have to drive himself, or urge himself, or drag himself to God's house, or to anything that he does as a Christian. The energy of the Spirit is moving in him. The Apostle Paul constantly makes this clear. At the end of the first chapter of the Epistle to the Colossians, he says, 'Whom we preach, warning every man, and teaching every man in all wisdom; that we may present every man perfect in Christ Jesus: whereunto I also labour, striving according to his working, which worketh in me mightily'. Similarly he says, 'the love of Christ constraineth me'. There was an energy moving him, carrying him along, and this is always characteristic of the Spirit. The Scriptures came into being in this way. Peter, in his Second Epistle, tells us that 'No scripture is of any private interpretation'. In other words it does not present a man's view of things. It is not a case of a man who has been studying, meditating, ruminating, and cogitating, who at last says, 'Now I have worked it out'. That is not how the Scriptures have come; but 'holy men of God spake as they were moved', 'carried along',

[277]

'borne along', 'energized by the Holy Ghost' (2 Peter 1:20–21). Our Christian life is to be lively; so if you are dragging yourself about and are lethargic you are probably quenching the Spirit.

Moreover, the Spirit, through His power, gives us ability to live and to witness. The apostles, after our Lord's death, were disconsolate, unhappy, miserable, feeling utterly helpless, so much so that Peter, as we are told at the beginning of John 21, turned to the others and said, 'I go a-fishing'. Listen to the conversation of the two men on the road to Emmaus: 'We trusted that it had been he which should have redeemed Israel' – and so on (Luke 24:21). That is the picture; and the Christian Church, had she continued in that condition, would not have held together for even a few weeks.

But look at what happened later. Peter, the one who denied his Lord but a few weeks previously, is now standing up in Jerusalem and charging the very rulers of the people, saying, 'You have put to death the Prince of life!' He condemns them and calls them to repentance. He preaches 'Jesus and the resurrection'. The difference is entirely due to the Spirit, the power of the Spirit. The Spirit enables us to witness. He teaches us how to witness, and gives us the ability to witness. He also tells us what to say.

A person sometimes says, 'I feel I am a Christian, but I cannot help anyone. I do not seem to know much.' But no Christian has the right to be in that state. It is not a question of human ability; but of the power of the Spirit given to us. This has been proved abundantly in the long history of the Christian Church. Some of the humblest members of the Church have been the means under God of helping some of the greatest. We have the example of the able, eloquent Apollos being helped by Priscilla and Aquila. We know the help that has been given to many a man of humble origin, like John Bunyan, of which the history of the Church supplies many striking examples. So there is no excuse. Have we this ability to live, to witness, and to pray?

The Spirit leads to prayer always; and He gives ability in prayer. Do you find it difficult to pray in private, and in public? It should not be so, for the Spirit energizes in this matter of prayer. 'We know not what we should pray for as we ought', but the Spirit helps our infirmities. He teaches us how to pray and leads us out in prayer; He enlarges us in prayer. What do we know of this in experience?

I am concerned about this not only in terms of our individual experiences, but also because of the whole state of the Church. Why is the Church so ineffective? My answer is that she lacks this power. Hence she is not praying and interceding as she ought, although the world is as it is, and there are terrible possibilities in the realm of nuclear science. The Church seems so lethargic, she has not got power; and it is largely because she does not know how truly to pray. And she cannot pray truly because the Spirit is not energizing her prayer. But when the Spirit comes He moves Christians to pray. Read the history of the great revivals in the Church, and you will find that, in revival, people begin to pray who have never prayed in public in their lives; and they pray in private as they have never prayed before. The Spirit coming in power gives the ability in prayer.

Another matter I must mention is 'boldness'. We are told in Acts, chapter 4, that when they observed 'the boldness of Peter and John'. They saw that they were 'ignorant and unlettered', and untutored men, but they also saw that they had boldness. It was the descent of the Spirit upon them at Pentecost that accounted for it. Peter had a natural courage, but face to face with death it failed him completely, and he denied his Lord. But not after Pentecost! On that day his fear of men vanished away. Boldness! And what the apostles prayed for was that 'with all boldness' they might be enabled to go on preaching the Gospel.

These, then, are some of the tests that we must apply to ourselves. 'Quench not the Spirit.' Are you quenching the Spirit? What about the life and the vigour? What about the warmth and the radiance? What about the joy and the praise and the thanksgiving? If they are not present, in some way or other, we are quenching the Spirit. The responsibility of Christians is very great. We have to start with the Church, not with the world outside. The chief trouble is in the Church. The masses are outside largely because we who are inside are not attracting them. We are failing to give the impression that we have the most glorious of all possessions. We give an impression of lethargy, of slowness and of dulness; there seems to be more life outside.

People say that you cannot get the young people to come to the church nowadays because they find the church dull. The church should be the most exciting and thrilling place in the world, and if she is not we are somehow or other 'quenching the Spirit'.

What are the ways in which we may quench the Spirit? We must examine ourselves in detail in this matter. There are some who are guilty of quenching the Spirit by limiting in their very thinking the possibilities of life in the Spirit. They put a limit upon the operations of the Spirit. In the first chapter of this Epistle we read in verse 13, 'In whom ye also trusted, after that ye heard the word of truth, the gospel of your salvation: in whom also after that ye believed (or, having believed), ye were sealed with that Holy Spirit of promise, which is the earnest of our inheritance until the redemption of the purchased possession'. The idea of sealing is repeated in chapter 4, verse 30: 'Grieve not the Holy Spirit of God, whereby ye are sealed until the day of redemption'. Or take the great statement in Romans: 'Ye have not received the spirit of bondage again to fear; but ye have received the Spirit of adoption, whereby we cry, Abba, Father. The Spirit himself also beareth witness with our spirit, that we are the children of God: and if children, then heirs; heirs of God, and joint-heirs with Christ' (8:15-17). Do we realize and believe these truths?

I am convinced that there are large numbers of Christian people who are quenching the Spirit unconsciously by denying these possibilities in their very understanding of the doctrine of the Spirit. There is nothing, I am convinced, that so 'quenches' the Spirit as the teaching which identifies the baptism of the Holy Ghost with regeneration. But it is a very commonly held teaching today, indeed it has been the popular view for many years. It is said that the baptism of the Holy Spirit is 'non-experimental', that it happens to every one at regeneration. So we say, 'Ah well, I am already baptized with the Spirit; it happened when I was born again, at my conversion; there is nothing for me to seek, I have got it all'. Got it all? Well, if you have 'got it all', I simply ask in the Name of God, why are you as you are? If you have 'got it all', why are you so unlike the Apostles, why are you so unlike the New Testament Christians?

The teaching that I have just mentioned is false. The apostles were regenerate before the day of Pentecost. The baptism of the Holy Ghost is not identical with regeneration; it is something separate. It matters not how long the interval between the two may be, there is a difference; there is an interval, they are not identical. But if you say that they are identical, you do not expect anything further. And if you do not believe that it is possible for you to experience the Spirit of God bearing direct witness with your own spirit that you are a child of God, obviously you are quenching the Spirit. That is why so many Christian people are miserable and unhappy; they do not know anything about crying out, 'Abba, Father'; or about 'the Spirit of adoption'. God is a Being away in the far distance; they do not know Him as a loving Father; they do not know that they are His children. They may believe it intellectually, theoretically; but Paul says, 'You have not received the spirit of bondage again to fear'. We are not to go about groaning and wondering whether we are Christians or not. We were in that state under the law; then we were wretched and we cried out, 'O wretched man that I am! who shall deliver me?' But no longer! 'We have received the Spirit of adoption, whereby we cry' – and it is an elemental cry that comes from the depth of the personality – 'Abba, Father'. We are now like a little child who has not seen his father for a long time; then the father suddenly appears and the child runs to meet him and cries out, 'Father!' 'Abba, Father!' If you deny this as a possibility, you not only lack the experience, but you are also quenching the Spirit. This witness of the Spirit is independent of our spirit. 'The Spirit beareth witness *with* our spirit' – over and above – 'that we are the children of God'.

The devil does not want us to know this; he would keep us trembling and unhappy and miserable. He succeeds with some even with respect to the very doctrine of the Spirit. He keeps them in a state of uncertainty. He says, 'To claim that the Spirit has given you direct assurance is presumption. You say you are a child of God, that you know that God is your Father, and that the Spirit has testified to it. That is enthusiasm! Ecstasy! Be careful; that is not the humility of the Christian man.' Christians are so much afraid of excesses and enthusiasm that they are only satisfied that they are Christians when they are really miserable.

What a tragedy! What blindness, what misunderstanding of Christian doctrine!

I am not advocating a glib, superficial, excitable, effervescent type of Christianity. I am referring to the 'witness of the Spirit', which at one and the same time humbles you, amazes you, and yet fills you 'with a joy unspeakable and full of glory'. Are you clear in your doctrine of the Spirit? Are you clear about the sealing and the earnest and the assurance and the testimony and the witness of the Spirit? If you have any doubts about these things, you are probably quenching the Spirit.

Secondly, there are those who say that they believe that these things are taught in the New Testament but that surely they were only for the first Christians. The Church was being inaugurated, and what happened at Pentecost was once and for ever, never to be repeated. Peter answered this view on the day of Pentecost: 'The promise is unto you, and to your children, and to as many as are afar off'. The blessing is to continue down the running centuries – 'you, your children, your descendants' – and on and on until the end of the age. Thank God it is as possible today as it was then. Many quench the Spirit in this way. But they are answered by Acts 2:39; and not only so, they are answered by every great revival in the history of the Church. Every revival is a repetition of Pentecost! God, blessed be His Name, has poured forth His Spirit many times since the day of Pentecost. Many revivals have occurred. Church history tells us of people who met together, not expecting anything in particular, when suddenly the Holy Spirit came down upon them and they were aware of a power and a presence filling the building. They were taken up, and out, of themselves; a repetition of Pentecost; and it has happened in the lives of many individuals. It still happens, thank God, quite apart from a general revival in the Church. To deny that is to quench the Spirit.

Then, thirdly, there are others who are guilty of the same denial of the working of the Spirit who say, 'I admit it is there, I cannot dispute it; but it is only meant for certain exceptional Christians; it is only meant for some great saints'. That is the heresy, the lie, taught by the Roman Catholic Church, which divides her people into two groups – the saints, the exceptional Christians, and the ordinary Christians. They do not expect anything from the latter for they have not gone in for the Christian life as a vocation. They talk about the 'religious' and the 'laity'. What a denial of New Testament teaching! The Apostle addresses every single member of the Church at Corinth as a saint! All New Testament Christians are 'called to be saints'; not only some whom you decide after many years to canonize and to call 'saints'. Every Christian is a saint; the word is not confined to certain special individuals. There is not a text in the whole of the New Testament which says that this blessing of the power and the fire of the Spirit is to be confined only to certain people, to exceptional saints, or preachers, or someone whom God wants to use in a special manner. No, it is 'to you, and your children, and to as many as are afar off'.

If we hold any one of these positions then we are guilty of quenching the Spirit. What do you expect? Let me be quite direct and practical. Do you have any expectation when you enter a Christian service? What is your mood, what kind of condition are you in, what is your attitude towards what you are doing? Do you go to a place of worship simply because it is Sunday morning? Is it just an item in the programme? And is it just a matter of singing some hymns, hearing the reading of the Scriptures, listening to a sermon, and so on? Just a matter of habit, repeating what you have done many times before? Is that the way in which you go into God's house? God have mercy upon you if it is!

Let me be personal. How do I enter a pulpit? Am I there simply because I was announced to preach? Simply because I am the minister of a church? And as the minister I am expected to preach Sunday by Sunday? God forgive me, it often has been so, but it never should be. We should all come together, not only to meet with God and each other, but to expect the gracious influences of His Spirit, regarding it as the highest privilege of our lives, not knowing what may happen, believing that at any moment He may come and the place be filled with His glory and with His presence and His radiance. Do you expect that? Does your doctrine cater for that? Has that got a place in your doctrine? If it has not, it is not surprising that the Church is as she is, and that the world is as it is. That is 'quenching the Spirit!' Our doctrine of the Spirit and His operations must be perfectly clear.

That leads me to the fourth illustration of the ways in which

[283]

we can quench the Spirit. Formalism is the greatest curse in the Church. I do not desire to criticize any particular section of the Church, as it is true of all the churches, unfortunately. But formalism is seen at its zenith in Roman Catholicism – the pomp, the ceremony, everything worked out to the minutest detail, with the processions and vestments, and so on, and the people sitting back and doing nothing while the great performance takes place before them. The people really do not enter into the service. Revivals do not occur in the Roman Catholic Church; they cannot do, there is no room left for such. Everything is controlled by men; the service is worked out in detail, and to the minute, everything perfect and in order. And there are those who imitate such methods in all sections of the Christian Church.

I throw out a question for your consideration: Is a prescribed liturgy compatible with the freedom of the Spirit? There is an answer to the question, and I give it myself immediately. The Holy Spirit can even use a liturgy! He has done so, He can break through it. But He has to break through it! The more set, formal, mechanical, repetitive the service, the less opportunity there is for the Spirit. If you read Church history in the light of this proposition you will find it is most illuminating.

Do not misunderstand me, but I have a feeling that the Christian Church today is dying of dignity, dying of decorum. Services are beautiful, and perfect, but where is the breath of the Spirit? We are so concerned about dignity, and so self-conscious; we are all unconsciously tending to imitate that Church to which I have already referred in which there are no revivals and which is still opposed to true reformation. Many others are imitating her in various shapes or forms; processions take place in free churches, and simple, godly preachers are anxious to become great church dignitaries. It was when this craving for dignity and decorum, and scholarship, learning and culture came into the churches about the middle of the last century that the Holy Spirit seemed to be withdrawn. Men began to 'quench the Spirit'. Formalism is always the greatest enemy of the power and the life and the freedom of the Spirit.

But this applies not only to Church services; it applies also to the type of life which we live. Christian people are in danger of being produced like postage stamps or peas in a pod, all the same.

[284]

They are 'converted', and then are given a certain teaching concerning sanctification. They soon become set and smug and glib. They know all the phrases and all the clichés; but there is no real life, no power, no freedom. They are merely formal Christians, and all are alike.

This seems to me to be a major problem confronting the Church. It is a simple fact, which can be proved statistically, that the so-called working-classes in this country, and in most other countries, are, speaking generally, outside the Christian Church. Thank God, there are such people in our churches; but speaking generally, the working-classes are missing. Our churches are filled with people who belong to a certain social class; and a process of inbreeding within that circle is taking place. This is surely the result of a formalism which produces a set type. But in the New Testament there are all types and kinds. And so it has been in every period of revival and of reformation. Formalism can grip us even in our personal lives, and it leads to a dislike of being disturbed. Our Christianity has a place in our programme; it has a part in our lives; we believe in doing this and that, and we thank God that we are as we are: and quite unconsciously we become Pharisees who thank God not only that we are as we are, but that we are not like those other people who are still outside. We go on in this smug, set, glib, formal way. We do not want to be disturbed; we do not feel that there is anything further for us. Hence we do not like the teaching that differentiates between regeneration and the baptism of the Spirit. For that means that, after all, we are not as we should be. We thought we were, however, and regarded the liberals and modernists and the people who were right outside as the people who alone were wrong. But now we begin to see that we ourselves need something; and we do not like the jolt. We fight against it; and that is 'quenching the Spirit'. If you are fighting against the New Testament teaching concerning the possibilities of life in the Spirit, because you are afraid of being disturbed, and of what it may lead to, you are quenching the Spirit.

That leads to another matter which I have already mentioned – the fear of excesses. Some Christians are so much afraid of the excesses of which others are guilty that they quench the Spirit. I am not saying that there are no excesses; excesses occur, and I do not defend them. They are wrong; they come from the devil pressing people to extremes. But you must not be so much afraid of them that you go to the other extreme and quench the Spirit altogether. You say 'I do not want to make a fool of myself'. That is right; you should not make a fool of yourself. But be careful lest in your fear of making a fool of yourself you never do anything at all, and you remain a useless Christian! That is what is happening to many because of fear of excesses.

I recall an incident in my own experience. A man put a question in a fellowship meeting which I used to hold in a church where I ministered. He was the type of man I am describing. He said, 'I am interested in that statement in the fourth chapter of the Epistle to the Philippians, "Let your moderation be known unto all men" '. Knowing my man I knew exactly what was in his mind. He had a feeling that some other members of the church were going a bit too far, taking their Christianity too seriously. They were coming to several week-night meetings in the church, and they were living for these things. He felt that this was going too far, and he thought he had found a text to support his position. But unfortunately for him he did not know the real meaning of the text. The translation found in the Authorised Version is not a good translation; he did not know that the real meaning is 'magnanimity', 'self-control', 'forbearance', in the sense that you do not lose your temper. But you see how the devil had come in. He thought he had provided the man with a text defining the right kind of Christian – the man who does not get excited about his faith, the man who is always 'moderate'. The devil as 'an angel of light' had given him a wrong interpretation in order to justify his quenching of the Spirit!

But this happens not only in individuals. There is an account in the life of Jonathan Goforth, the great Canadian missionary who was used of God in revival in Korea and other eastern countries early this century. It is said that, when he was passing through England in 1906, the authorities responsible for a certain well-known convention hesitated long as to whether they would ask him to speak because they did not want meetings which might go on for hours, even through the night, such as had been happening in Korea, to happen in their convention. The matter is mentioned in the official biography, *The Life of Jonathan*

Goforth, by Mrs. Goforth. In the outcome he was asked to speak in the convention but he was given to understand that he was now not in Korea, but somewhere else! Is that not quenching the Spirit? Why should the programme, the timetable, never be upset? Why must we say that the dignity and decorum must never be interfered with? God have mercy upon us! The fear of excesses is probably leading more people today to quench the Spirit than any other single factor.

Again, if you do not respond to the Spirit you are quenching Him. There is a hymn that expresses it thus:

> *Saviour, while my heart is tender,*
> *I would yield that heart to Thee.*

If He does come, and in His gracious influence gives you tenderness of heart, do not resist Him. Do not allow to happen to you what happened to the bride we read of in the Song of Solomon: 'I sleep, but my heart waketh: it is the voice of my beloved that knocketh, saying, Open to me, my sister, my love, my dove, my undefiled: for my head is filled with dew, and my locks with the drops of the night'. Then she replies, 'I have put off my coat; how shall I put it on? I have washed my feet; how shall I defile them? My beloved put in his hand by the hole of the door, and my bowels were moved for him. I rose up to open to my beloved; and my hands dropped with myrrh, and my fingers with sweet-smelling myrrh, upon the handles of the lock. I opened to my beloved; but my beloved had withdrawn himself, and was gone: my soul failed me when he spake: I sought him, but I could not find him; I called him, but he gave me no answer' (5:2–6).

Let that be a lesson to us! When He comes and speaks, when He brings His endearments, puts His hand as it were through the lock of the door, do not answer saying, 'I cannot rise now, I am tired and weary, I am in bed, I cannot get up as yet, I cannot put my clothes on, I cannot put anything on my feet, I cannot walk without anything on, I will defile my feet and will have to wash them again . . .' Do not resist Him when He comes. Receive Him, put everything on one side, welcome Him when you feel that the Spirit is dealing with you, calling you to repentance, or rebuking you for a certain sin. Listen to Him, thank Him, respond to Him. When He comes suggesting renewal or reformation, when He urges you to Bible study, to prayer, or work, whatever it is, do not quench Him, do not resist Him. Open the door at once, and open your arms! His visits may be rare, well, look forward to them, seek them, respond immediately. If you do not, you are quenching the Spirit, and you will have the unhappy experience that when you are seeking Him you will not be able to find Him. And when you are on your deathbed and are looking for Him you may not be able to find Him. Do not resist Him, His offers and His overtures; but rather welcome them with open arms whenever they come.

Yet another way in which we are guilty of quenching the Spirit is that we do not stir up the gift that is in us, we do not stir up the fire. Any fire tends to get filled with ashes, and you have to rake it out now and again; if you do not, your fire will go out. Get rid of the ashes! Paul puts it thus in writing to Timothy: 'Wherefore I put thee in remembrance that thou stir up the gift of God, which is in thee by the putting on of my hands' (2 Timothy 1:6). You can translate that, as we have seen, thus: 'I exhort thee to "fan the flame" (or to "stir into flame")'. Get hold of the bellows; get hold of a poker and do a bit of raking. Is the warmth diminishing, is the power becoming less? Well, get rid of the ashes and the dust; fan it into flame. Wake up; if you do not you are guilty of quenching the Spirit. Laziness and contentment with the little we have; not adding more fuel; not making an air-way; not giving opportunities for the Spirit, are ways of quenching the Spirit. The more you do, the more He will come; the more you stir yourself, the more He will stir you. This is the law of the spiritual life.

These, then, are some of the ways in which we are all guilty of quenching the Spirit. What fools we are even for our own sakes! But think of what it means to the Church, think of what it means to the world. The greatest of all needs today is the flame, the fire, the power of the Holy Ghost in individual Christians and in the Church as a whole. Beloved Christian people, 'Quench not the Spirit'; rather seek Him, make room for Him, make way for Him, yield yourselves to His gracious leadings and dealings.

21

Temptation and Sin

We move now to the consideration of another very fruitful source of trouble in the Christian life resulting from the 'wiles of the devil', namely, the confusion between temptation and sin. All who have any pastoral experience will agree that there is nothing, perhaps, on the purely practical level, which so frequently brings God's people into trouble, and into a condition of fear and of depression and a sense of frustration, as this particular matter. It includes such problems as evil thoughts, thoughts which may at times even be blasphemous, evil imaginations – the imagination tempted to play upon things that are wrong and evil and unworthy. James, in the first chapter of his Epistle, talks about 'filthiness' (verse 21). We read elsewhere of 'evil imaginations'. Such things are often mentioned in the Scriptures. We are told that before the Flood the condition of the human race was such that 'every imagination of the thoughts of (their) hearts was only evil continually'. There are also 'evil desires' which arise in thoughts and imaginations. The thought becomes a desire, the imagination leads to a lust.

The devil deals with this along certain lines. One line is to suggest that to be tempted at all is sin, in and of itself, and that the Christian should not even be tempted. The very fact that we are tempted is therefore indicative of the fact that we are perhaps not Christians at all, or at any rate very poor Christians. The devil comes and says, 'Obviously you are not a new creature, you have not been born again, you have not got a new nature. Temptation belonged to the old life and to the past; therefore the fact that you are still tempted is a proof that you are not really what you think you are.' So he comes and says that either the temptation in and of itself is sin, or else that as Christians we should not be tempted.

Perhaps his most subtle approach is to suggest to us that all these thoughts and imaginations and desires are entirely our own, that they arise within us, and are therefore proof positive that our nature is still vile and polluted and evil. He uses these various arguments with the intent of proving to us that we are not Christians, that we have never been Christians. Thus he depresses us and makes us feel entirely hopeless. The standard he sets up is that we should be in such a state and condition as to be entirely free from such temptations, and altogether delivered from them. The acceptance of such suggestions has often had a crippling effect upon many Christian people at one time or another.

How do we deal with this problem? These 'wiles of the devil' have to be analysed and isolated, and we have to show the appropriate remedy in each particular case. They must be taken one by one. The teaching which suggests that there is but one thing to do, namely, 'Let go and let God', is not New Testament teaching. These things have to be taken in detail one by one. It is the only way to deal with them. It is the Scriptural way; and it is the only way which works in practice.

The answer that is given us in the Scriptures is that we must start with the realization that as Christians we are neither perfect, nor sinless. If we think that the Christian is of necessity perfect, and entirely delivered from sin, we shall have no reply to give to the devil. But the teaching of the Scripture is that the Christian in this life and world is not sinless, is not perfect. The Scriptural position is stated very plainly in Romans 6:6: 'Knowing this, that our old man was crucified with him' – that is to say *with Christ* – 'that (in order that) the body of sin might be destroyed, that henceforth we should not serve sin'. We have died with Christ 'in order that' this body of sin, which, whether you take it as a description of the 'mass' of sin, or more correctly as the sin that tends to remain in the body – we have died with Christ in order that finally, ultimately, we may be delivered from it. The body of sin is to be 'disannulled', to be 'disintegrated', 'taken to pieces', 'rendered null and void'. In other words the teaching of the Scripture is that there is a relic or remnant of sin that remains in the body. In the first chapter of the Epistle of James the doctrine is stated very plainly. People were going astray about this whole matter of temptation even then. James says, 'Let no man say when he is tempted, I am tempted of God'. Some were ready to say so; but that is the devil's suggestion. He says, 'God cannot be tempted with evil, neither tempteth he any man. But every man is tempted when he is drawn away of his own lust, and enticed. Then when lust hath conceived, it bringeth forth sin: and sin, when it is finished, bringeth forth death' (1:13–15). There are what James calls 'lusts' remaining in the believer, in his body. Paul says to Christians in Romans 6, verses 11, 12 and 13: 'Likewise reckon ye also yourselves to be dead indeed unto sin, but alive unto God through Jesus Christ our Lord'. That is the Christian's position. But then the Apostle continues: 'Let not sin therefore reign in (have control of) your mortal body'. Do not let it control your mortal body, do not be controlled by certain tendencies in your mortal body. It is there, it is ever seeking to use the body. The Apostle continues, 'Neither yield ye your members as instruments of unrighteous-ness unto sin; but yield yourselves unto God, as those that are alive from the dead, and your members as instruments of righteousness unto God'. Notice the distinction between you yourself and the members of your body as instruments.

The Christian is not perfect in this life. He himself is saved, but his body is not yet saved. That is why the Apostle says again in Romans 8:23, 'We ourselves also, which have the first-fruits of the Spirit, even we ourselves groan within ourselves, waiting for the adoption, to wit, the redemption of our body'. The body is not yet redeemed, and will not be redeemed until our Lord returns and we are either resurrected from the dead or changed at that moment into the glorified state. Until then the body is not redeemed. Hence as long as we are in this life and in this world there will be this element of conflict, this fight against temptation and sin.

Having got rid of that difficulty, and having seen that the fact that we are tempted does not prove by any means that we are not Christians, we go on to the second element which is the activity of Satan himself. This is where Satan proves himself to be such a master in these matters. He hides himself altogether; he does not appear, he just whispers to us. We do not know where the voice comes from; we think it is our own true spiritual reasoning. 'Ah,' we say, 'I am tempted, but if I were truly Christian I would not be tempted. These thoughts, these imaginations, these desires are in me, and therefore I am unworthy, I am not a Christian at all.' While we are thinking in this way we forget the devil himself, the real source of most of our troubles. But the Apostle instructs us: 'Above all, taking the shield of faith, wherewith ye shall be able to quench all the fiery darts of the wicked one'. 'The fiery darts!' He is hurling them at us. But we, in our ignorance and our innocence in these matters, do not see him and are not aware of him. We think that all these arise within us from ourselves, and we are not aware that it is the devil hurling them at us from all directions – these fiery darts, these things that burst into flame, thoughts, imaginations, desires that come crowding, rushing in. It is the devil who throws them all; but he has concealed himself. There is nothing which is quite so disastrous as not to accept in its fulness the biblical teaching concerning the devil.

I am certain that one of the main causes of the ill state of the Church today is the fact that the devil is being forgotten. All is attributed to us; we have all become so psychological in our attitude and thinking. We are ignorant of this great objective fact, the being, the existence of the devil, the adversary, the accuser, and his 'fiery darts'. And, of course, because we are not aware of this we attribute all temptation to ourselves. So the devil in his wiliness will have succeeded admirably. We become depressed and discouraged, we feel that we are failures, and we do not know what to do. So the second answer is to remind ourselves of the devil himself, to expose him, to rip away the camouflage with which he always hides himself.

The third argument which the Scriptures bring to us is our Lord's temptation. He was the Son of God, sinless and perfect; and yet He was tempted. This can never be emphasized too frequently. The Gospels are very careful to record the accounts of His temptations, and particularly His temptation in the wilderness. But when that was finished, the devil only left Him 'for a season'. He came back to Him repeatedly. We are not given a full record of all our Lord's temptations. The devil pressed in upon Him, and followed Him all the way until the very end. The author of the Epistle to the Hebrews puts it thus: 'Wherefore in all things it behoved him to be made like unto his brethren, that he might be a merciful and faithful high priest in things pertaining to God, to make reconciliation for the sins of the people. For in that he himself hath suffered being tempted, he is able to succour them that are tempted' (Hebrews 2:17, 18). He is not content with saying it once. He repeats it in his fourth chapter, verses 14–15: 'Seeing then that we have a great high priest, that is passed into the heavens, Jesus the Son of God, let us hold fast our profession. For we have not an high priest which cannot be touched with the feeling of our infirmities; but was in all points tempted like as we are, yet without sin.' Tempted, remember, 'in all points like as we are', sin apart.

How prone we are to forget this! Our Lord's temptations were not a pretence; they were real; and in all points He was tempted exactly as you and I are tempted. Clearly, therefore, the fact that one is tempted does not presuppose any defect in the person, still less does it presuppose any sinfulness. Our Lord was tempted. As He was perfect, it is clear that His temptation came from the outside only, from the devil. But the important point is to notice that though He was perfect, harmless, free from sin, He nevertheless was tempted in all points like as we are. So the next time the devil comes to you and says, 'You are not a Christian at all because you are being tempted,' reply to him by saying, 'That does not prove anything of the sort; you tempted my Lord in exactly the same way.' It is a fundamental fallacy to assume that the fact that we are tempted means that there is any real defect in us. Our Lord Himself was tempted. 'Ah but,' you say, 'it cannot have been real, unless there was something within Him to correspond to it.' That is a still greater fallacy. The 'temptation' meant the suggestion and the enticement of the devil from the outside with all his power. Our Lord was tempted much more strongly than any one of us will ever be tempted. The devil brought out all his reserves in his attempt to shake Him. He did not succeed; but he tried with all his might.

So I come to my fourth and last answer to the devil at this

[293]

point. A temptation only becomes sin when we accept it, when we fondle it, when we enjoy it. The suggestion itself, the temptation, the feeling of desire is not sin. But to accept it and to enjoy it and to fondle it is sin. That is the vital point at which we must ever draw this distinction. The thing itself is not sin, but the acceptance of it and the enjoyment of it is definitely sin. Someone asks, 'How can I tell which it is?' I suggest certain tests that always apply to ourselves which will enable us to do this very thing.

Have you a consciousness that the thoughts and the imaginations and the desires come to you? Do you find sometimes that these thoughts or imaginations come to you perhaps as soon as you wake up in the morning, before you have started to think actively at all, and before you are fully awake? If so, they are not yours. You have not been thinking, you have not had time to think; yet they have already come. They are coming therefore from outside, and are 'the fiery darts of the wicked one'. Have you not also found very often that actually while you are reading the Bible these thoughts come? Clearly they are not yours for you are concentrating on reading the Bible. Perhaps when you have been on your knees in prayer, blasphemous thoughts have come or some ugly, foul, vile imagination. It is not yours. If you are concentrating on your prayer, your Bible-reading, or whatever it may be, and these things have arisen in your mind, that is a sure proof that their place of origin is not your heart, but the devil. At the most unexpected moments you find that this happens to you. Recognize it immediately, and, instead of being depressed, say, 'But I was concentrating on this or that and they came to me'. That is quite right: they do 'come' to you. We say that (do we not?) in regard to other spheres of thought or activity, and we seem to be quite clear about it. We say, 'It suddenly occurred to me'. What you mean is this: 'I really was not thinking about the thing at all, I was not working it out, but while I was doing something else, it suddenly dawned upon me'. In a similar manner the devil insinuates these thoughts, brings the suggestion, hurls it at you. So it is vital that you should be able to recognize that these things may come to you instead of being part of you.

But consider a second test. Can you say quite honestly that

you hate them, that you regard them as evil, and with utter detestation? These may seem to some to be trivial matters; but I can assure you that these simple questions have often been the means of delivering tormented souls. I could give you many illustrations from my own pastoral experience.

I adduce one example only to illustrate my point, and to show the necessity for working this out in detail. I remember a lady who was a very active church worker, the Superintendent of a church Sunday School, who was also a very good singer and skilled in teaching children to sing. Suddenly she dropped it all and was in great distress because she was plagued by evil thoughts, blasphemous thoughts, and therefore felt that she was not a Christian, and not fit to do any Christian work. She resigned from everything, no one could persuade her otherwise, and she was in an agony of soul. She remained in that condition for some considerable time, and gave signs of becoming physically ill in addition. Yet all that was necessary in her case was to put these simple points. I said to her, 'Do you hate these evil things?' 'I hate them with the whole of my being,' she said. 'Very well,' I replied, 'they are not yours.' But the devil had persuaded her that they were hers, that because she had the thoughts they therefore must be hers. I said, 'Here is the test. Do you hate them, do you regard them as evil?' 'Of course,' she replied. Then I went to my next point, 'Do you long to be rid of them?' She said, 'I would give the whole world if I could only stop it'. 'Well', I said, 'cannot you see that these things are coming to you, they are being hurled at you?' I said, 'These are "the fiery darts of the wicked one". They do not arise from yourself at all, but from the devil. But he has persuaded you that they come from within yourself, and therefore, of course, your defences are all down and you are completely defeated. You have got to recognize what is happening to you. If you can say that you hate them, that you long to be rid of them, and to be delivered and cleansed from them, and never have to countenance them again, then, I say, they are not yours, they do not belong to you.' And then I added a last and a final point: 'As you are tormented by these things, can you say quite honestly that you desire to know God, that your chief desire is to know God, to love Him and to serve Him, and ever to live to the praise of the glory of His grace? Can you say, just as you are, that your greatest desire is to be a true child of God and to know Him and to enjoy Him? If you can, I care not what the thoughts or imaginations or anything else may be, you are a child of God, and you are just being troubled and trapped and deceived by the wiles of the devil.' The lady was completely delivered.

We have still not finished with this matter of temptation; and I follow the tests which I have suggested by a word of exhortation. First, and most essential, we must learn to draw the distinctions which I have already been emphasizing, namely, the distinction between you yourself as a being and a personality, and what the devil is doing to you. It is good also at this point to remember what we are told later in our text about an 'evil day' – 'that ye may be able to stand in the evil day'. Sometimes the devil does what we are discussing almost like an avalanche. You will find that some of the greatest saints have recorded such experiences. It is not always so, but sometimes the devil comes, as it were from every direction with all his malignity and power, he trains his guns, as it were, upon us, and shoots his fiery darts at us. Luther felt that it was so on the famous occasion when he took up the ink-pot and threw it at the devil. He felt that the room was full of the devil who was suggesting evil things to him. This is the first way to handle the situation – draw that distinction!

Secondly, refuse to feel condemned. *You* have to do this; it will not be done for you. The devil is trying to rob you of your assurance; he is trying to make you think that you are not a Christian. He says, 'A Christian, with thoughts and imaginations such as you have at the present moment! The thing is inconceivable, you are not a Christian at all!' Take your stand and say: 'I am a Christian, and your proofs are not proofs; because, according to you, my Lord had a sinful nature, otherwise He would not have been tempted. You are tempting me as you tempted my Lord Himself and you cannot shake me. The fact that I am being attacked by you, far from proving that I am not a Christian is, in a sense, a proof that I am a Christian. You would not pay so much attention to me if I were not a Christian.' Round on him, attack him, refuse to be condemned. Do not allow him to raise the whole question of your salvation again;

[296]

stand again on justification by faith only, and say, 'I am saved, not by anything I do or have done or ever will do. I am not saved as the result of my being tempted or not being tempted; I am saved because the Son of God loved me, and gave Himself for me; and He has done it once and for ever; and whatever you do to me does not affect that most certain fact.' So stand on justification by faith and refuse to be condemned.

At this point you are beginning to obey the injunction of the Scripture to 'resist the devil'. James and Peter give us clear instruction about this matter. James in his Epistle gives this specific injunction: 'Submit yourselves therefore to God. Resist the devil, and he will flee from you' (4:7). Peter is equally clear about this: 'Be sober, be vigilant, because your adversary the devil, as a roaring lion, walketh about seeking whom he may devour' (1 Peter 5:8). What can you do? Are you to run away as quickly as you can? No! 'Whom resist steadfast in the faith, knowing that the same afflictions are accomplished in your brethren that are in the world.'

Again I must emphasize that it is essential that you should know how to put the counsel of James and Peter into practice. You have to come down to details. The devil as a roaring lion attacks you; or he shoots his darts at you. What are you to do? What I am about to say may seem to contradict what I have said so far, but, in my experience, it has often been the point of deliverance to many souls. You resist the devil by refusing to argue with him, and by refusing to reason with him. There is only one thing to do with the devil, and that is, to have nothing to do with him, to dismiss him. If you acknowledge his suggestion, his thought, and begin to try to argue he will defeat you every time. Adam and Eve were perfect, but the devil defeated them. Who are you to succeed when they failed? So, do not argue, turn from him; have nothing to do with him. What you have to realize is that these things are from the devil, and therefore, you must have nothing to do with them at all. Say to him, 'I have no dealings with you, I listen to nothing you say. You were a liar from the beginning, you are a liar still and the father of lies. I am not interested.' 'Ah but,' he will say, 'surely you believe the Scriptures?' Reply to him, 'I am not interested in it as you quote it; I am not interested in anything you say'. You may laugh at

[297]

that, but a day may come when you will be very grateful for what I have said. It is essential to reject the devil *in toto*. Remember that he can transform himself into 'an angel of light'. He knows the Scriptures much better than you do, and he will say, 'But what about this?' If you foolishly say, 'Very well, let us have a look at it', you are behaving in a foolish manner. Have nothing to do with him. 'Resist' means that you have nothing whatsoever to do with him. Tell him that he is a liar, take up 'the sword of the Spirit, which is the Word of God', and do what I have been saying. Do not take up any point, any word, any phrase; have nothing to do with him, and he will flee from you.

In addition, you can say to him, 'I am in Christ; the blood of Christ is on me, I am in the Kingdom of God; I do not belong to your realm any longer. I once did, but not now. I have been translated out of the kingdom of darkness into the kingdom of God's dear Son; I have been delivered from your dominion, and my inheritance is now among the children of light. There was once a time when I was in your clutches – no longer! The whole world lieth in the evil one, in you. I do not belong there. "Ye are of God, little children, and that evil one toucheth us not." You cannot touch me. No more am I going to be intimidated by you, no longer am I going to be alarmed, no longer am I going to receive your suggestions, no longer am I to be depressed by you. You are a liar, I have nothing to do with you, and you cannot touch me.' Then the devil can do nothing.

This is the literal teaching of the Scriptures; and, thank God, it is literally true! So you have to attack him in that way in detail. That is how to 'resist him, steadfast in the faith'. But above all, I say again, do not argue with him, do not reason, do not accept any of his suggestions for a moment, because you will always be defeated. Reject him and all his works, and everything that belongs to him, and he will not be able to touch you.

The last step in this exhortation is to remind yourself positively who you are and what you are. Remind yourself of your status and of your standing in Christ. Remind yourself of your prospects. This is the finest tonic for any weak Christian. This is positive. We have been dealing with the problem negatively, so far, and this is inevitable. But never stop at that, go on to the positive. Remind yourself of the truth about yourself as a Christian, that you are already saved, that you have already died with Christ, that you are 'in Christ', that you will never be more saved spiritually than you are now. If you are a Christian at all, you are 'in Christ', you have been crucified with Him. Thus to be crucified is not something you have to do, 'having believed'. Romans tell us what has happened to us, not what should happen to us. 'You have been' – it is in the aorist tense. 'Knowing this, that our old man *has been* crucified with Christ,' once and for ever. Remind yourself of that. Remind yourself that, as you died with Christ, you have also risen with Him, that you are seated with Him in the heavenly places, and that the devil is therefore attacking you in order to shake your confidence in your complete security in Christ.

Answer the devil therefore by redoubling your hold upon the truth, by making 'your calling and election sure'. Take a firm grasp of it, go back to the Scriptures and say, 'This is my position', and hold on to it and stand on it. That will then enable you to hate the suggestions and the thoughts and the insinuations of the devil still more. So that when he comes again you will be able to resist him at his first appearance, and you will not have the struggle that you had before. You have to continue to do this, and eventually you will have done it so well, and so successfully, that he will leave you alone at that point and will have to think of something else. This is the way in which this particular problem must invariably be dealt with by the Christian.

To complete this matter let me say an additional word about the question of doubts, even though it is covered in a sense by what I have already said. Doubts belong to the thoughts and suggestions put forward by the devil. But in a sense they constitute a special division. Doubts come to Christian people about the truth itself. I have known good Christian people who have been plagued by doubts even about the being of God or some other particular aspect of the Christian faith. Still more have they doubted God's love to them when they have experienced troubles and trials and tribulations. Or the devil may have come to them and attacked them more directly about their own belief, and said that they were hypocrites or humbugs or that Christianity can be entirely explained on psychological grounds. Thus he attacks us and raises doubts in order to try to undermine the whole position

[299]

of the Christian and his faith. Again, he produces the same arguments, suggesting that because we have doubts we have never been true believers, that if a man believes he can never be tempted by doubts; that they arise from ourselves, and therefore we have never been Christians.

The answer is exactly as before. Whatever the thoughts and the suggestions, remind the devil that you are well aware of his existence, and that he attacked the Son of God in exactly the same way. He came to the Son of God and said, '*If* Thou be the Son of God . . .' He raised a doubt. That is how he attacked our Lord. So when he comes to you and says, 'Are you sure that you are a child of God?' say to him, 'You are repeating what you did to my Lord; you tried that even on Him, so it is not surprising you are trying it on me'. That is the way to answer him.

Then, take the testimony of the saints, and you will find that some of the greatest saints have from time to time been plagued not by doubts, but by the temptation to doubt, by the thoughts that came to them. They tell us about them, and how they were able to resist the devil in this respect.

A final word of advice! If the devil has pressed you sorely and you are really shaken by him – and he can shake us when he brings out his reserves, he is so powerful – if he drives you into a corner, sometimes you will find that you will have to fall back on something like the following. Say to him, 'Well, all I know is this. I cannot answer you, but what I do know is that I want to believe, it is my desire to believe; and that proves that I am a child of God. Romans 8 tells me that "the carnal mind is enmity against God, is not subject to the law of God; neither indeed can be". I am not in that position, I am not at enmity against God. My desire is to know God. I cannot answer you, but I know that that is my desire; therefore I am not a "carnal" man. If I am not carnal, then I must be spiritual.' Then say further: 'In 1 Corinthians 2:14 I read that "the natural man receiveth not the things of the Spirit of God: for they are foolishness unto him; neither can he do so, for they are spiritually discerned". I do not know where I am; you have confused me. I know I am unworthy, and I do not know what is happening to me; but I do know this, that these things are not "foolishness" to me. These things are everything to me. Far from being "foolish" they are my greatest desire; there is nothing I want so much. I cannot answer you; but that is my desire. I know therefore that I am not a natural man; I must therefore be a spiritual man.'

You may have to meet him in that way, but thank God for the Scriptures which enable you to do so. Thank God for the ability the Spirit gives us to enable us to use this sword of the Spirit, which is the Word of God. And so you round upon the devil, and attack him, that whatever he may say, your deepest desire is to know God and the Lord Jesus Christ and the blessed Spirit, to be free from sin and to be a worthy disciple and a worthy Christian. Hold on to that and tell the devil that you are trusting solely to the blood of Christ. And then someone will be able in due course to write your epitaph and say, 'He was like the people in Revelation 12 – "they overcame him by the blood of the Lamb, and by the word of their testimony" '.

22

Discouragement

We are still dealing with the ways in which the devil attacks us in the realm of our experience. We have looked at this problem from different aspects – the standpoint of assurance, the quenching of the Spirit, and the whole problem of thoughts suggested to us by the devil.

We now move on to another group which can be subsumed under the heading of 'general discouragement'. We have been dealing hitherto with what we might call particular forms of discouragement with which the devil tries to afflict us all. If I were asked to hazard an opinion as to what is the most prevailing disease in the Church today I would suggest that it is discouragement. One reason for that is the whole state of the world, the whole state of society. We live in difficult and discouraging days. Some people, however, do not feel any discouragement. But that is due to a defect in their temperament. Their eyes are not open; they are not sensitive; they are probably so interested in their own activities that they cannot take a general view. But, speaking generally, these are very discouraging days for the Church and for the individual Christian; and the devil constantly works on this particular aspect of the Christian's life and experience.

Much space is given to a consideration of this matter in the Bible itself. Many of the psalms are entirely devoted to it; the psalmist is discouraged and he addresses his soul: 'Why art thou cast down, O my soul?' Many psalms deal with this trial in a wonderful way. But it is equally present in the New

Testament. The attempt to differentiate between the Old and the New in this respect is quite false. People say, 'But the Old Testament saints did not have the Holy Spirit as we have'. That is true, but that must not be interpreted to mean that Christians never know discouragement; for they do; and much attention is paid to the subject in the pages of the New Testament also.

This discouragement has many causes. The first, to which we have referred earlier, is the matter of temperament. Certain people are more subject to discouragement than others. You cannot help this, you are born with your temperament, and there is nothing wrong with temperament. I suggested in an earlier chapter that probably the best type of temperament was that praised so much by William Cowper, namely, that which knows something of this melancholic element but which is also capable of rising to the heights. It would be an interesting discussion to know which ultimately is the best kind of temperament to have, that of the extrovert or that of the introvert; that of the phlegmatic person with his tendency to be somewhat melancholic, or that of the complete extrovert, sanguine and optimistic. However, if one is born with the temperament that tends towards the more serious, despondent type, then the devil is likely to take full advantage of that fact.

One of the first things therefore that we all have to learn in the Christian life is to know ourselves. You cannot live properly with yourself if you do not know yourself. There are many people, it seems to me, who have never really known themselves. They have never looked at themselves truly, they have never recognized the type to which they belong, and therefore they are not aware that they have to be unusually careful at certain points. Get to know yourself, talk to yourself, and put up special guards at certain points. If you find it difficult to do this for yourself, then you must consult with others and ask their help. It is always easier to see things in other people than in ourselves. You must get to know your weaknesses, and your tendencies; and then, once you have known them, and can watch them, you are already a long way towards a complete victory over the devil and his wiles.

Furthermore, the melancholic temperament is particularly

subject to what I shall call the tendency to introspection and morbidity. This means the tendency to spend most of our time in looking inwards, in examining ourselves, and in always watching and observing our inward moods and states and conditions. 'But,' says someone, 'you have been emphasizing that we ought to examine ourselves and discover the truth about ourselves and our temperament.' It is just there that the wiles of the devil come in. Self-examination is commanded in the Scriptures. Any man or woman who never indulges in self-examination is of necessity a very poor Christian. The Apostle Paul, writing to the Corinthians in the Second Epistle and the last chapter, says, 'Examine your own selves'. The type of Christian who never examines himself at all is of necessity a very poor Christian. It means that he is self-satisfied, that he thinks he has got everything. But notice the words in the last chapter of the Epistle to the Galatians: 'If any man think himself to be something, when he is nothing, he deceiveth himself'. That is always the trouble with the man who does not examine himself at all.

But in the case of those given to self-examination, the devil, knowing that they are sensitive, spiritually-minded, and intelligent; and very much concerned to obey the Scriptural injunction to grow and to make progress in the Christian life – the devil, knowing all this, comes along and presses them on this very matter of self-examination. He drives them to it, he holds them to it, and he keeps them at it to such an extent that he succeeds in bringing them into a condition of utter depression. They feel hopeless; they are in a complete muddle, and know not what to do. That is, I suppose, one of the commonest causes of this condition; it is when you cross the line from self-examination to introspection.

The very term introspection is a good description; it means that your cameras and your telescopes, all your means and mechanisms of examination, are turned inwards upon the self. This leads to the accompanying condition of morbidity, which means that the soul is not able to function properly. It is a kind of paralysis, an organic disease of the soul and spirit. It is the result of overdoing something which is good and right in and of itself. That is where the wiles of the devil are active.

The devil rarely tempts this kind of person to commit some flagrant sin. But he succeeds with them by just turning them in so much upon themselves that they are utterly depressed and in a state of misery and paralysis and uselessness.

The answer to the devil at this point we shall deal with later when we come to the various parts of 'the whole armour of God;'* but I cannot leave it now without a word of encouragement to any such introspective, morbid soul. To the Christian who is tempted to say 'Why bother with all this? those people really need nothing but a good shaking!', I reply in words that Paul wrote to the Galatians: 'Bear ye one another's burdens, and so fulfil the law of Christ' (6:2). If you know nothing about this condition I assure you that it can be a terrible experience to pass through, and in any case it is very difficult to decide which of the two persons is in the better case, this morbid, introspective person, or the extrovert who never examines himself at all and who thinks he is something when he is nothing. 'Bear ye one another's burdens'; and at the same time, 'Every man shall bear his own burden.' Let us keep these thoughts in our minds.

We start with a general principle: depression is always wrong. A Christian has no right to be depressed. I put it like that deliberately because the realization of that truth is often the door of escape and of liberty. The tragedy is that when the devil plagues us and gets us into this state, we are not aware of it. We are so pre-occupied with self-analysis, and the cataloguing of the details of our deficiencies, that we do not see ourselves as a whole. Sometimes that is all that is necessary – we suddenly come to see ourselves, in the reading of the Scripture, or the listening to a sermon, or in conversation. We suddenly see ourselves as depressed and miserable Christians, sitting in a corner, while the men and women round and about us are going heedlessly to hell. We are so pre-occupied with ourselves, that we are utterly useless. Not only so, we realize that we are also obviously giving the impression that there is not much point in being Christian if this is what it leads to. So we are not only not helping others, we are barring the gate of entry into the kingdom of God against them. You suddenly

* In a future volume.

see yourself in that way, and you rise up and say, 'No more of this!' That is the way to start. Then go on to meet the devil with his own weapon. He will have been quoting Scripture: 'Examine yourselves, prove your own selves, that you may know whether you are in the faith or not'. Reply saying, 'Quite right, I must do this'. But then you must turn on the devil and say, 'But there are other scriptures'. And one that surely comes in immediately at this point is justification by faith only.

Why is a Christian depressed? It is because he has examined himself or herself in this minute way – it is always a matter of details, fine points, feeling the spiritual pulse, taking the spiritual temperature. Every conceivable investigation is carried out, and then the results are tabulated. Here, then, is the record; and it is very bad. The obvious conclusion drawn is, 'Well, am I a Christian at all? Have I ever really been a Christian? Is it possible?'

The devil's objective is to get us to entertain such a feeling. If he can make us examine ourselves in such a manner that it not only becomes introspection but leads us to the conclusion that we have never been Christians at all, he is perfectly satisfied. I am reminding you that the fundamental answer to him is that, whatever we may feel like, we are still Christians. But how do we prove that to ourselves? That is the real need at this point. The way to do so – and it is the reason why the Protestant Reformers saw that this is the fundamental article of a standing or a falling Church – is to remind yourself of justification by faith only! The devil says, 'Look at your record, there is only one conclusion to draw, you are not a Christian, you have never been a Christian'. Answer the devil by telling him that what makes a man a Christian is not anything that he finds in himself, it is 'Jesus' blood and righteousness'. Thank God for this, for if we all examined ourselves truly and tried to decide on the basis of our own life's record whether we are Christians or not, there would not be a single Christian! There is only one thing that makes us Christian – His righteousness, and nothing else.

Jesus, Thy blood and righteousness
My beauty are, my glorious dress.

So you must round on the devil and say, 'Yes, all that is absolutely true; but it does not prove that I am not a Christian, because, even as I am, I am still looking only unto Him and relying upon Him alone'. If you fail to do that, you are being defeated by the wiles of the devil, and you are guilty of introspection and morbidity.

How then are we to deal with this whole question of self-examination? Examine yourself, as the Scripture tells you to do; examine yourself in the light of the Scriptural teaching, then recognize the faults, the failures, the blemishes, everything, quite honestly. Then comes the crucial moment. Instead of sitting down and condemning yourself, and moaning and groaning and bewailing your failures, and spending your time turning in upon yourself and then discovering yet more defects, and continuing in this process of utter condemnation – instead of doing that, with the list of sins and failures in your hand, go to God. Get on your knees and confess it all to Him, and repent of it all, and express your sorrow and your regret. Take it to Him and say, 'It is true, I am hopeless, I am wrong'. But then do not stop there. Having confessed it all with shame and with honesty and true repentance, remember what He has said to you, and what He is still saying to you at that moment, if you but listen to Him instead of the devil. The devil will be whispering to you, perhaps even shouting at you; he will be saying that you have no right even to go into the presence of God because you are such a failure, and such a hopeless person. If you listen to the devil you will get off your knees as miserable as you were before. But listen to the voice of God! He is speaking to you at that moment, and this is what He is saying: 'If we confess our sins' – and this is for Christian people! – 'If we confess our sins, he is faithful and just to forgive us our sins, and to cleanse us from all unrighteousness' (1 John 1:9). Believe Him! Believe Him there and then! Thank Him immediately. Say: 'O God, I can scarcely believe it, but I do. I know Thy Word is true, and Thou art saying at this point that Thou art faithful, that Thou wouldest be unfaithful to Thine own Word if Thou didst not forgive me for Christ's sake. Thy justice is involved, Thou hast dealt with this very sin, this catalogue of sins, in Christ on the Cross; it is all forgiven.' Accept it, thank

God for it, rise to your feet and go on to live the Christian life as it should be lived. Realize more than ever your need of the strength and the power that comes to you only through the Holy Ghost, but remind yourself that a part of the gift of salvation is the gift of the Holy Spirit within you. Realize He is in you, realize what He can enable you to do, that though you are weak and frail and unworthy He can make you more than conqueror. Realize that He will mediate to you, and bring to you, the power of Christ. Remember that, such as you are, you are a member of the Body of Christ, and that He is the Head, and that the life and the power comes down through all the joints and all the parts, as the Apostle has been teaching in the fourth chapter and the sixteenth verse of this Ephesian Epistle. Remind yourself of all this, and get up, and get on.

But what you must never do is to sit in a corner going round and round in that whirlpool, that vortex of failure and defeat and self-condemnation. Introspection and morbidity are wrong, and indeed sinful, and the Christian has no right to be depressed in that way. Deliverance comes as you realize what the devil is trying to do with you, and that he has blinded you temporarily to justification by faith only. Justification by faith is always the place where you can get a foothold. Whenever you find yourself slipping down that slope of depression, the place at which you will always recover stability and get a foothold is justification by faith only. It defeats most of the wiles of the devil. Let us then be very certain about this, for it is the royal remedy, the invariably successful remedy against morbidity and introspection.

Are you already relieved? Are you released? Or are you still saying, 'Ah, yes, but if you only knew!'? Now if you say that, you have missed the whole point. There are no 'buts' and 'ifs' where justification by faith is concerned. It matters not what the truth about you may be; how black, how vile, how hopeless, how ignorant! No matter what you may say about yourself, throw it all in. Justification by faith means that in spite of what you are Christ died for you. 'While we were enemies,' 'while we were yet without strength, Christ died for us'. So if you bring in your 'buts' and 'ifs', you have not seen the truth. There is nothing of any value in any of us, and if you are looking to yourself in any sense you are in the hands of the devil, he has defeated you with his wiles. You must see clearly that, as you are, if you are looking to Christ, and relying only upon His perfect work on your behalf, you are saved. He saves you by the work He has completed on your behalf, and by that alone. That is the answer! You must get to that place, you must bring yourself there, you must compel yourself to get there; and having done so, rise up, and attack the devil and repulse him. Say, 'God's honour is involved in this matter, "He is faithful and just to forgive us our sins, and to cleanse us from all unrighteousness" '.

Closely akin to this is another way in which the devil often attacks us. It is not the same as that just dealt with, because it often afflicts people who are not given to introspection. It is a consciousness of lack of progress. It is not always as the result of examination, but it comes in various other ways. We may have a feeling that we are not making any progress in our grasp of truth, or in our understanding of truth and the way of salvation; we may feel that we are not growing much in grace and in the knowledge of the Lord, or in achievement. Sometimes this happens as the result of looking at other people rather than by a process of self-examination. We say, 'Those people seem to understand and to have grown in ways that I have not followed; they have much more than I have'. You may feel this when you meet other fellow-members of a church, or you may feel it sometimes as the result of reading. Of course I am not saying that a Christian should not read; but that, because reading is so valuable for the Christian, the devil is going to pay unusual attention to it. He causes people to read about certain great saints, and when they have done so he says, 'That is Christianity; where are you? That is the way to live the Christian life; where are you?' He comes to a preacher and causes him to read the journals of George Whitefield, and says, 'That is preaching; that is the way to be a Christian minister; what about you?' And the poor preacher feels at once that he has never really preached in his life, that he has done nothing! So the devil takes these excellent means, which are provided by God Himself, and by drawing these comparisons and contrasts

[309]

he makes us feel that we have made no progress, that we have nothing at all, that we do not understand, that we have never had an experience, that we have never achieved anything of value. And once more we are in a state of depression.

The answer to this is simply: Be yourself! You are never meant to be anything but yourself. Endless trouble is caused by our being anxious to be something we are not! How foolish that is in every realm! Even on the natural level it is wrong. There is nothing so foolish as to wish you were something that you are not – a desire to be tall or to be short, a desire to be of this colour or that colour, to have this power or that power. What a foolish thing it is! How useless, for you cannot change yourself! But more, why should you want to change? It is a wonderful thing to be yourself. You are an individual made by God. These things are not accidental. There is great value in individuality. If you made an analysis of all of us in detail and then picked out the points and put them in columns, you would find that they would balance up in a remarkable manner at the end. We tend to attach too much significance to certain things, and we do not realize the value of other things. But God sees matters in a different way. Things that the world never knows about are precious in the sight of God. Our Lord spoke the parable about the woman who put two mites into the collection, in order to teach that truth. The world pays no attention to two mites – two millions are marvellous, two mites are nothing; but not in the sight of God!

This is true of the whole of our personalities; so the way to answer the devil is to realize this principle, and to say, 'I am myself, and I am meant to be myself; and all God asks of me is that I do my best and my utmost as I am. I may not be meant to be a great corner-stone in the building, but it is necessary to have a number of loose stones to fill up the gaps between the big stones. I am only one of them perhaps, but if there were none of them, the others would not be able to sustain the wall, and the building would never go up.' In 1 Corinthians 12 there is a complete exposition of this matter. 'The less comely parts' are essential to the body. Do not despise or deride them, do not look down upon them. Every part of the body is essential to the functioning and the working of the whole. There is no such thing as an unimportant Christian, an unimportant church member; every one of us counts. There are some very quiet people in every church, but they often perform a great function by just being pleasant. They sometimes help much more than the more gifted members. The latter act in a different way; but all types are necessary.

Do not try to be something you are not meant to be; do not be jealous of someone who seems to be bigger or greater than yourself. Or, if you are bigger and greater, do not despise the others. 'Every man shall bear his own burden.' We bear one another's burdens, but we bear our own burdens also. God will only hold you responsible for what you have done with what He gave you. It is God who decided how much to give you. Be faithful with your one talent, it does not matter what it is, use it to the utmost. Be faithful with your five talents, if five are given to you. But what God desires is that every one of us should realize the privilege of being what we are. Though I am so unworthy and so small and insignificant, 'I am what I am by the grace of God', and God knows me, Christ died for me, even for me! I must not despise myself, and I must not be constantly comparing myself with others. I am to live my life with the temperament, the personality that God has given me. I intend to use it all to the utmost to the glory of God. I can do no more, and I know that God expects no more. Answer the devil in that way.

To be weary in well-doing is another very common manifestation of the wiles of the devil. As I have said previously, this is perhaps the commonest of all the manifestations at the present time. Christians are tempted to give way to weariness by the strain of life, the humdrum nature of the 'daily round and common task', the discouragements, the difficulties, the absence of striking happenings. We are living in evil days. They are bad days in every respect, not only in the world at large, but also in the Church. When you compare and contrast today with a hundred or two hundred years ago you see the difference. What days they were, with the Spirit of God outpoured in the great Evangelical Awakening of the eighteenth century, and tremendous things happening under the mighty Spirit of God in days of revival. And again in 1857, 1859 and 1860 even up to 1861 – what wonderful days! Then look at our days; what days of

[311]

discouragement they are, so little happening! Everything seems to be against us; new problems have arisen, militating against the Church and her work, and against the life of the individual Christian. The whole pace of life has increased, leading to strain and tiredness, women in the home feeling it as perhaps never before. All this tends to produce this condition of weariness and tiredness. The feeling begins to creep in, 'Is it worth while going on? Is there anything in it? Need I keep up this pace? Nothing seems to happen – well, let us slacken off a bit, let us take things a little more easily.' So the devil comes in with his wiles and insinuations. Throughout the country there are men and women, known to me, who are Sunday by Sunday preaching to small congregations. I was talking to a man recently who had been preaching the previous Sunday to four people. He said, 'Sometimes I begin to wonder whether it is worth while'. There are hundreds of such men scattered up and down this country. I remember going out of the pulpit one night some five or six years ago, when a man dashed in to my vestry saying that he was catching his train back to Newcastle-upon-Tyne. He had really come just to tell me one thing. He said, 'I just want you to know this: if ever the devil tries to discourage you, I want you to know that the thought of Westminster Chapel has often kept me going'. He said, 'I am a bit of a lay preacher up in my district, and, you know, the devil sometimes says to me, "Is it worth your doing it, there will only be three or four people there, perhaps nine or ten, just a handful; is it worth while going on?" ' He added, 'What has often made me go on has been just this, I have said to myself, That man is probably going up those steps into that pulpit at Westminster tonight to preach to a large congregation. We are in the same battle! I am going on, God is not interested in numbers.' Thus the devil comes in and tries to discourage us in various ways; and we begin to wonder whether it is worth while going on at all.

The individual Christian may feel this, even in his family. Perhaps you are the only Christian in your family and everything is against you. You are being misunderstood, and laughed at, and criticized, and you say, 'Well, I have been living before them as a Christian for years and it does not seem to help them, or to make any difference, I am only getting rebuffs on all sides; I wonder whether I should slacken off a bit. Must I go on like this? If I had only something to show it would be all right; but there is nothing to show, it is just a hard grind. I am fighting against everything the whole time.' The devil comes and says, 'Slacken off, give up'.

The Scripture gives us cogent answers to such a temptation; it brings to us great and glorious texts. 'Be not weary in well doing!' (Galatians 6:9). That is one answer. What you are doing is not only worth while, it is the most wonderful and most glorious thing in the world; it is 'well doing'. You are standing for truth, you are standing for Christ, you are standing for the kingdom of light against the kingdom of darkness. I know there is not much to show, but that does not matter. You are there; you are not the sun, perhaps, but you are a little match, and thank God for the light of a match where there is nothing but gloom and darkness and despair. 'Be not weary in well doing.' You are standing for everything that is noble and true and beautiful and right and holy in a world of shame and sin and darkness and vileness and foulness. Hold on to 'well doing'. 'In due season we shall reap, if we faint not.'

Then turn to Zechariah 4: 'Who hath despised the day of small things?' 'Ah but,' you say, 'what is there to show for my effort?' I agree that there is not much to show today, as there was very little to show in the time of Zechariah. That was the message after the Captivity when the returning exiles were only beginning to resettle. Little seemed to be happening. Facing them was a mountain of difficulties, and they said, 'We are moving on an inch or two perhaps, but we have to get over that mountain on to the other side before we can achieve much; it is a day of small things. If we did not move at all it would not make any difference; what is an inch, or half an inch, when you are confronted by a mountain?' But God's answer was, 'Who art thou, O great mountain . . . Thou shalt become a plain . . . Despise not the day of small things'. The small things are, nevertheless, the things of God. Some of God's things are very small, but they are God's; and if you do away with all the small things in the world the big things will soon collapse. In a great organization we may think that the only man who counts is the General Manager. Not so; you must have the office boy! This works out in every sphere of life. 'No chain is stronger than its weakest link'. 'Despise not the day of small things'. The farmer sows his seed in the ground. It happens, perhaps, to be a very disappointing kind of spring; there is no sunshine, no rain; it is cold and bleak, and dull; nothing happens. Has he wasted his energy because nothing seems to be happening? At last there is just a little sprouting, just a little appearance of life; but he says, 'What is that? That is nothing. I want to see a field of corn or wheat fully ripened. That is the only way I can be satisfied, and you show me just that little bit of greenness.' The answer is, 'Do not despise the day of small things'. That is God's way! 'The mills of God grind slowly, but they grind exceeding small.' 'That great mountain will be flattened into a plain.' Do not despise anything that happens in God's kingdom, whether it be your work or someone else's.

In other words, realize that all you are feeling is due to the devil and nothing else, that he is using this idea of bigness and greatness, which is so current today, the idea that if a thing is not big and great it is nothing. Do not believe it! It is a lie. Civilizations have often collapsed because of the neglect of small things. That is how the Roman Empire declined. People, or individuals who are prone to neglect details are doomed to disaster. 'Despise not the day of small things.'

Again: our Lord taught that 'men should always pray, and not faint'. The tendency to faint is ever present; but realize to whom you belong. 'Not by might, nor by power, but by my Spirit, saith the Lord of hosts.' However weak you are, however faint, that is always true. The Spirit of God is in you. Pray to God the Father, pray to God the Son, pray to God the Holy Spirit. 'Men should always pray, and not faint.' If you do not pray you will faint. So when you feel faint, go to God and talk to Him about it; ask Him to give you strength and power to go on with what you are doing, realizing that it is His work, that it is 'well doing'. And He will reply to you and say, 'Be not weary in well doing, for in due season we shall reap if we faint not'. There is a glorious harvest coming. 'Eye hath not seen, nor ear heard, neither hath entered into the heart of man, the things which God hath prepared for them that love him.' You may be having a hard and difficult time; perhaps you are being misunderstood and maligned, persecuted and trodden upon and kicked. And you are tired and weary, your health may be failing possibly, and you are almost at the point of exhaustion. Go on, I say, 'Be not weary in well doing, for in due season we shall reap'. A day is coming when you will be received with these wonderful words: 'Well done, thou good and faithful servant'. You went on, and kept on. Lift up your eyes, look to God, and you will receive strength from Him – 'They that wait upon the Lord shall renew their strength, they shall mount up with wings as eagles; they shall run, and not be weary; and they shall walk, and not faint' (Isaiah 40:31). If you are suffering with Christ now, you shall also reign with Him; you are 'an heir of God, and a joint-heir with Christ'.

Here is our last word on this matter. The Son of God was once in this world and He came in very lowly fashion. He was buffeted, jeered at, even misunderstood by His own mother and brothers. He was ill-treated by the religious authorities, the Pharisees, the scribes, the Sadducees, the doctors of the law. How little He seemed to accomplish! So little that even John the Baptist in a fit of depression sent his messengers asking, 'Art Thou he that should come, or look we for another?' John the Baptist was saying in effect, 'What are you doing up in Galilee? Why don't you go down to Jerusalem and be crowned as King and raise a great army and conquer the Romans? What are you doing? You are doing nothing, beyond preaching to a handful of common ordinary people. Who are they, what do they count?' That was the kind of life He had to live. He was very tired at times, so tired one day that He was too weary even to go into the village to buy provisions with the disciples, and so sat by the side of a well in Samaria. Another day He was so weary that He looked at people and said, 'How long shall I be with you, how long shall I suffer you?' Everything was against Him; He was misunderstood even by His own followers. They all forsook Him utterly and fled at the end, and He was left alone. But He went on. As the end approached He cries, 'If it be possible, let this cup pass from me: nevertheless, not my will but thine be done' – whatever it costs! He went on! And they killed Him and He died and was buried. But He rose again, He entered into heaven, and He is seated at the right hand of God in the glory with all power.

What I am saying is this – 'Cast aside that weight, and that sin that doth so easily beset you, looking unto Jesus, the author and finisher of our faith: who for the joy that was set before him endured the cross, despising the shame'. 'Ye have not yet resisted unto blood, striving against sin.' He did! In your weariness and tiredness, in your sins and failure, look unto Jesus, the Author, the Leader, the File-leader, the Finisher, the One who is at the head. You are following Him. Realize the greatness of your privilege. Go on, keep your eye steadfastly upon Him, praying and not fainting, not despising the day of small things, not being weary in well doing. If we suffer with Him, we shall also be glorified together with Him. And the 'crowning day' is coming, when you enter into your inheritance and spend your eternity in glory with Him!

23

Worry and Anxiety

One way in which the devil uses general discouragement very frequently is through worry and anxiety. Here is a subject in which temperament again plays its part. We have already seen that the devil knows us much better than we know ourselves, and he arranges his particular temptation and approach along the line of our temperament. Some Christians are naturally given to worry and to anxiety, and the devil, knowing this, presses them along that very line. He knows that they are conscientious, sensitive, highly-strung people who are never content with their achievements. He knows them to be perfectionists, never content with anything less than the best, so he comes and accuses them of continual failure to rise to the height of their ideal, and they end in the state and condition in which everything, practically, becomes a problem and a burden.

The Bible has much to say on this matter. It gives frequent warnings against what it calls 'the cares of this world'. Clearly it is something that has always afflicted God's people, and this type of person in particular. A classic example of this is the case of Martha. Our Lord turned to her and said, 'Martha, Martha, thou art careful and *troubled* about many things'. The word means 'distracted', 'turning hither and thither' so that she scarcely knew what she was doing. It illustrates the type of thing we are examining, a person's mind being filled and preoccupied with things pertaining to life in this world. These are perfectly legitimate things, and not only legitimate, but things which, generally speaking, are essential to life. This is often the particular problem of the housewife, the mother in the home who has a husband and children to look after and to care for. The devil fills the mind and the consciousness with these cares, these legitimate matters, so that they not only become a burden but crowd out spiritual thoughts and realities. Though the person is a Christian, the main outlook on life, and the main tenor of the life, almost ceases to be a spiritual one at all, and the time is given exclusively to these problems and cares.

If the devil can keep our minds from God and from the Lord Jesus Christ, if he can keep us from thinking about the soul, and about our growth and development, he is more than satisfied. And that is what he does with this type of person. Hence our Lord Himself more than once paid great attention to this particular matter. He does so, for example, in the Parable of the Sower. The danger is not merely that the devil may come and take away the Word at once; there is another type of person in whose case the devil brings in the cares and the affairs of this world, and the Word is 'choked'.

But there is a yet more solemn warning. Our Lord, in giving His prophecy of the course of history and the end of the world, finishes with the words 'Take heed to yourselves!' You need to be careful; you have to watch the wiles of the devil; 'lest at any time your hearts be overcharged with surfeiting and drunkenness'. 'Well,' you say, 'we are Christian people, we need not worry about being "overcharged with surfeiting and drunkenness".' But to 'surfeiting and drunkenness' the Lord adds 'and the cares of this life, and so that day come upon you unawares. For as a snare shall it come on all them that dwell on the face of the whole earth. Watch ye therefore, and pray always, that ye may be accounted worthy to escape all these things that shall come to pass, and to stand before the Son of man' (Luke 21:34-36). In other words the Apostle Paul's exhortation in our text is simply a repetition of what our Lord and Saviour Himself at the very end of His life, under the shadow of the Cross, was so careful to teach His followers. We have to pay great heed 'lest the cares of this life' render us unprepared for the momentous event that is coming.

How do we meet this particular manifestation of the wiles of the devil? I repeat that the first thing is to recognize the hand of the devil. That is all-important. We tend to look at the problems, the circumstances, the conditions, and we fail to see the hand behind them. The whole secret of victory is to realize that the problem is the devil and not the circumstances. We must realize that it is he who is trying to get us into this paralysed spiritual condition.

The next step is to reprimand ourselves; and we must do so for many reasons. One is that a Christian should never be agitated. The Christian has no business to be in what we call 'a dither'. He should never be out of control. That should always be one of the great differences between the Christian and the non-Christian. There should always be discipline in the life of the Christian. Show me a man who is always losing his self-control; then I say that if he is a Christian at all he is a very poor one. So we must reprimand ourselves and say, 'Why am I agitated? Does my Christianity make no difference to me?' We must pull ourselves up, and condemn ourselves and say, 'I have no right to be like this'. In other words, we have to preach to ourselves and say, 'You have allowed the devil once more to trip you; you have been looking at the circumstances. You cannot see that it is the devil who is crowding them in upon your mind in order to get you into this dither and this paralytic condition.' Thus you reprimand yourself for your failure and your folly.

The next step, as I have hinted, is the realization of the need of self-discipline, the essence of which is that we should always have a sense of proportion. That does not come to us automatically; we have to cultivate it quite deliberately. It is because we fail to do so that the devil gets his opportunity. The Christian should always be reconsidering his whole position in life and in this world, and having done so should always get his priorities right, and always have a sense of proportion. I am not sure but that this is one of the best definitions of the Christian life. The difference between the Christian and the non-Christian is that the life of the non-Christian is being determined and manipulated by the world, whereas the Christian is a man who is in charge, in control.

This is seen clearly in what the Apostle says about himself in 2 Timothy 1:12. He was in prison and everything, as it were, was against him. He gets discouraging messages from Timothy and others. If ever a man had a right to be overwhelmed, and to lose his balance and his self-control, it was the Apostle Paul. But he says, 'nevertheless, I am not ashamed'. What he means is, 'I am not put out', 'I am not in a dither', I am not making haste', 'I am not upside-down', 'I am not losing my balance'. Why? Because, 'I know whom I have believed, and am persuaded that he is able to keep that which I have committed unto him against that day'. Paul is a man whose life is under control. He is disciplined, he talks to himself, he keeps everything in proportion.

But let us go back to the example of Martha. 'Martha', says our Lord, 'you are troubled (busied, distracted) about many things. You are running back and forth from the kitchen to me, you are listening and going away, you do not know where you are, you are in a flurry, you are excited, you have lost control of yourself. But Mary has chosen that good part. It is a question of choice, Martha.'

It is not that it was wrong to prepare a meal as Martha was doing. She was concerned to entertain our Lord, and she felt that everything of the best must be provided, and so she needed the help of her sister. But Mary was sitting and listening to her Lord. Why did she not help? So Martha was excited and troubled. Our Lord tells Martha that it is a question of priorities, it is a question of choice. 'One thing is needful: and Mary hath chosen that good part.' Put that at the beginning, put that in the centre, make certain that that always has priority. If you keep that in the right place everything else will fall into its right position.

The illustrations I have given explain what I mean by a sense of proportion, the all-important matter at this point. But to achieve it you have to aim at it deliberately, and to discipline yourself. Mary had it, Martha lacked it. Our Lord tells Martha to discipline herself, and thereby she too will choose and obtain the 'good part'. Keep first things first, keep them at the centre. The family, the house, the home, the children, the husband, the work, the business, the profession – all these things are right and are very important, but they were never meant to be at the centre of life. It is God and my soul's relationship to Him that is to be in the centre. We are not primarily fathers or mothers or anything else; we are 'souls' in the sight of God. In a certain churchyard there is a tombstone on which are to be seen the words, 'Here lies So-and-so; born a man, died a grocer'. A man is never meant to die as a grocer, he is meant to be a man. We are all souls in the sight of God.

Keep these things in the first place, and then the devil will not have his opportunity. In the words of the Apostle Paul: 'In nothing be anxious' (Philippians 4:6, 7). You must not be worried about anything, you must not get into a dither about anything – it does not matter what it is. Paul's word 'nothing' is as all-inclusive as a word can be. It matters not what your problem is; however desperate, 'In nothing be anxious'. Repel anxious care, do not get alarmed and excited, do not get into a dither. 'In nothing be anxious; but in everything by prayer and supplication with thanksgiving let your requests be made known unto God. And the peace of God, which passeth all understanding, shall keep your hearts and minds through Christ Jesus.'

Another matter which is closely related to the need for self-discipline is the fear of the future, and here, in addition to the natural tendency to anxiety and worry, imagination plays a part. It is good to have an imagination; but it can be a burden and a problem. The people who lack imagination are fortunate in some respects though they lose so much in other respects. But a lively imagination can be used by the devil to force us to peer into the future. Our personal future in this world is quite unknown, so he will conjure up various dread possibilities. What is going to happen to us? What suffering shall we have to endure? And then comes the question, 'Shall we be able to stand it, will our faith hold, shall we be strong enough?' Timothy is the perfect example of this type of mentality which is naturally given to fear and anxiety, but especially fear of the future. The Apostle Paul was in prison, rumours were circulating that he was about to be put to death, there were troubles in the churches. Timothy was but a young man. What was going to happen? What future could there possibly be for the Church in such circumstances? Everything seemed to be going wrong. And so Timothy was fearful and filled with alarm and foreboding as he looked at the future. He was sending his frantic messages to the Apostle, asking why God had not set him at liberty, and why God allowed this, and so on. All these things rushed into his mind because he was looking into the future and allowing his imagination to run riot.

The way to meet the wiles of the devil in this particular respect is still much the same, except that I start with the very practical point that, apart from any other reason, to dwell on the future is an utter and complete waste of time. That is so because the thing you are worrying about may never happen. 'Do not cross your bridges until you arrive at them,' says common sense and the world's wisdom. But we as Christians often forget even that counsel. Worry in reference to the future is a waste of energy, and it is a sheer waste of time. Moreover, while you are worrying in this way about the future you are failing to live and to function as you ought in the present. So condemn yourself for it at once; recognize that it is a temptation from the devil. Do this same thing every time the temptation besets you – pull yourself up, address yourself, shake yourself, reprimand yourself, see how foolish you are to allow the devil to work you up into a frenzy over mere possibilities, and how you are paralysed in the present!

In addition, tell yourself that you are actually breaking a specific command of the Lord Jesus Christ Himself: 'Take no thought (no anxious thought) for the morrow'. He does not mean that you are not to make provision and to do what is necessary in life. He is referring to worry and anxiety – what are we going to wear? What are we going to eat? What is going to happen? He says that we must never have anxious care about tomorrow, that we are not to behave like the Gentiles. Note the contrast He draws between a non-Christian and a Christian. The nations of the world, the Gentiles, the unbelievers, are always thinking about the morrow. They live only for this world and this present life, concerned about what they are to wear, what they are to eat, what they are going to do tomorrow, and what is going to happen to them . . . The nations of the world, the Gentiles behave thus, the Lord says; but His disciples are not to be like that. They are children of His heavenly Father and therefore they should behave in an utterly different manner. Let us then, 'take no (anxious) thought for the morrow'. 'Sufficient unto the day is the evil thereof.'

But, in addition, let us remind ourselves that as Christians we have the Holy Spirit. You cannot be a Christian without having

the Spirit of God in you. 'If any man have not the Spirit of
Christ, he is none of his' (Romans 8:9). The Apostle Paul tells
Timothy that he seems to have forgotten this truth, that he is too
dependent upon him (Paul), and afraid of the future. But, says
the Apostle, 'God hath not given us the spirit of fear; but of
power, and of love, and of a sound mind' (2 Timothy 1:7). A
'sound mind' implies discipline, self-control, orderliness. Timothy,
says the Apostle, is denying the Holy Spirit that is in him, and
behaving as if he had not received the Spirit. A Christian should
not behave in such a fashion. 'Therefore endure hardness as a
good soldier of Jesus Christ', Paul proceeds to say to Timothy
in the next part of his letter. And it is in a similar way that we
have to speak to ourselves.

Furthermore, this fearfulness with respect to the future is not
only lack of faith; it is worse, it is unbelief. Let us examine it
and put the appropriate label on it; and let us chastise ourselves.
The whole art of defeating the wiles of the devil is to see that
he is at the back of it all; and then to look at yourself and to
say, 'What a fool I am to listen to him and to be deceived again'.
Address yourself and condemn yourself for being guilty of
unbelief. How? Question yourself about your heavenly Father in
whom you claim to believe. You seem to be forgetting Him, and
what our Lord says in His teaching in the Sermon on the Mount;
'Your heavenly Father knoweth that ye have need of all these
things' (Matthew 6:25-34). Why are you worried? If you believe
in Him at all, if you believe in Him as your Father, why not
believe that He knows your needs? Why not remind yourself
that 'the very hairs of your head are all numbered', that 'no
sparrow falls to the ground apart from your heavenly Father';
and 'how much greater value are ye than many sparrows'. But
fearfulness about the future is sheer unbelief and is to be condemned root and branch. Do you not believe that 'all things work
together for good to them that love God' (Romans 8:28)? If
you do believe this promise, why then are you frightened? You
are to believe the promises of the Scriptures; and if you do not
you are guilty of unbelief, as are all people who are guilty of this
craven fear. You are not trusting your Father; you do not
believe that He has loved you with an everlasting love; you do
not know that His care for you is infinitely beyond anything that

you can ever imagine, that He so loved you that He sent His only begotten Son to die for you.

Show yourself the unreasonableness of this fear and foreboding. Sustained by the divine logic of the Scriptures, turn to the devil and say, 'I am not going to be afraid of the future. The God who has done what He has for me already in His dear Son will not, can not, abandon me.' 'He that spared not his own Son, but delivered him up for us all, how shall he not with him also freely give us all things?' Turn that logic upon him and say, 'I am not afraid of the future; the God who saved me in the past, the God who is with me in the present, is the God who will always be with me.'

But let us turn now to another matter which arises out of the two we have already been considering – the whole problem of guidance. Here, again, is one of the commonest troubles. The fact is that they are all common, and the devil varies them. In this question of guidance we can include answers to prayer, and also the whole question of faith healing. They belong to the same category. Not surprisingly there is great interest in healing, guidance, and answers to prayer at the present time, for life is particularly difficult at the moment, and any conscientious Christian is always anxious to do what is right. There is a popular teaching which says, 'Pray to God. That is all you have to do; and you will be told exactly what to do, you will receive exact guidance.' Or if you are ill it says, 'Go to the Lord for healing'.

In these matters the devil, using all his wiliness, tries to persuade us to take a mechanical view and to believe that 'it is really quite simple', that there is no problem at all. You just go to God and you get your guidance; you pray to God and you get your desired answer. The 'prayer of faith', they say, surely guarantees that result. Then with regard to healing the argument is that 'it is never God's will that any of His children should be ill'. 'How can a loving Father allow any of His children to be ill?' 'It is always God's will that we should be well and healthy.' Therefore if you are ill, obviously you just ask God to heal you; and it must happen.

The result of such teaching is that, when these things do not happen, there is disappointment. You do not seem to be able to get your guidance, or you thought you had received your guidance but you found that things went wrong, and so you are in trouble, and are disappointed. The healing has not taken place in spite of fervent, believing prayer, as you thought. All this, plus the fear of taking the wrong decision, depresses the believer. He begins to turn in upon himself and says, 'Am I a Christian at all? If I were a true Christian, surely God would have answered me. Am I a Christian at all? If I am, then I am lacking in faith. There is something wrong with me somewhere. I do not know where it lies, but I am lacking in faith at some point.' Thus the devil encourages you to believe his lie; and he may use your friends in order to aggravate the condition.

Obviously this is not an easy problem; indeed it is one of the most difficult problems in the Christian life. I simply offer a number of suggestions by way of answer. The first is obviously that this whole matter is not as simple as some of our friends would have us believe. It is the chief characteristic of the cults that they always make everything 'quite simple'. You do this and the desired thing happens. 'You just go to God, and you get your guidance; you pray to God, and you are healed; you ask for God's will, He lets you know. It is as simple as that!' But it is clearly not as simple as that! If it were as simple as that, there would be no problem, and there would be no need for much of the teaching of the New Testament.

In the second place, it is clear that if it were as simple as is claimed, the Christian life would be machine-like, mechanical, automatic; it would be like pulling a lever and seeing the signal drop. But the Christian life is not like that. Not only so; if it were as simple as that, there would never be any growth in the Christian life. There is no growth and development in a machine; but where there is life there is growth and development. There is never any growth in the followers of the cults. Meet them twenty years after they joined the cults and you will find them exactly as they were at the beginning – if they are still in them! But there is certainly no growth; because there is no room for growth. All happens at once at the beginning, quite simply. But in the Christian faith you have 'babes in Christ', 'young men', 'old men' – there is growth and development and progress.

In the third place there is specific biblical teaching with respect to this matter. The Apostle Paul did not receive automatic guidance. He was sometimes in difficulties about his guidance. For example, in the sixteenth chapter of the Book of the Acts of the Apostles, we read in verse 6, 'Now when they had gone throughout Phrygia and the region of Galatia, and were forbidden of the Holy Ghost to preach the word in Asia, after they were come to Mysia, they assayed to go into Bithynia: but the Spirit suffered them not'. There is also the striking case of the Apostle and his 'thorn in the flesh' in 2 Corinthians 12. Three times he prayed to God with all faith and fervency that this be removed. But it was not removed; and he came to see why it was not removed. It was good for him – 'when I am weak, then am I strong'. He received the Lord's word of assurance, 'My grace is sufficient for thee'. So Paul says in effect, 'Whatever the thorn in the flesh may be, it does not matter, I am content to go on. Let everything minister to Thy glory and to Thy praise.' Trophimus likewise has to be left sick. Timothy is told to take a little wine for his stomach's sake. These are sheer facts in the teaching of the Scripture, and the subsequent history of God's saints and people teaches the same. There is nothing automatic about guidance and these other matters in the teaching of the Scripture or in the history of the Church.

'But,' asks someone, 'what about James' teaching concerning the prayer of faith? Are you not contradicting that?' Let us examine this question. The Epistle of James in its fifth chapter reads, 'Is any among you afflicted? let him pray. Is any merry? let him sing psalms. Is any sick among you? let him call for the elders of the church; and let them pray over him, anointing him with oil in the name of the Lord. And the prayer of faith shall save the sick, and the Lord shall raise him up; and if he have committed sins, they shall be forgiven him.' 'That,' says someone, 'is as plain as anything can be.' But I answer, that if again it is as simple as it would appear to be, why does it not always happen? That is the problem. People have lived who have believed James' words as intensely as possible; everything commanded in his Epistle has been done, but the sick person has not been healed. That should make us see at once that there may be something wrong with our interpretation of the passage.

But let me call attention to the parallel passage in the Gospel of Mark. 'And Jesus, answering, saith unto them, Have faith in God. For verily I say unto you, that whosoever shall say unto this mountain, Be thou removed, and be thou cast into the sea; and shall not doubt in his heart, but shall believe that those things which he saith shall come to pass; he shall have whatsoever he saith. Therefore I say unto you, What things soever ye desire, when ye pray, believe that ye receive them, and ye shall have them' (Mark 11:22-24). This statement is interpreted sometimes in the following way. If you have prayed to God, and you truly believe, do not stop at just asking God; thank Him at once, before you get off your knees. Thank God for having heard your prayer of faith, thank Him for what you know for certain is going to happen. 'That is the prayer of faith,' they say. But, again, we find that facts are very stubborn things. There are many unhappy and wretched Christians in the world who believe that kind of teaching whole-heartedly and honestly and sincerely, but the thing they desired has not happened, and they are perplexed. The reason is that they are misinterpreting the Scriptures.

What is 'the prayer of faith'? What is it that enables a man to believe that he is going to receive what he asks for? That is the crucial question, and the answer seems to be perfectly clear. You can never bring yourself to that persuasion. The fact that you say that you believe it, does not mean that it is true. You cannot force yourself in this matter, you cannot persuade yourself. I suggest that 'the prayer of faith' is a prayer that is always given, and indited by the Holy Spirit Himself. And when He gives it, there is no doubt, there is no uncertainty. You are not working yourself up to say 'I do believe', you are not persuading yourself. The Holy Spirit has made it absolutely certain to you.

There are two striking facts in the Book of the Acts of the Apostles concerning the healing worked by them. First, they never announced beforehand that they were going to heal! The modern faith-healers do so. They announce, 'On Wednesday there will be a healing service in the afternoon'. The Apostles never spoke in this fashion. I believe the explanation is that they never knew beforehand when the Lord would heal men by their means. They did not possess a kind of permanent power so that all they had to do at any given moment was as it were to press a button. This is what you find. As Peter and John were going

[327]

up to the temple at the hour of prayer, they saw the lame man at the gate. He looks up expecting to receive alms from them. Then Peter, 'fastening his eyes upon him with John, said, In the name of Jesus Christ of Nazareth rise up and walk'. What made Peter do that? I have no hesitation whatsoever in answering the question. He was given a commission, and at that moment. The command came, the Spirit told him, Christ said, as it were, 'I intend to heal through you'. And Peter knew the mind of the Lord.

You find the same principle in Acts 14 when Paul preached at Lystra. An impotent man was put to sit in front of him, and Paul 'perceiving that he had faith to be healed' spoke to him and healed him. The commission was given! Paul knew for certain that the man was to be healed. The Apostles never announced a healing beforehand, because they never knew when it was going to happen. Secondly, when the Apostles set out to heal they never failed. I am talking about the Book of the Acts of the Apostles after Pentecost, not about the Gospels. They never tried and failed. Your modern healers try and fail very often because they hold wrong teaching. They do not have the particular command, they have never had the particular commission; they believe that this power is in the Church and that you simply have to exercise it. You 'claim' the power, you act upon it. But there are more failures than successes. It is a misunderstanding of Scripture.

The 'prayer of faith' is a prayer that is given by the Spirit. You do not command it. You can never make yourself certain that you are certain to receive what you ask for. But God through the Spirit will at times give you that consciousness. Our Lord always had it; He knew. There was perfect accord between Him and His Father; and He was for ever doing His Father's works. He says, 'The works that I do, I do not of myself; but the Father that sent me, He doeth the works'. It is to be the same with us. It is only as we get into the condition in which we are sensitive to the Spirit that we shall be given authority, and certainty. We shall be given the commission, and then there never will be a failure. But if we experiment, and try to work up something in ourselves, there will be repeated failure and consequent dejection and unhappiness.

To summarize: we can say that these happenings are the

exceptions. God's normal way of guidance, and of healing, and of all these other matters, is through means. We are meant to get our guidance through the Scriptures, through an enlightened spiritual mind and understanding, through an enlightened reason, through an enlightened conscience. That is how God normally guides us. Thank God that He does so; and He gives us certainty through these methods. You read your Scriptures and absorb their teaching; and you apply it. If you are in trouble you go and consult others – pastors and teachers and older Christians. You bring all relevant factors together, and get the mind of the Church, as it were, upon them. And then, probably through circumstances, God will show you His will. And on top of all this, there is often such a thing as a pressure upon the mind and upon the heart, something you cannot get rid of. You sometimes wish you could, but you cannot. God is giving you some kind of general indication through a pressure on your mind that you are meant to do this or that, and you cannot get rid of the thought. These are the ways in which God normally guides His people.

So the ultimate rules of procedure, it seems to me, in this matter are as follows: Never make a claim in the presence of God; do not 'claim' healing, do not 'claim' guidance. We are not to 'claim' in the presence of God; but we come as humble suppliants. To claim is the fallacy of this modern teaching, and hence its confusion. Secondly, commit yourself and all your affairs to God, commit everything to God – illness, the future, guidance, everything. 'Take it to the Lord in prayer.' Tell Him that your one desire is to know His will and to do it. If you cannot be honest at that point, you might as well stop. Start with yourself and ask, 'Can I honestly say to God that I desire nothing but to know His will, and to do that will, whatever it is – whether I am to go abroad or stay at home, whether I am to be sick, or whether I am to be well; whether I am to get married or not to get married. Whatever it is, can I say honestly to God that my supreme desire is to know His will and to do it whatever it is?' Then remind yourself that God is your Father. Therefore leave it with God. Do not think too much about it after leaving it with God; it is His problem now, not yours. Do not pray to God, and then get up and start thinking again, and continue going round in circles. If you do so, you have not believed in your prayer. Leave the matter with God. Tell Him all honestly, and leave it with Him. Do not think too much about it now, but go on doing what you are meant to do. Do your work, be observant, keep your eyes open, be ready at any point for some indication of God's will. Be alert; but do not be anxious. Never be anxious. 'In nothing be anxious.' Refuse worry, refuse anxiety. Leave all with God, go on with your work.

Finally, never act against that inner voice. In other words you may find as the result of doing what I have been saying, that you have come to a point when everything seems to indicate that you should do some particular thing; but if there is a feeling within you that you should not, do not act. Always act as a whole. Never move until you are unanimous! 'Whatsoever is not of faith is sin.' Read the last verse of Romans 14 if there is any doubt. 'He that doubteth,' says the Apostle, 'is damned.' If there is a doubt left inside you which you cannot even understand, something almost intangible but nevertheless very powerful, do not act against it, whatever your mind and reason, or whatever else other people may say.

I often sum it up in the following way. A man seeking guidance and trying to carry out God's will in this world is like a train in Paddington Station or some other London railway terminus. There it is, everything is ready, the passengers are all in their seats, the power to begin the journey is present, but the train is not moving. Why not? The signal has not dropped! And the train does not move, though everything is ready, until that final signal has dropped. To me, the final signal is this deep consciousness within. Never act against it. Never act against your conscience, never act against this inward sense. But if that is clear and agrees with all the rest, go straight ahead. 'But,' says someone, 'what guarantee have I now that I am right? You have been shaking my confidence.' My reply is, that if you do what I have been saying, whatever the circumstances, you will not suffer, for you have acted as God's child should act. And God knowing you, and knowing your motives, will not punish you. For your own good He may prevent the thing you desire, and you will thank Him for doing so later on. But if you act scripturally, conscientiously and according to these rules, you can do no more; and I do not hesitate to assert that God expects no more of you. You have submitted to His will, whatever it may be, and anyone who does so will be blessed of God.

Let us then beware of the subtle teachings that are prevalent in the cults, and that in other ways would reduce the great mystery of God's relationship to His children, and our growth and development in grace, to something mechanical and machine-like. Let us 'quit ourselves as men' and use the means that God has given us. And if it be God's will for something unusual in any particular case, you can be sure that He will make it very plain and clear. There will be no question about it. If it is to be something miraculous, there will be the authority and the certainty that the Lord gave to His apostles; and He will give it to you. May God enable us to realize the truth concerning the 'wiles of the devil', that we may also realize our need of 'the whole armour of God', and the need to be 'strong in the Lord of hosts and in His mighty power'.

24

Self

We come now to the last sub-heading under this general heading of the attack upon the Christian in the realm of experience. I have deliberately kept it until the end in order that I might emphasize it, and because it throws light upon all we have been considering hitherto. It is the attack of the enemy upon us in the matter of self, or, the problem of self as it is made acute by the wiles of the devil.

I am surely right when I say that it is the universal testimony of the greatest saints that have ever adorned the Christian Church that the most subtle enemy they have had to face, and the last, is 'self', as their biographies and diaries testify. In the last analysis a man's greatest battle is that against himself.

According to the teaching of the Bible, self is responsible for all sin. The first 'fall' in God's creation was the fall of the devil. The devil was created perfect by God, and with unusual faculties, ability, power and understanding. He was a bright star in the firmament of God's creation. But he fell because of pride, which is nothing but a manifestation of self. He rebelled against God. He resented the fact that God was greater than himself. He wanted to be equal to God, as great as God and as important as God. The whole of evil ultimately emanates from this fact that self is present even in an angelic, a seraphic being. Self was the cause of the downfall, that pre-cosmic fall that has led to the whole problem of sin and evil.

After God had made the world and man, and had put man in

Paradise, man also fell. And the cause of man's failure was but a repetition of what had been true in the case of the devil. The devil knew the line that he must adopt; he knew the very thing that was likely to ensnare the man and the woman. So he went to the woman and he said in effect, 'Has God said that you should not eat of a certain tree? He has said so because He knows that if you eat of this tree of the knowledge of good and evil you will become as gods yourselves.' He played on pride, he played on self. He said, 'Eat that fruit and it will show you what you really are, and what your powers and possibilities really are'. So the cause of the fall of man was exactly the same as the cause of the fall of the devil, namely, self showing itself in this particular form of pride. It should not surprise us, therefore, that the devil in his wiliness constantly plays upon this particular aspect of our personality.

Throughout the Bible it is clear that self is the outstanding problem in human life. Hence we should always thank God that the Bible is not merely a Book of teaching but also a Book of history. In it we are given accounts of individual persons and individual nations, and as you read the Old Testament and the New there is no problem that raises its head more frequently than this horrible, terrible problem of self, whether seen in individuals, or groups, or nations. What havoc this whole problem of self has caused in the long history of the human race! Are you not surprised at what the Gospels reveal about the men who had the privilege of being in the innermost circle of our Lord's friends and associates? How pathetic to read about them that they were disputing among themselves as to which of them should be the greatest, even in His presence, despite all the privileges and blessings they enjoyed.

Our Lord has put particular emphasis upon this by constantly giving His picture of the Christian man in terms of a little child. He does so when women brought little children to Him to be blessed, and the disciples tried to stop them. But our Lord said, 'Suffer the little children to come unto me, and forbid them not; for of such is the kingdom of God'. 'Except ye be converted,' He says again, 'and become as little children, ye shall in no wise enter into the kingdom of God' (Matthew 18:3). He takes a little child and puts him in the midst. All along, and everywhere, He brings out this element of childlikeness as being the ultimate characteristic and hallmark of the true Christian.

But over and above His own teaching there is His own Person. He is 'the meek and lowly Jesus'. You cannot think of Him, you cannot look at Him, without at once being struck by this outstanding characteristic. 'The bruised reed he will not break, the smoking flax he will not quench.' His utter humility and his endeavours, from time to time, to get away from the crowds, and to hide Himself, are completely typical of His character. One cannot read the Four Gospels without being struck by the absence of ostentation and self-advertisement. He is the very negation of all that denotes pride. The meek and the lowly Jesus!

How well the devil knows our human weakness! There is no method, therefore, that he more frequently uses in order to try to mar God's work in the Church, and to spoil the testimony of Christ, than just to play on this problem of self as it is present in every one of us. The ways in which he does so are almost endless. He works on self in order to encourage pride. He tries to make us proud of our gifts, our brains, our understanding, our knowledge. In the church at Corinth, for example, there were the stronger brethren and the weaker brethren, and the men of knowledge and understanding despised the less gifted ones. How typical! The church was being divided up and ruined very largely because of this pride of knowledge and of understanding. How often this has happened! How often it still happens – pride in these particular gifts of intellect, perception, understanding, and knowledge!

A man may also be proud of his gift of facile speech. There is scarcely a more dangerous gift to possess than the gift of speech, and the ability to put things plainly and clearly, thereby influencing the hearers. How many a minister, a preacher, has been ruined because of his ready gift of speech!

Then think of the gift of singing! Is there anything that has done greater harm, perhaps, in the history of the Church than this particular gift? Have not choirs frequently quarrelled over the question of who is to have the pre-eminence? The ability to sing well is a great gift but a very dangerous one. It is a notorious cause of trouble. How subtle is the temptation to give prominence to your voice, to be just a little ahead of the whole

[334]

congregation or a little after them so that your voice stands out; or to adopt various other ways to destroy the harmony and unity of worship. These are some of the ways in which the devil uses these particular gifts to puff up our pride. This matter is dealt with clearly in the First Epistle to the Corinthians and especially in chapter 12. The Corinthian church was in trouble because of its spiritual gifts. Some were able to work miracles, some to speak with tongues, and so on; but others could not do so, and the result was a divided church.

But besides gifts, there is also the danger of working up pride in the matter of experience, and it shows us particularly clearly the wiliness and the subtlety of the devil. He can ruin a man's Christian life, as far as his enjoyment and usefulness in this world are concerned, by simply using the greatness of the experience a man may have had and puffing him up over it. He will make him boast of his spiritual experience. Some conversions are very dramatic, and some are not; and if it has happened to be a very dramatic experience the devil sees his opportunity at once. He will make this man talk about it excessively, and others in their folly will make him talk about it; they will put him forward as a kind of 'star turn', as we say, and the man, before he realizes it, is boasting of his experience – not boasting in the Lord any longer but boasting of himself and his own experience. The tendency to boast of one's spiritual experience can become so manipulated by the devil that I have even heard men boasting of their past sinfulness! Of course their object was to dramatize their experience, the great change that had taken place in their lives.

In this connection I always think of something that happened once in my presence which imprinted this danger upon my mind once and for ever. It shows how ridiculous this boasting can become. Early in my ministerial life in an open-air meeting where a number of men were called upon to give their experience, a man went forward to confess that he had been a drunkard and so on. He gave us many details, and then told us of how he had been entirely changed. He did it with much eloquence – even concerning the part that was sinful. When he had finished another man was called forward, and he began to speak thus: 'You have heard my brother telling of his experience of sin. Hah, he doesn't know what sin is! I will tell you about a life of sin'. So he began to boast of his former sinfulness! The meeting had degenerated into a competition in sin and almost in crime, as the second man tried to paint a blacker picture than the first man. It was all done in a spirit of pride and of boastfulness. The devil had come in at this most tender, delicate, sensitive point – the glory and the greatness of a great change in life produced by the Holy Spirit – and he had puffed up the speaker's pride. Indeed it was true of both of them. They were boasting of themselves and their past sinfulness. The result was that their testimony was utterly useless, and it seemed to me that the meeting was doing much more harm than good.

There is nothing about us that the devil cannot take hold of. It is because it has happened to 'us', because it is 'ours', because it is 'we' who have done it. And he will take even the most glorious gift and will twist it in this subtle manner. He will so bring self into it that the whole thing will be ruined.

Another form which this evil can take stems from the fact that various desires always tend to arise from self – the desire for importance, the desire for position. This is described in the Third Epistle of John as the desire for 'pre-eminence'. We are told there about a man called Diotrephes who, according to John, 'loved to have the pre-eminence'. He was a man who was doing harm in the church. He was a Christian man, a saved man, a good man, but he always liked to 'have the pre-eminence'; he liked to be the chief man.

This is not confined to men! In Philippians chapter 4, in the second verse Paul writes: 'I beseech Euodias, and beseech Syntyche, that they be of the same mind in the Lord. And I entreat thee, also, true yokefellow, help those women which laboured with me in the gospel, with Clement also, and with other my fellow-labourers, whose names are in the book of life.' Euodias and Syntyche were causing division in the church. They were both Christians, working for the same Lord; but they were also both coveting leadership, pre-eminence and importance. Thus the devil brings havoc into the life of the individual and into the life of the whole church. How essential it is that we should be aware of this, for this is still happening in individuals and in the Church of God!

All this leads above everything else to a spirit of self-satisfaction. The classic illustration of this is found in the case of the church of the Laodiceans in the third chapter of the Book of Revelation. The church was saying, 'I am rich, and increased with goods, and have need of nothing', and it did not know that it was 'wretched, and miserable, and poor, and blind, and naked'. In their self-satisfaction there was the feeling that everything was well and there was complete failure to realize their true state and condition, and therefore an entire neglect of self-examination. Such people never examine themselves. They think they 'have arrived'. They are perfect. What more can be desired? They are saved. They are not like the unbelievers outside. They never think of anyone except those who are outside. They never read about the saints; they never look at a standard higher than their own; they never apply the Scriptures.

Another way that this sin sometimes takes is to give us the feeling that we can never fall. Here, again, the Corinthian church supplies an illustration. The Apostle uses a very striking phrase in the tenth chapter of his First Epistle. He says to them, 'Wherefore let him that thinketh he standeth take heed lest he fall'. They felt that they could not fall. So the Apostle takes them back to the history of the children of Israel. Many, he says, were brought out of Egypt, even through the Red Sea, who never arrived in the land of Canaan, because they fell into this state of self-satisfaction. 'Wherefore let him that thinketh he standeth take heed lest he fall.' There is nothing more dangerous than for us to feel that we can never fall, that we can never sin, that nothing can ever go wrong with us. We hear of someone falling and say, 'What a terrible thing; fancy a Christian falling like that!' As a true Christian you should rather say to yourself, whenever you see someone falling, 'There, but for the grace of God, go I'. 'Let him that thinketh he standeth take heed lest he fall.' But the man who is puffed up with pride cannot imagine himself falling – it is impossible in his case, he has 'arrived', he is a perfect Christian.

Furthermore this condition leads to selfishness and self-centredness. Self is always interested in itself. Everything revolves round this particular entity; and it becomes the centre of a constellation. That in turn leads to jealousy and envy. This again was to be seen clearly in Corinth. The members with the lesser gifts were envying the others, feeling very jealous of them, wondering why they had not been given the same gifts, and in the end beginning to question God's goodness. Jealousy, envy, spite, malice, hatred, are all products of the spirit of self. To the extent that we are governed by self we are sensitive, and as such we can be easily hurt, easily depressed, and discouraged. Self is always watching for insults and slights. It is always hyper-sensitive. It is delicate, it is sensitized to everything; the slightest speck troubles it and alarms it. Self is totalitarian; it demands everything, and it is irritated and hurt if it does not get every-thing. As a consequence it becomes a most fruitful cause of quarrels and divisions and unhappiness in the life of the Church, in the life of the community, in the life of the State, and ultimately in the life of the whole world.

People are often amazed and surprised at such tragic results. They say, 'But we thought that when we became Christians we surely finished with all that!' Far from it! If it were so, why have we so many exhortations and so much teaching on the subject in the New Testament? The devil is still at work, and with his wiles he knows how to play upon our greatest weakness, which is self.

The answer to all this is found very simply and plainly in the Bible. The Bible always tells us to face ourselves honestly, and to realize the full truth about ourselves. That is the secret of it all. It is because we do not examine ourselves that we suffer from 'self'. The moment we examine ourselves honestly we discover that we have nothing to boast about. 'I am coming to examine you,' says Paul, in effect, to those Corinthians, 'and when I do come and examine you, I am not going to examine you in terms of speech and talking and statements – any fool can talk. I am coming to examine you, not in terms of speech, but in terms of power, for the kingdom of God is not in word, but in power' (1 Corinthians 4:20). I am going to make a thorough test, says the Apostle.

The First Epistle to the Corinthians, chapter 4, is full of the profoundest teaching with regard to this particular subject. In verses 6 and 7 Paul writes: 'And these things, brethren, I have in a figure transferred to myself and to Apollos for your sakes;

that ye might learn in us not to think of men above that which is written, that no one of you be puffed up for one against another. For who maketh thee to differ from another? and what hast thou that thou didst not receive? now if thou didst receive it, why dost thou glory, as if thou hadst not received it?'

The Apostle's argument is unanswerable. He says, in effect, to all Christians, 'You are boasting of your gifts and your superiority. But what are you boasting about? God's gifts, of which you are so proud? Why are you boasting about them? Have you produced them? Did you create them? Have you generated them? Are they the result of something that you have done? Stop and think for a moment, and realize that you have not made yourself what you are. If you have a great brain, it is no credit to you, you were born with it. If you have a wonderful singing voice, you have not produced it, it was given you. What are you boasting about? All that you have is not the result of your action and activity; it is something with which God has endowed you. 'Who maketh thee to differ from another? And what hast thou that thou didst not receive?' It is all the gift of God. If you are boasting about your personal appearance, your good looks, your abilities, or anything that you possess, stop and ask yourself: 'What am I boasting of? Why should I be proud of this? I have received it all, none of it is the result of anything I have done myself.' It is because we fail to do this that the devil with his wiles is able to puff us up and make us proud of the very gifts that God has given to us.

The most profound psychological understanding of man that can be found anywhere is found in the Bible. This is the ultimate and the only answer. We look at the great men of the world and we praise them and laud them. But we are wrong. We should praise God. It is God who makes a Shakespeare, not man; it is God who makes great generals, great statesmen. These men have been endowed with gifts. The great scientists have all been born with their gifts. Hence we should never glory in men, but in God who is able to give such gifts to men, and able to use men in the way He does. We should not boast in ourselves, we should not boast of others. We should see the great God over all who gives these various gifts as He wills. That is the secret.

But you must not stop at that point; we must go further and

ask this question: What do I really deserve? Examine yourself
and look at yourself as you really are, not as other people see
you, nor as you would have other people see you. Do not look
only at the figure you cut before society, but just look at yourself
and talk to yourself as you really are. Look into your spiritual
mirror. You know what people think of you. But what if they
knew all the thoughts which you fondle in your mind and
imagination, and in your heart? What if they knew of the things
you propose to yourself at times? Or what if they knew your
innermost secrets? 'No man is a hero to his valet' is a common
saying. And no man should be a hero to himself, because he is
still closer to himself even than his valet.

Realizing that, ask yourself, What do I really deserve? I have
nothing to boast of, what if I were treated according to my
deserts? What would happen to me? 'If thou, Lord, shouldest
mark iniquities, O Lord, who shall stand?' Realize, then, that
as Christians, we are what we are by the grace of God. The two
foolish men I have already mentioned, who were boasting about
their experiences, would have remained sinners were it not for
the grace of God. The grace of God had laid hold on them in
their drunkenness and had changed them and renewed them. Yet
they were boasting as if they had done it. People who give their
experiences publicly often tend to exaggerate them and build
them up in order to make themselves more wonderful; and thus
they detract from the all-important grace of God.

We are what we are by the grace of God. It is the special characteristic of the Apostle Paul that he emphasizes grace. He has
to defend himself occasionally, but he always restrains himself.
Referring to the resurrection appearances he says, 'And last of
all he was seen of me also, as of one born out of due time. For
I am the least of the apostles, and am not meet to be called an
apostle, because I persecuted the church of God. But by the grace
of God I am what I am' (1 Corinthians 15:8–10). Then in the
Second Epistle to the Corinthians he repeats that, saying in effect,
You are forcing me to boast. I do not want to boast, but you are
for ever glorying in men so much. You are so foolish, you are so
ignorant, that you are compelling me to boast. I must tell you
therefore what I have done (2 Corinthians 12:11). Paul always
kept the grace of God in view; it kept him humble; it kept his

spirit sweet; it kept him from the horrible sin of self and of pride and self-importance. Christians have nothing to boast of. We are what we are entirely as the result of the grace of God.

Let us work out the teaching of 1 Corinthians 12, and look at the Church as the Body of Christ. The central principle is that every part of the body is important. Of course every part is not as striking in appearance and does not seem to be so essential. The head, the eyes, hands and feet all seem to be essential and wonderful and important. But, says the Apostle, 'there are less comely parts'; there are parts we do not speak about, there are parts which we hide. But, says, Paul, the body cannot function without the less comely parts. The study of the body is a very salutary procedure. It is a very humbling but at the same time a very healthy thing to do. The less comely parts are as essential as the more comely parts. You do not boast about them; but you could not live without them. Well now, says Paul, apply all this to yourselves as members of the Christian Church. There are differences in gifts – some great, some apparently small, according to man's estimate. But, he says, do not estimate them according to man's estimate; estimate them in God's way. See that what matters is that you are a member of the Body of Christ, a little finger perhaps. That does not matter; you are there – a less comely part, but essential to the harmonious and healthy working of the body. The thing to concentrate on is not the particular part that you happen to be, but the fact that you *are* a part, that you have the privilege of being in the body, all the members of which are governed by the same Head, and necessary to the body's harmonious working. Rejoice in the fact that you are in the Body and a part of Christ. 'Ye are the body of Christ, and members in particular.' There is no such thing as an unimportant church member. Let not the devil fool us or mislead us. We are all of great value in the kingdom of God, and we must not indulge in artificial and ridiculous distinctions. Each member is essential to the harmonious working of the whole.

The only thing that matters ultimately is what God thinks of us; the only thing that matters is what Christ thinks of us. If we could but get hold of this principle it would revolutionize everything. We tend to be always wondering what people are thinking and saying; and so we become sensitive. They are not praising us

[341]

sufficiently, or they are criticizing us; and we are hurt and depressed. What misery and agony we all endure in life because of this horrible self, and this concern as to what people are thinking! There is only one answer to that. It is to be found in 1 Corinthians, chapter 4, beginning at the first verse, 'Let a man so account of us, as the ministers of Christ, and stewards of the mysteries of God. Moreover it is required in stewards, that a man be found faithful. But with me it is a very small thing that I should be judged of you, or of man's judgment: yea, I judge not mine own self. For I know nothing by myself; yet am I not hereby justified: but he that judgeth me is the Lord. Therefore judge nothing before the time, until the Lord come, who both will bring to light the hidden things of darkness, and will make manifest the counsels of the hearts: and then shall every man have praise of God.'

That is what should be true of all of us! 'With me it is a very small thing that I should be judged of you, or of man's judgment.' But the Apostle did not stop at that point. It is possible to read biographies of men who after a great struggle have come to the position of saying, 'To me, it is a very small thing that I be judged of you, or of man's judgment'. They had suffered because of their sensitive natures, because they were so troubled by what other people said and thought of them. They could not sleep at night because of it, and were in an agony, living in terms of reaction to other people's opinions and criticisms. They were hyper-sensitive. But after a terrible struggle they got over it and said, 'What do they matter after all? Who are they? They are poor judges in any case, and they cannot appreciate my work.' So they worked themselves into a position in which they insulated themselves against the criticisms of others. But in the process some of them became cynics. They retired into an innermost retreat in which they said, 'Of course, these people do not understand, they do not appreciate; that is their trouble. They are ignoramuses, they do not know.' So while, in a sense they were no longer reacting to criticism, they were in a yet more terrible condition because they were now living with themselves alone in the innermost sanctum. It is possible for a man to do that, and to be able to say, therefore, 'With me, it is a very small thing that I be judged of you, or of any man's judgment. I do not care what you think about me; you cannot hurt me any more.' He has insulated himself.

But the man is even more guilty of being a slave to self than he was before, for he has not taken that further step, 'Yea, I judge not mine own self'. The Apostle Paul had not only ceased to be troubled by other people's criticisms, he no longer even criticized himself. In other words he had stopped watching himself and living for himself. And this last step is essential. We have to learn to stop worrying about ourselves and our opinion of ourselves, leave alone that of other people. Self will feed self, and the way in which it does so is most subtle and ingenious; it brings out its compliments and praises us, and answers the criticisms. It is essential for us to reach that final stage in which self has stopped feeding self – 'Yea, I judge not mine own self'. And the only way to do so is that which the Apostle indicates. It is to realize that nothing matters but the judgment and the estimate and the opinion of the Lord Himself. 'I know nothing by myself; yet am I not hereby justified: but he that judgeth me is the Lord.' And He knows everything – 'the hidden things of darkness', 'the secrets of the heart'; they will all be brought forth. The one thing that matters is what I am like in His presence. So we can say with Horatius Bonar in one of his hymns:

> *Men heed thee, love thee, praise thee not;*
> *The Master praises; what are men?*

Or, still better, take a statement found in the Biography of George Müller of Bristol, the founder and establisher of Müller's Homes. He says quite solemnly, 'A day came when I died to George Müller completely, utterly, absolutely; all he was and all he had and possessed and all he hoped to be. I died utterly, absolutely to George Müller.' That is the secret, the final end and the death of self! And only as we reach that state shall we know true freedom, and be able to master the wiles of the devil in this particular respect.

But to complete the argument let us go on to realize how dishonouring self is, in all its manifestations, to God and His grace, and to the Gospel of our Lord and Saviour Jesus Christ. The world is watching us, and as it sees all this it says, 'Where is your Christianity? What is the value of it? What difference

[343]

does Christianity make?' They say, 'I see in those church people exactly what I see in people in the professions; every one trying to be great and pre-eminent, to be leaders. What is the difference between a church and a society, or a profession? There is none.' And so the Gospel is brought into disrepute. There is nothing that is more dishonouring to the Gospel, and especially to the doctrine of regeneration, and the new man in Christ Jesus, than the manifestation of this old principle of self which is the essential principle of sin and evil. Let us look at it then, and let us hate it with the whole of our being.

Finally, realizing its horrible nature, look at Him whom we are privileged to follow and to whom we belong. 'Let nothing be done through strife or vainglory; but in lowliness of mind let each esteem other better than themselves. Look not every man on his own things, but every man also on the things of others. Let this mind be in you, which was also in Christ Jesus, who, being in the form of God, thought it not robbery to be equal with God.' In other words He had been eternally in the form of God, but He did not look upon that as something that He must hold on to at all costs, and never let go – the signs and the manifestations of the glory. He did not regard that as a prize to be clutched at, and to be held on to at all costs. He did not say, 'I am giving up nothing, I demand my rights and my prerogatives'. He did the exact opposite – 'He made himself of no reputation, and took upon him the form of a servant, and was made in the likeness of men: and being found in fashion as a man, he humbled himself, and became obedient unto death, even the death of the cross' (Philippians 2:3–8). How can we ever forget that?

The Babe in the manger is the Lord of glory, the One through whom the heavens and the earth and everything else was made. He has humbled Himself to that! And there He is, brought up in poverty, unknown. There He is working with His hands as a carpenter – the One who had made with the same hands the whole cosmos – buffeted, jeered at, ignored. The Lord of glory! There He is! He is not considering Himself. That was the mind that was in Him, as He died in agony and in weakness and in shame upon a cruel Cross. He did it all that you and I might be redeemed from sin, from self, from this horrible, foul thing that has made the world what it is, and that has ruined God's glorious creation. He humbled Himself, did not consider Himself at all, became a nobody as it were, was regarded as a felon, was crucified with thieves, insult upon insult being heaped upon Him. He did not grumble, He went willingly. He made Himself of no reputation in order that you and I might be rescued and redeemed and become the children of God, heirs of God, and joint-heirs with Himself.

You cannot add to that. 'Let this mind be in you which was also in Christ Jesus.' He had only one controlling thought, it was to do the Father's will, no matter what it involved. It meant leaving heaven, leaving the glory, laying aside the signs of the glory; it meant being a little helpless Babe. Men rejected Him. 'He came unto his own, and his own received him not.' The Father is pleased, whatever men may do or think or say. That is what matters, to be serving God, to be of value in His Kingdom, to help in His great and glorious plan of salvation, His scheme of redemption. What matters is not what part or place you are playing, or what people think of you, or even what you think of yourself. 'The Master praises.' Look forward to the great day that is coming. The world may not have known about you, there may be no obituary notice about you in *The Times*. But when you appear in heaven your name will be known, and the Lord will say to you, 'Well done, thou good and faithful servant'. Unknown, unpraised by men, 'a mute inglorious Milton', 'some village Hampden' though you may have been. That does not matter. 'I knew you,' says the Lord, 'and I saw you. I saw your faithfulness and your loyalty. I knew that you were living for Me and My glory. Well done, thou good and faithful servant; enter thou into the joy of thy Lord.' 'Let this mind be in you, which was also in Christ Jesus.' If it is in you, the wiles of the devil will not be able to shake you. You will be able to answer him at every point in the way I have been trying to indicate, and so God will be well pleased with you, and will 'not be ashamed to be called your God'.

25

True and False Zeal

We come now to the third of the sections into which we have divided the manifestation of the wiles of the devil, namely, the wiles of the devil as they are brought to bear upon our conduct, our practice, and our behaviour. A rough but valuable division of our lives as Christians is to think of ourselves in terms of mind, heart and will; and nothing is more important, according to the Apostle Paul, than that we should realize that the devil, for his own ends and purposes, is concerned to bring us down at any one of these points. He generally starts with the mind. And then, as we have seen, he comes to the realm of experience and feeling, causing confusion and failure. But it does not stop even there. He does not leave us alone in the more practical matter of living, of application. He cares not where as long as he can bring us, and through us the whole of the Christian faith and message, into disrepute.

The Scriptures give considerable attention to this very matter. In the Old Testament much space is given to exhortation of the children of Israel to be holy. That is the meaning of the Ten Commandments, as also it is the whole meaning of the ceremonial law and the rules and regulations with which the life of that people was governed. The purpose of the whole can be summed up in the one sentence, 'Be ye holy, for I am holy'. The Israelites were God's people. They were recalcitrant and very slow to learn this truth, but it is the message which was preached to them by Moses and by Joshua, and then by all the prophets. They all preach this one message, that these children of Israel must never forget who they are, for God's name is upon them; and therefore they must live a life which corresponds to the exalted name and designation that has been given to them. There has been much misunderstanding concerning this, and especially in this twentieth century. Many who have emphasized the ethical teaching of the Bible have failed to realize that the context of the ethical teaching is the relationship of the people to God. It is not mere general morality. It is the peculiar ethic that applies to those who were called 'the people of God'.

The New Testament enforces the same teaching in a yet more striking manner. At the very beginning of His ministry our Lord preached what is commonly called 'The Sermon on the Mount'. The whole object and intent of that sermon is to remind us that because His disciples are God's people they are to live in a given manner. 'Let your light so shine before men that they may see your good works, and glorify your Father which is in heaven.' Our Lord gives detailed instructions as to how we are to live, and all because we are God's children. Christians are to be worthy of their Father which is in heaven. This matter of conduct and practice is put in the forefront, and so it continues throughout the whole of our Lord's teaching. Similarly in respect of the Epistles it is a commonplace to say that they all can be divided into two main sections – firstly, the doctrinal section, then a practical section urging the ethical application of all that has been laid down. That can be seen particularly clearly in the Epistle to the Ephesians. In the first three chapters we find pure doctrine. Then, at the beginning of chapter four, 'I therefore, the prisoner of the Lord, beseech you that ye walk worthy of the vocation wherewith ye are called', and so on. That is true of practically every Epistle in the New Testament, showing the all-importance of this practical aspect of our life as God's people here in this world. In the Book of Revelation, you will find that the last two chapters include this selfsame theme. There are warnings telling us that outside are the dogs, and that nothing unclean will be allowed to enter the Holy City (22:15).

The explanation of this emphasis, very largely, is that those who are outside, those who are not Christian, are always more interested in what we do than in what we are. We as God's people are the representatives of God and of His great purposes, and the people who are outside in their ignorance look at us and judge everything – the Father, the Lord Jesus Christ, and the Holy Spirit – in terms of us. They say, 'It is an easy thing to talk; but the question is, What are you like? What are you doing?' They apply that test to us in a very stringent and thorough manner, and we cannot blame them for doing so. We know that their standards and outlook are both at fault, nevertheless we have to take them as they are. They think that what makes a man a Christian is the life he lives, and therefore, if they find us failing in life and conduct and practice, they will regard the whole of the Christian message as being more or less worthless. They do not understand the doctrine of justification by faith only. They think that a Christian is merely a good man, a moral man, a man who lives a certain kind of life; so they will judge the whole of the Gospel in terms of our success or failure. It follows therefore that any failure on our part in this matter of conduct discredits the Gospel, discredits God and the Lord Jesus Christ, and all for which we stand.

The newspapers give us abundant proof of my contention constantly. If they find that a man who has committed a crime is a Sunday School teacher they never fail to report it. 'Sunday School teacher charged' is the heading in the newspaper report. That is simply the antagonism of the natural man, under the influence of the devil and his wiles, to God, to Christ, to the Church, to everything that is holy. They are always watchful of us, and the moment they find any lapse or blemish they are not slow to take it and to use it. Thus they attempt to bring the whole of the Gospel into disrepute. Obviously, therefore, this is something which the devil is most likely to employ. He always has attacked God's people along this line, and he will continue to do so. The history of the Church is a continuation of the history of the children of Israel. And if we fall, everything for which we contend is involved.

Let us note certain general lines of attack along which the devil comes to us. Firstly, the devil exercises his wiles by influencing our whole attitude to conduct and behaviour. The greatest thing in man is his mind, and if a man's thinking is wrong everything else will be wrong. 'As a man thinks, so he is'; and so he does. The devil's favourite method here again is to drive us from one extreme to the other. He delights to keep us from maintaining the balance of mind which is the essential glory of the Christian.

One extreme in this particular realm is that which is commonly known as antinomianism, which, according to the word's literal meaning, signifies opposition to the whole notion of law. It virtually claims that our conduct and practice are not related to the law of God. It argues thus: The Old Testament was concerned about morality, ethics, conduct, behaviour. That was the law. But under the Gospel the situation is quite different. The Gospel delivers us from law and sets us free. The Christian is no longer under the law, he is a free man. The devil comes to a man who has seen this truth, and presses him to such an extreme that he becomes an antinomian, namely, a man who is only interested in the faith of the Gospel in a purely intellectual manner. He is interested in the great doctrines; understands them and revels in them; and is prepared to argue about them and to defend them. But he stops at that and thinks that nothing more is necessary.

I recall an experience I once had in this respect with a man who belonged to another section of the Christian Church. He was very much interested in Christian doctrine and dogma and was always ready to argue about it and to defend it. I was once in the same company as this man, and even while we were arguing about the doctrines of the Christian faith he was drinking too much. It never seemed to occur to him that there was anything incongruous and contradictory in such action. His interest was purely intellectual. There are many such men, but not as many today as formerly.

But the devil has other approaches. One of the most subtle of them is the inculcation of a wrong understanding of the doctrine of justification by faith only, the cardinal doctrine of Protestantism. He comes to a man who has learned this doctrine and he so presses it, and drives the man to such an extreme, that he ends by saying 'What I do as a Christian does not matter. No one is ever justified by works; I am justified entirely by faith. My works then do not matter at all; I can do anything I like. If I believe in Christ all is well with me.' Such a view is, of course, nothing but a sheer travesty of the doctrine of justification by faith only.

In the same way the devil in his wiliness endeavours to confuse

Christians about 'the final perseverance of the saints', a most glorious doctrine! 'No man shall pluck them out of my hand!' The Gospel teaches that we are saved by grace, that salvation is of grace from beginning to end. We do not contribute to it at all. It is all of God. And in consequence the final perseverance of the saints is guaranteed. But the devil comes and says to us, 'What that really means is, you are free to do anything you like, it will not make any difference to you, your salvation is guaranteed'. So he traps us and tries to persuade us to presume upon these two glorious doctrines, and in fact to become rabid antinomians.

The danger is ever present, not to take the Word and its teaching as a whole, but to extract certain favourite texts and conveniently forget others: in other words, in this particular context, the devil tempts us to forget the teaching of the second chapter of the Epistle of James, that 'faith without works is dead'. Faith is not merely an intellectual assent; it involves the whole personality. It not only involves the mind, but the heart and the will and therefore every aspect of practice and behaviour. A man's faith is not concerned only with the realm of intellectual propositions, the whole man is engaged. So James very rightly argues that 'faith without works is dead'. 'Show me thy faith without thy works, and I will show thee my faith by my works,' says James. There is no contradiction between James and Paul. They both teach exactly the same thing. This selfsame emphasis is found everywhere in the teaching of the Apostle Paul; for which reason in his ethical exhortations he says in effect, 'If you claim to be Christians then you cannot be guilty of certain types of conduct. There is a consistency in the Christian life. Because you are justified by faith only, you are bound to live in a Christian manner.' He writes, for instance, in the second chapter of this Epistle to the Ephesians: 'We are his (God's) workmanship, created in Christ Jesus unto good works, which God hath before ordained that we should walk in them' (verse 10). If we believe in the doctrine of election we must believe that we are elected 'unto good works'. We have been 'born again' in order that we may do them. 'Faith without works is dead'; it is mere intellectual assent.

The same teaching is found in many other places in the Scripture, as, for example, in the First Epistle to the Corinthians, an Epistle which should safeguard us from this particular danger without any other addition at all. Certain Christians in Corinth were boasting about their knowledge, their understanding and their gifts, and yet the Apostle says that they were guilty of sins which the Gentiles would not even mention because they were so disgraceful. 'It is reported commonly that there is fornication among you, and such fornication as is not so much as named among the Gentiles, that one should have his father's wife. And ye are puffed up, and have not rather mourned, that he that hath done this deed might be taken away from among you' (5:1, 2). Sheer antinomianism! Puffed up with intellectual knowledge, they were allowing a sin which is not only a negation of faith, but something that even the pagan world regarded as abhorrent. Similar teaching is found in respect of the Communion Service in chapters 10 and 11 in this same Epistle.

The biblical answer to antinomianism is found in the Epistle to the Romans: 'Knowing this, that our old man is crucified with him, that (in order that) the body of sin might be destroyed, that henceforth we should not serve sin' (6:6). That is the whole object of salvation. Why did the Son of God die upon the Cross? He did so to 'purify unto himself a peculiar people, zealous of good works' (Titus 2:14). This is the object and purpose of salvation; not merely that we should enjoy Christian doctrine.

But our troubles are not ended. The devil, having failed to drive us into the position of the antinomian, now comes to us in an entirely different guise. He becomes concerned to drive us to the opposite extreme, into what is called legalism. He comes to us and says, 'Yes, everything that you have been taught against antinomianism is true; you must realize that in the Christian life the whole question of conduct and practice is absolutely central and all-important'. But he then tries to press us into a new kind of legalism. The history of the Church shows that one of the commonest forms of legalism is asceticism, as manifested in monasticism. It is exemplified in monks and monasteries, friars, and people who segregated themselves away from the world in order to live the Christian life. Short of that, and in principle, it is still found in the Protestant Churches. There is a good description of legalism at the beginning of the First Epistle to Timothy, chapter four: 'Now the Spirit speaketh expressly, that in the latter times some shall depart from the faith, giving heed to seducing spirits, and doctrines of devils; speaking lies in hypocrisy; having their conscience seared with a hot iron: forbidding to marry'. They say that sex is always sinful, and that a Christian should never get married, because that is pandering to the flesh. 'Forbidding to marry, and commanding to abstain from meats' – Christians must be vegetarians – 'which God hath created to be received with thanksgiving of them which believe and know the truth'. This is a typical account of what is meant by asceticism.

There is a similar description of asceticism at the end of the second chapter of Paul's Epistle to the Colossians where he puts it thus: 'Let no man beguile you of your reward in a voluntary humility and worshipping of angels, intruding into those things which he hath not seen, vainly puffed up by his fleshly mind, and not holding the Head, from which all the body by joints and bands having nourishment ministered, and knit together, increaseth with the increase of God. Wherefore if ye be dead with Christ from the rudiments of the world, why, as though living in the world, are ye subject to ordinances (touch not; taste not; handle not; which all are to perish with the using), after the commandments and doctrines of men? Which things have indeed a shew of wisdom in will worship, and humility, and neglecting of the body; not in any honour to the satisfying of the flesh' (verses 18–23). It is important we should know something of the danger of a false asceticism. People have argued that if you want to live the Christian life you cannot live in the world, you cannot be a businessman, you cannot belong to the professions. You have as it were to go out of the world; you have to join a monastery; you have to belong to some 'brotherhood'; you have to go and live in some isolated community, where alone can you live this life. Indeed some have gone even further; because the body went with them even to the cell they felt they had to put on a camel-hair shirt. Even then the body asserted itself, so they began to smite themselves and indulge in flagellations. They began to torment and to starve themselves. That is what is meant by legalism, it is a returning to a method which relies upon one's own works and activities in order to live the Christian life, and save one's soul.

This is not a theoretical matter. A movement in certain sections of the Christian Church at the present time is causing much unhappiness and havoc through a misunderstanding of New Testament doctrine. Its adherents misunderstand particularly the Second Epistle to the Corinthians, chapter 6 beginning at verse 14: 'Be ye not unequally yoked together with unbelievers: for what fellowship hath righteousness with unrighteousness? and what communion hath light with darkness?' – and especially, 'Wherefore come out from among them, and be ye separate, saith the Lord, and touch not the unclean thing; and I will receive you'. That is being interpreted as meaning that a man who is a Christian has no longer a right to be a member of any learned society if that society also includes unbelievers. For example, the edict has gone forth that if a Christian is a member of the Royal College of Physicians, which also contains people who are not Christians, he must resign his fellowship or his membership. 'Be ye not unequally yoked together with unbelievers,' they say. They prohibit people who are Christians even to eat with those who are not Christians. They go so far as to say that they are not even allowed to eat with other Christians who do not hold their particular point of view, even if they should be their own near relatives.

This has often been a source of trouble in the Church. It is perhaps not a major problem today, but I am old enough to remember a time when it was a source of trouble. I remember a very godly man, one of the most godly men I have ever known, who told me that as a young man he passed through a phase of legalism which expressed itself as follows. He believed that you should observe the Sabbath, the Lord's day, and that you should not do things you do on other days on the Lord's day. But the devil drove him to legalism to the following extreme. You may regard this as amusing, but it was a very real thing to the misguided man – he even put on his boots and tied them up on Saturday night. The argument was that you should do nothing on Sunday that you could do on Saturday; so on a Saturday night he tied up his boots and slept in them! Of course he discovered later that this was sheer legalism; but it took him some time to realize this and to obtain the balance of the Gospel itself. 'Let every man examine himself.' It is persons of the most honest type who are troubled by legalism. The commoner type of person is drawn to antinomianism. May God save us from both these extremes. What is your view of conduct and practice and behaviour? Where does this come in your normal thinking and arguing and reasoning? Let us beware lest the devil should drive us to one or the other of these extremes.

Now let us move to a second principle, or to a second group of problems under this heading of the devil's attack on our behaviour in general. Having decided our attitude and our point of view, we must examine ourselves with regard to our behaviour in general. Here again there are two obvious extremes. The first is what can be described as a general slackness. This means a failure in general to apply the truth to ourselves. One of the first things a Christian has to learn is that he must apply the truth to himself. It is not sufficient to listen to it, or to enjoy it. The Christian has to apply the truth to himself. James in the first chapter of his Epistle writes, 'Wherefore lay apart all filthiness and superfluity of naughtiness, and receive with meekness the engrafted word, which is able to save your souls. But be ye doers of the word, and not hearers only, deceiving your own selves. For if any be a hearer of the word, and not a doer, he is like unto a man beholding his natural face in a glass: for he beholdeth himself, and goeth his way, and straightway forgetteth what manner of man he was. But whoso looketh into the perfect law of liberty, and continueth therein, he being not a forgetful hearer, but a doer of the work, this man shall be blessed in his deed' (verses 21–25). A man reads the Bible, hears a sermon. He feels it is right, he follows the argument. But then he goes out and forgets all about it. He fails to apply it. There is nothing more useless than that, says James, and in his illustration he ridicules it. A man looks at his face in the glass, but then turns away and forgets all about it. We must go on looking, go on with the application. Remember, continue, go on speaking to yourself about it, in order that you may be delivered from this 'superfluity of naughtiness' with which the devil is always tempting us.

The Apostle Peter teaches the same truth in the first chapter of his Second Epistle. He says that 'we are given exceeding great and precious promises: that by these ye might be partakers of the divine nature, having escaped the corruption that is in the world through lust' (verse 4). We have been saved, we have been born again, we have been delivered, we have 'escaped the corruption that is in the world through lust'. Then he continues: 'And beside this (because of this), giving all diligence, add to your faith virtue; and to virtue knowledge; and to knowledge temperance; and to temperance patience; and to patience godliness; and to godliness brotherly kindness; and to brotherly kindness charity'. We have to 'add' these things, we have to give diligence to 'furnish out' our faith. Why? 'For if these things be in you and abound, they make you that ye shall neither be barren nor unfruitful in the knowledge of our Lord Jesus Christ. But he that lacketh these things is blind, and cannot see afar off, and hath forgotten that he was purged from his old sins. Wherefore the rather, brethren, give diligence to make your calling and election sure; for if ye do these things, ye shall never fall: for so an entrance shall be ministered unto you abundantly into the everlasting kingdom of our Lord and Saviour Jesus Christ.' There is no need to add to that! Note that the emphasis is on 'giving diligence'. But those who have a general spirit of slackness forget all this. They forget, says the Apostle Peter, that they have been purged from their old sins, and just go on living as if very little had happened to them. They have an intellectual faith which they remember on a Sunday, but which they do not seem to remember during the week; they do not apply it, they do not 'give diligence'. 'Add to your faith' – 'furnish it out'.

We can think of this evil also as arising from a lack of discipline in the Christian life. One of the first things we have to realize is that we have to discipline ourselves. 'Ah, but,' you say, 'I thought grace had come in, I thought that discipline was a matter of law, and that the difference between the man under the law and the Christian is that the Christian now knows freedom.' That, of course, is correct, but freedom does not mean that Christians live the Christian life automatically. The Christian is a man who is given responsibility; and being born again he has the power within him to live the new life. The Spirit is within him. God treats us not as machines but as men – 'Quit you as men'. We have to learn, and therefore we have to discipline ourselves. But many Christians fail to do so, and consequently they bring the whole Gospel into disrepute.

In practice this means that we have to discipline ourselves in the matter of time, as to how we use it. We have to safeguard sufficient time for the reading of God's Word. We shall never grow in grace except we know the Word of God. But the tendency of so many is to allow circumstances and other people to govern and control their lives. They do not take themselves in hand. They do not say, 'Now I must put this first. I have priorities, and whatever else I may do this day, I must read and study the Word of God because it is God's food for my soul.' This is the way of growth. It demands discipline, and sometimes a stern discipline. Likewise with the matter of prayer. Hence great emphasis is laid upon prayer in the Scriptures. Added to that is attendance at God's house. Passages about 'neglecting the assembling of yourselves together' were addressed to the early Christians because some of them were evidently thinking, 'As I am a Christian now, I do not need help any longer, I have arrived'. But they had not arrived, and they very soon showed it by their failure in their conduct, and practice, and ultimately even in their faith (Hebrews 10:25).

There is no greater cause of failure in the Christian life than a general slackness and failure to discipline the life. Read the accounts of all the great revivals in the Church, and especially of their beginnings, and you will always find that this idea of discipline had been restored. Take the famous example of what happened two hundred years ago in the Evangelical Awakening. What preceded that, humanly speaking, was the formation of the Holy Club in Oxford. The members of the club had not quite seen the truth yet, but they had seen the need of discipline. They realized that the vast majority of supposed Christians were not living as Christians at all. They called themselves Christians but there was very little difference between them and those who belonged to the world. But members of the Holy Club said, 'A Christian is a man who lives an ordered life'. So they began to discipline themselves, hence the term 'Methodist'. They began living a life according to a method. There is, of course, always the danger of the method becoming too important, and turning people into legalists. But the remedy for that is not to abandon method, but to exercise a balanced discipline, the realization that it is essential that we should order our lives according to the Scriptures.

It is of vital importance that we should make application of the truth constantly to ourselves. That involves self-examination frequently, even daily. We should always be reviewing our lives in the light of the teaching of the Scriptures, in the light of what we feel in the presence of God, in the light of the lives of the saints throughout the centuries. Discipline! Order! Self-examination! The devil tries to make the Christian negligent about these things and to say, 'I am a Christian now. I have been saved, I have gone forward at the end of a meeting, I have put my name on a card, all is well with me. I stood for Christ and therefore I have nothing to worry about.' That means slackness, the lack of discipline that brings the Gospel into such disrepute.

But then there is the exact opposite. The moment you realize the possibility of the danger just described, the devil will come to you and will tempt you to pursue what I am constrained to call a carnal zeal. Notice that I call it a 'carnal' zeal. Zeal is always good, but a carnal zeal in the Christian life is bad. I mean, that a man who has realized that he has been slack and has been doing nothing, now begins to become active and busy excessively. It is very difficult to tell which is the worse of these two conditions. There are many Christians who, quite unbeknown to themselves, are living on their own activities, living on their busy-ness, living on the organizations to which they belong, living according to a certain routine that is prescribed for them by someone else.

I have seen a great deal of this in my pastoral experience. I know of certain organizations where men and women are brought to a knowledge of the truth. Then they join a society, and in the charmed atmosphere of the society they never miss a meeting. They are full of good works, they take part in prayer meetings, they are active in personal evangelism. But shortly their time in that society and its atmosphere comes to an end for various reasons and they have to live more or less without much Christian fellowship in the great outside world. And very soon they lapse and fall, because they were dependent upon the atmosphere, the organization, the society. What a terrible danger this is! As long as they were in that atmosphere they were carried along by the momentum of the movement. But they had never really understood it. They were living on their own busy-ness, on their own activity, and their own carnal zeal. Suddenly, out in the world in entirely different circumstances, and left to themselves, they have nothing. The stimulus has gone, the momentum is not provided, and thus they begin to lose interest, become slack, and the next step is, perhaps, that they fall into sin and find themselves in a very grievous position. This constitutes a real danger for young people in particular. The devil tempts them through well-meaning people who say, 'Now that you are saved you must begin to get busy, you must be doing something'. And they put them into a certain mould. But they have no real understanding of their position; they have never reasoned it out gradually and spiritually. It is something artificial, and it is kept going by the artificial atmosphere in which they find themselves.

'We wrestle not against flesh and blood, but against principalities, against powers, against the rulers of the darkness of this world, against spiritual wickedness in high places.' The devil who can transform himself into an angel of light does not always incite to obvious sin. He knows that, if he came to a certain type of convert and confronted him with some terrible sin, the latter would recoil from it. So he just persuades him to be slack, not to be too keen, too zealous, 'not to make himself ridiculous' like some other Christians to whom he points. And so the victim becomes indolent, and does nothing; and gradually the whole temperature of his life falls and eventually he falls into sin.

As regards the other man who lives on his activities, we can apply what the Apostle says about his fellow-countrymen, 'I bear them record that they have a zeal of God, but not according to knowledge' (Romans 10:2). Zeal is not enough, busy-ness is not enough, activity is not enough. God forbid that you should be living on your own activity. If it stands between you and a knowledge of Him, and a growth in grace, and a development spiritually, it is but one of the 'wiles of the devil' to keep you ignorant and stunted.

The same applies to the type of Christian who says, 'Well, of course, I have not a great brain, I do not think, I do not read; I am a man who does things'. The devil has already manipulated him into a condition of inverted pride; and because he is living on his own activity and lacking in understanding, the devil will soon be tempting him in some more subtle manner and, not recognizing the temptation, he will soon fall.

[358]

The exhortation therefore is that we must be governed by the Scripture, we must keep to the divine balance, and avoid extremes. Not antinomianism, not legalism; not slackness, not a false zeal! What then? As the Apostle Peter puts it, we must 'Follow his (Christ's) steps'. There were no extremes in Him; He always did His Father's will. He never overdid anything on the one hand or on the other. He remained in the centre of God's will; and we are to follow His steps 'who did no wrong, neither was guile found in his mouth'. We are ever to 'look unto Jesus, the author and the finisher of our faith'.

May God bring home this all-important aspect of our Christian life. The world outside is watching us. 'Dearly beloved, I beseech you as strangers and pilgrims, abstain from fleshly lusts, which war against the soul; having your conversation honest among the Gentiles: that whereas they speak against you as evil-doers, they may by your good works, which they shall behold, glorify God in the day of visitation' (1 Peter 2:11, 12). May God give us such a sense of responsibility in the world that we live in today, that we shall realize that we are marked men and women, yea, that we are the children of God and the custodians of the faith, and that the world outside is judging even God Himself by what it sees in us. 'Take unto you the whole armour of God.' 'Be strong in the Lord, and in the power of his might', for nothing less than that will enable us to counter the wiles of the devil.

26

Worldliness

We look once more, and for the last time, at this great and momentous statement made by the Apostle Paul towards the end of the Epistle to the Ephesians. Having stated the great doctrines, and having worked out some of their practical implications, and their outworking in various departments of life, he felt it incumbent upon him to end with this powerful word of warning, this great call to battle. We have been examining it, and looking particularly at 'the wiles of the devil'. We have seen that we are fighting the devil himself, and all the forces he has with him – the principalities and powers, the rulers of the darkness of this world, the spiritual wickedness in high places – and we have seen in detail how the devil and these powers which he commands array themselves against us and attack us. We have seen how in his wiliness he attacks the mind of the believer, the experience of the believer, and how also he attacks us in the realm of conduct and practice and behaviour.

We come finally to another aspect of this matter, and look at what is commonly known as 'worldliness'.

The main trouble with worldliness is that in and of itself it pertains to things which are not sinful. It is that condition in which we allow things which are legitimate and right to play too big a part, and have too big a place, in our life and experience as Christians. It is because these things are not sinful in and of themselves that they constitute such a danger.

Our Lord Himself dealt with this matter, because it is one of the most subtle dangers confronting the Christian. He did so, for instance, in the Parable of the Sower, where we read: 'He also that received seed among thorns is he that heareth the word; and the care of this world, and the deceitfulness of riches, choke the word, and he becometh unfruitful' (Matthew 13:22). That is exactly what is meant by worldliness. But, still more strikingly, just under the shadow of the Cross at the end of His life, when our Lord gives a preview of history, He says: 'And take heed to yourselves, lest at any time your hearts be overcharged with surfeiting, and drunkenness, and cares of this life, and so that day come upon you unawares' (Luke 21:34). He is talking about the ultimate end of history, the climax of the ages which is to come as a 'snare', suddenly and unexpectedly. So He exhorts His followers to be careful. This is a word that speaks to us today. Notice that He says that we must 'take heed' – 'take heed to yourselves'. You must never allow not only 'surfeiting and drunkenness' but the 'cares of this life' so to ensnare you, and to occupy you, that 'that day come upon you unawares'.

Then there is the passage in the Second Epistle to the Corinthians, chapter 6: 'Be ye not unequally yoked together with unbelievers: for what fellowship hath righteousness with unrighteousness? And what communion hath light with darkness? And what concord hath Christ with Belial? Or what part hath he that believeth with an infidel? Wherefore come out from among them, and be ye separate, saith the Lord, and touch not the unclean thing; and I will receive you, and will be a Father unto you, and ye shall be my sons and daughters, saith the Lord Almighty.' This statement deals with the same problem, not in the Jewish legalistic manner to which we have already referred, and which is being evidenced at the present time in certain sections of the Church, but in the true and balanced way which the Scripture teaches.

A further illustration, a very striking one, is found in Paul's First Epistle to Timothy: 'For the love of money is the root of all evil: which while some coveted after, they have erred from the faith, and pierced themselves through with many sorrows. But thou, O man of God, flee these things; and follow after righteousness, godliness, faith, love, patience, meekness. Fight the good fight of faith, lay hold on eternal life whereunto thou

[361]

art also called, and hast professed a good profession before many witnesses' (6:10–12). These warnings and exhortations were necessary in the early Church. And Paul further says: 'Godliness with contentment is great gain' – people are always concerned about gain – 'for we brought nothing into this world, and it is certain we can carry nothing out. And having food and raiment let us be therewith content. But they that will be rich fall into temptation and a snare, and into many foolish and hurtful lusts, which drown men in destruction and perdition' (6:7–9).

But in many respects the most famous warning of all is that found in the Second Epistle to Timothy: 'For Demas hath forsaken me, having loved this present world, and is departed unto Thessalonica' (4:10). Then there is the striking and solemn warning in the First Epistle of John, chapter 2, verse 15: 'Love not the world, neither the things that are in the world. If any man love the world, the love of the Father is not in him.' Notice the contrasts and opposites. It is clear, then, that this is a route along which the devil very frequently attacks God's people.

Now this can show itself in the Church in general as well as in the life of the individual Christian. Hence the warning to the Church in James, chapter 2: 'My brethren, have not the faith of our Lord Jesus Christ, the Lord of glory, with respect of persons. For if there come unto your assembly a man with a gold ring, in goodly apparel, and there come in also a poor man in vile raiment; and ye have respect to him that weareth the gay clothing, and say unto him, Sit thou here in a good place; and say to the poor, Stand thou there, or sit here under my footstool: are ye not then partial in yourselves, and are become judges of evil thoughts? Hearken, my beloved brethren, Hath not God chosen the poor of this world rich in faith, and heirs of the kingdom which he hath promised to them that love him?' (verses 1–5). The New Testament draws a distinction between the Church and every other realm in life; and the moment we ignore this and regard the Church as but the spiritual aspect of the State, we are heading straight for worldliness in the Church. It can be carried further, so that the divisions the world recognizes outside may become recognized in the Church. The moment we bring the categories of the world into the Church, the moment the Church becomes 'worldly' in her social distinctions, in her way of conducting her affairs – raising funds and similar things – the moment she brings in the worldly idea, the worldly method, she is guilty of worldliness. Nothing, perhaps, has been such a brake upon the advance of Christianity, and the work of the Church, as this spirit of worldliness entering into the Church of God, and turning her into something which is so essentially different from the primitive pattern found in the New Testament.

But, leaving the Church in general, let us look at this as it affects the individual. Worldliness is that state in which our thinking is governed by the mind and the outlook of the world. Let me show how subtle it is. We are dealing with Christians because Christians only can be guilty of worldliness. The man who is not a Christian is not guilty of it because he cannot be anything else. Worldliness can only be true of God's people; it is that state in which their thinking is still determined by the mind and the outlook of the world.

If we go to such people and talk to them or question them about the way of salvation they are perfectly clear; all is well with them. Their thinking in *that* respect has been changed. They have seen it, they have been convicted by the Word of God. They are no longer trying to make themselves Christians, they have seen the truth about justification by faith only. On the matter of salvation they have an entirely new outlook, and they are thinking in a spiritual manner. But the devil comes in at that point. He knows that it is no use tempting them any longer about the way of salvation, and he does not do so. What he does now is to see to it that in the remainder of their lives they are still using the old categories, still thinking in the old terms, their outlook still being governed by that which governed them before they ever became Christians. In other words they are living in two compartments. In the matter of the intellectual apprehension of salvation they are spiritual; in the remainder of their lives they more or less go on living exactly as they were before. The devil worked thus with people in the early Church, and he has been doing so throughout the running centuries. It is the failure to realize that the whole of our thinking must be Christian, the whole of our outlook must be spiritual. We must not live in compartments. Everything I do and all my activities must ultimately be controlled by my relationship to God in Jesus Christ, that is to say, by my spiritual Christian outlook. Otherwise I become guilty of worldliness.

Worldliness shows itself in various ways. One is what is called 'worldly wisdom' and calculation. Instead of being governed by the plain teaching of the Scripture we begin to argue and to reason and to question. Instead of obeying the spiritual leadings which come to us through the Word, and through the Spirit, we apply our natural minds and outlook to our lives. So we tone down everything, and we are so afraid of going to excess, and becoming guilty of enthusiasm, that we on the other hand become worldly-wise. Those who have ever read John Bunyan's *The Pilgrim's Progress* will know all about 'Mr Worldly-Wiseman'. He is always in evidence; he is one of the devil's tools, and he comes to us and tries to reduce everything from the spiritual to the worldly level.

But there is another way in which worldliness shows itself. Everything in this world has been given to us by God, and is meant for our use. Indeed, everything is meant for our enjoyment. Everything is made and created by God, therefore obviously all such things are not only good but are perfectly legitimate for the Christian man. The use of these things becomes worldliness when we allow things that are perfectly right and legitimate in themselves to take too much of our time, too much of our attention, too much of our interest, too much of our enthusiasm.

This applies to literature, art, music, games – anything you like to think of. I am not, of course, talking about a man's means of livelihood. A man has to live and to earn his bread. I am dealing rather with the man's use of his leisure; and leisure is essential for everyone. These things I name offer themselves to us and they are perfectly legitimate. The Christian is not to cut himself off from them; he is not to segregate himself and to go out of life; he is not to say that he has no interest in general culture, for all things are given by God. All abilities, every power that man has ever exercised, all ultimately come from God. Everything produced by these powers is right in and of itself, unless, of course, it is turned to sinful purposes and uses. But it becomes worldliness if it absorbs us too much. If my interest in these things becomes central in my life, and takes the first place, or drives out the spiritual and my concentration on the eternal, then I am guilty of worldliness.

[364]

'The cares of this world' are inevitable in this world, and they are right in themselves. It is right for a husband or a wife to be concerned about the well-being of those in the family circle, and about food and clothing and the home. These 'cares' are inevitable. But if your life is dominated by them, if you spend all your time with these things, if they are constantly coming between you and your reading of the Word of God and prayer and fellowship with God, or the practice of the Christian life in some active form, then they become worldliness, and a hindrance. And the devil, of course, has always seen to it through the centuries that God's people are trapped and ensnared by these things which are right in and of themselves. He so exaggerates them and their import-ance, and so rouses an interest in them in us, that they become a hindrance to our growth in grace. That is what is meant by worldliness.

Then, of course, and in a much more obvious form, worldliness can appear as love of ease and indolence. That means not only the enjoyment of all God's good gifts in this world, but a tendency to live for them, a tendency to make them the main preoccupation of our life, the result being that the tone and the level and the quality of our spiritual life is lowered. We become lethargic spiritually, we become cold, we become unmoved. We are in a position of compromise; we are no longer thrilled by the things of the Spirit of God and gripped and moved by them. We have lost 'our first love'.

How, then, are we to avoid worldliness? The first answer is that we must never cease to remind ourselves that one of the first objects of salvation is to deliver us out of 'this present evil world' (Galatians 1:4). This thought is central everywhere in the New Testament. Christ died on the Cross not merely to save us from hell, but that we might be 'delivered out of this present evil world'. The world in its mind and thought and outlook is under the dominion of the devil. It belongs to him, he is 'the god of this world', 'the prince of the power of the air, the spirit that now worketh in the children of disobedience'. To be Christian is to be 'delivered out of this present evil world'. We must make that basic and fundamental in our thinking. If we fail to do so, the devil is sure to trap us in this matter of worldliness.

The same truth is emphasized in the Apostle Peter's phrase, 'Dearly beloved, I beseech you as strangers and pilgrims' – that is the Christian view of life in this world – 'abstain from fleshly lusts, which war against the soul' (1 Peter 2:11). The Christian is a stranger in this world. Such a statement is not popular today, I know indeed that it is most unpopular. This is the butt of the jokes of the comedians against religion – 'pie-in-the-sky!' We do not expect such people to understand it. But God forbid that we should take our view of the Christian life from them! The beginning of Christian understanding is that 'Our citizenship is in heaven' (Philippians 3:20). Heaven is where we belong. That is the essential difference between a Christian and a non-Christian. The Christian is a man who belongs to a different realm, the realm of God, the kingdom of God. He has been 'translated from the kingdom of darkness into the kingdom of God's dear Son' (Colossians 1:13). He is a stranger here, a journeyman, a pilgrim, a wayfarer. That is the Christian view of life, and if we keep this in the forefront of our minds we have gone most of the way already to defeat the devil as he attacks us in this matter of worldliness.

The Apostle Paul states this particularly clearly in 1 Corinthians 7:31: 'And they that use this world, as not abusing it'. You cannot add to that! It is the difference between using the world and abusing it. We are meant to use the world. We are not meant to be monks or anchorites or hermits. That is the whole error of monasticism. We do not go out of the world. It was a grand truth that was revealed to Luther – that you can be a good Christian wherever you are, and however humble your task. If you are but brushing the floor or washing it, you can do that to the glory of God. Every task is sacred. So we do not divide up Christians into the religious and the laity. We are all 'called to be saints'; not merely a few special people. And we realize that everything is here to be used: but you must not abuse it – 'using this world, as not abusing it'. Indeed the entire seventh chapter of the First Epistle to the Corinthians is most instructive in this very matter that we are considering. If we can always keep to that line we shall never go astray. 'Use' but do not 'abuse'. You abuse the world when you allow it to govern you, when you get too thrilled and excited about it, when it makes you forget the spiritual.

[366]

Finally take the word of the Apostle John in his First Epistle, chapter 3, verse 3: 'Every man that hath this hope in him purifieth himself, even as he is pure'. That is what we have always to bear in mind. If we are truly Christian we say that we are destined for God's realm. 'It doth not yet appear what we shall be; but we know that, when he shall appear, we shall be like him; for we shall see him as he is.' The world is too much with us. There is so much that is good and attractive in it, there is so much that is legitimate; but the devil as an angel of light will try to make us abuse it. He will so press it, so fool us with an interest in it, that quite unbeknown to ourselves we shall gradually cease to be interested in that other spiritual realm. We shall have forgotten about 'the hope', and the 'inheritance', we shall have forgotten our separation, we shall have forgotten that we are the children of God even now, and that we are going to see Him and be like Him.

That is how we are to deal with the subtle temptation of worldliness! You may have a beautiful home – well, just remind yourself that it is not permanent, that you will have to leave it. It is not an 'end', it is a place where you spend but a night. Christians are all travellers and pilgrims and strangers. The whole of life is nothing but – as one of the poets puts it – spending a night in an inn, paying your bill in the morning and going on. That is the theme of the whole Bible. The Christian is a pilgrim, and life is a Pilgrim's Progress. We do not belong here. This world is *Vanity Fair* through which we are passing. We do not build permanently here. No, keep moving, keep your eye on your ultimate destiny, remind yourself of who you are. Do not be over-attracted by the Fair, do not spend too much time at any of its stalls as you are passing by. You are entitled to look at them, you are entitled to use this world, but you must not abuse it. Never forget where are you going, and who you are, and the family to which you belong. Keep these things in the forefront of your mind, says the Bible, and you will already have defeated the wiles of the devil in this matter of worldliness.

The final problem arises in connection with the actual committing of sin. People have come to me in distress because they have fallen into sin. The trouble arose because they did not realize that it was sin when they first looked at it. Such is the devil's subtlety that he can make you sin even while you are trying to do good. I have known troubles, and almost tragedies, arise through one Christian trying to help another Christian with the best possible motives. The one Christian went to the other in trouble; the former was naturally sympathetic and wanted to do everything to help. But it ended in sin. Great care needs to be exercised in this matter. Men should be most cautious when they try to help women who come to them with their spiritual troubles, and vice versa. You may say, 'I understand, I am strong'. But the Scripture says, 'Let him that thinketh he standeth take heed lest he fall'. Even when you are doing good, the devil with all his wiles comes in and incites and tempts to sin. This is a very important matter for all Christians, and especially important, perhaps, for ministers and for those who are in pastoral charge of others. That is why it should always be in the forefront of instruction given to ministerial students.

There are many other ways in which evil can befall the Christian. Setting out to do good you may suddenly find yourself tempted, and falling because of the very fact that you were doing good. It is obvious that this is a method which the devil will frequently use. Nothing pleases him, nothing pleases the world, more than to see a Christian falling. Look at the glee and delight in the newspapers when such a thing happens; how they emphasize it and parade it and put it into the headlines. Of course! It is a defeat of God, they think, and a defeat of Christ. A Christian, with all his claims, failing, falling into sin! That is why the Bible has so much to say about this matter.

The First Epistle to the Corinthians is the chief treatise on this subject, and especially chapters 5 and 6. The Apostle reminds the Corinthian believers of who they are and what they are; how the Spirit of God dwells in them. That is the way to face it all. In Galatians, chapter 5, we find the same thing: 'Walk in the Spirit, and ye shall not fulfil the lust of the flesh' (verse 16). It is the only way. Again Paul writing to Timothy says: 'Holding faith, and a good conscience; which some having put away concerning faith have made shipwreck' (1 Timothy 1:19). You must not only 'hold faith', but also 'a good conscience'. Faith and works must never be separated; they must always go together. Do not neglect this aspect, says Paul, for 'some having put away

[368]

the good conscience have made shipwreck'; they have fallen into grievous sin and have caused great trouble.

But some of the strongest statements in this respect are found in the First Epistle of John. 'If we say that we have fellowship with him (God), and walk in darkness, we lie, and do not the truth' (1:6). Again, in the fourth verse of the second chapter: 'He that saith, I know him, and keepeth not his commandments, is a liar, and the truth is not in him'. That is Scriptural holiness preaching; not an appeal to us to receive holiness as a gift, but to be honest and consistent. If you say that you belong to Him, and know Him, but are not keeping His commandments, you are a liar! Such is the manliness of Scripture. If you believe in 'calling a spade a spade', well, there it is! If you say, 'I know Him', but are not keeping His commandments, you are a bare-faced liar!

The Scriptural warnings in this connection are essential because these things, as Peter puts it, 'war against the soul'. They war against the best interests of the soul and the happiness of the soul. Sin leads to shame, to misery, to unhappiness. That in turn makes us doubt, perhaps, whether we have ever been Christians. The devil torments us and makes us doubt whether we can be forgiven again. We say, 'Before, I did not know, now I do know, so how can I ever be forgiven?' Then we begin to feel that we shall never be able to stand in future. 'If I failed then, why should not I fall the next time?' And we begin to feel that our whole position is hopeless. We become depressed, despondent, discouraged, utterly hopeless, and the devil says, 'Why not give up? You are a complete failure. You are not a Christian.' Thus these things 'war against the soul', as we have seen also under the heading of experience.

But let me remind you of the way in which we must answer the devil. The answer is: 'If we confess our sins, he is faithful and just to forgive us our sins, and to cleanse us from all unrighteousness' (1 John 1:9). Again, 'My little children, these things write I unto you, that ye sin not. And' (or 'but') 'if any man sin, we have an advocate with the Father, Jesus Christ the righteous: and he is the propitiation for our sins; and not for ours only, but also for the sins of the whole world' (1 John 2:1, 2). That means that if you should fall into sin be especially careful not to listen to the

[369]

devil, to his accusations, to his discouragements. Turn on him and say, 'You are the accuser of the brethren, and whatever you say is a lie'. Turn to God and repent. Express your sorrow, realize what you have done, and how you have not only let yourself down, but also the Church of God, and Christ. Make yourself feel that you are a cad because you have also besmirched the Family name and the Family honour. Do not spare yourself. Then, having repented, believe God's Word. Remember, I say again, that you are justified by faith always, and never by your works; therefore believe God when He tells you that He is 'faithful and just to forgive your sins, and to cleanse you from all unrighteousness'. Believe God; do not believe the devil! Believe God, accept His forgiveness, thank Him for it, rise up, stand on your feet, go on as a man, watch and pray, and continue the fight. That is the only way to deal with it. Do not grovel in the dust; do not listen to the devil, to the voice of the accuser; do not be depressed. But having repented, believe the word of forgiveness, feel that you are washed again in the blood of Christ, and go forward, being circumspect and careful as to where you place your feet.

These are the ways in which the devil comes and attacks us. 'We wrestle not against flesh and blood, but against principalities, against powers, against the rulers of the darkness of this world, against spiritual wickedness in high places.' Oh! the malignity, the subtlety, the power and the ingenuity of the devil! 'Wherefore take unto you the whole armour of God, that ye may be able to withstand in the evil day.'

What does the apostle mean by 'the evil day?' All we have been considering is the permanent position of the Christian; but there are times when it is even worse. For his own subtle, evil purposes, the devil sometimes attacks us with unusual force and might. The 'evil day' means a Satanic attack. There are days in the lives of Christian people when hell is, as it were, let loose, when the devil seems to marshal all his forces against us from all directions. It is something unusual and exceptional. There is no need to be alarmed, for it is all catered for; but let us not forget it. The greatest saints have given descriptions of these evil days, when the devil, having failed to catch them along the usual lines, made an unusual effort so that they were not given a moment's peace. It might go on for weeks with scarcely any intermission at all. The evil day!

How do you react to all this? Do you feel that it is based on imagination, and that it has nothing at all to do with you? Do you say that since you have become a Christian you have never known any of these troubles and problems? If so you are so completely and utterly defeated by the wiles of the devil that you do not even know it. I cannot imagine anything more hopeless than that! Indeed I would question whether such a person is a Christian at all. For the devil is 'the adversary' and 'the accuser of the brethren'; and he even attacked our Lord Himself.

Are you discouraged and depressed by it all? What has been the effect of all these studies upon you? Are you saying to yourself, 'I am disappointed with this Christian life. I thought it was going to solve all my problems; but it seems to become worse and worse, and more and more subtle. Who am I to contend with all this?' If you are depressed and discouraged the fact is that you have not understood the truth; you have missed the whole point of the message. The apostle not only warns us, he also shows us how all these problems can be dealt with. He does not remind us of them to depress us, but in order to show us the way of triumph and of victory. You have got to realize the position in which you are placed; if you do not, you are a fool. That is what really happened to this country, and all the free world, before the Second World War. Not believing the truth about Hitler and his machinations and all his schemes, we were very nearly defeated. So let us make sure that we know and realize what is happening to us. Paul was anxious that the Ephesians should realize this.

But that is only one side of the matter; it does not stop there. We are reminded of the power of the Name of the Lord! Here is the answer: 'Be strong in the Lord!' The Lord is always the answer. Everything is in Him. The foe is mighty, subtle, powerful, and ingenious. But we belong to One who is much mightier, and who has already defeated the devil and all his hordes.

Our Gospel teaches us about an Incarnation! The God whom we adore, in the Son came into this world. He lived as a man, and He has met the devil and the principalities and powers, the rulers of the darkness of this world and the spiritual wickedness in high places. He has met them all in the flesh as a man, 'tempted in all points like as we are, yet without sin' (Hebrews 4:15). He was able to say at the end of His life, 'The prince of this world cometh and hath nothing in me' (John 14:30). Nothing at all! All that you and I are battling against He has met. He has defeated them all, every one of them. At every point He was victorious, both in His life, and in His death. Listen to Him: 'Now is the judgment of this world: now shall the prince of this world be cast out'. As the result of His death (John 12:31), 'the prince of this world' has been cast out. As the Apostle Paul says in Colossians 2:15 in reference to the Cross: 'And having spoiled principalities and powers, he made a show of them openly, triumphing over them in it'. On the Cross of Calvary our Lord gave the final mortal wound to the devil and all his forces. He has 'made an open show of them'. He triumphed over them in his death on Calvary's hill.

If, then, you remain afraid of the wiles of the devil and all his powers, remember the One who has conquered him by His life, by His death, and by His resurrection; and who is now seated at the right hand of God. All rule and authority and power are given unto Him, everything is under His hands, and He has sent us the Holy Spirit. So as John is able to say, 'Greater is he that is in you, than he that is in the world' (1 John 4:4). The devil and these forces are controlling men in the world; but 'greater is he that is in you than he that is in the world'. 'Christ in you'. The Holy Spirit is in you. God takes up His abode in you. Remember all this. We are not left to ourselves.

Remember, too, your relationship to Him. As John writes again in that First Epistle: 'We know that whosoever is born of God sinneth not' – does not keep on doing it, is not constantly defeated – 'but he that is begotten of God keepeth himself, and that wicked one toucheth him not. And we know that we are of God, and the whole world lieth in wickedness', in the wicked one (1 John 5:18, 19). We do not lie in the wicked one, because we are 'of God', and the devil cannot 'touch' us. Let him do what he will he cannot 'touch' us; he will never get us back into his dominion. Do not let him frighten you, therefore; do not be alarmed by him as you realize these truths concerning him. Say to yourself, 'I am strong in the Lord, and in the power of His might. I am covered with the whole armour of God; therefore, though I wrestle against principalities and powers, against the rulers of the darkness of this world, against spiritual wickedness in heavenly places, I am not afraid. Having taken unto me the whole armour of God I am able to stand in the evil day, and having done all, to stand, confident that neither life, nor death, nor the devil, nor hell, nor any other creature, or power, shall be able to separate me from the love of God which is in Christ Jesus our Lord.' 'Finally, my brethren, be strong in the Lord, and in the power of his might. Put on the whole armour of God, that ye may be able to stand against the wiles of the devil.'